T

CATTLE

TOWNS

LIBRARY MEDIA CENTER
ALBUQUERQUE ACADEMY.

THE

CATTLE

TOWNS

Robert R. Dykstra

University of Nebraska Press
Lincoln and London

27020
LIBRARY MEDIA CENTER
ALBUQUERQUE ACADEMY

© Copyright 1968 by Robert R. Dykstra
All rights reserved
Manufactured in the United States of America

First Bison Book edition: October 1983
Most recent printing indicated by the first digit below:
1   2   3   4   5   6   7   8   9   10

Library of Congress Cataloging in Publication Data

Dykstra, Robert R., 1930–
   The cattle towns.
    Originally published: 1st ed. New York : Knopf, 1968.
    Includes bibliographical references and index.
    1. Cattle trade – Kansas – History – 19th century.
2. Cities and towns – Kansas – History – 19th century.
3. Frontier and pioneer life – Kansas – History – 19th
century. 4. Kansas – History. I. Title.
HD9433.U5K215 1983   978.1'031   83-6485
ISBN 0-8032-6561-1 (pbk.)

Reprinted by arrangement with Alfred A. Knopf, Inc.

Two sections of *The Cattle Towns* appeared, in different form, in
Agricultural History, and one in the *Kansas Historical Quarterly.*
Each is reprinted with the kind permission of the respective pub-
lisher.

LIBRARY MEDIA CENTER
ALBUQUERQUE ACADEMY

978.1031
Dyk

FOR

Allan G. Bogue

CONTENTS

ILLUSTRATIONS

Unless otherwise credited, all illustrations are courtesy of
the Kansas State Historical Society, Topeka.

Following page 206

Joseph G. McCoy
Theodore C. Henry
William ("Dutch Bill") Greiffenstein
Robert M. Wright
Alonzo B. Webster (Courtesy Boot Hill Museum, Inc.,
    Dodge City)
Marshall M. Murdock

Abilene in 1867
Abilene two or three years later

Smoky Hill Crossing near Ellsworth
Ellsworth in 1872

Main and Douglas, Wichita, 1870
Same view five years later
Bird's-eye view of Wichita

Front Street, Dodge City
Bird's-eye view of Dodge City
Caldwell in the mid-1880's

Stockyard at Ellsworth
Railway depot at Wichita

MAPS

THE
CATTLE
TOWNS

INTRODUCTION

Town–Building &
the Texas Cattle Trade

[1]

"**B**Y GOLLY, there's this you got to say for 'em," exclaims one of Sinclair Lewis's minor but representative characters: "Every small American town is trying to get population and modern ideals. And darn if a lot of 'em don't put it across! . . . You don't want to just look at what these small towns are, you want to look at what they're aiming to become."[1]

This observation seems to emphasize two important truths: that small communities reflect human motives, of which ambition is surely the most obvious, and also that large communities do not germinate from impersonal circumstance alone. Despite the advertised appeal of collective intimacy and intimacy with nature, most American small towns would be cities if they could. The frontier townsman's term for this impulse, expressed as a program, was "town-building." Modern students of urbanization—some of them historians—tend to de-emphasize the human factor in urban growth. But they seldom reckon with the marked fluidity of frontier periods, when the

---

[1] Sinclair Lewis: *Babbitt* (New York, 1922), p. 119.

opportunities for *recruiting* the acknowledged attributes of city status—population, major transportation facilities, capital investment—were perhaps better than they would ever be again. Even geographical advantage, that most important of fortuitous variables, required human agency for translation into urban prosperity. To the dedicated town-builder this appeared self-evident.

Richard C. Wade's study of St. Louis and four Ohio Valley cities in their first decades of growth vividly documents the successful urban impulse on the frontier. On the other hand, Lewis Atherton's description of life in the midwestern country towns of the late nineteenth and early twentieth centuries in a sense catalogues its failures.[2] But if we could distribute these communities on a scale according to their success in achieving urban growth—Wade's to the upper end, Atherton's to the lower—it seems apparent that while we gain something from this raw discrimination of extremes, much is still to be said about what lies between: the collective experience of numberless villages and towns that may be thought of as aspirants to city status, whose destinies for longer or shorter periods and in greater or lesser degree hung in a precarious balance between urban "success" and small town "failure."

Considering the peculiar domination of entrepreneurial motives in American history, remarkably few writers have treated the urban impulse in the small community with anything but an amused dismissal of pretensions. In the present study this impulse serves as the central theme—which is to say that I have taken it, and the social imperatives proceeding from it, seriously. By giving it thematic preference over "local progress" I believe I have freed my materials from a traditional form of de-

[2] Richard C. Wade: *The Urban Frontier: The Rise of Western Cities, 1790–1830* (Cambridge, Mass., 1959); Lewis Atherton: *Main Street on the Middle Border* (Bloomington, Ind., 1954).

terminism that, in the long run, has not proved very useful in specific cases.

Few, I think, will dispute that much remains unknown about the evolution of social organization in America. In this respect the main intent of this book has been to expose to view the interaction of personal and impersonal factors —or "social process"—and I have tried to do this by offering a rather less circumscribed intimacy with local experience than is usually exploited in historical analysis. My focal point is that critical moment in the lives of five frankly ambitious frontier settlements when their decision-makers fought hard to avoid a conventional community fate.

[2]

THE KANSAS CATTLE TRADING CENTER or "cattle town" of the 1870's and 1880's has up to now belonged more to the imagination than to history. The lively rendezvous of cowboy, cattleman, gambler, and city marshal is currently a theatrical image only tenuously connected with tradition. Catering to a popular fascination with violence, the idea of the cattle town seems at every brow-level to be scarcely more than a gathering of taut characters with itchy trigger fingers.[3]

[3] The first attempt to deal at any length with the major cattle towns as social units was Floyd Benjamin Streeter's *Prairie Trails and Cow Towns* (Boston, 1936). Although an academic product, it is nevertheless long on violence and short on useful community detail. The most recent survey, Harry Sinclair Drago's *Wild, Woolly and Wicked: The History of the Kansas Cow Towns and the Texas Cattle Trade* (New York, 1960), is a blatantly popular treatment and no improvement on Streeter.

I have discovered, incidentally, that the term "cow town," used above and by many other writers (myself formerly included), was never employed by self-respecting cattle town people themselves—to judge by their spokesmen. It was originally a mildly derogatory term that appeared in the mid-1880's. For an example of its use see the letter of a Dodge City critic in the Topeka *Commonwealth*, June 17, 1885.

As a historical reality the cattle town has much more to offer. It was, technically speaking, an interior market facility situated at the juncture of railroad and Texas cattle trail where drovers sold their livestock to buyers. That its economic organization did not envision a primary dependence upon local agriculture, but rather "commerce," in all cases both stimulated and sustained the urban impulse. Through the medium of the range cattle trade townsmen sought the rare prize of city status.

The simple correlation was stated time and time again. "Since the inception of this immense business, Abilene and the Texas cattle trade have been synonymous," wrote a booster of that town to a St. Louis newspaper, "and in consequence from an insignificant frontier railroad station the place has grown to one of great importance."[4] "This will be the great shipping point for the Texas Cattle trade for 1872," insisted an Ellsworth realtor late that same season, "and those wishing town lots that are desirable will find this a good time to purchase." "This is essentially a cattle point," a Caldwell editor declared; "no less than 100,000 head of cattle will be shipped from this point during the season of 1880. . . . Caldwell is destined to be the largest town in the State of Kansas, and that, too, before five years will have passed by."[5]

The collective experience of the five cattle towns examined here spans the entire period of the Texas cattle trade in post-Civil War Kansas—the years from 1867

[4] The quoted dispatch, since it was of local interest, was reprinted in the Abilene *Chronicle*, June 15, 1871. This was common editorial practice, as any person who has worked with nineteenth-century newspapers knows, and many of the newspaper citations in the present work are to such republished pieces. For the sake of brevity, fully explicit citations are avoided in such cases. Wherever it seems especially useful, however, the origins of reprinted articles have been indicated.

[5] Ellsworth *Reporter*, Dec. 14, 1871 ff. (advertisement); Caldwell *Post*, Nov. 27, 1879.

through 1885. Any scrutiny of the cattle town as a type must include the two most famous of them: Abilene, first of the principal cattle trading centers, and Dodge City, the longest lived. Of the remaining—Ellsworth, Wichita, and Caldwell—all enjoyed reputations as being among the most important range cattle markets in the West. Not least important in governing their selection, finally, is the rich collection of extant materials on each. If this work is at all meaningful, it is to a great extent because so much of what the cattle town people had to say for themselves somehow survived the years of incredible change from their day to ours.

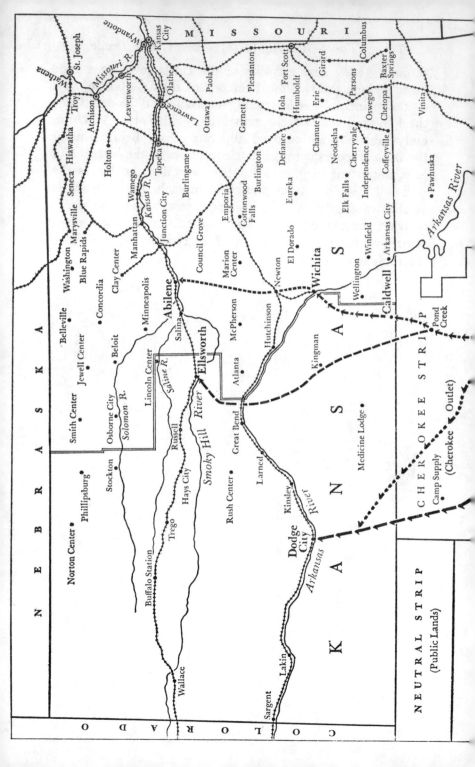

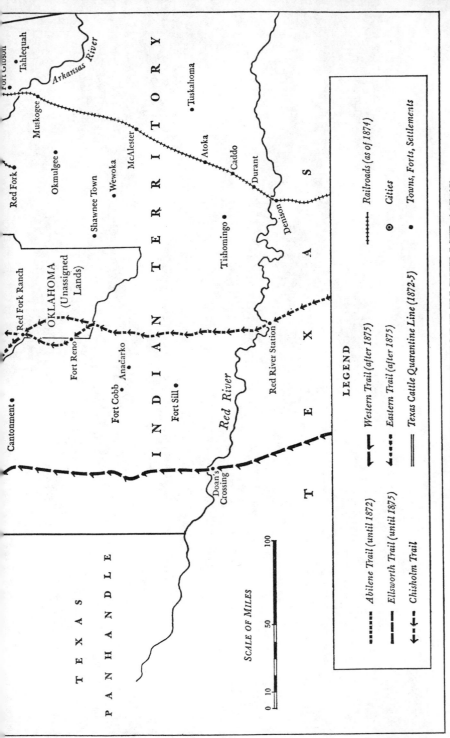

KANSAS AND INDIAN TERRITORY IN THE MID-1870'S

LEGEND

.... Abilene Trail (until 1872)
– – – Ellsworth Trail (until 1875)
←–←– Chisholm Trail

▼ Western Trail (after 1875)
◄--- Eastern Trail (after 1875)
═══ Texas Cattle Quarantine Line (1872-5)

+++++ Railroads (as of 1874)
◉ Cities
• Towns, Forts, Settlements

SCALE OF MILES

0   10   50   100

I

Beginnings

[1]

IN THE SUMMER of 1855 national attention focused on Kansas. Within a shallow crescent of settlement beyond the Missouri line roving slavery and anti-slavery forces clashed tentatively in a confrontation that would soon enlist Americans everywhere. Far less conspicuously, meanwhile, frontiersmen with more routine pursuits in mind moved up the valley of the Smoky Hill River a scant hundred miles to the west, poking a thin finger of settlement through the rich bluestem grasslands to the very edge of the Great Plains.

Firstcomers to the region a day or two upstream from Fort Riley squatted along streambeds tributary to the shallow and meandering Smoky Hill, both for easy access to water and timber and, with the ancient prejudice of forest folk, because they believed the rolling uplands unfruitful. More hunters or trappers than farmers, they and their families sheltered within untidy bottomland groves, among ash, elm, hackberry, occasional bur oaks and walnuts, and of course the familiar cottonwoods, always more numerous and usually rising taller than the rest, their sparse pale leaves fluttering aimlessly in the persistent prairie winds. These scattered pioneer vanguards of the general population advance lived grim and isolated lives. Not over half a dozen families had infiltrated the area at the time of its organization as Dickinson County early in 1857.[1] But soon that inevitable frontier figure, the townsite speculator, came among them. To the riverside straggle of corn patches and dugout huts, modest emblems of civilization in those parts, he brought a certain new pace and tone.

The village called Abilene was already six years old when discovered by the Texas cattle trade. The original settler near the site, a restless migrant from Illinois, Timothy F. Hersey, established a claim on the bare west bank of Mud Creek just north of the Smoky Hill in July 1857, where a river-hugging wagon track, the so-called military road, dropped southwestward from Junction City toward its distant intersection with the Santa Fe Trail. Three years later one Charles H. Thompson descended the road from Leavenworth County to join him there, acquiring the government quarter-section on the creekbank opposite. Thompson bought his tract at the Junction City land office by filing a military bounty warrant purchased from the widow of a War of 1812 soldier, the widow having earned it by virtue of a recent congressional act granting quarter-sections to veterans or their survivors.

Charley Thompson's new property was an edge of prairie sloping imperceptibly south toward the timbered, mile-wide Smoky Hill bottom and the low, irregular limestone bluffs rising beyond. The tract altogether impressed its owner with urban possibilities, lying as it did near the center of the county beside the increasingly busy military road. In the spring of 1861 he hired a surveyor to stake out a town on part of his land and had it ruled off into the usual neat grid of blocks and streets. He filed a plat with the county register of deeds on June 7 and promptly

[1] For a good reconstruction of the early pioneer experience in Dickinson County see Edward G. Nelson: *The Company and the Community* (Lawrence, Kan., 1956), chaps. vi, viii.

began selling lots. Six months later he boasted glowingly
that his development, named Abilene, already contained
a store, a blacksmith shop, hotel, post office, and several
families.[2]

Abilene represented but one of several townsites in
the area, all of them awaiting the golden touch of population settlement. In the usual manner of the frontier town
speculator, each Dickinson County promoter sought to
obtain for his site the exclusive political, economic, and
psychological advantages that came with having the
county seat. In Dickinson's original organization, this
prize went to Newport, a development of somewhat
grandiose proportions situated beside the Smoky Hill in
the northeast quarter of the county. For some reason
Newport drifted into decline. Promoters of rival sites
called for relocating the county seat during the winter of
1861–62. In February 1862, the state legislature scheduled a plebiscite on the question, and the electioneers
came forth. While far to the east General McClellan
hammered at the gates of Richmond and General Buell
lumbered toward Chattanooga, Dickinson County residents fought out their own civil war.

The contenders were Abilene and two other village
sites—Smoky Hill, near the defunct Newport, and Uniontown, on the south side of the river. Uniontown promoters banked on winning, with less population in their
area, by virtue of a north side split between Abilene and
Smoky Hill. But through some stratagem Charley Thompson induced the north-siders on Chapman Creek to transfer their allegiance from nearby Smoky Hill to the more

[2] Abilene *Chronicle*, Mar. 3, 1870, July 14, 1876; A. T. Andreas:
History of the State of Kansas (Chicago, 1883), p. 685; J. B. Ed-
wards: *Early Days in Abilene* (Abilene, 1940), p. 13; Robert W.
Baughman: *Kansas in Maps* (Topeka, 1961), especially p. 67; *U.S.
Statutes*, X, 701–02; Dickinson Co. Deeds (Register of Deeds Office,
Abilene), A, 70–71, 96, H, 506; Dickinson Co. Plats (ibid.), A, 1;
Junction City *Union*, Feb. 6, 1862.

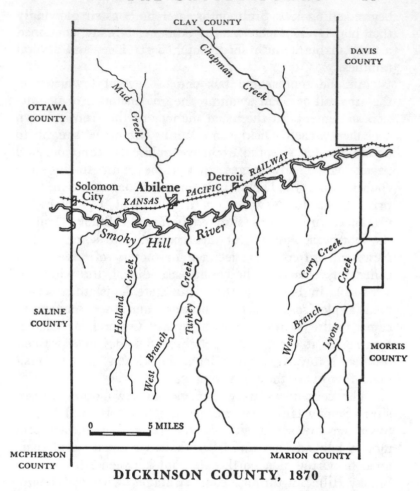

DICKINSON COUNTY, 1870

distant Abilene. The result on August 5 was seven votes for Smoky Hill, twenty-eight for Uniontown, and sixty-six for Abilene.[3] Following its defeat Uniontown rapidly

[3] Abilene *Chronicle*, July 14, 1876; Andreas: *History of Kansas*, p. 685; *Laws of Kansas*, 1862, pp. 441–42; Dickinson Co. Commissioners Journal, 1861–83 (microfilm copy, Kansas State Historical Society, Topeka [cited hereafter as KSHS]), p. 11.

reverted to farmland, although the hamlet of Smoky Hill, later christened Detroit, remained in a state of latent insurgency under the leadership of its aggressive chief proprietor, William H. Lamb. In 1865 a trio of local speculators founded the village of Solomon City to the west of Abilene. The route of the Union Pacific Railway, Eastern Division, which in the spring of 1867 swept conveniently along the north bank of the Smoky Hill River on the trace of the military road, left the towns of Detroit, Abilene, and Solomon—all three effortlessly rail-road-blessed—to contend for permanent supremacy within Dickinson County.[4]

Despite the visionary expectations of Charley Thompson, Dickinson's seat of government remained a mere cluster of ragged shelters crouching randomly at the junction of creek and railroad track. The hoped-for boom had not occurred. It was still, in the often quoted description of Joseph G. McCoy, a "small, dead place, consisting of about one dozen log huts" when he stepped off the train at Abilene with a scheme that was to prove its regeneration.[5]

Like many another enterpriser in that postwar era of opportunity, Joe McCoy represented a happy combination of personal initiative and economic privilege. Born to moderately wealthy parents near Springfield, Illinois, he grew to manhood on his father's farm, avoided Civil War military service, and withdrew from college to pursue the profits in wartime livestock trading in emulation of his two elder brothers. By 1867 young McCoy was

[4] Abilene *Reflector*, Sept. 10, 1908; Andreas: *History of Kansas,*. pp. 685, 691.

[5] Joseph G. McCoy: *Historic Sketches of the Cattle Trade of the West and Southwest*, ed. Ralph P. Bieber (Glendale, Calif., 1940), p. 116. (All references will be to Bieber's exhaustively annotated edition of this well-known work.) For the appearance of Abilene in early 1867 see also Bieber: "Introduction," ibid., p. 58; C. F. Gross to J. B. Edwards, May 29, 1922, Edwards Papers, KSHS.

shipping animals to markets as distant as New Orleans and New York. Early that year he joined his brothers' flourishing Springfield livestock firm. During his first season with William K. McCoy and Brothers the company did a business of $2.5 million with one local bank alone. In this period, as Joe McCoy later admitted, the firm's resources, financially, "were not limited."[6]

In the spring of 1866, as a demobilized nation found solace from the shattering experience of war in the old routines of field and shop, dollar-starved Texans resumed their prewar traffic in southern cattle. Up from the vast ranges of the Southwest they prodded their half-wild, massively horned animals, bound for northern market places and sky-high beef prices. Cattle driving in America was almost as old as America itself, but this year many participants in the venerable enterprise felt desperately frustrated.

The problem stemmed from the fact that Texas cattle were known to be carriers of the lethal splenic fever—commonly called "Spanish" or "Texas" fever—to which the rugged longhorns themselves were practically immune but which invariably wrought havoc among northern herds. Much as the Texans might pooh-pooh northern fears or interpret them as a mere front for sectional discrimination, midwesterners had correctly identified the secondary source of the disease. Southern cattle were widely recognized as safe for importation only in winter, when the miniscule tick that transmitted splenic fever was dead. In the summer and autumn of 1866 Texas drovers were rebuffed by so-called quarantine statutes forbidding entry into east Kansas and southwest Missouri, in some cases locally enforced by vigilante action.

⁶ Joseph G. McCoy: "Historic and Biographic Sketch," *Kansas Magazine*, II (1909), 49; McCoy: *Historic Sketches*, p. 111; Bieber: "Introduction," ibid., pp. 17–19; Gross to Edwards, Apr. 13, 1922, Edwards Papers.

Northern prices for Texas beef might be high, but the old overland routes to market remained closed.[7]

If historians today tend to honor Joe McCoy as the unassisted originator of the frontier cattle market, it is mainly because they have accepted his own account of his personal vision. In his book, published in 1874, McCoy credited no one but himself. "This young man," he wrote, speaking of himself in the third person, "conceived the idea of opening up an outlet for Texan cattle . . . a market whereat the southern drover and northern buyer would meet upon an equal footing, and both be undisturbed by mobs or swindling thieves." We now know that he owed much to conversations with two men with firsthand knowledge of Texas livestock conditions, Charles F. Gross and W. W. Sugg. But it has not yet been emphasized that as the Union Pacific tracks inched across central Kansas, others were already implementing plans for a cattle market beyond the settled portion of the state months before McCoy himself arrived on the scene.[8]

Circumstantial evidence suggests that a small group of wealthy and important enterprisers caused the inclusion of certain key provisions in the 1867 Act for the Protection of Stock from Disease that materially paved the way for McCoy's project. Early that year it became apparent that the Union Pacific would shortly extend its line to the center of Ellsworth County, where, as we shall see, plans for locating the town of Ellsworth were already afoot. At the same time, Kansans agitated for or against repealing an 1861 statute forbidding the summertime

[7] T. R. Havins: "Texas Fever," *Southwestern Historical Quarterly*, LII (1948), 147–62; McCoy: *Historic Sketches*, chap. ii; Bieber: "Introduction," ibid., pp. 46–51.

[8] McCoy: *Historic Sketches*, p. 112; Bieber: "Introduction," ibid., p. 54. Bieber more than once contradicts McCoy's claim to complete originality, and also cites the existence of the Topeka Live Stock Company, a more detailed account of which follows. But he does not give this revision of McCoy's own account the emphasis it obviously deserves.

driving of longhorns into the state. In February 1867, a
bill that would have opened roughly the western third of
Kansas to Texas cattle passed the house of representatives
almost unanimously. The members of the senate, however, altered the proposed "quarantine zone" into which
Texas stock could be driven so as to encompass only the
unsettled southwest quarter of the state. More important,
they brought its vertical boundary—the quarantine line
or "deadline," as it came to be called—substantially eastward to the west edge of Dickinson County. They also
added a proviso allowing railroad shipment of longhorns
through the state, and further specified that any incorporated and properly bonded group could survey a trail
from the quarantine zone to a cattle market on the Union
Pacific tracks for the shipment of such stock.

The house, in turn, provided—and the senate subsequently agreed—that this cattle market could not be east
of a line running through Ellsworth County, a change
that obviously benefited the proposed Ellsworth townsite.
Only two house members cast negative votes on this al-
teration. One of them was Representative Charley
Thompson from Abilene, who probably had viewed in the
senate proposal the possibility of his own town's becoming the chosen cattle market, only to have it now snatched
from his grasp. McCoy himself later denounced this bill
as a plot to set up an Ellsworth monopoly on the cattle
trade, which was doubtless Thompson's interpretation as
well.

On February 26, 1867, Governor Samuel J. Crawford
signed the bill into law. On the very next day those possibly instrumental in effecting the cattle market provision
of the act revealed their identities by incorporating themselves as the Topeka Live Stock Company. They included
former governor Thomas Carney, the man who had been
his secretary of state, another who had served on Car-

ney's personal staff, a fourth former public official who was now a government beef contractor, and two members of the 1867 senate. The latter were George W. Veale, who sat on the committee that devised the bill's original cattle market provision, and John Walter Scott, a member of the committee producing the final version of the provision. A week after incorporating, the Topeka Live Stock Company addressed a circular to Texas cattle drovers, inviting them to take advantage of a new trail it was laying out to an unnamed depot on the Union Pacific tracks. Here the company was to construct a shipping yard. The circular promised drovers that agents would meet them at the Kansas line and guide them in over the new route. This announcement went out through the mails to the cattle- men and newspapers of Texas.

Scattered Indian raids along the frontier early that summer, as well as Texans' suspicion of something about which they possessed only sketchy information, con- demned the scheme. Most early drovers turned east to Baxter Springs. For its part, the Topeka Company did not persevere with efforts to establish a cattle market, per- haps because it could not come to satisfactory shipping terms with the Union Pacific management, or, if it had Ellsworth in mind, because of the turbulent situation there (to be discussed presently).

In the meantime Joe McCoy had arrived in Kansas, a slender figure in unpretentious garb—heavy boots, short topcoat, black slouch hat—the goatee that hid a weak chin lending age to his twenty-nine years, his bland, ascetic visage concealing qualities both good and bad: a brilliant entrepreneurial imagination, a tenacious fixity of purpose, but also a somewhat undisciplined ego that fre- quently impelled him to an overconfidence in his personal mastery. After a trip to the end of the railroad line and long conversations with several knowledgeable parties, he

LIBRARY MEDIA CENTER
ALBUQUERQUE ACADEMY

decided to implement his own scheme for a Texas cattle mart. When put into effect, it proved identical to that proposed earlier by the Topeka group.[9]

Without denying him his due, it seems important to note that McCoy also exaggerated the independence of his role. His endeavor, far from being a lonely plunge, had behind it the full resources of the fraternal business partnership to which he belonged. McCoy family tradition remembers Joe as only the Kansas manager of the venture, "while James staid on his farm on Spring Creek [in Illinois] and fattened the cattle, and William looked after the sales in New York City."[1]

The three brothers' profits, besides a good opportunity to purchase livestock themselves from the herds attracted to their Kansas market, were to materialize as fees paid by railroads for the privilege of shipping longhorns east. In St. Louis the younger McCoy obtained a verbal commit-

[9] *House Journal*, 1867, especially pp. 306, 445, 869–71; *Senate Journal*, 1867, especially pp. 375, 386, 422–25, 581–82, 715; *Laws of Kansas*, 1867, pp. 263–67; Secretary of State Corporations Register (KSHS), I, 312; McCoy: *Historic Sketches*, pp. 111–13, 115, 130; Bieber: "Introduction," ibid., pp. 52–54. For data on most of the Topeka incorporators see S. Lewis and Co.: *United States Biographical Dictionary: Kansas Volume* (Chicago, 1879), pp. 206–07; Biographical Publishing Co.: *Portrait and Biographical Record of Southeastern Kansas* (Chicago, 1894), pp. 115–16; *Collections of the Kansas State Historical Society*, X (1907–08), 250, 252, 269, XI (1909–10), 5 n. For some especially good observations on McCoy's personality see Gross to Edwards, May 4, 1925, Edwards Papers.

[1] Edwin H. Van Patten: "A Brief History of David McCoy and Family," *Journal of the Illinois State Historical Society*, XIV (1921), 126. When the Abilene venture finally failed it broke all the brothers, not just Joseph. Writes Van Patten (ibid.): "They never got over their financial down fall but all died poor men, leaving their children as the only heritage to society." Charles Gross felt that McCoy was unfair in not stressing this in his book: "Joes Entire fortune was wiped out but so also was the fortune of Wm K McCoy and James McCoy his Brothers who gave of their substance *their all* and let Joe spend it. I should have Expected him to have given them *more mention*." Gross to Edwards, May 4, 1925, Edwards Papers.

ment from Union Pacific officials for payment of about five dollars for every car of cattle loaded at the chosen site. He reached a similar agreement with another company for shipment from the Missouri River to Chicago.

Satisfied with these arrangements, McCoy now turned to locating his market. He had initially favored the flourishing town of Junction City; now some contention there over the price of land for a good stockyard impelled him farther west. Bypassing Abilene, he thought Solomon City and Salina likely points but found that the leading citizens of those places shared the popular antipathy to Texas cattle that had been overridden in spring's legislative session. In June, therefore, he retraced his route and came to favorable terms with Charley Thompson, proprietor of Abilene.

In light of Thompson's intimate knowledge of the 1867 quarantine statute, McCoy could hardly have remained unaware that bringing fresh Texas cattle to Abilene would be clearly illegal. But he was not to let his plans be frustrated by a law that many Kansans considered unconstitutional in its infringement of interstate commerce. During a brief visit to Topeka he persuaded Governor Crawford—who had signed the act into law but who was, he later admitted, convinced of the general economic importance of McCoy's idea—to write him a "semi-official" endorsement of the Abilene location; and at a later date McCoy also obtained Crawford's approval of a trail surveyed over forbidden ground to Abilene.

With the normal livestock shipping season half over, McCoy now urgently turned to providing the necessary facilities at Abilene. He bought 250 acres adjoining the town for a large stockyard and made plans for immediately erecting a barn, a small office building, a set of livestock scales, an elegant hotel with attached livery stable, and a bank. He also sent an agent deep into Indian Territory to contact the startled and initially skeptical owners of northbound herds. By mid-August Texas longhorns nibbled the lush upland grasses of Dickinson County awaiting buyers, and on September 5 the first twenty carloads moved out, bound for the Chicago stockyards. Abilene was in business as a cattle town.[2]

While townsmen rejoiced over the economic endowment reflected in McCoy's enterprise, a number of settlers east of town viewed with justifiable alarm the invasion of their county by fever-laden livestock. In July or early August, preceding the arrival of the first herds, these irate farmers met near Abilene and organized themselves into a protective association for the purpose of blocking the importation of Texas cattle—by force, if necessary. Catching wind of this development, McCoy requested a hearing at which the pros and cons of the issue might be discussed. The spokesman for the group agreed. On an appointed evening McCoy met with the farmers, bringing with him several Texans who had arrived at Abilene ahead of their herds. He addressed the assembly, promising honest compensation for domestic stock that died of splenic fever, pointing out the splendid opportunities for purchasing cheap cattle, and insisting that the influx of transients connected with the cattle trade would offer a direct consumer market for farm products of all types.

As McCoy spoke, the Texans accompanying him moved among the settlers, contracting for butter, eggs, vegetables, and feed grain, offering seductive prices. Hostility weakened. At the close of the session the farmers' leader explained his own change of heart to his fellows. "Gentlemen," he concluded, "if I can make any money out of this cattle trade I am not afraid of Spanish fever,

[2] McCoy: "Historic and Biographic Sketch," 45–55; McCoy: *Historic Sketches*, pp. 111–25, 168–69; Bieber: "Introduction," ibid., pp. 54–56; Junction City *Union*, June 8, July 20, Aug. 31, Nov. 2, 1867; New York *Tribune*, Nov. 6, 1867; Topeka *Capital*, Aug. 30, 1908; Kansas City *Star*, Nov. 19, 1911; Topeka *Journal*, Mar. 8, 1913.

but if I can't make any money out of this cattle trade then I am damned 'fraid of Spanish fever." The protective association dissolved, and although much adverse feeling persisted, the first herds arrived at Abilene unmolested.[3]

In nearby Detroit, however, that town's principal citizen, Will Lamb, rallied remaining anti-cattle trade sentiment. On August 31 he scratched an angry note to Governor Crawford laying out his case. "If I mistake not," Lamb observed,

> there is a State law prohibiting any person or persons driving Texas cattle inside the limits of civilization on the frontier: If there is such a law why not enforce it; for there is now, and will be still coming, several thousand head of Texas Cattle in this immediate vicinity. . . . As a mass the settlers are against it. there are some very fine herds of cattle in this part of Kansas, and now to have the Texas cattle fever break out among them would indeed be to[o] bad. We are all afraid and ask your advice in regard to the matter.

A week later Lamb received Crawford's reply, a request for detailed information. He furnished the governor a hasty bill of particulars. "There are several of those men at Abilene in this Texas cattle business," he wrote.

> I do not think that I can get the names of any of them, but one McCoy & Bro. they are shipping those cattle to Leavenworth.
> They say that those Gentlemen who are driving said Texas Cattle into this County, have filed with the Governor & Sect of State a bond, in the sum of fifty thousand dollars ($50,000) for all damages that may occur to citizens in this part of Kansas. Also they have the written consent of all settlers *within five miles of Abilene*, to

³ McCoy: *Historic Sketches*, pp. 135–37.

drive, and *herd* there *Cattle* in that *Vacinity;* Yet that does not *protect Our cattle* from contagious decease, ariseing from Texas Stock. If this is the facts of their case please answer and let us Know; If it is false We will commence suit against them Immediately.

Please to let me Know whether they have filed any Bonds to that effect or not.

Crawford's answer has not survived, but having already thrown his support behind McCoy's venture, the governor felt disposed to do little. He may have justified inaction on the grounds that quarantine law enforcement remained a strictly local responsibility. Dickinson County's officials, however, also ignored the situation. Newton Blair, a local farmer, laid a complaint before a justice of the peace and found him unwilling to act on it. Inquiring around, he discovered all local magistrates hesitant to prosecute save one whose election was in doubt. "We have no Prosecuting Attorney for this Co," he wrote Governor Crawford, adding that the county attorneys holding office on either side of Dickinson had been bribed not to prosecute. "In fact," he concluded, "all the officers from whom those Cattle-Men thought they had anything to fear are bought up."

Will Lamb complained to the governor again in November, urging him to intervene because civil violence impended. He alleged that the Texas cattlemen, whom he described as unreconstructed Confederates, had threatened settlers with bodily harm should they pose active objections to incoming herds. Crawford simply forwarded this communication to Henry H. Hazlett, an Abilene grocer serving as county sheriff. Hazlett, no doubt personally impressed by subsidiary profits from the cattle trade, assured the governor that Lamb's assertions were

all both singly and collectiv[e]ly false. There has been at no time this Summer any feeling existing that would tend towards a Collision between the resident Citizens and the Drovers, but on the Contrary the best of feeling preva[i]led among all Parties and never before in the annuals of Kansas has there been found so great a number of loose men togeather and so little cause for trouble or complaint. . . .

The Settlers in the County . . . have with a very fiew exceptions . . . gone in to the Texas Stock Business and have purchased more or less of that class of Stock to raise and fatten for Market. . . . There are no Cattel here now. And no Texas Men. The former having all been sold or gone in to Market and the latter to there homes, and in consequence the Farmers and others are complaining of dull times and all will look anxiously for the return of Spring to us[h]er in again the Texas Men with there Texas Cattel.[4]

In 1867 Abilene captured the tailings of a desultory trail driving season. Only some thirty-five thousand head reached Abilene, of which from eighteen to twenty thousand left McCoy's stockyard for points east.[5] These numbers served well enough as a fair portent for 1868. But Sheriff Hazlett's glib dismissal notwithstanding, rural opposition remained a definite threat. If ignored, it could very well solidify into a full-throated demand for local enforcement of the quarantine law—or failing this, for the political replacement of officials who refused to act. Such repercussions promised a most effective destruction of Abilene's fledgling cattle trade. At the very least anti-cattle agitation could inhibit the drovers, many of whom

[4] William H. Lamb to Samuel J. Crawford, Aug. 31, Sept. 10, 1867, Governors' Correspondence (Livestock), KSHS; Newton Blair to Crawford, Oct. 7, 1867, ibid.; H. H. Hazlett to Crawford, Nov. 19, 1867, ibid. No evidence exists that McCoy posted the bond mentioned in the September 10 letter and required by the 1867 Texas cattle statute.

[5] McCoy: *Historic Sketches*, p. 122 *n.* McCoy himself bought "about 3,000 head" and shipped them to Chicago, but lost heavily on the deal. Ibid., pp. 173–74.

would surely prove skittish about pasturing their valuable property within a pocket of rural antagonism. They might well take their herds elsewhere.

As a matter of fact, the businessmen of Junction City, viewing the retail profits attending McCoy's cattle trade, had already launched an effort to lure it away from Abilene. Publicizing Dickinson County's hostility to the trade now comprised an important part of their plan. On the other side of Abilene, Solomon City posed a second nearby threat to McCoy's monopoly. The Solomonites had rebuffed Joe McCoy the previous summer, but by autumn had changed their minds. In November 1867, they announced the completion of their own stockyard, thereby anticipating "a very large proportion of the cattle trade of the next season." But this radical about-face also worked to Abilene's advantage. While setting themselves to compete with Abilene, Solomon's businessmen now proved just as eager as their down-river neighbors to keep Dickinson County open to Texas cattle.[6]

Abilene's small but growing business community rallied around McCoy in the spring of 1868. Hostile farmers clamored for a county-wide assembly that would organize appropriate action on the Texas cattle question. The Abilene men responded to this threat by calling upon their new competitors at Solomon City. They promised Solomonites half of all Texas cattle attracted to Dickinson County the coming summer in return for help in manipulating the cattle trade meeting. The Solomon City men agreed.

On a Saturday afternoon in April, farmers and businessmen descended from wagons and buggies beside the Smoky Hill at Humbarger's Ford, the cattle crossing immediately south of Abilene. Abilene's Tim Hersey called the meeting to order. Will Lamb and his outnumbered

[6] McCoy: *Historic Sketches*, pp. 189–90, 191–92 *n.;* Junction City *Union*, Nov. 9, 1867, Feb. 29, Mar. 21, 1868.

supporters evidently expected a democratic expression of alternatives; things turned out quite differently. A Solomon City innkeeper took the chair. Elected secretary was Theodore C. Henry, an ambitious young Abilene realtor whose public debut this day prefaced fully fifteen years' prominence in local affairs. The chair appointed a committee of five—four of them Abilene or Solomon businessmen—to draft resolutions expressing the general sentiment. The committee retired without even awaiting discussion from the floor. During its absence, in the words of Henry's report, "the propriety and objections to the presence of [the] cattle trade were urged in an animated discussion." To little avail. The committee reappeared and announced that whereas the experience of 1867

> induces belief that the facts justify the withdrawal of all objections on the part of the farmers and citizens of Dickinson Co., to the continuation of the trade, therefore
>
> *Resolved*, That we, the citizens of Dickinson county, invite and encourage the presence of the trade, as beneficial to every permanent interest of our people.
>
> *Resolved*, That every endeavor that we can command, be exerted to allow those engaged in, and connected with this trade, a peaceable and undisturbed entry into our county, that they may avail themselves of our facilities for shipment and transportation to the markets of the east.

Promptly adopted, the resolutions were ordered mailed to newspapers in Salina, Junction City, and Texas itself for the widest possible effect. As T. C. Henry piously, if ungrammatically, concluded his report: "The Convention fully determined that no unwise and proscriptive legislation [that is, the quarantine law] should influence the citizens of Dickinson county, to refrain from conceding every right and privilege that the citizens of whatever State is morally and naturally entitled to."[7]

---

[7] Detroit *Western News*, Feb. 11, 1870; Junction City *Union*, Apr. 11, 1868. Ironically, Theodore C. Henry, as we shall see in Chapter

The outcome at Humbarger's Ford no doubt cheered McCoy, and in preparing for a busy new cattle season he also felt pleased by the railroad's having accepted his enterprise as a permanent success. Union Pacific officials signed an agreement extending in written form—for at least another two years, thought McCoy, who drafted the contract himself—the lucrative 1867 agreement.

In much larger numbers than the previous season the longhorns of 1868 drew on toward Abilene. Drovers that year funneled many herds through Indian Territory on the trail laid out by the half-breed Cherokee trader, Jesse Chisholm. The first Texas cattle reached Dickinson County in the last week of April. By mid-June shipments already totaled three thousand head, with about ten thousand more roaming the outlying uplands awaiting sale or transport. At the end of the month the demand for cattle cars outran the railroad's supply of them.[8]

But local hostility had not really been killed. For one thing, the men of Abilene promptly broke their promise to share the cattle shipping business with Solomon City. Vigilant townsmen met the very first herd that started for Solomon and diverted it to McCoy's stockyard, a slight Solomonites were not to forget. More important, local domestic livestock began dying of splenic fever. This time the rural uprising proved serious. "When the settlers near Abilene began to lose cattle from the fever," recalled McCoy's young assistant, Charley Gross, "Hell was to pay. . . . The farmers had but few cattle [and] little money & to see their small stock of cattle die off was to them almost unbearable, it was almost open gun war."

VIII, was instrumental in ousting the cattle trade from Dickinson County in 1871–72. McCoy, without mentioning this meeting, also tells of invitation circulars broadcast in early 1868. McCoy: *Historic Sketches*, pp. 181–82.

[8] Gross to Edwards, May 4, 1925, Edwards Papers; McCoy: *Historic Sketches*, pp. 159–63 n., 181–82, 192, 199, 249–51.

At the end of August the Junction City newspaper confirmed that "At Abilene a great many native cattle have died, and the feeling is growing very strong among the farmers against the Texas cattle business."

Joe McCoy fully reaffirmed his earlier promise to make good on local stock losses, the total value of which amounted to about $4,500 that summer. He asked the drovers to contribute a share of this amount, but they stubbornly clung to the Texan notion that longhorns had no connection with the disease. Professor John Gamgee, a celebrated London veterinary surgeon who toured splenic fever areas that summer under the auspices of the U.S. Department of Agriculture, visited Dickinson County late in August and helped convince them otherwise. The Texans finally levied a tax on themselves of five cents per head of cattle owned. They raised by this means about $1,200, which McCoy himself increased by $3,300 to cover the amount claimed. With this voluntary payment of damages, testified Charley Gross, "a partial peace was obtained."[9]

McCoy deftly handled yet another emergency that summer, a flat market for Texas cattle occasioned by splenic fever devastation in Illinois. He responded with his characteristic inventiveness, organizing an advertising campaign that included what was apparently history's first Wild West show, a collection of three buffalo, an elk, and three wild ponies, all chased around an enclosure by a pair of costumed Mexican vaqueros before delighted audiences in St. Louis and Chicago. To the same end McCoy sponsored a western buffalo hunt for Illinois cattle buyers, afterwards entertaining them at Abilene. As a result, or simply because of a natural lapse of splenic fever, the last steer on the Abilene market was gone before

[9] Detroit *Western News*, Feb. 11, 1870; Gross to Edwards, Apr. 13, 1922, Edwards Papers; Junction City *Union*, Aug. 29, 1868; McCoy: *Historic Sketches*, pp. 219–20, 226–27.

cold weather set in. "Abilene is deserted," a citizen reported to the Junction City newspaper, "but will be so only for a few months." As weary townsmen contemplated the snug profits of a successful retail season, they laid plans for the next spring's inundation of consumers.

From St. Louis the board of directors of the Union Pacific, Eastern Division—shortly to change its name to the Kansas Pacific Railway—reported to stockholders that the number of Texas cattle shipped eastward over the line during the year, "chiefly from the stock yards at Abilene," came to 52,920 head. "This cattle trade," they cautiously confided,

> has grown into very considerable importance within the past two years, and already adds largely to the east-bound freight of the road. With the additional facilities for shipment, which your Board believe it to the interests of the Company to provide, a very large increase of this business is expected.

It seemed true indeed, as Joe McCoy later recollected, that "The year of 1868 closed with Abilene's success as a cattle market of no mean proportions assured beyond cavil or doubt."[1]

[2]

SIXTY MILES SOUTHWEST of Abilene a second prospective cattle town—Ellsworth—straddled the tracks of the railway. Near here, back in the late fifties, the military road from Junction City, after slicing across from Salina, rejoined the Smoky Hill River at the ford known as Smoky Hill Crossing. On the north bank of the ford, in the center of what would become Ellsworth County, an enterprising

[1] McCoy: *Historic Sketches*, pp. 245–49; Junction City *Union*, Oct. 17, Dec. 12, 1868; Kansas Pacific Railway Co.: *Annual Report . . . 1868* (St. Louis, 1869), p. 12.

frontiersman had erected a dirt-roofed log hut that served as a primitive inn.

The hectic war years retarded new immigration into the area and local raids accompanying the Indian troubles of 1864–65 prompted the evacuation of what few residents there were. In June 1864, with the mails west of Salina in chaotic shape, the western military authorities briefly turned their attention from the Confederate threat and moved to re-establish security along the important communicaton routes on the frontier. A cavalry force, finding the cabin at Smoky Hill Crossing abandoned, paused to build a crude blockhouse at the ford. Moving on, they left behind a small detachment to provide regular escort for stagecoaches and wagon trains between that point and Fort Zarah. Later in the summer, with the Indians far from subdued, a larger garrison occupied the tiny outpost, which became a permanent part of the frontier defenses of Kansas. At the close of the Civil War troops relocated the post a mile upstream and christened it Fort Harker. Settlement immediately resumed under its benevolent proximity.[2]

In the autumn of 1866, at about the time the railroad tracks reached Junction City, a group of businessmen met there and drew up plans for a townsite development in the path of the road west of Salina. One of them later recalled that the proposed Ellsworth County location was originally envisioned as "the nucleus of an as yet undeveloped agricultural country." But more likely immediately motives arose from the presence of the military gar-

[2] Charles J. Lyon: *Compendious History of Ellsworth County* (Ellsworth, 1879), pp. 24–30; Andreas: *History of Kansas*, p. 1274; U.S. War Dept.: *The War of the Rebellion: A Compilation of the Official Records of the Union and Confederate Armies* (Washington, D.C., 1880–1901), Ser. I, XXXIV, pt. 4, 205, 402, 404, XLI, pt. 1, 189–90, pt. 2, 545, 630, XLVIII, pt. 1, 462, pt. 2, 277; Francis Paul Prucha: *A Guide to the Military Posts of the United States, 1789–1895* (Madison, Wis., 1964), p. 78.

rison and foreknowledge that the tracks would halt there for a time, transforming the potential development into an entrepôt serving New Mexico, Denver, and the army posts of west and southwest Kansas. Those interested in the scheme formed a corporation on January 15, 1867, and completed their organization as the Ellsworth Town Company in April. A few days later the military authorities upgraded Fort Harker to a status equivalent to Forts Leavenworth and Riley through an order that its temporary buildings be rebuilt with permanent materials. This happy event did not go unnoticed. The expenditure of army funds, noted the Junction City editor, would contribute to the new townsite's rapid growth. "We regard the order as of peculiar significance to that point," he wrote.

> The employment of four or five hundred mechanics during the next year and a half or two years, together with the terminus of the railroad at that point, will combine to make one of the largest and liveliest points in Kansas; to say nothing of the current expenditures of a military post of such importance. From the Atlantic westward, the selections by the military of points for their operations have, without exception, been changed to large, populous, and important cities and towns—thus certifying to the wisdom which moves competent military commanders in such matters.[3]

A mile west of the fort a flat strip of land lay squeezed between rounded bluffs and a riverbank deeply cut but anchored by protruding cottonwoods. On this ground, overlooking a broad spread of bottomland that termi-

[3] Topeka *Commonwealth*, Feb. 18, 1872; Corporations Register, I, 276; Junction City *Union*, Apr. 13, 20, 1867. The belief that the site of an army post represented an ideal place for a future town development had by this time evidently become part of the frontier speculator's dogma. For an interesting discussion see Wichita *Eagle*, Apr. 1, 1875.

nated to the south in a line of bare hills, the Ellsworth promoters decided to locate their town. In March 1867, they had it surveyed, then sought to obtain title. They found that the desired land lay mainly on two quarter-sections. One owner, a Davis County resident, obligingly sold his entire 160 acres to the company for $100. The other owner proved more difficult. A prominent Junction City hotelman, he did not relinquish his quarter-section until May 4, and then only for $2,800, forcing the town-site speculators to meet his terms by reason of their haste to implement their plans. They filed their plat on May 5 with the register of deeds at Salina, and commenced the sale of town lots. Two weeks later the company president visited the site and reported that commercial buildings were springing up like magic, information that the town was to remain for some time a railroad terminus acting as a magnet for scores of itinerant merchants.[4]

Suddenly an unkind fate struck Ellsworth's proprietors a series of rapid, disastrous blows. On June 8 the Smoky Hill belied its normal placidity and inundated the little boom town with several feet of water, ruining stocks of goods and sweeping many of the jerry-built stores and cottages from their foundations. The inhabitants hastily moved to higher ground to the northwest, where the proprietors had already obtained another quarter-section from an Ohio entryman for $1,400. This "Addition to Ellsworth," which became the original townsite for all practical purposes, was surveyed in early July and a plat filed on July 18. A special act of the state legislature subse-

[4] Ellsworth Co. Deeds (Register of Deeds Office, Ellsworth), A, 532, B, 23–25; Ellsworth Co. Plats (ibid.), A, 2; Andreas: *History of Kansas*, p. 1276; Junction City *Union*, May 11, 25, 1867. What the original "owners" actually sold, of course, were their *claims* to the land rather than ownership, since the federal government was sometimes as much as years behind in issuing patents. The Junction City hotelman's claim, incidentally, was evidently invalidated a year or two after its sale, so that the $2,800 had been spent for nothing.

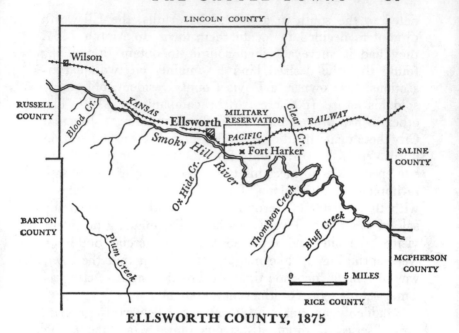

ELLSWORTH COUNTY, 1875

quently legalized transfer of titles from the earlier site to the new. But scarcely had the waters subsided than a party of Cheyenne marauders swept through the county, raiding one night to within a quarter mile of town and sending frightful rumors up the railroad line that both town and fort had been massacred. Then followed a visitation of dread Asiatic cholera that killed some two hundred soldiers and civilians and emptied the community of most of its panic-stricken residents, understandably deterring further population increase. The final blow of the season fell that autumn, when the railroad line moved on west. By November, with trains running regularly to Fort Hays, the end-of-track boom at Ellsworth had collapsed.[5]

[5] Andreas: *History of Kansas*, pp. 1276–77; Ellsworth Co. Deeds, A, 531, B, 30–31; Ellsworth Co. Plats, A, 2–3; *Laws of Kansas*, 1869,

In a desperate bid to retain the value of their investment, the townsite promoters in January 1868 sought and obtained a charter for the Ellsworth and Pacific Railroad Company. They then petitioned Congress and the army to withdraw support from the proposed Kansas Pacific extension to Denver and to give it instead to their own line, which would run from Ellsworth to the West Coast via Santa Fe. Even with Governor Crawford as a charter stockholder, the grandly conceived E. & P. never went anywhere. This defeat was only partially mitigated in March by an order that all government freight would be unloaded at Fort Harker rather than Hays. A newspaperman accompanying an excursion train out to the end of the line in June brutally disparaged Ellsworth's future. "One of the Agents of the [National] Land Company," he observed,

> had already been sent up to Pond creek, or Fort Wallace, to lay out a town near that point. Thitherward the people of Hays and Ellsworth, also, are already looking, and many are making arrangements to move to that point, whenever the line of the road is definitely settled and the town laid out. It is their only hope. There will continue to be some little business at Ellsworth and Hays, as long as the forts remain there, but not enough to support over one fourth the present number of business houses. Business has been over done in these frontier towns, and a reaction, painful, but undoubtedly healthful, is taking place. . . .
>
> Ellsworth is the county seat of Ellsworth county, and although in a little better looking country than farther west, it is by no means a farming coun[tr]y. A little land has been cultivated along the creeks, but with indifferent success, there not being enough rain to produce good crops, and there being not enough water for irrigation.

pp. 261–62; Junction City *Union*, June 15, July 6, 20, 27, Aug. 3, 24, Nov. 30 (train schedule), 1867; Leavenworth *Conservative*, July 6, 26, 27, 1867.

The railroad company have an engine house here, with four stalls, and also have a blacksmith shop. The trade of the fort, together with a share of the New Mexican trade, constitute about all the business, which is by no means large. Persons wishing to invest in real estate can do so in Ellsworth just now at greatly reduced rates.

A month later the once-solicitous Junction City editor announced derisively that "Ellsworth is puking, and this time most of her people are coming down to Abilene"— the booming new cattle town. Ellsworth County's fledgling agricultural community suffered miserably poor crops that year, and to top things off the Indians returned in the autumn, forcing settlers to congregate for defense at Fort Harker and beg army rations. Ellsworth's newspaper editor, who had arrived only months before, gave up and deserted the dispirited little town. Not surprisingly, the businessmen who remained felt their common economic salvation lay in acquiring a share of Abilene's cattle trade. During the winter of 1868–69 they laid plans to dislodge it.[6]

Like the unsuccessful Topeka group of 1867, the Ellsworthites made their influence felt in the state legislature. On March 2, 1869, accordingly, Governor James M. Harvey approved an act establishing a state highway to Ellsworth from Fort Cobb, Indian Territory, especially designed for livestock. Drovers importing Texas cattle over this road were to be exempted from the regulations and penalties of the quarantine law. A month later six Ellsworth citizens serving as city or county officials petitioned Governor Harvey to cause the enforcement of this same splenic fever statute to which Ellsworth was now

[6] Corporations Register, I, 450–51; Leavenworth Bulletin: *The Ellsworth and Pacific Railroad* (Leavenworth, 1868); Junction City *Union*, Mar. 21, July 18, 1868; Lawrence *Tribune*, June 19, 1868; Adolph Roenigk (ed.): *Pioneer History of Kansas* (Denver, 1933), pp. 86–87; Kansas State Board of Agriculture: *Biennial Report . . . 1878* (Topeka, 1878), p. 212.

doubly immune. "The Law was passed in 1867," they reminded him, ". . . prohibiting Texas cattle from being driven East beyond a certain boundary. The Law has been violated daily since that time, and your petitioners pray your Excellency that you have the Laws faithfully carried out and justice done." According to Joe McCoy's recollection, they also tried to induce Dickinson County settlers to protest the illegally positioned Abilene cattle market.[7]

As spring arrived one Ellsworth businessman spoke publicly of having "an assurance of the cattle trade," and William Sigerson and Company of St. Louis began work on a large stockyard and a structure to hold the requisite banking facilities. The Kansas Pacific Railway added the necessary siding. Circulars and posters advertising these improvements went out to all corners of Texas, and on May 31 agents left for that state to guide herds up the new state road. For the first time in over a year the townsmen's spirits soared. "It was supposed," wrote an excited news correspondent, "that when the railroad was extended west of the town, Ellsworth would die, but instead she prospered." By autumn, however, the town's good prospects had once again proven ill founded, perhaps due in part to Indian raids early in the summer that kept many a wary cattleman from driving so far west. In September, when it should have been at the height of its shipping activity, Ellsworth was pictured by a passing newspaperman as back in the doldrums again.[8]

Meanwhile, several prominent Ellsworth County settlers had developed an incipient dairy cattle industry.

[7] *Laws of Kansas*, 1869, pp. 217–18; M. Newton to J. M. Harvey, Apr. 3, 1869 (enclosing petition), Governors' Correspondence (Livestock); McCoy: *Historic Sketches*, p. 130.

[8] Junction City *Union*, May 15, Sept. 25, 1869; Leavenworth *Times and Conservative*, June 5, 6, 1869. The railroad reported no 1869 cattle shipments from towns west of Brookville. Kansas Pacific; *Annual Report . . . 1870* (St. Louis, 1871), p. 19.

While townsmen yearned for the Texas cattle trade, these rural enterprisers opposed it for fear of splenic fever. In 1870 drovers brought at least a few herds of longhorns into Ellsworth County, evidently aiming either for the empty Ellsworth stockyard or for more northerly ranges and shipping points. Several of these visitors were fined for violating the quarantine line, which protected the eastern half of the county, by a local official who was himself a dairyman of consequence. "Persons driving Texas cattle will do well to take this [as a] warning," wrote a spokesman for domestic stock interests to the Junction City paper, "as some half dozen of farmers have lost by the 'Texas fever' and are in no humor to be trifled with."

This mood was shortly to be tested. In their report to stockholders that winter the Kansas Pacific directors revealed preparations to make Ellsworth a principal shipping point for 1871, a policy dictated by an accurate guess that the Abilene cattle trail would soon be blocked by the advancing agricultural frontier. In January 1871, the road's general freight agent, although he gave Abilene featured billing, advised drovers that "The stock yards at Ellsworth . . . are also to be again opened, under charge of an experienced cattle man." The company itself then bought the stockyard, repairing and enlarging it. That summer, for the first time, a significant portion of the Texas herds driven into Kansas came to Ellsworth. By July hundreds of trail-weary longhorns cropped grass on the empty uplands of the county, and in town new store buildings had sprung up in response to their salubrious presence. A total of 28,500 head, or over 18 per cent of all cattle handled by the Kansas Pacific that season, boarded the cars at Ellsworth. During the winter the railroad managers declared that, with the traffic in Texas livestock at an all-time high, in the coming year "the larger part of the cattle shipments of the company" would originate from the new cattle town.[9]

As Ellsworth's businessmen briskly surveyed the local scene they probably felt little concern about remaining rural antagonism to Texas cattle. As in Dickinson County during the first years of Abilene's cattle trade, many of Ellsworth County's domestic stock raisers had been struck by the profits to be had on "wintered" Texas beef —that is, animals bought cheaply in the local cattle town market in the autumn, fed usually by being turned loose to forage for themselves in the winter, and sold again, heavier and free of splenic fever, in late spring. Such stockmen, in favoring Texas cattle, thus put themselves in league with the townsmen. This left as critics of the trade only those relatively few local cattlemen still dealing exclusively in domestic stock, together with a comparatively slow-growing aggregation of conventional farmers. For many a settler intending primarily to raise crops instead of cattle, concern about splenic fever took second place to trampled fields—fields unfenced because of the scarcity of native timber and the expense of wire. These farmers feared both the summertime inundation of southern herds and, as demonstrated in the exceptionally bitter cold season of 1871–72, depredations by free-ranging wintered stock. With grass buried beneath the snow and streams frozen, some forty thousand hungry and thirsty longhorns invaded Ellsworth County farmsteads to gobble stacked hay, to strip fruit and forest saplings, and to

[9] C. C. Hutchinson: *Resources of Kansas* (Topeka, 1871), pp. 103–05; Leavenworth *Times and Conservative*, June 5, 1869; Junction City *Union*, Sept. 10, 1870; Kansas Pacific: *Annual Report 1870*, p. 8; ibid. *1871* (St. Louis, 1872), p. 8; ibid. *1872* (St. Louis, 1873), p. 20; Wichita *Vidette*, Feb. 25, 1871; Topeka *Commonwealth*, May 30, July 16, 1871. The figure for the total Kansas Pacific shipment of 1871 varies; that given in the Abilene *Chronicle*, Feb. 1, 1872, was used here and represents the period May-November 1871.

drink from ice-skimmed water holes meant for domestic animals. The famished cattle often refused to be driven away, and angry settlers killed some of them. That winter both stockmen's and farmers' protective associations organized for action, but the issue subsided with the return of spring.

Harassed farmers looked to the imposition in Ellsworth County of new legal penalties for those who allowed their livestock to roam at will. In early March 1872, the governor of Kansas approved a "herd law" act that, if locally implemented, would force cattle raisers to restrict their animals rather than requiring farmers to fence their fields. This new statute gave the board of commissioners governing each county arbitrary power to declare the herd law in effect. Townsmen, mobilized to encourage the Texas cattle trade, and local stockmen, for the most part handling Texas cattle without benefit of fenced ranges, both opposed the herd law's concept of justice, and were, of course, militantly against its imposition. Of Ellsworth County's three commissioners, one was an Ellsworth tavern keeper and another a stockman who allowed his cattle to forage each winter. Only one of them expressed much sympathy with the farmers' viewpoint. No herd law, consequently, emerged from the board that spring. On May 10 the farmers' protective association members apparently considered pressing for the law, but, the planting season being upon them, they did not meet again till autumn.[1]

With Ellsworth anticipating the bulk of the cattle trade on the Kansas Pacific line that spring, new faces appeared weekly within its business community. Many peripatetic frontier tradesmen calculatingly shifted operations down the track, just as they had deserted Ellsworth four or five years before, to cash in on the expected

[1] Ellsworth *Reporter*, Dec. 21, 28, 1871, Jan. 11, 25, Feb. 22, 29, Mar. 7, 14, Apr. 4, May 9, 1872; *Laws of Kansas*, 1872, pp. 384–85.

influx of transients. "Half of Abilene will be here in two months," the editor of the recently established Ellsworth *Reporter* observed in March, himself a testimony to the town's resurgence. On June 1, the first stock shipment of the season left the Ellsworth loading pens, and by mid-month the countryside swarmed with an estimated 100,-000 head destined for sale.

A correspondent for a Kansas City newspaper documented the community change wrought by Texas cattle. "As you observe," he reported to his readers, "I am at Ellsworth, but not the Ellsworth of last year, for it has become thoroughly revolutionized, and to-day is the Abilene of last year. This is really the cattle mart of the great West." Wrote another who in early July came to see for himself: "Ellsworth has her cattle trade, the same that rendered Abilene so famous, and wherever that is there will be money."[2]

[3]

SOME EIGHTY-FIVE MILES due south of Abilene the wide and smoothly flowing Arkansas River arches resolutely downward to be met by the current of a lesser stream, the Little Arkansas. In the late sixties, immediately below this juncture, herd after herd of market-bound Texas cattle thrashed through the waters, swept over the river's shallow, cottonwood-fringed left bank, and slowly ascended toward the vast prairie skyline to the north. At this point a third major cattle town sprouted beside the flattened sod. Its name was Wichita.

The first white men had arrived in the area just before the Civil War, mainly trappers and buffalo hunters who left little mark on the broad grasslands. Then in early 1864 the peaceable Wichita Indians, weary refugees from

[2] Ellsworth *Reporter*, Mar. 21, June 6, 20, 27, 1872; Leavenworth *Commercial*, July 7, 1872.

Confederate-sympathizing tribes to the south, settled at the site, accompanied by several ambitious traders. One of these traders, the renowned Jesse Chisholm, marked out a route from the Wichita village to a point deep in Indian Territory over which the great herds were to move a few years later.[3]

In 1867 the Wichitas returned home. Potential speculators recognized the deserted site as an ideal location for a city, not only because of its situation beside the cattle trail now extending up to Abilene, but also because of its choice position in relation to the new quarantine line. Although, as we have seen, Governor Crawford specifically endorsed it as a summertime Texas cattle market, Abilene was strictly off limits; most other towns on the Kansas Pacific line could receive Texas cattle only by observing certain stringent conditions. But the site at the mouth of the Little Arkansas lay just at the edge of the free zone—the completely unrestricted southwest quarter of the state. Should the 1867 law ever be enforced, drovers bringing cattle up the Chisholm Trail during the summer season would have to stop their northward momentum at this precise point unless they chose to deviate from the established route.

By all rights, therefore, Wichita's emergence as an urban development should have occurred sooner than it did, despite the early lack of a railroad in the area. The delay was caused by a tangle of land disposal questions in south-central Kansas that for a time seriously inhibited speculators from exploiting the site.[4]

To the Osage Indians belonged the aboriginal claim

[3] Andreas: *History of Kansas*, pp. 1384–85; O. H. Bentley (ed.): *History of Wichita and Sedgwick County* (Chicago, 1910), I, 125; Wichita *Vidette*, Aug. 13, 1870; Wichita *Eagle*, Mar. 1, 1890.

[4] For a good general treatment of this land question see Paul Wallace Gates: *Fifty Million Acres: Conflicts Over Kansas Land Policy* (Ithaca, N.Y., 1954), chap. vi. A satisfactory grasp of many of the complexities, however, requires recourse to the original materials.

to the region. In an 1865 treaty the tribesmen condition-
ally relinquished part of their domain, including a broad
swath of Kansas embracing the juncture of the two
Arkansas rivers. Congress delayed the treaty with
changes that had to be ratified by the Osages, and the
document did not receive final approval until January
1867. For the land-hungry, its terms proved difficult. The
treaty disallowed cheap acquisition through conventional
pre-empting or homesteading procedures, and curiously
extended purchase privileges only to a relatively few very
early squatters on the tract. Among the most disappointed were prospective townsite proprietors.

With hardly anyone happy about the old one, agitation for a new Osage treaty stirred Kansans in the winter of
1867–68. In April 1868, President Andrew Johnson accordingly appointed a commission to negotiate a new
agreement with the Osages.[5] Anticipating liberalized
provisions for land procurement, new squatters zealously
infiltrated the tract. The eagerly expectant included townsite speculators with designs on the confluence of the
rivers.

On April 23, as the treaty commissioners hastened to
Osage headquarters in Indian Territory, a group of men
gathered at Emporia to form the Wichita Town and Land
Company. Among them, or at least lending his name and
influence to the group, was none other than Governor
Crawford. The assembled stockholders envisaged a gi-
gantic development—one with 640 acres, or an entire section, surveyed into town lots and streets, plus an additional half-section of suburban five-acre lots, including
"suitable locations for Public Buildings, churches,
Schools & Parks." As emphasized by speakers, the economy of the proposed metropolis was to center on the
Texas cattle trade, and the speculators directed their pro-

[5] *U.S. Statutes*, XIV, 687–93; *House Exec. Doc. No. 310*, 40 Cong.,
2 sess., pt. 1, *passim*, pt. 3, pp. 27–28.

visional president "to issue a circular setting forth the advantages of the town as a depot for the sale of southern cattle." They then dispatched David S. Munger, a Topeka businessman, on ahead to establish the nucleus of urban growth at the site with a store and hotel. When the Osages signed a new treaty, late in May, Dave Munger was in place.[6]

In June, however, amid stormy revelations in Congress, the truth emerged that the negotiators, with a patent disregard for the public interest, had arranged to sell the entire Osage reserve to a railroad corporation. Presumably the Wichita promoters could have bought their lands just as readily from the railroad as from the government, though certainly not as cheaply. Governor Crawford was one of the most vocal of the many outraged Kansans. The new treaty failed of ratification, but when Congress finally made the Osage lands available by a resolution early in 1869, the terms seemed little better than in the 1865 treaty: for sale only to those squatters already on the land, who were given two years within which to purchase individual quarter-section claims at $1.25 per acre. Since these terms allowed no possibility for the extensive urban development anticipated in the spring of 1868, many of the original Wichita promoters lost interest. But some of them retained individual financial interests in the tract held by Munger, who persisted in his intention to gain title and eventually to plat it as a townsite.[7]

[6] Emporia *News*, Apr. 24, 1868; John P. Edwards: *Historical Atlas of Sedgwick County* (Philadelphia, 1882), p. 10; Chapman Bros.: *Portrait and Biographical Album of Sedgwick County* (Chicago, 1888), p. 160; Andreas: *History of Kansas*, p. 1389; Topeka *Leader*, May 7, 1868; D. S. Munger to A. F. Horner, May 24, 1868, Horner Papers, KSHS.

[7] Gates: *Fifty Million Acres*, pp. 198–206; *U.S. Statutes*, XVI, 55–56. Lack of an entry for the Wichita Town and Land Company in the Secretary of State Corporations Register reveals that its members never

General Land Office regulations supplementing the 1869 congressional resolution specified that acquisition be accomplished according to pre-emption procedures. Each claimant was to file a statement of intent at the nearest land office, thus gaining permission to purchase six months thereafter. The office at Humboldt, Kansas, began accepting initial entries in August 1869; most of the settlers at Wichita immediately filed and began waiting out their six-month residence requirements.

That autumn Wichita received an important addition to its population with the arrival of William ("Dutch Bill") Greiffenstein, a German-born Indian trader who had spent his entire adult life on the frontier. A large, untidy man with watery eyes (he had once been badly snow-blinded), given to cigars and a long-stemmed German pipe, he was by the look of his gray hair and whiskers an old man. Actually he was forty-one. Greiffenstein was also very nearly broke; the army recently had run him out of Indian Territory for allegedly selling ammunition to the tribesmen and had confiscated his goods. Friends urged him to get a fresh start at Wichita, advice he followed, buying an improved claim from an original pre-empter and opening a modest mercantile business. Although not permitted to purchase title to his land

---

completed their intended incorporation. W. W. H. Lawrence, president of the Wichita Company, was also secretary of the Kansas Live Stock Company which in 1867, as we have seen, proposed to establish a cattle market on the Union Pacific line. That corporation's charter included "the improvement of a town site" as among its stated aims and Sedgwick County as within the area in which it intended to do business. But its possible connection with the Wichita endeavor remains obscure. The early chroniclers of Wichita displayed only an incomplete knowledge of the first townsite company. According to the Wichita *Vidette*, Aug. 13, 1870: "In 1868 Gen. Lawrence . . . and others, began talking about laying out a town; but it seems that the land could not be obtained for that purpose." See also Edwards: *Historical Atlas of Sedgwick County*, p. 10: "For some reason . . . they disbanded, and left others to reap the benefits."

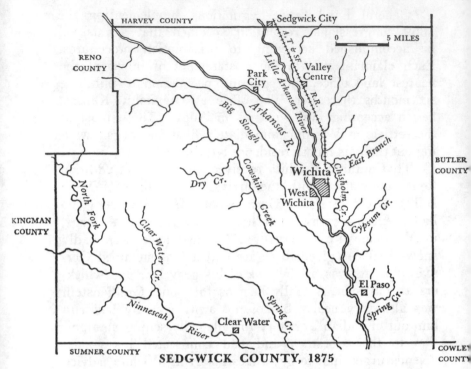

SEDGWICK COUNTY, 1875

under the limited provisions then in force, he evidently expected—as did others—that pre-emption would shortly be extended to latecomers like himself.

In the spring of 1870, having fulfilled the formal residence provision, Dave Munger paid the required $200 and gained title to his quarter-section. He was already selling town lots in his tract without the legal niceties of a regular plat, and that gave the shrewd Greiffenstein an idea. He decided to gain control of the project to be known as Wichita by platting an alternate townsite on land owned by one Eli Waterman, whose tract lay between Munger's property and his own claim. Waterman had paid for his quarter-section in February, thus obtaining the first actual title at the site; now he agreed to transfer the east half of his purchase to Greiffenstein for $2,000. Greiffenstein hastily had the ground surveyed, entering a town plat, drawn up on brown paper sacking from his store, at the courthouse at Eldorado on March 25, 1870. A few hours later the distressed Munger filed his own plat at the courthouse and within the week had persuaded his competitor, possibly with cash, to agree that the two plats together would constitute the honorific "Original Town Site."

Munger entered a formal statement to this effect in the records at Eldorado, but Greiffenstein had not capitulated. As expected, Congress in July extended pre-emption privileges to all newcomers on the Osage lands. That winter Greiffenstein purchased his pre-empted claim and had it staked out as a town addition. In a short time, as Munger looked on helplessly, Greiffenstein began diverting urban development his way. Within four years his holdings were the nucleus around which the town's growth mushroomed.[8]

Despite the uncertain future of the Osage lands during 1868 and early 1869, Wichita's population had been growing, sheltered by a military garrison temporarily posted there to guard against Indian raids. In August 1869, a visiting newspaper correspondent described Wichita as already "a town consisting of two or three hundred inhabitants" surrounded by a farming community of as many more. At the same time a cocky Wichitan boasted to readers of another paper: "I know of no better site to invest [in] than here. We have . . . the great Texas

[8] *U.S. Statutes*, XVI, 362; Sedgwick Co. Deeds (Register of Deeds Office, Wichita), A, 24, 83, 275; Sedgwick Co. Plats (ibid.), G-1, 16, I-J-O, 19, M-1, 2; Sedgwick Co. Patents (ibid.), A, 127, E, 481; *U.S. Biographical Dictionary*, pp. 749–50; Bentley: *History of Wichita*, I, 239; D. B. Emmert: *Wichita City Directory and Immigrant's Guide* (Kansas City, 1878), pp. 15–16; Topeka *Commonwealth*, Jan. 7, May 10, 27, 1870; Wichita *Eagle*, Oct. 24, Dec. 12, 1872, Jan. 16, 1873, Apr. 6, 1876, Sept. 28, 1899, Mar. 27, 1900, Mar. 25, 1910.

cattle trail [extending] from Red River to Abilene." Indeed, the only thing lacking in Wichita's development as a cattle trading center was a railroad. As another visitor noted in May 1870:

> A road here now would command nearly all of the immense cattle trade of western Kansas, as they could be taken from here to St. Louis or Chicago as cheaply as from Abilene, and with the advantage of one hundred miles [less] distance to drive, and not having to pass through any settlements south of this point.

Citizens, he added, remained "sanguine that they will have two railroads running to this point within eighteen months."

One of the roads expected shortly to reach Wichita was the Atchison, Topeka and Santa Fe, which had been inching southwestward from Topeka since 1868. In the spring of 1870 Thomas J. Peter, its general manager as well as one of the line's largest stockholders, passed through Wichita with a survey party, laying out a possible route to the west boundary of the state. He evidently told Wichitans that the Santa Fe was considering building through their settlement, but he must have added that a substantial local subsidy like those his company had acquired elsewhere would help change possibility into fact.[9]

With three other railroads also showing interest in Wichita, its citizens decided to induce a speedy resolution. They urged that the newly organized Sedgwick County—in which their town enjoyed the status of county seat—float a bond issue for the purchase of $200,000 worth of stock in the first of the four companies to extend its rails to Wichita. In October 1870, after being

[9] Hortense Balderston Campbell: "Camp Beecher," *Kansas Historical Quarterly*, III (1934), 172–85; Andreas: *History of Kansas*, p. 1385; Wichita *Eagle*, Dec. 12, 1872, Apr. 6, 1876; Lawrence *Tribune*, Aug. 19, 1869; Topeka *Commonwealth*, May 4, 27, 1870.

bombarded with pro-railroad rhetoric from the town's little newspaper, Sedgwick settlers obliged by voting a handsome majority to the bonds. This seemed a generous bait; Wichitans expected at least one of the railroad companies to snap it up. But in their view the monetary inducement was only frosting on the cake. "The immense cattle trade of this point," insisted one of Wichita's most dedicated promoters, real estate developer James R. Mead, "would furnish all the business one road could attend to, loading east with cattle and returning loaded with lumber, merchandise and the multitudes of people seeking homes in our broad . . . and fertile valleys."

The expected competition failed to materialize. None of the four companies bid for the prize. The Santa Fe officials indeed seemed intent on exploiting the Texas cattle trade. But they evidently saw no good reason to build so far south as Wichita when the Abilene trail could be tapped north of that point. The Santa Fe, complained Wichita's editor two weeks after the bonds had been approved, "will stop at Doyle creek for several years, trusting that Texas cattle drovers will be directed toward their road, and thus enable them, without extending their line further for a time, to secure this trade." He pointed out that any one of the other railroads specified in the bond proposition could undercut the Santa Fe's cattle trade operation simply by meeting the Chisholm Trail at Wichita. But none of them expressed interest.

Sedgwick County's bonds went begging that winter. With the other roads definitely out of contention, Wichita's best hope still appeared to be the Santa Fe, its management having decided to intersect the trail at Newton in the then extreme northeast corner of Sedgwick County. Apparently T. J. Peter urged the directors to dip south to Wichita, but was overruled despite his firsthand observations about the town's traffic potential. In the

spring of 1871 the rails of the Santa Fe approached Newton, there to pause a while before the push west.¹

So near, yet still so very far. With their expectations of
urban importance now fast dissipating before the chill
logic of impending reality, some of the townsfolk panicked. What chance had Wichita as a viable community,
with a booming railhead and cattle town in the same
county a mere twenty-five miles to the north? James
Mead, for one, conjured up the desperate vision of
Wichita as a mere county seat town, or perhaps not even
that, since there were rivals too for this relatively modest
asset. On June 2, 1871, he dispatched a laconic message
to T. J. Peter, asking his conditions for building at least a
trunk line to Wichita. Peter's reply was equally terse and
to the point: "IN ANSWER TO YOURS OF 2D WILL SAY, IF
YOUR PEOPLE WILL ORGANIZE A LOCAL COMPANY AND VOTE
$200,000 OF COUNTY BONDS, I WILL BUILD A RAILROAD TO
WICHITA WITHIN SIX MONTHS." These terms meant that
since the Santa Fe directorship, as such, remained unin-
terested, a completely new company must be formed. But
this company would not qualify for the 1870 bonds, not
being one of the four roads specified in that proposition.
Wichitans would have to persuade Sedgwick's residents
to vote a completely new bond issue. They decided to
try.

On June 16 Mead and a few others hastened north to
confer with Peter in Topeka, and, if the Santa Fe directors remained adamant, to organize the suggested "local
company." Corporate disinterest still prevailed, so with
both Peter and the equally visionary Santa Fe director,
Cyrus K. Holliday, entering personally into the scheme,

¹ Wichita *Vidette*, Aug. 13, Oct. 13, 20, 1870; Sedgwick Co. Commissioners Journal, 1870–74 (transcript, KSHS), pp. 2, 4; Topeka
Commonwealth, Oct. 11, 1870; *Atchison, Topeka, and Santa Fe Railroad [Report for 1870]* (Boston, 1871), p. 11; Glenn Danford Bradley:
The Story of the Santa Fe (Boston, 1920), pp. 84–85.

a charter for the Wichita and South Western Rail Road Company—in effect a Santa Fe subsidiary—was filed with the secretary of state on June 22. The directors included Peter, who would supervise construction, Holliday, James Mead, and ten other Sedgwick County capitalists. Back in Wichita four days later, the directors named Mead company president, and he and two others were chosen to circulate a petition for a new county vote on $200,000 worth of railroad bonds.[2]

The agony of those striving to manipulate Wichita's fortunes was far from over, however. Now they confronted the perplexities of county politics. As originally organized, Sedgwick County contained four incipient urban centers, spaced at roughly ten-mile intervals from north to South: Newton, Sedgwick City, Park City, and Wichita. Wichita and Park City had not been on the best of terms for some time. Being nearest the center of the county, these two fought a bitter county seat contest in the spring of 1870. Wichita triumphed, although the struggle invited much lively speculation about which place had cast the greater number of fraudulent votes. Park Citians subsequently applauded the defeat of bonds to finance permanent county buildings at Wichita, and continued to nourish expectations of gaining the county seat. When the 1870 railroad bonds came up for ratification, Park City opposed them without a dissenting ballot, wanting no part in promoting her rival's pretensions as a cattle town. Besides, it cherished ideas of becoming a cattle trading center itself in time. In 1870 and again in 1871 its citizens sought to divert the Chisholm Trail from Wichita by encouraging drovers to follow a special Park City cutoff. In the second year they obtained important aid in this effort. An agent of the Kansas Pacific Railway

[2] Chapman Bros.: *Portrait and Biographical Album*, p. 161; Wichita *Tribune*, June 22, July 6, 1871.

covertly marked out a trail to his company's tracks west of Abilene via Park City in an attempt to cripple the Santa Fe's cattle trade at Newton.

As a result of this continuing menace, Wichitans planned that Park City should in no way benefit from the new railroad line into the county. They chose this moment, in fact, to destroy their up-river challenger completely. No Park Citian sat on the board of directors of the new railroad company, although it included one representative each from Sedgwick City and Newton. At the June meeting at which officers were chosen, two uneasy Park City promoters appeared and offered to deliver their town's votes in favor of an even larger bond issue if they could be guaranteed the road would touch there; this deal was rejected. The two warily lent their names to a petition in favor of calling a bond election. But as approved by the county commissioners several days later, the bond proposal denied Park City any assurances, specifying that the new railroad should start "at or near the town of Newton . . . [and run] by the way of Sedgwick City, building and maintaining a Station thereat, to the town of Wichita."

Park Citians immediately declared war. Realizing that the votes they controlled were far too few to defeat the proposition, they campaigned vigorously throughout the county. The Wichitans cleverly neutralized this desperate effort in secret negotiations with the community leaders of Newton, the additional votes from Newton being enough to swing the election. By the terms of their agreement, Newtonians would approve Wichita's railroad bonds. In return Wichitans pledged not to oppose a planned secession of Sedgwick's northern townships, which would go to help make up a new county with Newton as county seat. On August 11, 1871, therefore, the second bond issue won a resounding majority. The vote sealed Park City's fate. Bypassed by the railroad, its businessmen lost all hope of urban importance. Soon they began packing up to find opportunities elsewhere, and within several years Park City had virtually returned to a state of nature.[3]

Compared with other problems Wichitans met in acquiring the cattle trade, initial rural opposition to Texas stock proved almost insignificant. Townsmen nevertheless acknowledged the problem. Their aims were two: first, to keep the growing farm population of the neighborhood from inducing the state legislature to move the quarantine line any farther west; second, to keep them from discouraging incoming drovers by lawsuits or vigilante action. As a Wichita editor phrased the problem: "It is generally known that the trail can be prevented from coming through or near here if any one objects; and the farmers will most certainly object if their crops are damaged by Texas cattle." The same could have been said for splenic fever losses among domestic stock.

In August 1870, Wichita's farsighted businessmen "made arrangements" with the settlers along the trail from Cowskin Creek southwest of Wichita to a point fifteen miles above town, thereby ensuring the unmolested passage of Texas cattle. Early in 1871 they raised a contingency fund to pay any local damage claims levied against drovers during the coming trail driving season.

Like rural dwellers elsewhere, Sedgwick County farmers looked to a herd law as the best means of redress against trespassing longhorns. Since the very first meetings of Sedgwick's board of commissioners in the spring of 1870, settlers had enjoyed the dubious protection of a

[3] Edwards: *Historical Atlas of Sedgwick County*, pp. 8, 11; Sedgwick Commissioners Journal, pp. 4 (Wauculla Twp. vote), 17, 29, 31; Wichita *Vidette*, Aug. 25, Sept. 1, 1870; Topeka *Commonwealth*, Nov. 17, 1870; Wichita *Tribune*, Apr. 6, 20, June 1, July 6, 13, Aug. 3, 1871; Wichita *Eagle*, Feb. 7, 1879, Feb. 28, 1884. Harvey County, with Newton as its county seat, was formally organized by legislative action on February 29, 1872.

"night herd law" that forbade the running at large of animals during the hours of darkness. Then, in April of the following year, Sedgwick's citizens ratified the new round-the-clock herd law provided by the 1871 legislature. When the legislature of 1872 repealed this act and replaced it with a herd law that differed from the first statute mainly in requiring no public ratification, local farmers immediately demanded it and the county commissioners obliged. As farmers were to learn, however, enforcement was another matter entirely.[4]

Quarantine line agitation seemed a more serious challenge. In May 1871, aroused farmers near Sedgwick City threatened to divert drovers to the Park City cutoff by closing the regular trail, arguing that northbound Texas herds violated the 1867 deadline. A Sedgwick City justice of the peace, acting on complaints, had some drovers arrested and impounded their cattle. William B. Hutchison, a Wichita editor who doubled as United States commissioner for the district, promptly had the arresting constable and the justice arrested in turn, confiscating their warrants and ordering the offending cattlemen and herds released on grounds that the 1867 law was unconstitutional. He hailed the two officials before him and bound them over to appear in federal court at Topeka. On complaint of the officials and their neighbors, however, Governor Harvey obtained their release from this judgment and Hutchison's discharge from office.

[4] Wichita *Tribune*, May 11, 1871; Wichita *Vidette*, Aug. 25, 1870, Jan. 5, 12, 1871; *Kansas Statutes*, 1868, pp. 1001–02; *Laws of Kansas*, 1871, pp. 208–11; ibid., 1872, pp. 384–85; Sedgwick Co. Journal, pp. 1–2, 18, 85, 91; Wichita *Eagle*, Apr. 19, 26, 1872. The 1872 herd law was not subsequently enforced, the false claim being made that notice of its local enactment had not been printed in four consecutive issues of a local newspaper. See discussion in Wichita *Beacon*, Nov. 10, 1875.

The herds continued their customary amble up the trail through Wichita, as they had since 1867, without further legal hindrance that season. In early 1872 the state legislature considered new quarantine legislation, causing some concern in Wichita. But with one of the city's most forceful personalities in the house of representatives, the new quarantine line, radically altered in most other areas, merely retraced its old course through the south half of Sedgwick County, leaving Wichita's status as a potential cattle town unchanged.[5]

At long last, in May 1872, the railroad tracks arrived. The first train rumbled to a stop amid wild celebrants clustered about the town's new depot, and nothing appeared to stand between Wichita and the urban impetus of its first cattle trading season. With Abilene now out of the picture as a cattle market, most of the drovers bringing longhorns over the Chisholm Trail reined in at Wichita. The town captured top honors as a shipping point for 1872, sending off fully 70,600 head—a figure nearly double the total shipped that season from Ellsworth, Wichita's main competitor up on the Kansas Pacific line. As a Topeka correspondent visiting the new cattle town observed dryly, "The business is now so well established here that stupendous efforts will be required to draw it away."[6]

[4]

EVEN AS WICHITANS prepared to welcome their first railroad train, the main line of the Santa Fe pushed west

[5] Wichita *Tribune*, May 18, 1871; George M. Weeks to Harvey, May 23, 1871 (enclosing petition), Governors' Correspondence (Livestock); Harvey to Weeks, May 31, 1871, Governors' Letters (KSHS), I, 69; *Laws of Kansas*, 1872, pp. 387–91.

[6] Wichita *Eagle*, May 17, Oct. 24, 1872, Jan. 23, 1873; Kansas Pacific: *Annual Report . . . 1873* (St. Louis, 1874), p. 18.

from Newton; to qualify for its government land grant the company's tracks had to reach Colorado before another spring rolled round. Rail traffic opened to Hutchinson on June 17. That very same day two liquor dealers, reckoning potential sales to work crews, pitched a store tent beside the line of survey a few miles west of Fort Dodge near a pre-emptor's low-slung sod shack. A pair of grading contractors joined them later that day with a small general supply store. Within the month several other such merchants propped up temporary business houses on the bald incline above the Arkansas River. From here they occasionally squinted south across the wide, brushy riverbed to the pale buffalo grass stretching away as far as the eye could follow, where instead of a horizon, land and sky merged in a faint lavender haze. This gentle bluff, with its magnificent vista, would be the heart of the cattle town called Dodge City.

Situated in the southwest quarter of Kansas, the region that became Ford County, with Dodge as its capital, experienced an intimate association with merchants, teamsters, and soldiers long before its settlement. Here the venerable Santa Fe Trail skirted the north bank of the Arkansas before swinging south toward its ultimate destination. From 1850 to 1854 a handful of soldiers sojourned at the crossing, providing protection for wagon trains. During the Indian uprising of 1864–65 interest in its safety revived.

In March 1865, the military commander at Santa Fe dispatched troops to occupy the strategic Arkansas River crossing. His colleague at Leavenworth simultaneously launched a force against the Indians, ordering his men to establish and garrison a post near the spot. In April a detachment of cavalry thereupon founded Fort Dodge not far from the remains of the earlier outpost. With hostilities continuing well into the seventies, the fort remained a man-made fixture on a vast and empty landscape.

Civilization finally arrived in the form of the little settlement immediately upstream from the post.[7]

Given the site's location adjoining trail, railroad, and fort, together with its proximity—as the southernmost point on the Santa Fe line—to the vast buffalo ranges of the Southwest, men with a speculative turn of mind were not blind to its measure of commercial promise. Although the settlement lay a half-mile within the Osage reserve, townsite promoters were no longer inhibited by the peculiarities of Osage land acquisition. An innocuous rider to the Indian Appropriation Bill of 1871, with origins in a congressional conference committee that included Representative Sidney Clarke of Kansas, provided that "the laws of the United States relating to town sites be extended over all the lands obtained of the Osage Indians in the State of Kansas."

Early in July 1872, a few Fort Dodge officers, including the post commander, together with several local merchants and army contractors, formed a corporation to develop the site. On August 15, a month before the railroad opened for business at the budding settlement, the group completed its formal organization as the Dodge City Town Company. Seeking acquisition under the townsite purchase act of 1867, they first planned a development of 320 acres "more or less." The regulations, however, required that such an extensive tract be shared among one to two hundred occupants, forcing the Dodge City promoters to offer a more realistic proposition. As finally entered, the plat encompassed a modest eighty-seven acres.

According to the 1867 provisions, the proprietors had

[7] Dodge City *Democrat*, June 19, 1903; Robert M. Wright: *Dodge City: The Cowboy Capital* (Wichita, 1913), pp. 12–16; Ida Ellen Rath: *Early Ford County* (North Newton, Kan., 1964), pp. 15–17; War Dept.: *War of the Rebellion*, Ser. I, XLVIII, pt. 1, 408, 1082, 1211–12, 1224, 1246, pt. 2, 74–75; Prucha: *Military Posts*, pp. 57, 72.

to have the local county judge act as a trustee. The election of all Ford County's officers having been challenged in the courts, progress lapsed. Finally the group obtained the agency of the probate judge of nearby Ellis County as "ex-officio" probate judge of Ford, and this officer entered the $108.75 purchase price at the Wichita land office on June 25, 1873. In compliance with state regulations covering townsite acquisition, the judge then appointed three commissioners to resurvey the site and, after thirty days' notice, to apportion it among those entitled to ownership. He then levied a tax assessment to reimburse himself for the entry fee and to pay other expenses. With these matters settled and the new plat filed at the Hays City courthouse, in August the judge deeded the townsite to its nineteen occupants. The town company, in the meantime, had increased its membership to include some interested newcomers. On August 30 the individual title holders transferred their allotments to the company for consolidated exploitation.[8]

In the interim Dodge City had become a mecca for buffalo hunters. The effect was staggering. Robert M. Wright, one of the townsite proprietors, bought and shipped east over 200,000 buffalo hides that first winter of 1872–73. Wright recalled that

Dodge was in the very heart of the buffalo country. Hardly had the railroad reached there, long before a depot could be built (they had an office in a box car), [than] business began; and such a business! Dozens of cars a day were loaded with hides and meat, and dozens of car-loads of grain, flour, and provisions arrived each

[8] *U.S. Statutes*, XIV, 541–42, XVI, 557; *House Misc. Doc. No. 45*, 47 Cong., 2 sess., pt. 4, p. 301; Corporations Register, IV, 474–75; ibid., Amendments, A, 47; Dodge City *Democrat*, Jan. 1, 1887, June 19, 1903; Wright: *Dodge City*, pp. 9, 339–40; *Kansas Statutes*, 1868, pp. 1074–75; Ford Co. Deeds (Register of Deeds Office, Dodge City), A, 13–15, 62–63, 491–95, 550; Ford Co. Plats (ibid.), A, 47, 49.

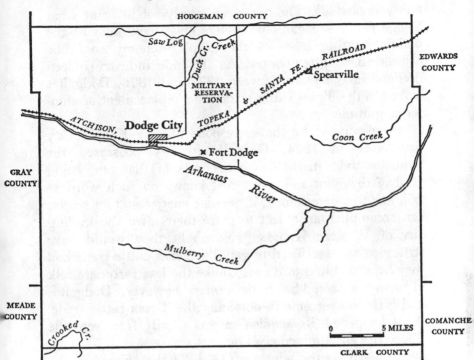

HODGEMAN COUNTY

Saw Log

Duck Cr. Creek

SANTA FE. RAILROAD

EDWARDS COUNTY

Spearville

MILITARY RESERVA-TION

ATCHISON,

Dodge City

& TOPEKA

Coon Creek

× Fort Dodge

GRAY COUNTY

Arkansas River

Mulberry Creek

MEADE COUNTY

Crooked Cr.

0   5 MILES

COMANCHE COUNTY

CLARK COUNTY

FORD COUNTY, 1880

day. The streets of Dodge were lined with wagons, bringing in hides and meat and getting supplies from early morning to late at night. . . .

I have been to several mining camps where rich strikes had been made, but I never saw any town to equal Dodge.

Dodge City's buffalo boom was not yet a year old when a visitor sounded a negative note, observing that "from the way the carcasses are strewn over the vast plains, the American bison will soon be numbered among the things of the past." Whether the writer was speaking specifically of the southwestern range serviced by Dodge, or just about buffalo in general, the truth of the prediction was obvious. The comment merely set in print what Dodge City's sagacious promoters must have known: the buffalo hunting basis of the town's economy could be considered only temporary. As the hide industry indeed declined in the years between 1872 and 1876, Dodgeites looked to the Texas cattle trade for a replacement of similar magnitude.

As described by the correspondent of a Kansas City newspaper in 1874, Dodge's citizenry possessed the requisite civic attributes by the tests of that era, being "full of that vim and pluck that knows no such word as fail, and . . . determined, if genuine energy and enterprise can accomplish an object to make their town the leading city of Western Kansas."[9] No doubt they would have struggled and sacrificed to gain the Texas cattle trade had they been required to do so. Unlike the less fortunate folk of many a would-be cattle center, however, Dodgeites had little to overcome in obtaining the Texas cattle trade. As it happened, its acquisition was wholly free from the difficulties encountered elsewhere.

As early as the winter of 1874–75 the officers of the Santa Fe Railroad acknowledged the need for a new shipping site. "The country about Wichita is becoming so well settled," they reported to stockholders, "that the tendency will be to drive more cattle to Great Bend; and it may be necessary, the coming season, to prepare a point of shipment still farther west." The road, as a matter of fact, had already built a small stockyard at Dodge City, although shipments from it before 1876 were so small as to escape official mention.

That year the company's corporate eye settled on Dodge as the best potential shipping center on the line. Noting that Great Bend would be shut out by an impending change in the quarantine limit for Texas cattle, rail

[9] Wright: *Dodge City*, pp. 76–77, 140; Topeka *Commonwealth*, Apr. 17, 1873; Dodge City *Messenger*, Feb. 26, 1874.

officials predicted in early 1876 that the fine range below Dodge would "no doubt be largely occupied the coming year." They also commented on new measures taken by the military south of Dodge to forestall Indian depredations, "which danger has hitherto prevented the cattle-trail from spreading so far westward." Dodge City's shipments rose to 9,540 that season, a figure second only to Wichita's. In October 1876, the town's businessmen were described as already dependent "upon the Texas cattle trade for support."[1]

Early in 1877, with the Chisholm Trail to Wichita choked off by rural settlement and new quarantine legislation, Dodge City anticipated its first important season as a cattle center. The Santa Fe contributed a new stockyard—the largest on the entire system except for Wichita's—as well as an expenditure of $374 for "Locating Texas cattle at Dodge City." In the spring of that year townsmen mounted a "general effort" to welcome the trade. "The citizens of Dodge City," insisted the editor there,

> . . . have adopted wholesome measures whereby the cattle men can be treated upon general principles of equity and reciprocity.
>
> The business men have reduced the prices of the liquors, cigars, tobacco, etc., for the especial trade of the cattle men. Reductions have also been made in prices generally. Accommodations for a large influx of people are being made by the hotels and restaurants, and with a view to the adage of "live and let live." Trustworthy men . . . will be in readiness to assist in showing the best pasturage, where water and other accommodations can be found. . . .

[1] Atchison, Topeka and Santa Fe Railroad Co.: *Annual Report* . . . *1874* (Boston, 1875), pp. 27–28, 36; ibid. *1875* (Boston, 1876), pp. 28–29; ibid. *1877* (Boston, 1878), p. 26; Dodge City *Times*, Oct. 14, 1876. According to George M. Hoover, substantial numbers of Texas cattle were first received at Dodge late in 1875. Dodge City *Democrat*, June 19, 1903.

Our citizens do not intend that anything shall be omitted.

Despite these irresistible inducements, the first drovers to arrive at Dodge that season, distressingly enough, lingered awhile and then trailed their herd on toward the Kansas Pacific tracks at Ellis. Not, townsmen were happy to learn, without considerable trouble from anti-cattle farmers in that area. Dodge City's own rural neighbors remained confined to the northeast corner of Ford County. Though there was probably some rural disappointment that the new 1877 quarantine line did not extend into the county, settlement posed no immediate threat to the trail approaching Dodge from the south. Nor were farmers yet numerous enough to apply pressure for a local herd law.[2]

The season's first cattle shipment left Dodge in June. "The grass is remarkably fine," reported an observer, "the water plenty, drinks two for a quarter and no grangers. These facts make Dodge City THE cattle point." A writer in the Kansas City *Times* pronounced it "the great bovine market of the world." By year's end the statistics proved such statements to be no mere propaganda. With its 22,-940 head loaded that season—over a quarter of the Santa Fe's total shipments—Dodge left its Santa Fe competitors of 1877 far behind. "It may appear improbable, but is nevertheless a fact," Dodge City's editor boasted, "that during one month of the past season the business of the A. T. & S. F. road at this place excelled that done by the same road for the same month at the great commercial city of Wichita, with its 5,000 inhabitants."[3]

[2] Santa Fe: *Annual Report 1877*, pp. 35, 81; Dodge City *Times*, Oct. 14, 1876, Mar. 24, May 12, June 2, 9, 16, Aug. 18, 1877.

[3] Dodge City *Times*, June 9, 16, July 7, Dec. 22, 1877; Santa Fe: *Annual Report 1877*, p. 26. The grand total of tonnage shipped eastward from Dodge by the railroad that year was exceeded only by eastward shipments from Osage City and Wichita. Ibid., p. 65.

[5]

A FIFTH CATTLE TOWN—Caldwell—sprang up beside the Chisholm Trail in the creek-veined prairie two days' journey south of Wichita.

Early in the winter of 1870–71 a number of Wichita merchants and real estate dealers, at the suggestion of Charles H. Stone, a cattle speculator, banded together to found a town on the south line of the state near the Chisholm or another trail over which Texas drovers regularly brought their herds. As the early promoters of Wichita had dispatched David Munger down the trail to pre-empt land, sell to passing cattlemen, and form the nucleus of settlement, so Stone prepared to function at the new site as resident partner with James H. Dagner, a Wichita liquor wholesaler.[4]

That a commercial location at the juncture of cattle trail and Kansas line would provide thirsty Texans with their first chance to buy whisky legally since crossing Red River obviously seemed an important ingredient of the promoters' thought—or at least of Dagner's. But presumably most of the group nursed broader visions. Such a location had manifest attractions for promotion as a full-fledged cattle shipping center. A cattle town at the spot would mean many miles less for drovers to bring their cattle—130 miles off the distance to Abilene, nearly 50 miles less than to Wichita. An added inducement was a well-founded supposition that, with white settlement barred from Indian Territory, the promoters of a cattle market on the state line could exploit permanent pasturage for holding Texas cattle no matter how many farmers crowded the Kansas side. Moreover, since the stockyard

---

[4] Caldwell *Messenger*, Sept. 3, 1953. The excellent historical account printed in this issue of the *Messenger* was obviously taken from an earlier narrative. Neither I nor the current Caldwell editor was able to locate the original, however.

could be built right up to the state boundary if necessary, there need be no concern over herd laws or quarantine lines. Like Wichita, its location astride the trail meant that it lacked only a railroad for transformation into a cattle town. Wichita's experience was showing that this need could be met with sufficient cash and courage. And, as with Wichita in the interim before rails arrived, townsmen could make a more than decent living supplying the trail drivers. What more ideal spot for a frontier version of metropolitan growth?

Profits beckoned. Late in 1870 Charley Stone and Jim Dagner rode south over the deserted, hoof-scarred trace of the Chisholm Trail to the nether end of Sumner County. They could take their pick of the terrain; the first settler had arrived in the area only that year. Just above the state line the cattle trail tilted down to cross a lightly timbered meadow and two deeply channeled creeks before mounting into Indian Territory. Here, on the slope overlooking the twin streambeds, Stone and Dagner felt they stood on an ideal site.

So pleased were they that they immediately broke off prospecting and rode back to Wichita. Stone returned briefly with a survey party and staked the new town of Caldwell off into lots in January 1871. He returned once again late in February with teams and a work crew. From cottonwood and hackberry trees felled at creekside he and his men raised a log house beside the cattle trail that Stone thereafter managed for himself and Dagner as, to quote an old-timer, "a grocery store, with liquid groceries predominating." Back in Wichita the promoters sold shares in the townsite venture, and advertised for settlers with some success. In May, an editor having observed that "business must be somewhat lively in that town," Wichitans expressed fear that a general exodus from Wichita to Caldwell might take place.[5]

[5] Caldwell *Messenger*, Sept. 3, 1953; Wichita *Vidette*, Feb. 25,

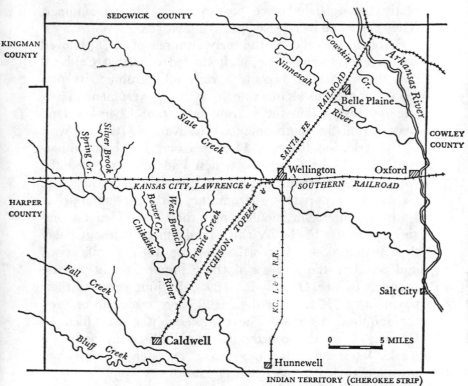

SUMNER COUNTY, 1880

The Caldwell boom soon subsided, however, and the
tiny collection of saloons and supply stores eked out its
first two years on the seasonal trade provided by herds
passing north to Abilene, Ellsworth, and Wichita. "Caldwell, Sumner county, is growing," a Wichita editor reported in the fall of 1872. "The cattle trail running di-

Mar. 11, 1871; Wichita *Tribune*, Mar. 15, 1871 ff. (Osage Land and
Insurance Agency ad), May 18, July 6, 20, 1871; Andreas: *History
of Kansas*, pp. 1502–03; John P. Edwards: *Historical Atlas of Sumner
County* (Philadelphia, 1883), p: 8; G. D. Freeman: *Midnight and
Noonday, or the Incidental History of Southern Kansas* (Caldwell,
1892), pp. 11–12, 22–26, 43.

rectly through the place has given it life all summer. They expect an incre[a]sed growth next year."

And so they did. In the early summer of 1873, buoyed by the expectation—false, as it turned out—that Caldwell was imminently to become a railroad terminus, its promoters moved to secure title from the government. Their site lay just within the narrow border of Cherokee land that skirted the south boundary of Kansas. Its sale, west of the Arkansas River, at $1.50 per acre had been authorized in 1872 by Congress, which had also extended the conventional townsite acquisition provisions to the strip. Caldwell's proprietors, unfamiliar with the appropriate statutes, suffered a rebuff when they attempted an outright purchase at the Wichita land office. Without delay they then proceeded according to the 1867 specifications and acquired the services of the Sumner County probate judge as trustee. On July 22, 1873, the judge entered their payment of $174.40 for the 116.25-acre tract and ordered the required resurvey. The completed plat was filed on October 2 at the courthouse in Wellington, and two weeks later the judge began the transfer of individual town lots to their respective occupants.[6]

Caldwell lay much too far from the center of Sumner County to permit county seat anticipations, but its promoters occupied themselves with a variety of vexations nonetheless. For one thing, they had to retain the cattle trail—both as a source of everyday prosperity, and for the sake of their future hopes for Caldwell as a shipping center—in the face of growing rural opposition to the driving of Texas stock through Sumner County. By early

[6] Wichita *Eagle*, Oct. 24, 1872; *House Misc. Doc. No. 45*, pt. 4, p. 304; *U.S. Statutes*, XVII, 98; Caldwell *Messenger*, Sept. 3, 1953; Sumner Co. Deeds (Register of Deeds Office, Wellington), B, 37, 40, 51–52 ff.; Sumner Co. Plats (ibid.), I, 23, II, 29; Sumner Co. Land Office Receipts (ibid.), A, 133; Sumner Co. Patents (ibid.), VI, 397.

1874 local farmers offered some considerable resistance. A visiting editor in July of that year advised Caldwellites to forget about the cattle trade and orient themselves instead to local agriculture. "The encroachment of the cornfields on the great trail," he suggested,

> is the beginning of the end. Where the long horned bovines trampled last year, the glittering plow share is at work this summer, and next season the fiat will go forth, thus far shalt thou go and no farther. . . . At any rate the cattle drive through Sumner county will cease, and soon be a thing of the past. These fertile lands can not long remain idly waiting for the plow. The conflict will soon be ended, for corn is King.

The 1874 agricultural disaster experienced everywhere on the Kansas frontier no doubt gave Caldwell a new lease on life by easing the press of rural settlement on the trail, although nearly depopulating the town itself. But rural antagonism was not easily or completely overcome. Early in 1875 fifty-five Sumner County farmers petitioned the state legislature, asking that the quarantine line for Texas cattle, which since 1872 had lain just east of the Chisholm Trail, be extended beyond the county. This effort to close Sumner to southern cattle failed, but in 1876 the quarantine line was indeed pushed west over the objections of both Wichita and Caldwell. This move, together with the rise of Dodge City as a cattle center in the west, apparently doomed Caldwell to an obscure fate.[7]

Yet the idea of Caldwell as a cattle shipping center still seemed feasible, provided rails could be had. The Chisholm Trail to the Kansas line, although falling into disuse as drovers increasingly patronized the Western

[7] Wellington *Press*, July 2, 1874; Edwards: *Historical Atlas of Sumner County*, p. 9; Wichita *Eagle*, Feb. 4, 1875.

Trail to Dodge City, remained open as before. Not surprisingly, railroads were the main preoccupation of Caldwellites throughout the seventies.

If the original proprietors of Caldwell had expected the Atchison, Topeka and Santa Fe to extend south from Wichita in 1872, they reaped disappointment. In the winter of 1872–73 Sumner County's settlers excitedly anticipated a railroad into Wellington, the county seat, but nothing came of it. In the summer of 1873 hopes at Caldwell rose again, on rumors that a company planned to lay track through Wellington to Caldwell. In July the road's president submitted a formal proposition asking $150,000 in county bonds. Caldwell's Charley Stone was one of the most active in promoting a bond issue, but the scheme never got to a public vote. Caldwellites tried that autumn to help interest the Santa Fe in pushing its Wichita branch to Caldwell as a means of better exploiting and keeping the cattle trade. In mid-1874 the company actually prospected a tentative route into Sumner County. This venture also fell through.

In the winter of 1874–75 Caldwellites banded together in support of a locally initiated railroad that would run from Caldwell via Wellington to a point on the Leavenworth, Lawrence and Galveston tracks above Humboldt. A group incorporated itself and advertised for subscription of capital stock, and delegations sought financial aid in the other counties through which the line would pass. Enthusiasm was sufficient but funds—in the wake of the great agricultural disaster—were not. After some months the project died the death of former Sumner County railroad propositions.

In the spring of 1877, as Caldwell slumbered beside a Chisholm Trail now closed at the state line to Texas cattle, hope briefly revived. Two separate railroad schemes agitated the county. During the summer residents approved county bond issues for both roads, but neither then accepted these inducements to build.[8]

Finally in September 1878, the president and chief engineer of the Kansas City, Burlington and Southwestern Railway visited Wellington, asking subsidies for a road that would enter Sumner from the east and run via Wellington to the west or south line of the county. Scarcely had this proposal agitated everybody than a Santa Fe official appeared on the scene. This gentleman offered a proposition for extending his company's Wichita branch to Caldwell—thereby recapturing, before some other line did so, the Chisholm Trail cattle traffic now closed to Wichita, but it nonetheless expected a local subsidy. Visits by rival railroad officials ensued in bewildering succession. Caldwell's citizens, having been promised the Santa Fe terminal, worked feverishly for this proposition over the other. In response to alternate petitions the commissioners of Sumner County scheduled bond elections on these proposals for December 31, 1878. Technically, both roads could be voted subsidies in the amount of $4,000 per mile of track laid within the county. For the thrifty settlers of Sumner, however, it was a question of aid to either one road or the other.

In the ensuing weeks the electioneering grew fierce. As New Year's Eve approached Caldwellites brought into play a weapon commonly sprung upon an impressionable public by town-promoters in such times of crisis: a newspaper. With the son of a local real estate dealer as editor, and the father's land office partner as his temporary associate, the first issue of the Caldwell *Post* emerged on December 28 as a straightforward Santa Fe

[8] Edwards: *Historical Atlas of Sumner County*, p. 8; Wichita *Eagle*, Oct. 3, 1873, June 25, 1874; Wellington *Press*, Dec. 24, 1874, Jan. 14, 1875. For good examples of the prevailing tone of Sumner's citizens on railroads during the seventies see letters in the Wichita *Eagle*, Feb. 27, July 17, 1873.

propaganda piece. The counting of ballots three days
later disclosed a majority of 665 for the Santa Fe proposition and sound defeat for its rival.[9]

Real estate values in Caldwell promptly soared, and
through 1879 the settlement expanded under the benign
influence of its promised rails. But the dilatory pace of
the Santa Fe builders soon distressed Caldwellites impatient to entertain the Texas cattle trade that summer.
Pushing south from Wichita, the tracks reached Wellington in the middle of September. But the company's main
effort then shifted toward Arkansas City, which lay on the
state line thirty miles to the east.

An end to Santa Fe indifference finally came with a
challenge from yet another railroad corporation, the Kansas City, Lawrence and Southern. This road, under a subsidiary organization, in mid-1879 won township bond aid
for a proposal to build through Wellington on its way
west. The approach of the K.C.L. & S. early in 1880, and a
threat by Caldwell citizens to entice the tracks their way,
prodded the Santa Fe into action. News of the start of
work between Wellington and Caldwell reached town on
February 20, lifting both spirits and land values. "Town
lots went up fifty per cent," exclaimed the *Post*'s editor.
"More lots changed hands on Saturday [February 21]
than any other one day in the history of Caldwell."
Taunting Dodge City with having now "lost the cattle
trade," he succinctly expressed the local consensus:

[9] Edwards: *Historical Atlas of Sumner County*, p. 8; Andreas:
History of Kansas, p. 1503; Caldwell *Post*, Jan. 2, 9, Apr. 17, 1879.
The reason for the Santa Fe's interest in a line to Caldwell—when it
already commanded the cattle shipping at Dodge City—was explained
fairly logically by a Wichita editor: "The object of the [new] road is
to reach out for the Texas cattle trade. The pasturage is so uncertain
on the western ranges, that the stock men . . . would gladly come
further east, where the range is always good, if they can get the
necessary shipping facilities." (Quoted in ibid., July 17, 1879.) The
Santa Fe branch to Caldwell was technically known as the Cowley,
Sumner and Fort Smith Railroad.

"Caldwell is sure to be the King of Cattle Shipping points."[1]

Caldwell's orgy of self-congratulation had scarcely subsided than townsfolk confronted a new crisis. In March the K.C.L. & S. laid track from the east edge of the county into Wellington. The corporation's officers then chartered the Sumner County Railroad Company for the purpose of building a branch road south to the state line. This startling development, news of which broke upon Caldwell a few days later, meant that the K.C.L. & S. planned to cash in on the Texas cattle trade by promoting a rival shipping center within the county. Obtaining confirmation from the officials themselves, the alarmed Caldwellites met the challenge as best they knew how. Convening in emergency session on April 8, they urgently agreed that the K.C.L. & S. threat could be neutralized only by inducing the company to build to Caldwell.

The following day a citizens' committee called upon the road's chief engineer at Wellington, and on April 11 he arrived in Caldwell to look over the ground and to hear what financial terms the townsfolk felt prepared to offer. A second meeting convened. Those present desperately resolved to raise all the local bond aid that could legally be extended. At the same time the assembled citizens pledged individual donations totaling 280 acres of outlying real estate, 919 town lots, and $1,100 in cash. "More money and land can be raised if necessary," Caldwell's editor noted anxiously. On April 15 the Caldwell city council appropriated $5,000 in community scrip to reimburse influence payments already made by a group of five businessmen, and later that year two Caldwellites claimed similar expenditures of $657.50 more.

But all went for nought. By May the K.C.L. & S. officials had decided to run their branch from Wellington to

[1] Santa Fe: *Annual Report . . . 1879* (Boston, 1880), p. 24; Edwards: *Historical Atlas of Sumner County*, pp. 8–9; Caldwell *Post*, Jan. 2, 1879 ff., Jan. 22, Feb. 26, Mar. 11, 1880.

a point just east of Caldwell in return for $28,000 in bonds from the respective townships thus favored. Without even awaiting the outcome of ratification elections their tracklayers moved from Wellington to the state line, where the town of Hunnewell was then platted as a cattle shipping center.[2]

With their own branch railroad now approaching from the north, Caldwell's citizens staunchly pressed ahead with efforts to gain the bulk of the Texas cattle once again attracted up the Chisholm Trail. On June 1 the rails arrived in Caldwell. The first carloads of cattle left the town's only partially completed stockyard on June 16—fulfilling at last the ten-year-old vision of men whose roles as Caldwell promoters, with the exception of Charley Stone, had long since fallen to other actors.[3]

Through the summer of 1880 cattle shipments proceeded steadily from both Caldwell and Hunnewell, spurred by a ruinous rate war between the competing railroads concerned. Cattlemen and other railroad users of south-central Kansas rejoiced; railroad officialdom did not. In September the Santa Fe line completed negotiations for purchasing the K.C.L. & S., and the rockbottom shipping charges that had advertised Caldwell and her nearby rival far and wide abruptly rose. Thereafter the Atchison, Topeka and Santa Fe controlled the cattle shipments of both Caldwell and Hunnewell. Had Caldwell not been forced, as it was, to share the Chisholm Trail traffic with her neighbor, it might have enjoyed the greatest volume of cattle trading business in the history of the

[2] Edwards: *Historical Atlas of Sumner County*, p. 9; Andreas: *History of Kansas*, p. 1509; Caldwell *Post*, Apr. 8, 15, Oct. 14, 1880; Wellington *Democrat*, May 5, 12, June 16, 1880.

[3] Caldwell *Post*, June 3, 1880; Caldwell *Commercial*, June 17, 1880. By 1879 Stone, again a cattle dealer, resided at Independence; he continued, however, to speculate in Caldwell real estate in the years following. Caldwell *Post*, Apr. 10, June 5, 1879; Andreas: *History of Kansas*, p. 1504.

Kansas cattle towns. As it was, Caldwellites would have occasion to invoke regretful memories of "the mistake of 1880, when the town of Hunnewell was started."[4]

But for the moment, at least, the community prospect seemed bright. Like forward-looking townsfolk everywhere in that nineteenth-century America of the urban possibility, bright prospects were all that cattle town people ever asked.

[4] Caldwell *Post*, Apr. 22, 1880; Caldwell *Commercial*, Sept. 9, 16, 1880; Sante Fe: *Annual Report . . . 1880* (Boston, 1881), p. 6; Henry V. Poor: *Manual of the Railroads of the United States for 1881* (New York, 1881), p. 737.

II

Cattle Town Enterprise

[1]

"WE ARE HERE," observed a philosophical Dodge City editor, and he included his fellow citizens in the plural pronoun, "to live and get rich—if we can."[1] This candid statement of the businessman's ethic exposed the impulse that brought the cattle town people together in the first place and mainly motivated them thereafter. Entrepreneurship remained a general matrix to which virtually all other aspects of local life were fixed in one way or another.

[2]

CENTRAL TO THE COMMUNITY economic base was of course the cattleman. The source of this enterpriser's operations, the thing that attracted him to the Kansas markets year after year and finally led him to large-scale ranching within and on the periphery of the state, was the difference between the worth of cattle on their native prairies and what northern buyers would pay.[2] Some

[1] Dodge City *Times*, May 28, 1885.

[2] The three standard works on the western range cattle industry are Ernest Staples Osgood: *The Day of the Cattleman* (Minneapolis, 1929); Edward Everett Dale: *The Range Cattle Industry* (Norman, Okla., 1930); Louis Pelzer: *The Cattlemen's Frontier* (Glendale, Calif., 1936). Although too concerned with the merely colorful, Wayne

truly spectacular profits in the early days of trail driving inspired drovers of succeeding seasons. In 1868, for example, M. A. Withers brought north a herd of six hundred steers valued at about $8 to $10 a head, or $5,400, in Texas. Reaching Abilene without much loss, Withers sold the herd for $16,800. He figured his expenses at $4 per head. His net profit therefore totaled about $9,000—a "snug sum" for one season's work in those days. Another Texan, James F. Ellison, drove a mixed herd of about 750 head to Abilene the following year, also earning a $9,000 profit. Drovers in later years made up for lower profits per head by trailing larger herds. George F. Hindes brought a herd to Wichita in 1872 and estimated his net profit at $15,000.[3]

The livestock buyers who congregated each season at the cattle towns, some of them simply cattle speculators, represented three groups of secondary purchasers: the ranchers of Colorado, the Dakotas, Wyoming, and Montana, where a demand persisted for yearlings and two-year-olds as stock cattle; the feeders of the Middle West who until about 1880 commonly bought full-grown steers for final fattening; and the packinghouses of eastern terminal markets that sought beef steers for slaughter. The drover could—and many did—decline to sell to cattle town buyers and instead choose to ship his own finished beef to a terminal market for sale, or trust his animals to a livestock commission merchant who would do it for him. These terminal markets often held out the promise of greatest profits. In mid-1870, a season that witnessed the

---

Gard's *The Chisholm Trail* (Norman, Okla., 1954) remains the best general work on this aspect of the subject. Beyond these principal monographs the pertinent literature is vast. See the admirable bibliographical essay in Ray Allen Billington: *Westward Expansion: A History of the American Frontier* (3rd edn.; New York, 1967), pp. 877–82.

[3] J. Marvin Hunter (ed.): *The Trail Drivers of Texas* (2nd edn.; Nashville, Tenn., 1925), pp. 96–98, 477, 823–24.

highest maximum beef prices ever paid at Chicago during
the cattle town era, a 900-pound steer worth $11 to $14 in
Texas could be sold at Abilene for $20 to $25, but might
bring an additional $10 at Chicago or St. Louis. The same
animal sold at New York might net $70 or more.[4]

Despite its attractions, livestock shipping to terminal
markets broke the financial back of many an enterprising
drover, rancher, and speculator. The operation involved
heavy rail freight charges, to say nothing of the risk of
sudden market slumps between cattle town loading pen
and urban destination. The average cattleman preferred
to sell "on his own ground," as Joseph G. McCoy phrased
it, shipping only if compelled by absolute necessity. This
remained true throughout the period, the Chicago stockyards being characterized by a Caldwell editor in 1885 as
"that fitful but last resort market" for the really desperate
seller.[5]

In any case, the cattleman's was a business in which
losses could be appalling. Whether in a year of poor cattle town demand he courted the sudden death of shipping
to a terminal or instead suffered the slow agony of awaiting a local price upturn, the cattleman found himself at the
mercy of both national livestock and money markets. The
dangers these presented dwarfed the menace of the rustlers and redskins of tradition, as the debacle of 1873
illustrates.

The drive from Texas was a relatively large one that
year although an oversupply of cattle in the North, a
short midwestern corn crop that curtailed feeding, and
"close" financial affairs everywhere in the nation presaged
a poor market. Few buyers visited Ellsworth, Wichita,
and other cattle towns; incoming drovers therefore held

[4] Osgood: *Day of the Cattleman*, p. 95; Abilene *Chronicle*, Sept. 22,
1870.

[5] Joseph G. McCoy: *Historic Sketches of the Cattle Trade of the
West and Southwest*, ed. Ralph P. Bieber (Glendale, Calif., 1940), p.
168; Caldwell *Journal*, Sept. 10, 1885.

their herds on nearby ranges, hoping for an upturn of demand in the autumn. Their current expenses required bank loans, however. Joe McCoy estimated that by September 1, 1873, Texas drovers in Kansas were collectively some $1,500,000 in debt. The greater portion of the amount would come due before frost.[6]

On Thursday, September 18, the New York office of Jay Cooke and Company closed its doors, triggering the collapse of one of the nation's most respected financial empires. Thus began the disastrous Panic of 1873. As the news reached the cattle towns by wire, frantic drovers now unable to gain extensions on their loans began shipping their herds off to terminal markets for desperation sales. Daily shipping totals mounted fantastically. At Wichita on Sunday, September 21, some 2,400 head went out, and nearly as many left Ellsworth four days later. Cattle prices disintegrated completely, but panic shipping continued. Toward the end of October a writer from Wichita summarized the cattleman's dilemma:

> The majority of drovers are still indebted for their cattle purchased in Texas. To sell to buyers here at less than cost, or ship on their own account to Kansas City and other eastern markets, and there meet with a like fate, and take certified checks, subject to a discount on the streets of 20 per cent, for currency, as many of them have done, means bankruptcy. . . . To sell or not to sell, that's the all important question. Notes given in banks whereby to raise funds for the payment of hands, subsistence and the like, are about maturing and must be promptly met. This class of dealers must sell, as one remarked to me, "if it takes the hair off." So sacrifices are made, and cattle men, as well as cattle, are slaughtered every day.

One Texan, Joseph Cotulla, sold out at Wichita and reckoned his loss at $7,000. A livestock dealer shipped a herd

[6] McCoy: *Historic Sketches*, pp. 308–10. See also the pre-season letter from Texas in Ellsworth *Reporter*, Mar. 20, 1873.

from Wichita for which he had paid $17,000; he lost fully
$10,000 on the transaction. In just three weeks' time a
single firm of livestock traders suffered losses totaling
$180,000.[7]

While the 1873 disaster proved unique in its general
destructiveness, the occasional collapse of financial institutions such as Kansas City's First National and Mastin
banks in the late seventies continued to hurt individual
stock raisers severely, even as trailing gave way to the
somewhat more stable ranching.[8] To these national and
regional economic vicissitudes add such routine hazards
as stock disease and inclement weather and one discovers
an enterprise more often resembling gambling than legitimate business. "So deep and firm [nevertheless] does the
habit and incentive to trade and speculation take hold
upon its votaries," wrote the knowledgeable Joe McCoy
of the cattleman as a type,

> that few men, after beginning, are ever willing to quit the
> business of stock trading and shipping, or exchange it for
> any other business. . . . If he succeeds, no matter how well
> at first, it only serves to make him determined to retrieve
> his losses in the same vocation in which he sustained it.
> Bankruptcy and financial ruin is the only means that will
> put a stop to his operations.[9]

[3]

TWO MAJOR SERVICES contributed directly to the cattleman's activity, without which there would have been no

[7] Wichita *Eagle*, Sept. 25, Oct. 30, Nov. 27, 1873; Ellsworth
Reporter, Sept. 25, 1873; Hunter: *Trail Drivers*, p. 318; McCoy:
Historic Sketches, p. 310.

[8] Dodge City *Globe*, Feb. 5, Aug. 6, 1878. For the special commitment of these two institutions to the cattle trade see McCoy: *Historic
Sketches*, pp. 366–68, 370–71.

[9] McCoy: *Historic Sketches*, p. 322.

cattle trade as the Kansas market towns came to know it. One of these was the railroad. Railroad aid to cattlemen normally included the services of a company-owned stockyard, a station with telegraph facilities, and a small force of supervisory personnel. The railroad's major role, of course, was as a provider of eastward transportation to the feeders and slaughterhouses of the Middle West and East.

To imply that all livestock sold at the cattle towns was thereupon shipped east by rail would be a mistake, since many buyers, especially territorial ranchers, walked purchases to their destinations. According to McCoy, driving cattle from Abilene northwestward became quite as usual as driving from Texas to that market town. In 1871, for instance, cattlemen sold an estimated 190,000 head at Abilene, of which only 40,000 went out by rail. In 1882 buyers at Dodge City purchased approximately 200,000 head, but only about 65,000 of this number left town on the cars.[1] These examples notwithstanding, the railroads' commercial involvement in the cattle town livestock market remained a considerable one.

Perhaps the most fundamental link between the railroad and the cattle trade, from the railroad point of view, was the sorely needed eastbound traffic western livestock provided. A continuing burden to roads operating in frontier regions, the imbalance of westbound over eastbound freight reflected the typical underdeveloped area's need for goods far in excess of its ability to furnish a compensating volume of products in return. This meant that eastbound trains commonly hauled empty freight cars. Management recognized this waste factor as a profit stealer to be eradicated only when the areas served became fully

[1] McCoy: *Historic Sketches*, p. 144; Abilene *Chronicle*, Feb. 1, 1872; Dodge City *Globe*, Jan. 2, 1883.

settled and productive.[2] In the meantime officials eagerly grasped at anything resembling a fairly stable source of important eastbound freight.

When implementing his Abilene project in the summer of 1867, Joe McCoy gained a measure of cooperation from extremely skeptical railroad officers primarily because of their urgent desire for "freight going east." In its report to stockholders at the end of 1868 the Kansas Pacific management observed enthusiastically that while westbound freight tonnage still exceeded more than twice that headed in the opposite direction, the Texas cattle trade "already adds largely to the east-bound freight of the road." Figures provided by the Santa Fe reveal much the same traffic imbalance that a vigorous cattle commerce helped alleviate. In 1874 and from 1876 through the next decade, excepting only 1884, eastbound tonnage lagged greatly behind westbound. More important, the gross receipts from eastbound freight fell far below those from westbound freight even in 1884. In 1881 the freight differential peaked at $5,501,969—westbound receipts being that year over four times as much as eastbound receipts. The freight traffic imbalance thus comprised a very serious matter of dollars and cents.[3]

Fees received for carrying animals from cattle town stockyards varied considerably with the town's location, since rates were in "per ton per mile" form, and depended even more on the existence or the lack of rail competition. For the first few years of the era the Kansas Pacific enjoyed a virtual monopoly on cattle town shipments. In the autumn of 1867 it charged $100 per carload to carry cattle from Abilene to St. Louis, and $150 to Chicago. By the

[2] See Kansas Pacific Railway Co.: *Annual Report . . . 1869* (St. Louis, 1870), p. 9; Atchison, Topeka and Santa Fe Railroad Co.: *Annual Report . . . 1882* (Boston, 1882), p. 17.

[3] McCoy: *Historic Sketches*, p. 114; Kansas Pacific: *Annual Report . . . 1868* (St. Louis, 1869), p. 12. See also the appropriate figures in the Santa Fe's annual reports for 1874–86.

fall of 1870 the "special rates" offered stockmen who desired to ship from Abilene ranged from $6 to $7 per head, or from $120 to $140 per car. After the Kansas Pacific received some substantial shipping competition, rates dropped sharply. In 1872 the Santa Fe's charges from the new cattle town of Wichita were $30 per car to Missouri River points and $100 per car to Chicago. To meet this challenge the Kansas Pacific slashed its rates, the average paid at Ellsworth that season being only $29.96 per car. In 1873 the Ellsworth average rate dropped to $29.67, but rose again in 1874 to $34.97. These charges never again reached earlier levels. During the late 1870's and the 1880's rates from Dodge City or Caldwell to Kansas City stabilized at about $40 per carload, or $2 per head, with shipping charges to terminal markets farther east proportionately higher.[4]

All the cattle carried east by the railroads did not, of course, come from the Kansas cattle towns; yet such shipments usually totaled enough to merit special attention. In 1872, for instance, gross receipts from cattle shipments at Ellsworth reached $60,155, or nearly 25 per cent of the Kansas Pacific's total gross cattle shipping receipts. In that season of initial competition from the Santa Fe, however, this amount was reckoned by management to be "below the cost of doing the business." The following year, because of "a better understanding between the various [railway] lines and stock shippers," the Kansas Pacific earned more satisfactory returns. Although loading considerably fewer cattle, Ellsworth's contribution to the road's total gross cattle shipping receipts rose slightly to $60,571.05, or over 26 per cent of the total—verifica-

---

[4] New York *Tribune*, Nov. 6, 1867; Abilene *Chronicle*, Sept. 22, 1870; Wichita *Eagle*, Oct. 24, 1872; Kansas Pacific: *Annual Report . . . 1873* (St. Louis, 1874), p. 18; ibid. *1874* (St. Louis, 1875), p. 14; Dodge City *Globe*, May 13, 1879, Oct. 18, 1881; Caldwell *Journal*, May 29, 1884.

tion, incidentally, that poor profits for cattlemen did not necessarily mean railway profit losses.[5] In 1874, finally, with Ellsworth in decline as a cattle center, the receipts there fell by nearly half, to $32,345, but still 15 per cent of the company's total cattle shipping receipts. The statistics also showed that the loss of receipts at Ellsworth was only partially being made up elsewhere.[6]

Banking comprised a second enterprise directly supporting the cattle trade. As McCoy pointed out, the sums exchanged in stock transactions often reached enormous proportions, even by the early 1870's. Transfers of $1,000 to $20,000 became seasonally common, with as much as $50,000 to $100,000 occasionally changing hands in a single sale. Cattle town deposit and exchange facilities, providing both security and convenience, accordingly became a necessity. Credit also represented an important need. In the early days, when drovers bought herds in Texas on extended terms, likely as not to be paid for only upon their return with money in hand, loans to meet current expenses comprised about all the cattleman might require. The drover sought loans to pay off employees, to replenish supplies expended on the trail, and to pay living expenses incurred while he himself sojourned in town awaiting satisfactory buyers. By the mid-seventies, however, the demand for cattle in Texas enabled ranchers of that state to require payment for cattle on shorter time.

[5] Kansas Pacific: *Annual Report . . . 1872* (St. Louis, 1873), p. 19; ibid. *1873*, p. 17.
[6] Calculated from Kansas Pacific: *Annual Report 1873*, p. 18; ibid. *1874*, p. 14. A lack of comparable statistics for the Santa Fe makes the same kind of analysis for that road impossible. Local editors, however, sometimes reported cattle receipts, obtaining the information from railroad officials. In 1881 the figure was as high as $62,880 at Dodge City, and about $52,000 at Caldwell. During 1883 the cattle receipts at Dodge climbed to $134,080. Dodge City *Globe*, Nov. 22, 1881, Dec. 11, 1883; Caldwell *Post*, Dec. 15, 1881.

Many drovers therefore obligated themselves to pay off immediately upon arrival at the cattle town. If, as was common, profitable sales could not be made immediately, the herd would have to be paid for by a loan. If the cattleman elected to ship directly to a terminal market, moreover, he needed to pay rail charges, and these too must be met by loans.

Bankers' profits came from discounting the large volume of paper passing over their counters, and, of course, in interest charges from large short-term loans. Although cattle town credit institutions existed that in customary frontier fashion looked primarily to land mortgages, the larger and more immediate profits in cattle loans beckoned alluringly to the enterprising financier. "A fabulous interest is paid for cash," reported a visitor to Wichita in 1873, "and banks are as fat a thing as gold mines." In another two years the cattle trade had largely deserted Wichita for Dodge City and other points. Discounters and lenders felt the effect. "We called on two of the banks. . . ," another visitor recorded. "The officers seem cheerful, but they miss the clank of the Texas spur to a considerable extent." These paired observations succinctly captured the cattle town banking experience.

The cattleman's growing credit needs attracted both peripatetic frontier lenders and representatives of large and respected institutions. Joe McCoy early began referring Texas cattlemen at Abilene to the First National Bank of Kansas City, and by 1870 that facility's business with drovers had so increased that it opened an office in Abilene. Over $900,000 passed over the counter in its first two months of operation there. The establishment of resident banks soon followed, some of the larger businessmen putting to use, as capital, profits already garnered from the cattle trade. The Wichita Savings Bank, with merchant Sol H. Kohn as its moving force, declared a 10 per cent dividend on its paid-up capital stock just six months after commencing business.[7]

The Panic of 1873—its deleterious effects on cattle-men also affecting their creditors—curtailed this general development to some degree. Wichita's First National Bank, for one, suffered intensely from too deep a commitment to the cattle trade. Cattlemen held most of its loans, aggregating at the inception of the panic about $220,000, and the institution never recovered from their collective bankruptcy. Its president later admitted that it was during this financial crisis "that the axe was laid at the roots of this bank." In August 1876, the bank went into voluntary liquidation and its president to jail for having lapsed into fraudulent practices while trying to repair the damage.[8]

During the depression of the 1870's cattle town commercial houses sometimes engaged in banking as subsidiary operations. The Dodge City firm of Wright, Beverley and Company carried on such an activity, apparently in order to capture the cattleman's mercantile patronage by providing him with a necessary service rather than by specifically seeking discount or interest profits. "Our remittances to banks in Leavenworth," recalled the company's senior member, Robert M. Wright, "were frequently as high as fifty thousand dollars. This was owing to stock men depositing their whole pile with us, and drawing against it as they needed it." The firm thus furnished free security and bookkeeping. The company's major competitor, the York-Parker-Draper Mer-

[7] McCoy: *Historic Sketches*, pp. 363–66; Wichita *Eagle*, Apr. 3, July 17, 1873, July 8, 1875; Abilene *Chronicle*, Sept. 15, Oct. 13, 1870.

[8] Using materials on failed national banks in the National Archives, George L. Anderson has examined the aborted career of this credit institution in some detail. See his "From Cattle to Wheat: The Impact of Agricultural Developments on Banking in Early Wichita," *Agricultural History*, XXXIII (1959), 3–15.

cantile Company, its principal personnel being alumni of an east Kansas financial institution, also carried on a banking service in connection with its commercial trade.[9]

The final phase of cattle town banking came after 1880, when the great western cattle boom saw the rise of ranching in close proximity to Dodge City and Caldwell. The latter's Stock Exchange Bank, founded in 1881 by neighboring Cherokee Strip cattlemen, illustrated a tighter interdependence of credit and cattle than earlier, in that depositors and borrowers were to a large extent evidently identical.[1] The Bank of Dodge City, established in 1882 by several of that town's wealthiest merchants, many of them cattle speculators, also represented this development but to a lesser degree.[2]

[4]

ENTERPRISES THAT ATTENDED to the personnel of the cattle trade rather than the trade itself remained the life's blood of the cattle town economic organism. For most local businessmen, the principal attraction of the commerce in

[9] Robert M. Wright: *Dodge City: The Cowboy Capital* (Wichita, 1913), p. 158; Dodge City *Globe*, Jan. 1, Sept. 17, 1878 ff. (ad), Apr. 19, 1881; A. T. Andreas: *History of the State of Kansas* (Chicago, 1883), p. 1561.

[1] Andreas: *History of Kansas*, p. 1503; Caldwell *Commercial*, Oct. 27, Nov. 17, 1881; Caldwell *Post*, Oct. 27, 1881. That depositors and borrowers were largely identical seems verified by the fact that its semi-annual statements, as published in the local press, often show loans virtually equal to deposits. See especially those statements in Caldwell *Post*, Jan. 25, 1883; Caldwell *Journal*, July 26, 1883, Jan. 24, 1884, Jan. 29, July 23, 1885, Jan. 7, 1886.

[2] Dodge City *Globe*, June 20, 1882; Dodge City *Times*, June 22, 1882. While more characteristic of the later years, this development is also seen in the early period in the Powers Bank at Ellsworth, which represented a combination of stock raising with banking. For details see McCoy: *Historic Sketches*, pp. 372–74; Andreas: *History of Kansas*, pp. 1277, 1280; Ellsworth *Reporter*, Nov. 7, 1872, May 8, 1873, Apr. 16, 30, 1874, June 3, 1875.

livestock was its need for associated consumer goods and services. Those with something to sell viewed it as a market for everything from cabbages to dance hall queens.

The cattle trade consumer group initially consisted of transients who populated a cattle town between late spring and October or November, depending on the briskness of the autumn's shipping season. Although enthusiastic local editors probably exaggerated, the numbers of those usually passing through town each good season must have been well into four figures.[3] A cattle town, however, might be virtually vacant of temporary residents from December through April, which imposed a decided unevenness on things. The development of ranching in the 1880's modified this picture a good deal. With shorter, and often multiple, drives then being made to cattle towns by ranchers and drovers, businessmen enjoyed a more consistent supply of transient consumers. Cowboys and stockmen from relatively nearby ranches, in fact, often became frequent visitors. Even this did not mean the end of periodic influxes, since the arrival of herds from Texas—especially from the Panhandle—continued regularly throughout the era, and autumn remained a favored shipping time even for ranchers.[4] By and large, however, the spectacular summertime influx of earlier years slacked off toward the end of the period, the seasonal heights and depths leveled out, and all forms of business enterprise benefited from an increased stability.

The transient consumer group, the core of which con-

[3] A citizen of Abilene was supposed to have counted four thousand persons on Texas Street in one day. (Adolph Roenigk [ed.], *Pioneer History of Kansas* [Denver, 1933], p. 36.) In specific calculations of summertime visitors connected directly with the cattle trade, Abilene's editor in 1870 and a Dodge City editor in 1878 both arrived at the figure 1,500 as representative of sojourning cowboys, owners, and buyers. The latter writer broke this number down into 1,300 cowboys and 250 owners and buyers. Abilene *Chronicle*, Nov. 24, 1870; Dodge City *Globe*, May 7, 1878.

[4] See for example Dodge City *Globe*, Dec. 16, 1884.

sisted of Texans, posed certain unique problems for those who wished to exploit it. Since, as Joe McCoy testified, the average Texan distrusted the northerners with whom he came into contact, local businessmen persisted in special efforts to achieve rapport with him. Persons well known and well liked by the Texans, for example, found themselves always in demand by cattle town merchants seeking sales personnel. The names given commercial establishments also reflected this entrepreneurial courtship. "As at Newton," reported a visitor to Abilene,

> Texas names are prominent on the fronts of saloons and other "business houses," mingled with sign board allusions to the cattle business. A clothing dealer implores you to buy your "outfit" at the sign of the "Long Horns;" the leading gambling house is of course the "Alamo," and "Lone Stars" shine in every direction.[5]

Among goods sold in the transient market, groceries evidently outclassed any other single item in value.[6] While it is not possible to isolate cattle trade sales from purchases by residents, rural settlers, or smaller retailers, cattle trade consumption reportedly was always high. As herds approached town from the south, local grocers regularly solicited orders from their crews to replace supplies expended on the trail. Owners who arrived by rail in advance of their herds often bought groceries in bulk and dispatched them to meet the incoming outfits. Thereafter sales were made to the various herders' camps during the period when cattle grazed on outlying prairies awaiting

---

[5] McCoy: *Historic Sketches*, pp. 128, 213; Topeka *Record*, Aug. 5, 1871.

[6] According to the only known value estimate of goods sold at a cattle town—a listing for Ellsworth in 1874—groceries comprised 31 per cent of the total. (Kansas State Board of Agriculture: *Annual Report . . . 1874* [Topeka, 1874], p. 143.) The fact that 1874 was a very poor commercial season for Ellsworth, however, and that it was already in sharp decline as a cattle market, virtually destroys the usefulness of this rare compilation for present purposes.

sale. Grocery sales to the cattle trade also were made indirectly through purchases by restaurateurs and hotel proprietors who fed the drovers, buyers, and other cattle trade transients sojourning in town.

Although there were large grocery houses at each of the cattle towns, Wichita found itself in an especially strategic position for furnishing provisions to advancing herds, being for a time the first town on the Chisholm Trail north of Red River to be served by a railroad. Its grocers thus had first crack at even those herds driven on to Ellsworth in the years 1872–75. In 1872, for example, W. A. Thomas and Company of Wichita sold $100,000 worth of groceries, of which nearly a quarter of the total went directly to trail outfits. "This firm expects to do a big jobbing trade the coming season," reported a correspondent early in 1873, "and are making arrangements to sell $50,000 [worth] to the cattle trade alone." That season it indeed furnished no less than seventy different herders' camps, its sales averaging $12,000 per month.[7]

Clothing followed only groceries as a cattle town commercial product of importance. Cowboys with two or three months' accumulated wages—perhaps $60 to $90 each[8]—accounted for this to a great extent, since their

[7] Wichita *Eagle*, Feb. 6, June 26, 1873.

[8] Lacking concrete contemporary estimates, we can only guess at this "typical" sum. In 1880 Joe McCoy, in contributing to the federal agricultural census, reckoned the average cowboy's wage at $25 to $30 per month; the latter figure indeed is often mentioned as applying in various years throughout the period. (U.S. Census Office: *Tenth Census of the United States: 1880* [Washington, D.C., 1883], III, 974; Hunter: *Trail Drivers*, pp. 59, 135, 147, 235, 367, 535, 735, 882.) An approximate average of the length of time a herd spent on the trail completes this rough estimate. In 1870 the typical herd at Abilene was said to have been two months on the trail. In 1880, when many herds originated in the Panhandle, McCoy estimated thirty-five days. (Abilene *Chronicle*, Sept. 22, 1870; *Tenth Census*, III, 975.) Since most cowboys probably began work before the actual drive commenced, and some were retained after the drive ended to hold the herd while the owner awaited a buyer, an estimate of from two to three months' wages, or

first major expenditure upon hitting town was on fresh clothes. "Straightway after settling with their employers," wrote McCoy, "the barber shop is visited. . . . Next a clothing store . . . is 'gone through,' and the cowboy emerges a new man in outward appearance, everything being new, not excepting the hat, and boots with star decorations about the tops; also a new—, well, in short everything new." Clothiers discovered the enormous profits to be acquired as early as September 1867, when the first Texas cattle had barely cleared Abilene's new stockyard.[9] Throughout the cattle town era newly, expensively, and often grotesquely garbed cowhands fresh from the trail or range persisted as a part of the local color invariably commented upon by sightseers.

Jacob Karatofsky, a young German-born dry goods and clothing merchant, for several years paid a close and rather conservative attention to the cattle town clothing trade. He first appeared in Abilene in the spring of 1869 with an assortment of dry goods and "notions." The following year his new Great Western Store at the busy corner of Texas and Cedar streets, a prime location for tapping the transient trade, offered for sale what thereafter remained his staple items: "Dry Goods, Clothing, Boots, Shoes, Hats, Caps, and Gents' Furnishing Goods." Karatofsky also carried ladies' fancy dress goods, perhaps catering thereby to the expensive tastes of transient prostitutes. In the spring of 1872, after having briefly experimented with a subsidiary line of groceries, he followed the cattle trade to Ellsworth. In August, however, he

---

$60 to $90, seems not unreasonable. For trail bosses the typical sum may have been $200 to $300; McCoy estimated that these supervisory personnel averaged about $90, although the amount usually mentioned is $100. Ibid., 974; Hunter: *Trail Drivers*, pp. 367, 783, 853.

[9] McCoy: *Historic Sketches*, p. 204; New York *Tribune*, Nov. 6, 1867. For proof that the propensity to outfit themselves anew remained a cowboy characteristic to the last, see the Caldwell *Journal*, Sept. 17, 1885.

closed out both his Ellsworth and Abilene stores and transferred operations to the promising new cattle town of Wichita. Here he opened two stores, offering the usual dry goods and men's and women's clothing. In the fall of 1874, responding intelligently to omens that the trade was in a decline at Wichita, Karatofsky sought greener pastures elsewhere. After first prospecting in Texas itself, he resumed business at Hot Springs, Arkansas, a growing resort center probably offering a much better market for the distaff side of his commercial line. Thus ended a restless but apparently profitable six years' flirtation with the cattle trade.[1]

Bootmaking represented a unique specialty within the cattle town clothing business. Together with the occasional wagonmaker, brewer, or saddler, the bootmaker personified the cattle town manufacturer specifically oriented to the transient trade. Both cowboys and cattlemen demanded footwear tailored according to Texan tastes. Abilene's Thomas C. McInerney was one of the first to capitalize on this specialized demand. During the flush summer seasons this enterprising businessman employed from ten to twenty men to help him turn out high-heeled, red-topped boots spangled with Lone Star and crescent moon devices. These sold for $12 to $20 a pair. Another of the most successful bootmakers was John Mueller, whose "sign of the Big Boot" was displayed to Texans for several years. Mueller first opened in business at Ellsworth in the early seventies and found trade exceptionally brisk. At the end of May 1874, with the sea-

[1] U.S. Manuscript Census, 1870: Kansas (KSHS), Dickinson Co., Grant Twp., p. 18; Leavenworth Times and Conservative, June 25, 1869; Abilene Chronicle, Sept. 1 ff. (ad), Nov. 24, 1870, May 18 ff. (ad), Oct. 12, Dec. 14, 21, 1871, Mar. 28, Apr. 11, May 2, Aug. 8, 1872; Ellsworth Reporter, May 2, June 20, 1872; Wichita Eagle, Aug. 16, Oct. 31, Nov. 7, 14 ff. (ad), 28, 1872, June 5, 1873, Nov. 5, 1874; Roenigk: Pioneer History, p. 35; O. H. Bentley (ed.): History of Wichita and Sedgwick County (Chicago, 1910), I, 266, 435–36.

son's herds just beginning to arrive near town, he had already sold over a hundred pairs of cowboy boots that year. When the cattle trade failed at Ellsworth he promptly removed to Dodge City, where he amalgamated for a time with a rival bootmaker. Late in 1880 Mueller finally sold out and turned his full attention to a growing herd of livestock that betrayed its economic origins by wearing the "Big Boot" brand.[2]

Except for grocers, clothing and dry goods merchants, and bootmakers, few successful cattle town businessmen evidently specialized by choice. The popular mercantile inclination was toward a "general" line of products. At its most modest level this might reflect the combination of only one or two types of goods. Shrewder merchants combined clothing, groceries, and camp equipment as a means of comprising a drovers' and ranchers' "outfitting establishment" in the broadest sense of that term. The largest operators, finally, included enough miscellaneous merchandise to attract the custom of the farmer and the permanent resident as well. In establishing this secondary source of profits they thereby created something of a market for their goods during the comparatively slack winter seasons.[3]

One of the earliest "general" merchants to orient his business operations to the Texas cattle trade was Mayer Goldsoll. Having immigrated from Russia as a mature married man, Goldsoll made his home in St. Louis and normally spent only the summer months personally supervising his cattle town facilities. He first appeared at

[2] J. B. Edwards: *Early Days in Abilene* (Abilene, 1940), p. 8; Roenigk: *Pioneer History*, p. 41; Ellsworth *Reporter*, May 29, July 31, 1873, May 28, 1874; Dodge City *Times*, June 23, Dec. 15, 22, 1877; Dodge City *Globe*, Jan. 15, 1878.

[3] Good examples of such operators include Abilene's Henry H. Hazlett, Ellsworth's Jerome Beebe, and Caldwell's W. N. Hubbell. See especially Abilene *Chronicle*, Apr. 21, 1870 ff. (ad); Ellsworth *Reporter*, Feb. 12, 1874 ff. (ad); Caldwell *Commercial*, May 13, 1880.

Ellsworth in 1867 or 1868, opening a general store known as the Old Reliable House. Perhaps impatient with the delay in the cattle trade's arrival there, in 1871 he operated a branch house at Abilene, the Texas Store, that offered fancy clothing, men's furnishing goods, boots, guns and ammunition, and watches. His Abilene profits evidently prompted him to open a second branch at Russell that winter, where he supplied Texas cattlemen herding stock in the Solomon River valley. When Abilene's cattle trade dwindled in 1872 Goldsoll closed his branch there and opened another at Denison, Texas, foreseeing that new railhead's subsequent emergence as a cattle shipping point of considerable importance.

With Ellsworth by this time commanding a good share of the cattle trade, Goldsoll for the next few years offered there the "largest stock in Western Kansas, of Fancy and Staple Groceries and Provisions, also Liquors, Cigars and Tobacco." In addition he advertised clothing, boots, shoes, blankets, luggage, jewelry and watches, silverware, cutlery, pistols, musical instruments, and toys. It was said that he could furnish "anything you may call for, from a $500 diamond to a pint of salt." Goldsoll created a faithful clientele by extending liberal credit to drovers during slack periods. His sales at Ellsworth in 1873 totaled $150,000, the monthly average amounting to $30,000 that summer, and early in 1874 he enlarged his store there. That season his establishment required the services of five full-time employees, one for each department (jewelry, groceries, clothing, and accounts) plus a general floorwalker.

Personnel losses and the inexorable shifts of the cattle trade caused changes in Goldsoll's operations. In 1874 he opened a branch at Brenham, Texas, the outlet at Russell having been cut off from the cattle trade. Barney W. Applebaum, who had been with Goldsoll since he first en-

tered business at Ellsworth, left him early in 1873 to buy
into a partnership with Jake Karatofsky at Wichita. Two
years later, with Karatofsky gone, Applebaum decided to
follow the cattle trade to Great Bend and open his own
house there. Goldsoll had the same idea that spring, and
talked Applebaum into co-managing a branch store there
with S. E. Isaacson, a clerk transferred down from the
Ellsworth facility. Applebaum agreed, and the arrangement gave Goldsoll control of branch houses in four cattle towns, two in Kansas and two in Texas. The 1875
cattle season proved the last at both Ellsworth and Great
Bend, however, and Goldsoll entrenched himself at the
short-lived cattle town of Ellis for the seasons of 1876 and
1877. He evidently remained permanently in St. Louis
thereafter and turned his talents to other enterprises, having been one of the most persistent exploiters of the cattle
town transient.[4]

If Mayer Goldsoll can be considered an example of
the large cattle town merchant in the first half of the era,
Dodge City's Bob Wright serves as his counterpart in the
last half of the period, when the development of Texas
and Indian Territory ranching added a new dimension to
commercial exploitation of the cattle trade.[5] Trimly built,
with a deceptively boyish expression, Wright had come
by his initial credentials as a self-made businessman the
hard way—operating far out on the frontier. As such he

[4] Ellsworth Co. Commissioners Journal, 1867–87 (transcript,
KSHS), pp. 48, 83; U.S. Manuscript Census, 1870: Kansas, Ellsworth
Co., 1st section, p. 5; Abilene *Chronicle*, May 18, 1871 ff. (ad), Jan.
18, 1872; Ellsworth *Reporter*, Dec. 14, 1871 ff. (ad), Jan. 25 ff. (ad),
Dec. 26, 1872, Mar. 20, 27, May 1, 8, 29, June 5, July 17, 1873,
May 7, 14, 21, July 30, 1874, Jan. 28, May 13, 1875; Topeka *Com-
monwealth*, July 1, 1873; Wichita *Eagle*, June 5, 1873; Wichita
Beacon, May 5, June 9, 1875; Dodge City *Times*, Oct. 14, 1876, Sept.
1, 1877; Andreas: *History of Kansas*, p. 1277.

[5] By the end of the era Bob Wright was shipping huge consignments
to ranches even in midwinter. Dodge City *Cowboy*, Jan. 31, 1885.

was every inch a natural leader of western men, commanding respect from the shaggiest buffalo hunter to governors and congressmen. Born a Marylander, he had migrated alone to the frontier while still in his teens to spend the war years in Colorado and western Kansas as a freighter, the manager of a line of stage stations, and a wood and hay contractor for various army posts. This rugged, often solitary career required of him a sideline as Indian fighter ("A man might as well be dead as to lose his property," he once told a comrade when weighing the alternatives of massacre or flight). In 1866 he moved to the vicinity of Fort Dodge, where the following year he won appointment as post trader. In 1872 Wright, now aged thirty-one, was an original proprietor of the Dodge City townsite. In partnershop with Charles Rath he shipped great quantities of buffalo hides from the new settlement, at the same time outfitting the hunters with camp equipment, clothing, groceries, and other necessities. When the buffalo gave out in the mid-seventies he and Rath, like the rest of the resident business community, turned gratefully to the cattle trade.

By 1877 Wright and Rath were said to be doing a retail trade of $250,000 annually. In November of that year, however, they dissolved their commercial relationship. Wright thereupon amalgamated with one of the firm's salesmen, Henry M. Beverley, a popular Texan and former cattle drover who had worked earlier for Mayer Goldsoll at Ellsworth. A third man, Charles H. Lane, joined these two as a junior partner. In the winter of 1877–78 the firm employed the services of a number of talented clerks. S. E. Isaacson, seasoned graduate of Mayer Goldsoll's Ellsworth and Great Bend facilities, managed the clothing department while one Sam Samuels took charge of firearms and jewelry. All hands utilized experience or special relationships with the transients.

"Judge Beverley has sold a few goods this week," a reporter noted in 1878, "—perhaps eight or ten thousand dollars worth. The Texas drovers seem [to] think a heap of the 'Old Jedge.'" Samuels's particular forte was dealing with Mexican cowhands, since he spoke fluent Spanish. "Wright, Beverley & Co's store was a perfect bee-hive last Tuesday," wrote an observer. "About thirty Mexican customers dropped in at the same time and purchased goods to the amount of seven or eight hundred dollars. The Mexicans look upon Sam Samuels as their Moses in this strange land." Besides this resident sales force the firm employed a Texan to ride out and solicit trade from the incoming herds, a practice common to the large cattle town mercantile houses.

With a trade area that embraced the huge Panhandle ranches, the firm boasted in 1879 that besides maintaining *"the largest and fullest line of Groceries and Tobacco west of Kansas City"* it could accommodate those desiring

> ANYTHING or EVERYTHING from a PAPER OF PINS to A PORTABLE HOUSE, GROCERIES, PROVISIONS FOR YOUR CAMP, RANCH OR FARM; CLOTHING, HATS, CAPS, BOOTS AND SHOES, UNDERCLOTHING, OVERALLS, and all kinds of FURNISHING GOODS; STUDEBAKER WAGONS, the best in the market, A GENUINE CALIFORNIA OR TEXAS SADDLE, A NOBBY SIDE SADDLE, A SETT OF HARNESS, A RIFLE, CARBINE, PISTOL OR FESTIVE BOWIE KNIFE, CAMP EQUIPPAGE of any kind, a full assortment of BUILDING HARDWARE.

In 1880 the company opened a branch store at Fort Griffin, Texas, to permit a better exploitation of the ranch and trail trade, a chief attraction of the new arrangement being that stockmen could buy goods at Griffin but pay for them at the store in Dodge after cattle driven there had been disposed of. That Wright and his associates also performed an informal banking service for their clientele has already been mentioned.[6]

Like Goldsoll's firm before it, the Wright Company proved a source of trained cattle town businessmen. In 1879 Charley Lane withdrew from the firm and the following year went into business with Sam Samuels at Caldwell. Samuels later served with another large outfitter there. In 1884 Henry Beverley relinquished his interest in the firm but stayed on as manager of the store until establishing his own clothing house at Dodge in 1885. Bob Wright, clearly the guiding genius of the company, remained in business at Dodge City even after the cattle trade's demise, publicly acknowledged as the wealthiest member of the community.[7]

Although each of the cattle towns contained the usual complement of doctors, laundresses, barbers, druggists, contractors, realtors, liverymen, blacksmiths, and—of

[6] Wright: *Dodge City, passim;* Ida Ellen Rath: *The Rath Trail* (Wichita, 1961), chap. x; Dodge City *Messenger*, Feb. 26, 1874; Dodge City *Times*, June 9, Nov. 24, Dec. 22, 1877, June 8, July 13, 1878, May 17, 1879 ff. (ad), Mar. 13, 1880; Dodge City *Globe*, Jan. 1, 1878, Feb. 24, 1880; Andreas: *History of Kansas*, p. 1562.

A body of business records from the R. M. Wright firm has survived, a microfilm copy of which is held by the Kansas State Historical Society. This consists of a Sales Book (1879–81), a Ledger (1883–85), and a Petty Ledger (1885–87). While some sophisticated speculative conclusions might emerge from a very painstaking and extended analysis of these fragments, their failure to synchronize makes definitive estimates of the firm's commercial success especially difficult. Be that as it may, from balance sheets for the years 1883 and 1884 it would appear that the net worth of the company increased during the two-year period from $27,185.66 to $47,326.75—or by $20,141.09—which figure is roughly equivalent to undivided profit. (Ledger, pp. 4, 114.) The balance sheets themselves are subject to question, however, since they are not fully verifiable—due to the lack of the corresponding journal and cash book—and also are marred by inconsistent entry nomenclature and categories.

[7] Dodge City *Globe*, June 10, 1879, June 1, 1880, Oct. 27, 1885; Dodge City *Times*, Mar. 13, 1884; Dodge City *Democrat*, Sept. 26, Oct. 3, 1885; Dodge City *Cowboy*, Aug. 29, 1885; Caldwell *Commercial*, May 27, Sept. 30, 1880.

course—lawyers, the keepers of hotels provided a service peculiarly necessary to the cattle town. Joe McCoy, whose own Drovers Cottage he considered as important a lure to the early cattle trade as his small banking office, revealed the importance of hotel facilities when he lent his advice to the would-be market town of Newton: "Mc-Coy says that the cattle business would desert Abilene if comfortable hotel accommodations were available at Newton," it was reported.[8] Such a factor indeed influenced Texans weighing the advantages of one cattle town over another, but profits from the seasonal influx of transients formed an incentive more important from the individual hotelman's view.

Wichita's eight hotels and five boardinghouses enjoyed a phenomenal business in the early seventies. From July 1, 1872, through March of 1873 daily registrations at its three largest establishments totaled 19,410. One of these, the mammoth three-story brick Douglas Avenue House, accommodated 1,260 guests from June 1 through mid-July 1873. Enticements to cattle trade transients appeared regularly in newspaper advertisements and blurbs. "Stock Dealers make this House their headquarters," it was hopefully said of Beede's Hotel at Ellsworth. Caldwell's Moreland House proclaimed itself "The Home of the Cowboy." Some cattle town hotels maintained "stock registers" in their lobbies as a means of capturing the cattleman's custom. Here drovers could enter their names, local addresses, and the numbers and characteristics of livestock they had to sell. Buyers then consulted these registers as aids to finding the herds from which they wished to purchase.[9]

[8] Topeka *Commonwealth*, Aug. 15, 1871. For another such statement on the importance of hotels to the Texans see Wichita *Eagle*, Apr. 19, 1872.

[9] Wichita *Eagle*, Apr. 3, July 17, 1873; Ellsworth *Reporter*, Dec. 14, 1871 ff. (ad); Caldwell *Post*, Jan. 26, 1882 ff. (ad). See descriptions of the stock registers at Ellsworth's Grand Central Hotel and

The earliest and most famous of the large cattle town hotels was the Drovers Cottage, put up by Joe McCoy at Abilene in 1867 at an estimated cost—including furnishings and an adjoining stable—of $15,000. Though alterations later changed its appearance, as originally built it was a boxlike wooden structure, forty by sixty feet, three stories high, enclosing forty or fifty spacious, well-appointed chambers, a bar, restaurant, and billiard room. In exterior design it was vaguely Italianate, spare of ornamentation except for a shallow gable at one end and green louvered shutters hung to either side of its windows, the clapboards painted a delicate beige. It fronted the railroad tracks a block west of the stockyard, and the patrons relaxing along its lengthy veranda enjoyed in shade and comfort the only free entertainment regularly to be had in town—watching the trains arrive, load, and depart. The Drovers Cottage was easily Abilene's most impressive structure throughout the cattle trade era, looming on the low skyline above weedy vacant lots and a scattering of pitch-roofed residences, barns, and stores.

Opening his hotel just in time for the 1868 cattle season, McCoy brought from St. Louis an experienced couple, Mr. and Mrs. James W. Gore, to manage it for him. Lou Gore, through her motherly concern for sick and down-and-out cowboys, soon became a general favorite with the Texans and thus an excellent advertisement for both hotel and town. Within a year McCoy had leased the Cottage to Jim Gore at a rent of nearly $1,000 a month. In July 1869, he sold the hotel to another entrepreneur, from whom Gore continued to lease. Business was so good that Gore himself bought the establishment in February 1870; eight months later he sold it again to a prosperous cattle dealer from Texas, Moses B. George.

Dodge City's Dodge House—printed by coincidence exactly ten years apart. Ellsworth *Reporter*, June 12, 1873; Dodge City *Globe*, June 12, 1883.

George ordered extensive additions, running the total cost of its construction up to about $40,000. In 1871 the hotel measured seventy by ninety feet, contained nearly a hundred rooms, could accommodate one hundred and seventy-five guests, and maintained stabling for fifty carriages and a hundred horses.

In early 1872, with the cattle trade expected to shift from Abilene, the businessmen of Ellsworth formed a corporation to underwrite the construction of a large new hotel, hoping thereby to fix the trade at their town. In exchange for a $4,000 subsidy, George agreed to put up a structure worth $10,000 and have it ready to welcome the season's first cattlemen. His plan was simple. House moving was not yet a lost art, certainly not on the frontier, and George had the Drovers Cottage detached from its Abilene moorings and shipped to Ellsworth by flat car, leaving behind only its smaller rear wing. He retained the Gores to manage the reconstituted Cottage, which reopened in May, proving just as popular with the Texans as ever.

In 1873 George sold back to Jim Gore both the Drovers Cottage and its Abilene remnant, but at Ellsworth Gore's business declined sharply in response to competition from the new, even more elegant, and more conveniently located Grand Central Hotel. In 1874 Gore evidently considered transferring his operations up to Russell, and set his fully insured establishment on fire in an effort to raise the necessary cash. Someone sounded the alarm before the conflagration could do much damage, however, and Gore collected only a small claim. In 1875 he tried the same thing again, but a night watchman discovered the incendiary device. Gore spent one night in jail before being turned loose and told to leave town. He was well liked, and to townsmen the only criminal content of his act had been to pose a fire threat to the business district. The Gores returned unmolested to Abilene, where in the eighties they continued to manage what remained there of the original Drovers Cottage.[1]

[5]

WHAT COULD BE termed the cattle town "entertainment industry" deserves consideration as a major purveyor of goods and services. Although virtuous exceptions of course existed, the average cowboy's self-indulgent profligacy proved so unusual as to become a great western tradition. As Joe McCoy wrote in the early seventies: "The barroom, the theater, the gambling room, the bawdy house, the dance house, each and all come in for their full share of attention. . . . Such is the manner in which the cowboy spends his hard-earned dollars." This characteristic remained even after trailing gave way to ranching. "The cowboy spends his money recklessly," observed a visitor to Dodge in 1884. "He is a jovial, careless fellow bent on having a big time regardless of expense. He will make away with the wages of a half year in a few weeks, and then go back to his herds for another six months." Cowboys themselves verified such opinions. Reminisced an old-timer who drove cattle to Caldwell in 1882 and 1884: "Like most of the boys of the early days, I had to sow my wild oats, and I regret to say that I also sowed all of the money I made right along with the oats."

Cattle owners could be just as abandoned as their employees and usually enjoyed greater wherewithal for doing so. Texas drovers, McCoy testified, "do not hesitate to squander tens, fifties, and hundreds for the gratification of their appetites or passions." In 1871, for example, John James Haynes and his partner drove north a thou-

[1] McCoy: *Historic Sketches*, pp. 186–88 (with Bieber's documentary summary, footnote 279); Hunter: *Trail Drivers*, pp. 454–55; Junction City *Union*, July 17, 1869; Ellsworth *Reporter*, Jan. 11, 25, Feb. 29, May 16, 23, June 27, 1872, May 21, June 11, 18, 1874, May 6, 1875; Secretary of State Corporations Register (KSHS), IV, 110–11.

sand head of yearlings bought on credit. "We reached Abilene, Kansas," Haynes recalled, "with our yearlings in good shape, and we sold them for eight dollars per head. We found ourselves in possession of $8,000, and had started out without a dollar. But any old trail driver who found himself rich in Abilene, Kansas, in 1871, knows the rest."

Such remarks identify these transients as innately thriftless, but a Wichita resident offered an alternate explanation in which there must have been much truth. As soon as a Texas owner sold his herd, this observer noted, he left town. "The rest, who await the fattening of their herds . . . ," he added,

> tarry patiently in town the livelong day, loitering princi-
> pally on the benches erected for their accommodation in
> front of the different dry goods and grocery stores, whit-
> tling thoughtfully with their jackknives, and at times
> evincing the propensities of our town, that "everything
> goes" in our midst; they indulge in innocent amusements
> that abound, I presume through no love of spending
> money, but as an incentive to while away the dull hours
> which hang heavily on their hands.[2]

The saloon appeared to be the most obvious source of indoor relaxation for cowboys and cattlemen alike. Awed visitors, especially those from parts east of Kansas City, often exaggerated the numbers of these convivial facilities. In Abilene's busiest cattle season, 1871, the town possessed eleven taverns, including the bars operated in the Drovers Cottage and the Planters Hotel. At Ellsworth in 1873 there were no more than ten.[3] Wichita admitted to fifteen that same year. Dodge City's saloons numbered

[2] McCoy: *Historic Sketches*, pp. 127, 205; Dodge City *Cowboy*, July 12, 1884; Hunter: *Trail Drivers*, pp. 47, 245; Wichita *Eagle*, Aug. 21, 1873.

[3] Edwards: *Early Days in Abilene*, p. 10. The Board of Agriculture's *Annual Report 1874*, p. 143, fails to list any Ellsworth taverns, but "other mercantile pursuits" included only ten houses.

eight in 1878 and fourteen in 1879, declining to thirteen by 1882. Caldwell apparently reached a high point in 1880 with eleven, a figure that dropped thereafter to six or seven in response to state prohibition.[4]

Cattle town saloons varied considerably in character. They ranged from the usual dingy hole-in-the-wall to Dodge City's tastefully functional Long Branch to the rococo elegance of Abilene's finest, the celebrated Alamo, whose triple set of glass doors opened onto a brightly lit array of felt-topped gaming tables flanked by a gleaming brass-mounted bar and walls hung with ornate mirrors and sham Renaissance nudes. The men who operated them also varied. At one extreme stood such types as Ben Thompson and Phil Coe, a couple of frontier drifters who owned the Bull's Head Saloon at Abilene for a short time in 1871. If they made money it was primarily by trading on the fellow feeling of their Texan compatriots.[5] Other tavern keepers pursued profits in a more systematic manner, the really enterprising among them finally shifting to liquor wholesaling and other businesses. George M. Hoover, whose tent saloon was the first commercial structure at the site of Dodge City, embodied this kind of success. His product sold well there from the first, and soon he and his partner wholesaled the stuff to more remote points. When Texans replaced the buffalo hunters, Hoover's facility reportedly proved "a popular place with cattle men." Retaining his wholesale trade, he later gave up the retailing of liquor entirely and helped found the Bank of Dodge City, serving as its charter president. By 1885 George Hoover enjoyed a reputation as the second largest

[4] Wichita *Eagle*, Apr. 3, 1873; Dodge City *Times*, June 22, 1878, Aug. 3, 1882; Dodge City *Globe*, Sept. 2, 1879; Caldwell *Post*, June 3, 1880; Caldwell *Commercial*, Dec. 28, 1882; Caldwell *Journal*, Feb. 7, 1884.

[5] Stuart Henry: *Conquering Our Great American Plains* (New York, 1930), p. 267; W. M. Walton: *Life and Adventures of Ben Thompson, the Famous Texan* (Austin, 1884), pp. 103–08.

taxpayer in Ford County, just behind merchant Bob Wright.[6]

Professional gambling was quite closely associated with cattle town taverns throughout the period. Sometimes a saloon owner himself sponsored the gaming that occurred in his establishment, while at other such places itinerant professionals played independently. Card games —poker, monte, and faro predominating—appear to have been the most popular, with dice games such as chuck-a-luck and hazard running a close second. Keno, a game similar to bingo, was a special case in that ideally it demanded special accommodation so that large numbers might play.[7]

One suspects that individual gambling, at least, proved less lucrative than tradition would have it. For one thing, professional gamblers held high status among cattle town transients, probably tempting many with only marginal skill to adopt the sporting life as an occupation. Furthermore, the gambler's income remained especially subject to variations in the local economic picture. "Business," wrote an observer of the gamblers at Ellsworth in 1873, ". . . is rather slack with them just now, owing to the

[6] Gerald Gribble: "George M. Hoover, Dodge City Pioneer" (M.A. thesis, University of Wichita, 1940); Topeka *Commonwealth*, Apr. 17, 1873; Dodge City *Messenger*, Feb. 26, 1874; Dodge City *Times*, Dec. 22, 1877, June 22, 1882; Dodge City *Globe*, June 13, 1882; Dodge City *Cowboy*, Aug. 29, 1885. Hoover's Saloon Account Book (1883–85), now held by the Kansas State Historical Society, does not allow a calculation of profits, since the prices paid for liquor and related products sold by Hoover are not given. Nevertheless, these fragmentary data reveal that for the period April 1883 through March 1885 (when he discontinued this business), Hoover's raw income from liquor and saloon supplies totaled $65,341.12. His largest monthly sales occurred in October of each year—$6,228.67 in 1883 and $5,523.59 in 1884—which coincided with the periods of greatest cattle-shipping activity.

[7] Ellsworth *Reporter*, July 3, 1873; Topeka *Record*, Aug. 5, 1871; Wichita *Eagle*, June 24, 1875; Dodge City *Times*, Sept. 1, 1877, June 8, 1878.

scarcity of cash, but good times are anticipated as soon as the cattle sales commence." "Gambling was better last week than it has been in Dodge for many a day," announced an editor of that place in the slack autumn of 1877—a hopeful indication, he felt, that money was at last becoming more plentiful.[8]

Alongside the saloonmen and gamblers, prostitutes comprised a third profession offering diversion to transients. Late in 1867, Abilene's first cattle season, a few girls traveled up the line from points east; but in the following spring, recalled Joe McCoy's assistant, "they came in swarms, & as the weather was warm 4 or 5 girls could Huddle together in a tent very Comfortably." For the next two decades they remained a fixture of cattle town life.

Reports on the numbers of prostitutes must often be discounted. Even Abilene's worst enemy, the editor of a rival town during a county seat contest, charged the community of 1869 with harboring but three brothels and twenty-one whores. Caldwell's police court docket, which supposedly listed all resident prostitutes, displays the names of only twenty-five for the period April through August 1880. Then, too, the numbers fluctuated as the cattle season waxed and waned. Wichita apparently possessed three brothels and thirteen prostitutes in August 1872. At the height of livestock shipping the following month this figure rose to four establishments and fourteen girls. In November, with the cattlemen and cowboys rapidly deserting Wichita, only two brothels and six girls survived.[9]

[8] Dodge City *Globe*, June 3, 1879; Ellsworth *Reporter*, July 3, 1873; Dodge City *Times*, Oct. 16, 1877.

[9] C. F. Gross to J. B. Edwards, May 29, 1922, Mar. 31, 1925, Edwards Papers, KSHS; Detroit *Western News*, Feb. 11, 1870; Caldwell Police Court Docket, 1879–89 (microfilm copy, KSHS), I, *passim;* city marshal's reports, August–November 1872, in Wichita Miscellaneous Papers, 1871–81, microfilm copy, KSHS. (These figures did

The cattle town dance house, representing a kind of entertainment emporium, remains to be considered. The dance house primarily existed to provide female companionship. Here ladies of easy virtue might mix with their prospective clientele within a socially accredited, if not morally approved, format. "Men of every grade assemble at the local dance house," noted a Dodge City visitor. ". . . Even the Mayor of the city indulges in the giddy dance with the girls and with his cigar in one corner of his mouth and his hat tilted to one side, he makes a charming looking officer." A prominent Wichita dance hall, wrote a Topeka newspaperman,

> is patronized mainly by cattle herders, though all classes visit it; the respectable mostly from curiosity. . . . The Texan, with mammoth spurs on his boots . . . and a broad brimmed *sombrero* on his head, is seen dancing by the side of a well-dressed, gentlemanly appearing stranger from some eastern city; both having painted and jeweled courtezans for partners.[1]

The women glimpsed in such places might include those employed only to stimulate the purchase of liquor at the bar; others might be unmarried girls who worked locally as servants.[2] But a large percentage, if not most, were prostitutes, a portion of whom usually belonged to the establishment. Stripped of its glamor, the typical dance house, in the words of a Dodge resident,

---

not include the prostitutes of West Wichita, however.) A Dodge City editor in 1878 and another Dodgeite in 1879 estimated the number of local prostitutes at forty and forty-seven, respectively; in light of the documentary evidence for other cattle towns these figures appear highly exaggerated, and may have been intended as humorous. Dodge City *Times*, Aug. 17, 1878; Dodge City *Globe*, Sept. 2, 1879.

[1] Dodge City *Times*, Sept. 1, 1877; Topeka *Commonwealth*, Oct. 17, 1872.

[2] Kansas City *Times*, Sept. 10, 1883; Samuel J. Crumbine: *Frontier Doctor* (Philadelphia, 1948), p. 26; Eddie Foy and Alvin F. Harlow: *Clowning Through Life* (New York, 1928), p. 106. All these eyewitness references are to Dodge City.

was a long frame building, with a hall and bar in front and sleeping rooms in the rear. The hall was nightly used for dancing, and was frequented by prostitutes, who belonged to the house and for the benefit of it solicited the male visitors to dance. The rooms in the rear were occupied, both during the dancing hours and after, and both day and night by the women for the purpose of prostitution.[3]

Dance house proprietors usually earned a combined income from dancing fees (if these were in effect), bar sales, and prostitution. Since the average house apparently contained gambling tables, the owner also enjoyed a cut of the profits from this source.

Each of the major cattle towns contained such a facility at one time or another. Abilene evidently had no dance house until 1871—and it flourished only that single season—but Ellsworth, where local prostitution predated the cattle trade, harbored one at least as early as 1869. For a brief period two such establishments graced Wichita, one of them run by the colorful Joseph ("Rowdy Joe") Lowe and his wife Kate; the other was operated by Ed T. ("Red") Beard. Red's mistress, like both of the Lowes, was a recent graduate of Ellsworth high life. As at Ellsworth, a Dodge City dance house already existed when the cattle trade arrived, one such facility flourishing there just six months after the community's founding. For a brief time during the cattle trade era Dodge contained three dance halls, but the usual number was two —one of them staffed by white females and patronized by white males, the other staffed by Negro females and patronized by whites and Negroes alike. Caldwell received its one and only dance house in 1880, when, the railroad tracks having just entered town, a notorious Wichita couple, George and Margaret Woods, unloaded a two-story bagnio from a flatcar and saw to its reconstitution there. The following year the Woodses opened a second facility

[3] Dodge City *Globe*, Feb. 17, 1879.

at nearby Hunnewell in order to nip the transient trade effectively at either shipping center.[4] In more ways than one, such bold entrepreneurs of sin resembled those who tapped the cattle trade in less disreputable style.

[6]

THAT THE CATTLE TOWN ECONOMIC STRUCTURE included others than businessmen scarcely needs emphasis. The following table, employing data from the manuscript federal census converted so far as possible into occupational categories, shows the composition of the urban work forces of Abilene in 1870 and Dodge City in 1880, two fully operating cattle centers actually in the midst of shipping seasons.[5]

[4] Edwards: *Early Days in Abilene*, p. 8; Roenigk: *Pioneer History*, p. 38; Junction City *Union*, July 24, Aug. 27, 1869, Jan. 15, 1870; Manuscript Census, 1870: Kansas, Ellsworth Co., 1st section, pp. 8, 12; Wichita *Eagle*, July 26, 1872, Nov. 13, 27, 1873; Topeka *Commonwealth*, Feb. 11, 1873; Dodge City *Globe*, June 4, 1878; Dodge City *Times*, June 8, 22, Oct. 19, 1878; Dodge City *Cowboy*, Aug. 9, 23, Sept. 6, 1884; Caldwell *Post*, Apr. 8, 22, May 20, 1880; Caldwell *Commercial*, Aug. 25, 1881.

[5] U.S. Manuscript Census, 1870: Kansas, Dickinson Co., Grant Twp., pp. 1–6, 8–12, 17–22; ibid., 1880: Kansas (microfilm copy, KSHS), Ford Co., City of Dodge City. These are the two best censuses for our purposes; with the possible exception of that for Caldwell in 1880 the other cattle town federal censuses were taken where the cattle trade was not yet fully developed, and the pertinent Kansas censuses, on the other hand, were taken in the early spring and thus are of limited value in assessing the summer-oriented cattle town economic base. In the extraction of data I omitted all agricultural occupations, including those having to do with cattle. The occupational categories of Tables 1 and 2 were adapted from Bureau of the Census: *Classified Index of Occupations and Industries* (Washington, D.C., 1960), pp. xv–xx and *passim*. Changes consisted of combining "clerical and kindred workers" with "sales workers," and "private household workers" with "service workers," because of the great difficulty in differentiating such types of employment in the 1870 and 1880 censuses. As it is, much interpolation was required in separating, for instance, blacksmiths who were proprietors from blacksmiths who were employees. We cannot, unfortunately, compare this table with any

Although in size the urban work force at Dodge was nearly twice that of Abilene's ten years before, the percentage figures are at least roughly comparable and would seem to represent something approaching typicality. And it is clear that in neither case were the first two groups, composed mainly of business and professional men, col-

TABLE 1

THE CATTLE TOWN WORK FORCE

OCCUPATIONAL GROUPS	ABILENE, 1870		DODGE, 1880	
	No.	%	No.	%
Professional and technical workers	17	6.2	21	4.7
Proprietors, managers, and officials	54	19.9	60	13.6
Clerical and sales workers	18	6.6	41	9.3
Craftsmen and foremen	58	21.3	79	17.9
Operatives	10	3.7	42	9.5
Household and service workers	66	24.3	86	19.4
Laborers	49	18.0	113	25.6
TOTALS	272		442	

lectively dominant in number. But it is also clear that the rewards of labor congregated at the upper end of the scale. Table 2 is a breakdown by occupational group of those members of Abilene's urban work force who reported real estate and personal property valuations to the census-taker in 1870.[6]

"typical" nineteenth-century occupational profile; neither have the published occupational groupings of 1870 and 1880 been converted into the useful current categories nor have other local studies (to my knowledge) done so with raw census data.

[6] Of the censuses pertinent to the cattle towns, only the federal census of 1870 and the Kansas census of 1875 list property valuations; thus that for Abilene in 1870 provides the only useful cattle town

Thus in the Abilene of mid-1870 business and professional men comprised only 26 per cent of the work force but accounted for over 82 per cent and over 85 per cent respectively of the real and personal property valuations reported. These figures demonstrate a substantially un-

TABLE 2

DISTRIBUTION OF PROPERTY VALUATIONS

ABILENE, 1870				
OCCUPATIONAL GROUPS	Real Property $	%	Personal Property $	%
Professional and technical workers	11,625	7.6	4,825	5.1
Proprietors, managers, and officials	114,880	74.6	76,650	80.6
Clerical and sales workers	400	0.3	4,700	5.0
Craftsmen and foremen	15,755	10.2	2,365	2.5
Operatives	910	0.6	200	0.2
Household and service workers	3,400	2.2	4,525	4.7
Laborers	7,000	4.5	1,860	1.9
TOTALS	$153,970		$95,125	

equal distribution of income within the cattle town economic system.

It seems beyond all question, however, that entrepreneurial values predominated at the cattle towns. The only challenge of these values, as we shall see, came from

analysis. For the impracticability of attempting to employ tax records for analyses of economic worth see Merle Curti *et al.*: *The Making of an American Community: A Case Study of Democracy in a Frontier County* (Stanford, 1959), p. 456.

a moral reform impulse that was itself partly entrepreneurial in origin. In any event, the only rhetoric resembling a conflict of labor and capital that was to emerge in the cattle trading era came from farmers, but even here the theme was merely an incipient one.

Certainly the general cultural environment of nineteenth-century America militated against invidious class comparisons. But locally speaking, the existence of a relatively large craftsman-foreman group was probably important, consisting as it did of skilled employees who no doubt identified far more with the businessmen above them than with the unskilled workers on the lower end of the occupation ladder. And the cattle towns were also relatively free of large-scale employing units that might have induced the social and political coalescence of labor; the Wichita of 1875, reflecting the cattle town at its most urban stage, contained but four manufacturing concerns employing twenty-one workers among them.[7] Finally it can be assumed that except for Negroes, unskilled status was not a fixed affair by any means.[8] Some laborers (as well as other workers) were evidently farmers only temporarily employed in town. Many more came from the ranks of the young, unattached males who collectively loomed so large in the cattle town demographic profile. Nearly a quarter of the household and service workers at Dodge City in 1880, for example, were white

[7] Kansas Manuscript Census, 1875 (KSHS): Sedgwick Co., City of Wichita, schedule 3. The only discernible trade union activity came at the end of the cattle trading period when the Knights of Labor appeared among railroad employees at Caldwell late in 1885.

[8] Both narrative and statistical data agree in identifying Negroes as the one ethnic group systematically relegated, economically as well as socially, to the lowest stratum of cattle town society. At Abilene in 1870 and Dodge in 1880 a combined total of thirty-five nonwhites reported occupations to the census takers. Of these all but one, a Negro woman who operated a restaurant at Dodge, were either household and service workers or laborers. All of those reporting real or personal property valuations at Abilene in 1870 were Caucasians.

teen-agers. In such persons the expectations of upward mobility remained strong, denying any psychological income from a challenge of the economic order.

The cattle town, therefore, was at base truly an entrepreneurial organism. If its business and professional men maintained an overriding influence in cattle town affairs it was also true that they were the men who had the most to gain and—perhaps even more important—the most to lose.

III

The Adjustment to Violence

[1]

A S LEGEND AND LITERATURE have made all the world aware, the cattle town people confronted a peculiar social problem: personal violence. The traditional concept of the cattle trading center as an arena for almost unlimited homicide is not a twentieth-century product. Notoriety was a contemporary thing, born of the same vigorous sensationalism that underlies the present-day image.[1] Three of the five major cattle towns, in fact,

[1] The concept of huge cattle town homicide rates long ago passed unchallenged into serious scholarship. Ray Allen Billington, dean of frontier historians, writes of cattle town violence: "Mobs of mounted cowboys 'took over' by day, their six-shooters roaring while respectable citizens cowered behind locked doors. . . . Seldom did a group of drovers leave without contributing to the population of 'boot hill' . . . for barroom brawls, drunken duels, and chance shootings were so common that no one bothered to punish the murderers." To Vernon L. Parrington, such cattle town personalities as Wild Bill Hickok aptly symbolized Gilded Age extravagance: "All things were held cheap, and human life the cheapest of all." Although Lewis Atherton recently questioned the legendary propensities of western cattlemen and their employees to resort to gunplay, no authority has critically examined violence in the shipping centers where a large share of the cattle industry's homicides are presumed to have occurred. Harvey Wish even implies that the Hollywood conception of the "bold, wicked" cattle

suffered from violent reputations even before their careers as cattle trading centers.

Ellsworth, which did not receive large numbers of longhorns until 1871, earned an unenviable community image immediately after its founding in 1867. Filled with a heterogeneous collection of teamsters, railroad workers, army scouts, soldiers, and the usual disreputable hangers-on—itinerant liquor dealers, gamblers, prostitutes—it was the scene of at least eight homicides during its first year of existence, all delightedly recorded by newspaper editors in better regulated towns up the line.[2]

Dodge City experienced a similar early notoriety that it never outlived. Established four years before becoming an important reception point for Texas cattle, it entertained the same type of transients as had Ellsworth, plus a lethal increment of buffalo hunters. During its first year, 1872–73, news correspondents reported the violent deaths there of nine men, with another three as possibles. A quarter of a century later George M. Hoover, whose memory remained accurate about other matters, reported the true figure to have been fifteen. A year after its first settlement the commandant at nearby Fort Dodge finally had to intervene and rescue the town from a band of pseudo-vigilante terrorists.[3]

town—with its "feuding bad men," its "swift, straight-shooting" peace officers, and its "vigilante hanging[s]"—is an accurate portrayal. Billington: *Westward Expansion: A History of the American Frontier* (3rd edn.; New York, 1967), p. 678; Parrington: *Main Currents in American Thought* (New York, 1927–30), III, 15–16; Atherton: *The Cattle Kings* (Bloomington, Ind., 1961), pp. 35 ff.; Wish: *Society and Thought in Modern America* (2nd edn.; New York, 1962), pp. 73, 75.

[2] Junction City *Union*, July 13, Sept. 28, Oct. 5, 1867, Mar. 7, 1868; Leavenworth *Conservative*, Aug. 20, 27, 28, 1867; Topeka *Leader*, Apr. 16, 1868; A. T. Andreas: *History of the State of Kansas* (Chicago, 1883), p. 1277. Newspaper citations (as also in the following two footnotes) are the first and most complete reports of homicides. Duplicated, garbled, and fragmentary versions often appeared elsewhere.

[3] Topeka *Commonwealth*, Sept. 8, Dec. 7, 31, 1872, Jan. 23, Feb. 2,

Caldwell suffered much the same public relations fate. In the nine years between its founding in 1871 and its emergence as a cattle center in 1880, an assortment of vagrant whisky peddlers, livestock rustlers, and other frontier riffraff infested the tiny border community and its environs. Several murders and lynchings made its name a synonym for violence that, as in the cases of Ellsworth and Dodge, the passage of time never erased.[4]

Primary responsibility for these initial homicides must be laid to the lack of any systematic efforts to suppress violence in these as yet municipally unorganized communities. Although the subsequent arrival of the Texas cattle trade hardly promised an end to the kind of transients who caused trouble, a new factor altered the situation considerably. The community economic base increasingly featured a variety of more or less orthodox businessmen interested in maximizing profits in a rational manner. By and large the cattle town business firm represented a substantial investment over earlier enterprises both in stock and plant outlay, even the characteristic tent or shack saloon of earlier years giving way to a measure of bibulous elegance most attractive to drovers, buyers, and cowhands. Homicide, it seemed obvious enough, could easily lead to riot, and riot to property destruction —arson being particularly feared in those pre-brick days of almost prohibitive fire insurance rates.

In addition, as their profits mounted cattle town business

11, June 7, 1873; Abilene *Chronicle*, Feb. 20, 1873; Dodge City *Democrat*, June 19, 1903; Richard I. Dodge to Thomas A. Osborn, June 4, July 5, 1873, Governors' Correspondence (Cities and Towns), KSHS; Osborn to Dodge, June 4, 1873, ibid.; Robert M. Wright: *Dodge City: The Cowboy Capital* (Wichita, 1913), pp. 171–72.

[4] Topeka *Commonwealth*, Apr. 21, 1872; Wichita *Eagle*, Apr. 26, June 21, July 5, 1872; Wellington *Press*, June 25, July 30, Aug. 6, Sept. 3, Oct. 15, 1874; G. D. Freeman: *Midnight and Noonday, or the Incidental History of Southern Kansas* (Caldwell, 1892), *passim*.

and professional men increasingly invested surplus earnings in local opportunities, and such commitments caused an entrepreneur to identify the community's well-being with his own. Although the desire to suppress disorder could be, and was, rationalized in terms of making the town a good place to raise a family, townsfolk also feared that publicity about local violence inhibited the immigration of solid citizens, hard money, and permanent industry. "During the coming season," wrote a Wichita editor,

> Wichita desires law and order, with their consequent peace and security, and not bloodshed and a name that will cause a thrill of horror whenever mentioned and which will effectually deter the most desirable class of people from coming among us. Right speedily will the latter follow if the former are not maintained.

On the eve of his town's first cattle shipping season a Caldwell editor warned fellow citizens of the same danger. "We know," he reflected,

> that persons will frequent the city, at times, who, reckless in regard to law and order, having no interest in the good name and welfare of the place, acknowledge only their own inclinations and whims as their sole rule and guide for their conduct. Should this element . . . get the upper hand . . . then we may be certain that business men, men with capital and men having families, whom they love and respect, will steer clear of this place, and go to other localities, where law and order is the watchword of the day. Nothing would more surely kill the rapid growth, the substantial growth of our city.[5]

Essentially entrepreneurial motives, in short, provided a powerful impetus for the systematic suppression of violence.

[5] Wichita *Eagle*, June 7, 1872; Caldwell *Post*, Mar. 25, 1880.

[2]

LEGEND IMPLIES that the cattle town people found themselves almost at the mercy of armed visitors, but such was not really the case. Responsible vigilante action always remained a decisive deterrent to any attempted terrorism by transients. The Kansas code empowered mayors to call upon all male inhabitants between the ages of eighteen and fifty to aid in enforcing the law. Yet local authorities held this alternative in reserve as an extraordinary measure to be used only when regular law enforcement had broken down—as at Ellsworth in 1873, at Wichita the following year, and at Dodge City and Caldwell in 1881.[6] Whether justified by circumstances or not, collective citizen action invariably created ill feeling among the transients, most of whom, cowboys and drovers alike, were clannish Texans easily roused to a kind of ethnocentric defensiveness. The withdrawal of herds—and consumers —from an "unfriendly" shipping center always remained a possibility. The problem for the cattle town people was not to rid themselves of visitors prone to violence, but to suppress the violence while retaining the visitors.

The community problem was unique in this respect, but the initial steps toward order were strictly conventional. Although many routine advantages accrued to communities that incorporated themselves as municipalities under Kansas law, at the cattle towns the immediate impetus to legal organization was fear of transient vio-

[6] *Compiled Laws of Kansas*, 1879, p. 191. The Ellsworth affair will be treated later in detail. For the other incidents see Wichita *Eagle*, July 9, 16, 1874; O. H. Bentley (ed.): *History of Wichita and Sedgwick County* (Chicago, 1910), II, 464–66; Caldwell *Post*, Dec. 22, 1881; Caldwell *Commercial*, Jan. 26, 1882; Freeman: *Midnight and Noonday*, chaps. xli–ii; Dodge City *Globe*, Apr. 19, May 10, 1881; Dodge City *Times*, Apr. 21, June 9, 1881; Caldwell *Commercial*, Apr. 21, 1881.

lence. Except in the case of Abilene, actual or anticipated acquisition of the cattle trade coincided roughly with municipal incorporation. The earliest city council proceedings at each town dealt with statutory limitations on disorder and violence, and the hiring of police officers was always among the first municipal business transacted.

The Abilene business community suffered through its first full cattle shipping season, 1868, without an attempt at control. In the summer of 1869 it became apparent that neither county nor township law enforcement officials felt responsible for coping with the special problems of the settlement. "While we were in Abilene," recorded one cowboy visitor of that summer, "we found the town was full of all sorts of desperate characters, and I remember one day one of these bad men rode his horse into a saloon, pulled his gun on the bartenders, and all quit business. When he came out several others began to shoot up the town." It was probably after such an incident as this that forty-four business and professional men petitioned their probate judge to grant the town corporate status. The judge favored the request in early September. But, recalled Theodore C. Henry, the land agent chosen as provisional mayor, "the [cattle shipping] season was so nearly closed by that time that active government was not attemp[t]ed." On May 2, 1870, a few weeks before the arrival of the new season's first herds, the governing council reconvened, drafting ordinances treating misdemeanors associated with transient disorder and creating a police force to enforce them.[7]

[7] J. Marvin Hunter (ed.): *The Trail Drivers of Texas* (2nd edn.; Nashville, Tenn., 1925), p. 503; T. C. Henry: "Thomas James Smith, of Abilene," *Transactions of the Kansas State Historical Society*, IX (1905–06), 528; Abilene Council Record, 1870–76 (microfilm copy, KSHS), p. 29; Abilene *Chronicle*, May 12, 1870.

Ellsworth's municipal organization resulted directly from an act of violence during its first cattle season. Earlier the community made do with county and township officers, since the town was the only substantial population center in the county. Following a fatal saloon gunfight in 1868 the county commissioners ordered the sheriff to "receive such business as the Town authorities may transfer to him." With an "assurance of the cattle trade" that turned out to be premature, Ellsworthites launched a vigilante action early in 1869 against some disorderly elements; but, as an inauspicious harbinger of things to come, a stray Texas cowboy shot and killed a local law officer in an Ellsworth dance house later that summer. The year 1871 was the town's first major cattle season, and on June 18 one of its two township constables was shot and seriously wounded. Whether or not the offender was a cattle trade transient, as is likely, the encounter moved Ellsworth's businessmen to press for its organization as a city of the third class. The required plebiscite was accomplished so hastily as to be illegal, necessitating special approval by the state legislature that winter. The charter mayor, a realtor like Abilene's T. C. Henry, met with his council for the first time on July 27, 1871, their only act being to appoint a city marshal and a clerk. At their second meeting on August 4 they passed the necessary law enforcement ordinances.[8]

Wichita wisely organized in anticipation of cattle trade violence rather than waiting for it to occur. Some of its substantial residents had settled at the site as early as 1868 and had already gained two years' experience with

[8] Junction City *Union*, Mar. 7, 1868, May 15, Aug. 7, 1869; Ellsworth Co. Commissioners Journal, 1867–87 (transcript, KSHS), pp. 34, 121–22, 125, 129–30; Leavenworth *Times and Conservative*, Aug. 4, 1869; Topeka *Commonwealth*, Nov. 24, 1869; Salina *Journal*, Feb. 23, 1871; Ellsworth Council Record, 1871–80 (microfilm copy, KSHS), pp. 1, 5–6; Ellsworth Ordinances, 1871–80 (microfilm copy, KSHS), 1st Ser., nos. 1 ff.; *Laws of Kansas*, 1872, p. 33.

Texans passing by on the trail to Abilene. The town proprietors filed plats on March 25, 1870. Less than four
months later the residents incorporated their settlement,
with an attorney specializing in land claims as provisional
mayor. The first meeting of the council on July 22 dealt
with setting the limits of the town. Three days later it met
again and addressed the problem of transient disorder,
appointing a city marshal and passing the usual ordinances.[9]

Like early Ellsworth, Dodge City lay within an almost
vacant area. Its citizens accordingly dominated the
affairs of the county and sought, as at Ellsworth, the
cheap expedient of having county and township law enforcement authorities suppress community disorder. The
Kansas code forbade the sale of liquor in unorganized
regions. So anxious, therefore, were townsmen to organize
their county during the winter of 1872–73 that in sub-
mitting the required petition and census return to the
governor they represented transients as bona fide residents. The governor and legislature declared Ford
County duly organized, but the Santa Fe Railroad, fearing high local tax assessments on its property, took the
matter of the fraudulent census to court. While lawyers
argued the case through 1873, Dodge City residents went
ahead and organized a county government. Despite the
patent validity of the railroad's case, a sympathetic legislature specifically legalized the organization of Ford
County on March 7, 1874. Two days later the county
commissioners passed their first measure aimed at the
suppression of violence at the county seat with a resolution "that any person or persons found carrying concealed
weapons in the city of Dodge or violating the laws of the
State shall be dealt with according to law." In the fol-

[9] Wichita Council Record, 1870–81 (microfilm copy, KSHS), A,
25–26; Wichita *Vidette*, Aug. 13, 1870.

lowing year the town received a number of cattle herds for shipment. Expecting that a full complement of cattle trade transients would descend upon them the coming spring, townsmen obtained municipal organization as a third class city in the autumn of 1875. The newly elected mayor, a restaurant proprietor, assembled his councilmen on December 24 to pass the usual regulatory and enforcement ordinances.[1]

At Caldwell no sooner had bonds been voted for the acquisition of a railroad that would turn the community into a cattle shipping center than its local editor brought up the question of organization. "We think we have enough inhabitants to incorporate," he insisted, "and it would insure better protection to the citizens of the town than the present system. . . . Strangers generally give towns unincorporated a wide berth. People who have money to invest go where they are protected by law, and where good society and order reign." The business community responded promptly. It failed, in an attempt at expediency, to obtain immediate corporate status from the state legislature that spring, however, and routine action by the district court dragged on into the middle of summer. On July 22, 1879, the appropriate judge finally granted Caldwell its incorporation. Citizens thereupon elected a dry goods and grocery merchant as mayor, and he convened the city council for the first time in mid-August. The councilmen immediately provided for the

[1] *Kansas Statutes*, 1868, pp. 386–87; Thomas A. Osborn to Herman J. Fringer, Apr. 8, 1873, Governors' Letters (KSHS), II, 21; Richard I. Dodge to Osborn, July 5, 1873, Governors' Correspondence; Dodge City *Messenger*, Feb. 26, 1874; *Kansas Reports*, XII, 441–47; Ford Co. Commissioners Journal, 1873–85 (microfilm copy, KSHS), pp. 2, 4, 18, 25; Dodge City *Democrat*, June 19, 1903. The Dodge City council proceedings in their original form are no longer extant for the cattle trade period; after early 1877 they may be followed in the newspaper. For the original organization of the city council see Dodge City Ordinances, 1875–86 (microfilm copy, KSHS), pp. 1 ff.

suppression of violence and the establishment of a police force.[2]

STATUTES DESIGNED for the regulation of disorder in each of the Kansas cattle towns differed only in minor details from place to place and did not, of course, vary greatly from those of municipalities everywhere. State law already set penalties for many offenses, and municipal statutes routinely forbade vagrancy, disorderly conduct, intoxication, fighting, disturbing the peace, and resisting arrest. Discharging firearms within city limits was invariably proscribed, as was the carrying of dangerous weapons of any type, concealed or otherwise, by persons other than law enforcement officers. Local lawmakers also banned gambling, prostitution, and the frequenting of prostitutes. So much for statutory limits on disorder. Supplementary nuances, however, were sometimes unique, reflecting the heightened pertinence of these routine legal measures for the cattle town people.

The carrying of six-shooters by cattle trade transients proved of major concern. A long-standing state law prohibited any vagrant, intoxicated person, or former Confederate soldier from carrying "a pistol, bowie-knife, dirk or other deadly weapon" on pain of up to $100 fine and three months in jail. Cattle town authorities tended to ignore this severe injunction, preferring blanket ordinances against the carrying of arms by anyone and establishing a system for easy compliance. Wichita's evolving approach to the firearms problem provides an example. In 1871 the city marshal erected two signs warning against the carrying of firearms. In 1872 the toll-keepers at the privately operated Chisholm Trail bridge were sworn in as unpaid special policemen charged with exchanging metal tokens

[2] Caldwell *Post*, Jan. 2, 16, Feb. 20, Apr. 3, May 1, July 24, Aug. 21, 1879.

for weapons as riders entered town. This measure evidently proved unsuccessful, since in 1873 signboards ordered visitors to "LEAVE YOUR REVOLVERS AT POLICE HEADQUARTERS, AND GET A CHECK."[3]

State law already forbade both prostitution and gambling if the latter involved special tables and devices[4]— two kinds of professional amusement that, however socially obnoxious, cattle town businessmen considered absolutely indispensable to their hold on the Texas cattle trade. City fathers pragmatically softened the harsh punishments specified for those who would follow these illegal callings, their aim being local regulation rather than prohibition.

Of course these municipal statutes also ensured that all monetary penalties extracted from minor transgressors would accrue to the city's treasury rather than to that of the state. As misdemeanors, most routine misbehavior was handled in cattle town police courts. At Wichita in the twelve months following March 1, 1874, for instance, magistrates handed down a total of 439 convictions, all but 8 of them for misdemeanors. Only 12 of these cases were heard in district court, 53 by justices of the peace, and 374—or 85 per cent—in the Wichita police court.[5] Police court fines thus constituted no small portion of the cattle town municipal income.

Of most importance was the establishment of the ac-

[3] *Kansas Statutes*, 1868, p. 378; Wichita Council Record, A, 90, 186–87; Andreas: *History of Kansas*, p. 1390. Not that these measures were universally effective. Newspaper editors often complained of laxity in enforcement of firearms statutes.

[4] *Kansas Statutes*, 1868, pp. 370–72, 377–78. These provisions remained in effect throughout the cattle trade period, as did that covering dangerous weapons.

[5] Kansas Manuscript Census, 1875 (KSHS): Sedgwick Co., City of Wichita, schedule 4. These are only true court cases, not including regular assessments on illegal enterprises (discussed below); with these added, the number of police court "convictions" for May–November 1874 totaled 590. Wichita *Beacon*, Dec. 9, 1874.

tual police machinery. Tradition relegates cattle town law enforcement to fast-drawing city marshals, each of whom operated virtually single-handedly in a sort of free-agent status, mainly motivated and guided by a personal commitment against lawlessness, divorced from prosaic police duties and the discipline or direction of a municipal employer. The image violates reality. In no case did any cattle town depend upon a lone marshal for its law enforcement. Police bodies of up to five men—carefully ranked as marshal, assistant marshal, and policemen—customarily supervised cattle trading seasons. Mayors appointed candidates to police posts at least annually, the chosen officers then being subjected to the often rigorous supervision of city councilmen who ratified appointments, determined pay and allowances, and removed officers at their discretion.

Local ordinances laid out the specific duties of the city marshal and his staff. The code drafted at Abilene in 1870 for the first cattle town police force remained fairly typical. The marshal, as "captain of police," was to supervise the city jail, maintain a "police record" of all persons arrested and confined, together with their offenses and ultimate dispositions, and "have charge of and control the entire police force of the town." The "several members of the town police" were to keep the peace, being specifically authorized to "enter any saloon, billiard hall or other place of public resort or amusement, and to arrest and confine in the jail of the town any person guilty of disorderly conduct or drunken[n]ess, who may refuse to be restored to order and quiet." An arresting officer was to report his action to some magistrate having jurisdiction within twenty-four hours of any arrest.[6]

⁶ *Compiled Laws of Kansas*, 1879, pp. 166, 169, 180–81, 190–91, 200–01; Abilene *Chronicle*, May 12, 1870. Succeeding years of cattle town experience with law enforcement personnel led to more detailed supervisory regulations—especially in light of officers' continuing pro-

A few months after passage of this measure Abilene councilmen also invested their city marshal, Thomas J. Smith, with the duties of street commissioner at no increase in pay, a post bestowed on Marshal James B. ("Wild Bill") Hickok the following season. This less than glamorous office became a customary additional responsibility for cattle town lawmen. The job entailed investigating complaints about street obstructions, defects, and nuisances, both animate and inanimate, and seeing to their removal. Sometimes the police themselves hired others to perform this part of their task, such as the young Negro deputy employed by the Ellsworth force in 1873 "to arrest swine found at large," in the words of a waggish newspaperman. During winter months—periods of little law enforcement business—policemen might be made to earn their wages by direct attention to the streets. Thus at Wichita in early 1875 councilmen abolished the formal position of street commissioner and set the town's lawmen, including one Wyatt Earp, to repairing thoroughfares and sidewalks pending the advent of a new cattle season.[7] Cattle town officers also acted as municipal sanitary inspectors each spring, and often made winter surveys of chimneys and flues. A man was sometimes added to the force specifically as a night watchman with the primary duty of keeping an eye out for fires. City fathers also occasionally employed "special" policemen to supervise particular trouble spots such as a theater or dance house, or allowed owners to do so.

Municipal contributions to support police officers

pensities to give their own interpretations of the law, to engage in supplementary wage-earning, to gamble (although state law forbade them to do so), and to drink excessively while on duty. The code imposed on the uniformed Dodge City force in 1882 represents an epitome of the effort to regularize both procedures and discipline. See Dodge City *Times*, June 22, 1882.

[7] Abilene Council Record, p. 38; Abilene *Chronicle*, June 29, 1871; Ellsworth *Reporter*, July 3, 17, 1873; Wichita *Eagle*, Jan. 28, 1875.

constituted by far the largest cattle town expenditure for salaries. In the last three quarters of 1871, for example, the salaries of Abilene's police force amounted to 48 per cent of the town's total expenditure. For the same period at Caldwell in 1880 the proportion was 33 per cent. At Dodge City for the twelve months after April 9, 1884, police remuneration totaled 42 per cent of all expenditure.

In terms of specific salaries, Ellsworth's experience was probably typical. Through her first two years as a cattle center the scheduled allowances for her mayor, councilmen, treasurer, clerk, and city attorney, not counting special fees, totaled $1,410. During the same period police salaries were paid on a monthly basis, continually being adjusted to accord with the amount of police business. Except for one lapse from the pattern, the city marshal earned $150 per month during the cattle trading season (roughly June to November), and half that sum during the winter and spring—theoretically, therefore, $1,275 per year. In mid-1874, when other municipal salaries were drastically cut back to $725, the marshal's summer pay dropped to $100 per month. The salaries of his staff during the cattle trading years came to be fixed at $75 each per month. The city fathers manipulated this expense by simply adding policemen in the summer and removing them each autumn. Every member of the force in addition to his salary was normally allowed $2.50 for each arrest he made, a fee paid by the convicted lawbreaker as a part of court costs.[8]

Experience soon indicated that whoring, gambling, and overindulgence in liquor were the three main causes of cattle town violence, and it seemed only fair that those enterprises that most stimulated this lethal circumstance should heavily subsidize its suppression. Saloon

[8] Abilene *Chronicle*, Jan. 11, 1872; Caldwell *Commercial*, Jan. 20, 1881; Dodge City *Globe*, Apr. 14, 1885; Ellsworth Ordinances, *passim*.

keepers already paid relatively high annual license fees into municipal coffers in accordance with state law.⁹ But prostitution and professional gambling, legally nonexistent, contributed nothing at all. It was soon decided that they too should join in supporting local police machinery, and consequently a system for covert regular assessment was devised.

The taxation of such underworld businesses clearly bears the stamp of the large urban center, from which it probably migrated to the western frontier. A New Englander who later sat on the United States Supreme Court, for example, introduced such taxation into a California mining camp in 1850. Although not publicized, the system was not unknown to Kansas. The law of 1871 establishing provisions for third-class cities, under which all the cattle towns functioned for periods, expressly forbade the practice.¹

Joseph G. McCoy, innovative father of the cattle trade at Abilene, deserves credit for instituting the system there after his election as mayor in 1871. Apparently acting on behalf of the saloon owners among his supporters, he forestalled an attempt to increase the liquor license fee and instead persuaded his councilmen to make up the difference by a covert assessment of gamblers and prostitutes. These fines remained in force throughout Abilene's last summer as a major cattle town. Always forward-look-

⁹ Besides meeting other requirements, Kansas saloon keepers had to purchase annual licenses, costing anywhere from $100 to $500, from their boards of county commissioners or, if operating within corporate towns, their city councils. (*Kansas Statutes*, 1868, pp. 399–400.) Few cattle town administrations ever required the legal maximum. Other businessmen normally had to buy annual municipal licenses, but these usually amounted to from $5 to $20 for most occupations. Even if assessed at the minimum $100 figure, therefore, tavern owners paid relatively high annual fees.

¹ Carl Brent Swisher: *Stephen J. Field: Craftsman of the Law* (Washington, D.C., 1930), p. 33; *Compiled Laws of Kansas*, 1879, pp. 194–95.

ing, Wichita's authorities evidently introduced the system there in August of the town's first shipping season, 1872. The taxing of prostitutes commenced at Ellsworth in the autumn of the same year, the community's first important cattle season, with gamblers' fines added to regular civic revenues in the spring of 1873. Despite ample precedent from the older cattle centers, Dodge City—with its mayor probably on better personal terms than elsewhere with the disreputable elements—imposed illegal assessments only in 1878, when, in the midst of a desultory third cattle season and with the city deeply in debt, angry taxpayers convened and insisted on it. Caldwell's administrators, who invariably took their cue from Wichita, responded rapidly to precedent. In early 1880, six months after formally organizing itself and before the start of its first shipping season, the municipality began taxing gamblers regularly and in April extended the system to prostitutes.[2]

The technical machinery involved did not vary substantially from place to place. If those on the books did not already provide them, new city ordinances introduced low minimum fines for prostitution and gambling convictions. These minimums then served as fees to be collected monthly. They usually amounted to from $5 to $10 for whores, the same for professional gamblers, and double these amounts or sometimes even higher for owners of brothels or places where professional gaming was sponsored. The proceeds of these fines, together with

[2] Abilene Council Record, pp. 69, 71, 94; Abilene *Chronicle*, May 12, 18, June 1, 22, July 20, 27, 1871; Wichita Council Record, A, 247; city marshal's reports of fines collected, 1872, in Wichita Miscellaneous Papers, 1871–81, microfilm copy, KSHS; Ellsworth Police Court Docket, 1872–84 (microfilm copy, KSHS), pp. 83–94, 96; Ellsworth *Reporter*, June 12, 26, 1873; Topeka *Commonwealth*, July 1, 1873; Dodge City *Globe*, May 21, July 9, 1878; Dodge City *Times*, Aug. 3, 10, 17, Sept. 7, 1878; Caldwell Police Court Docket, 1879–89 (microfilm copy, KSHS), I, *passim*.

tavern license fees and the income from routine misdemeanor convictions, evidently more than carried the weight of multiple peace officers. Wichita, in fact, by setting its illegal assessments rather higher than the norm and also altering its saloon license fees to monthly payments for easier collection, made the most of the system. Its spokesman boasted openly that the city thereby required no general business taxes such as were common elsewhere, a fact thought highly encouraging to prospective immigrants.[3]

As elsewhere on the nineteenth-century frontier, the cattle town people, when it came to the matter of actual court action, tended to be lenient toward perpetrators of violence. This made penalties essentially discretionary and heightened the importance of selecting good law officers. Police judges customarily prosecuted participants in nonfatal encounters only for carrying weapons, being drunk and disorderly, or some other such light misdemeanor, although sending these cases to district court for comparatively severe assault and battery convictions always remained an alternative.[4]

Generally speaking, the same leniency was granted to

[3] Wichita *Eagle*, Dec. 26, 1872, Sept. 28, 1873, Oct. 8, 1874; Bentley: *History of Wichita*, I, 238. The specific fees levied on the illegal elements at three of the cattle towns are on record. Those for Ellsworth prostitutes can be seen in its police court docket; for Wichita's gamblers and prostitutes in the city marshal's reports (through April 1873) and thereafter in the police judge's reports, Wichita Miscellaneous Papers; and for Caldwell's gamblers and prostitutes in its police court docket. In most cases they must be extracted from the midst of routine police court fines, but can be identified by the regularity with which the same names appear in the record together with the unvarying amounts levied.

[4] For examples of lenient treatment in such cases see Abilene *Chronicle*, June 22, 1871; Wichita *Eagle*, May 29, 1873; Caldwell *Post*, June 10, 1880. For a complete analysis of district court cases at Wichita during the cattle trading years see James W. Spradling: "The Problem of Law and Order in Wichita and Sedgwick County, 1870–1875" (M.A. thesis, University of Wichita, 1952), chap. v and appendix.

homicides. Only three persons ever earned the death sentence for cattle town killings, and none of these was ultimately executed by the state.[5] Besides these three convictions, certain citizens of Abilene lynched one person as a penalty for murder.[6] None of the three crimes for which these four men were punished was a gunfight or even a shooting homicide. In such cases townsfolk invariably were inclined to be forgiving, especially if the perpetrator could cite youth, intoxication, or some other extenuating circumstance. Of particular appeal was word that a youthful killer came from a good family, so that, with typical Victorian sentimentalism, it could be said of him that he fell temporarily upon evil ways. "We have no personal ill-will against the accused," mused Abilene's

[5] The two murders for which the three were convicted consisted of the killing of an itinerant painter by two men in Wichita in an attempt to defraud an insurance company, and the killing of a Dodge City tailor by an apparently unbalanced young white man who violated general social norms by having a Negro common-law wife. Wichita *Eagle*, Jan. 1, Feb. 19, May 21 ff., 1874; Dodge City *Globe*, Sept. 9, 1879, Jan. 13, 27, 1880; Dodge City *Times*, Sept. 13, 1879, Jan. 17, Feb. 28, 1880; Caldwell *Post*, Mar. 1, 1883; Topeka *Commonwealth*, May 23, 1885.

Not only did the Kansas governor remit the supreme penalty in these three cases, but there were no legal hangings whatever in Kansas between 1870 and 1887—or practically the entire cattle trade era. Louise Barry: "Legal Hangings in Kansas," *Kansas Historical Quarterly*, XVIII (1950), 279–301.

[6] The murder victim was yet another tailor, killed for his savings. (Abilene *Chronicle*, Feb. 15, 29, 1872; J. B. Edwards: *Early Days in Abilene* [Abilene, 1940], p. 11.) An angry editor emphasized the irony of the Abilene lynching: "Some who were loudly in favor of hanging Elsizer [the late suspect] are among the very men who have hitherto associated with gamblers and known murderers . . . but not a word were they ever heard to utter in favor of hanging such scoundrels with the blood of many victims dripping from their guilty hands." (Abilene *Chronicle*, Feb. 29, 1872.) A participant in the lynching, apparently reflecting a certain segment of cattle town opinion, years later conceded that gunshot homicides resulting from quarrels were somehow considered legitimate. "But," he added, "to kill for money—it was too much." C. F. Gross to J. B. Edwards, Apr. 13, 1922, Edwards Papers, KSHS.

editor of a young Texan just acquitted of murder. "If he now reforms his life it will give us pleasure to note the fact, as it will certainly rejoice the hearts of his father and good mother, who are said to be highly respectable people." Another cowboy, a Georgian named Bob Shaw, wounded while trying to kill Dodge City's marshal, was exonerated by citizens as well as the authorities. "Shaw is not a desperado as would seem from this case," the local editor hastened to make clear. "Parties who have known him say he never was known to make a six-shooter play before this. . . . Shaw's family are highly respectable people, and he has concluded to quit the far west and go back to live under the parental roof."[7]

A need to retain the good will—and the trade—of cattle town transients provided a more important motive for leniency. None of the four killers severely dealt with by cattle town justice was a cattleman or cowboy, and several specific incidents highlighted the fact that in the minds of a vocal citizen minority, at least, the law ought to rest lightly on Texans. At Wichita in 1874, for example, a group of cowboys calculatingly murdered a Negro laborer. When neither city nor county authorities moved to apprehend the killers, a local editor fumed. "If the law and its officers are powerless," he warned, "the sooner we know it the better. . . . A thousand men can be raised in Wichita and in this county, in three hours' notice, who will stand by their vindications." This stricture immediately provoked the wrath of many businessmen, who pounced on the surprised journalist for irresponsibly inflaming the public mind against those from whom they feared a retaliatory boycott.

Again, at Caldwell in 1882 two taut young fugitives from Texas justice who had come up the trail as cowboys gunned down the city marshal and fled into Indian Ter-

[7] Abilene *Chronicle*, June 8, 1871; Dodge City *Times*, Nov. 17, 1877.

ritory. The mayor hastily formed an impromptu posse, urging his volunteers to secure such horses as they needed from those hitched along the sidewalk. The Texans to whom the mounts belonged, however, refused to let them be requisitioned—and were supported by several businessmen. Nor could the intended pursuers learn the two killers' names or to which cattle outfit they belonged although, as an angry editor reported, "one or more persons knew all about them, but refused to give any information, fearing, perhaps, they might lose six bits of trade if they 'gave away' a cowboy, no matter what crime he might commit." During the following year at Dodge City, to cite a third instance, only the outspoken intervention of the influential Robert M. Wright kept boycott-obsessed businessmen from having the city marshal indicted for killing a cowboy who had been firing his pistol promiscuously.[8]

[4]

THE EXTENT to which the choice of law enforcement personnel proved crucial in the cattle town adjustment to violence is evident in several unfortunate cases. Many different types of men served as cattle town law officers, from respected local citizens to virtually unknown transients.[9] It is not true that lawmen all displayed a marked proficiency in that brand of personal combat known as gunfighting, but a military background or some other demonstration of familiarity with firearms, plus "nerve" and "pluck," were obvious requisites. Sometimes the desire for competency caused city fathers to hire men from

[8] Wichita *Eagle*, May 28, June 4, 1874; Caldwell *Commercial*, June 29, 1882; Dodge City *Globe*, July 10, 17, 1883; Dodge City *Times*, July 12, 1883; Wright: *Dodge City*, pp. 173–74.

[9] For an encyclopedic catalogue of documents pertaining to many cattle town peace officers see Nyle H. Miller and Joseph W. Snell (eds.): *Why the West Was Wild* (Topeka, 1963).

those same disreputable elements they were supposed to govern. Lapsing into drunk and disorderly conduct became a routine occupational hazard with many such lawmen. Local authorities also risked the chance that such an individual would prove overly prone to the employment of violence as a deterrent, or that for the sort of discretionary firmness called for he might substitute mere bullying. This kind of "zealousness" often precipitated, rather than dispelled, trouble. At his worst, such an officer might display actual criminal propensities.

Caldwell's experience with city marshals proved especially distressing. By 1882 community opinion had split over whether a demonstrated gunfighter or a good local citizen would make the better law officer for the town. After various unsatisfactory experiments with both types, the advocates of the former triumphed. The city administration hired three polished gunfighters just up from Texas to administer justice. One of these, unknown to the community, was a graduate of the notorious Billy the Kid gang in New Mexico. Soon winning promotion to marshal, this young man, Henry N. Brown, though considered a bit quick on the trigger, gave Caldwell nearly two years of satisfactory service—until he was captured with his assistant marshal and two other comrades after trying to rob the bank at nearby Medicine Lodge and killing its president and cashier. All were killed in turn by angry citizens of that place. The damning notoriety brought upon Caldwell by the gunmen in whom it had placed its trust more than offset any previous benefits from Marshal Brown's efforts to contain violence.[1]

Avoiding untrustworthy candidates was only one problem in officer procurement. Since the rationale behind cattle town law enforcement was the prevention of acts of violence rather than repression of those who

[1] Freeman: *Midnight and Noonday*, chaps. xxxiv–vi; Miller and Snell: *Why the West Was Wild*, pp. 67–84, 91–97.

were potential transgressors, both intelligence and a proper temperament were required. Treading the narrow margin between prevention and suppression, the ideal lawman promised no leniency for major infractions but at the same time avoided a hostile attitude that might simply provoke antagonism among those governed and serve as a standing challenge to physical encounter. Few officers existed with the natural qualifications of Abilene's popular Tom Smith, who kept his pistol concealed and often triumphed over violators of the peace merely with his fists.[2]

In a variety of ways, therefore, economic, social, and psychological themes complicated the cattle town law enforcement problem. Ellsworth's experience in the 1873 cattle season tragically illustrated nearly all the complexities.

"The great droves cover the hills and knolls," an Ellsworth correspondent wrote to a Topeka paper on June 2, 1873, "and the valleys are dark with them for miles around." Thousands of cattle but few buyers—that was the situation as an absolutely flat market congested the outlying range and inundated Ellsworth itself with drovers and cowboys who, lacking prompt cattle sales, found their visits necessarily prolonged.

An early onslaught of ninety-degree temperatures contributed a special misery. Day after day the sun blazed down from cloudless skies on a town still largely clustered about its central business district, two uneven rows of low buildings that faced one another across a treeless, weedy plaza and the railroad tracks. Would it never rain? In sweltering offices and shops collarless, shirt-sleeved businessmen grimly totted up credit sales to drovers. Their enervated wives, most of them still in homes that were merely narrow apartments above the stores,

[2] Henry: "Thomas James Smith," *passim;* Miller and Snell: *Why the West Was Wild,* pp. 576–80.

closed windows and curtains to the midday heat and dust that rose from the street, coping with fretful babies, absently permitting older children to escape to the depleted waters of the Smoky Hill. On benches in front of the town's four hotels, cattlemen glumly considered pulling out for Wichita where, word had it, the ranges were far less dry though cattle prices just as low. Their off-duty cowhands wandered or lounged along South Main Street's board sidewalk, tending to congregate beneath the wooden awning of Jerome Beebe's mercantile house, where they idly contemplated the grubby railroad depot across the way or, if they had the money, occasionally turned aside into one of the adjacent saloons.

Local night life, given the lack of cash in circulation, was not what it might have been. Professional gamblers, for example, suffered badly from the slump. Yet, with evening, high-heeled boots drummed the sidewalk more resolutely and voices floated raucously on the still air. Toward nine o'clock the noise subsided somewhat as many quit the saloons for the Ellsworth Theatre to slouch on bare plank seats amid clouds of cigar smoke and applaud vaudeville troupes imported from St. Joseph, Kansas City, or St. Louis. Later still, while citizens sought relief in fitful sleep, transients adjourned to the dance house on the riverbank east of town where they drank, waltzed, and bedded the girls until finally drifting back to hotels or cow camps in the pink dawn that heralded yet another insufferable day.

The heat, the general economic anxiety, the transients' aimlessness, all added up to trouble. The desperate cattle price situation culminated everywhere in the Panic of 1873. In Ellsworth it also turned out to be one of the two most fatal cattle town seasons on record.[3]

[3] Topeka *Commonwealth*, June 4, July 1, 1873; Ellsworth *Reporter*, July 3, 1873, Jan. 8, 1880. Floyd Benjamin Streeter, the first scholar to be interested in the cattle towns as such, four times published his ac-

In the early daylight hours of June 11 startled residents awoke to the sound of gunfire as drunken Texans indulged in some playful shooting at signboards. Later that morning Ellsworth's city fathers convened in special session, irritably vowing to suppress such goings-on at the outset, before someone got hurt. They beefed up the police force to five men, all reputedly experienced gunfighters. To meet the costs of this enlarged force they passed an ordinance that in effect extended to gamblers the regular fines imposed on prostitutes the previous autumn. The reinforced police then sallied forth. They arrested several Texans, including two prominent gunmen, Ben Thompson and his younger brother Billy, on various charges— carrying deadly weapons, being drunk, conducting themselves in a disorderly manner, disturbing the peace—and roughly escorted them across the plaza to the police court to suffer fines ranging from $15 to $35. Having successfully tested their mettle, the police a week later again displayed a new aggressiveness by putting a bullet through the thigh of a visitor unwise enough to argue with them.

Resentment flared dangerously among the transients, especially within the gambling fraternity. Ellsworth's newspaper editor ventured a cautious warning. If the gamblers, he wrote, "desire to continue their business in this city, they should use their influence to preserve good order." They were, in fact, doing just the opposite. Apparently the new municipal tax weighed heavily on them in that slack season, and the attitude of the police, whom

count of the 1873 violence at Ellsworth. Unfortunately, it lends little in the way of perceptive insight into the social context of the law enforcement problem. See his "Tragedies of a Cow Town," *The Aerend: A Kansas Quarterly*, V (1934), 81–96, 145–62; *Prairie Trails and Cow Towns* (Boston, 1936), pp. 115–42; *The Kaw: The Heart of a Nation* (New York, 1941), pp. 138–48; *Ben Thompson: Man with a Gun* (New York, 1957), pp. 92–115.

their contributions were helping maintain, added insult to injury.

Especially exasperating was one John ("Happy Jack") Morco. A less appropriate policeman is hard to imagine. Morco arrived in town that spring from the West Coast, where for several years he had drifted about evading apprehension on a murder charge. On June 9 he was tried in Ellsworth's police court for vagrancy. His appointment as an officer can only be ascribed to an overly hasty response to the June 11 emergency. A sour, childishly volatile subliterate (he could not write his own name), Morco had a crude mouth and a challenging demeanor—in short, a positive talent for provoking the Texans, drovers and gamblers alike, to frustrated rage. On June 30 he mixed briefly with Billy Thompson, who received his second court conviction of the season. From about this date on there ensued, in the recollection of an Ellsworth attorney, "a state of war between the police and the Texans," a group that included "some of the more wealthy cattlemen."[4]

The citizens of Ellsworth nevertheless seemed solidly behind the police, interpreting Texan discontent as sheer orneriness and applauding what they considered a commendable zeal on the part of Morco and his colleagues. In an election held June 21 to replace a prematurely retiring mayor, a realtor named James Miller won office on a promise to continue tough law enforcement. He defeated James W. Gore, proprietor of the Drovers Cottage, who, as a man economically dependent on the transients in a direct way, evidently urged an official policy of tact and

[4] Ellsworth Council Record, p. 87; Ellsworth Police Docket, pp. 112, 115–21, 142; Topeka *Commonwealth*, July 1, 1873; Ellsworth *Reporter*, June 12, 26, July 3, 1873; reminiscences of Ira E. Lloyd in ibid., Aug. 8, 15, 1957. Lloyd, who had arrived in Ellsworth late that June, is not always accurate in details, but provides many good insights into the law enforcement troubles of midsummer 1873, being a harsh critic of the police.

moderation.[5] Gore was already a city council member, the others being another hotelman, a bootmaker, a druggist, and a building contractor. All apparently harbored doubts about the entrepreneurial wisdom of police zealousness.

On the evening of July 1 the council met with Miller for the first time, hearing a short address by him on "the necessity of preserving good order," as the newspaper paraphrased his remarks. The councilmen reviewed the recent endeavors of the police, but evidently at Miller's urging sustained them by taking no action except to fix policemen's salaries. Many businessmen, especially the saloon owners, continued to be upset by police enthusiasm. In mid-July, responding to continued complaints, the councilmen moved to re-establish good community relations with the Texans by cutting the size of the force, aiming particularly at the removal of the obnoxious Jack Morco. On Jim Gore's motion they dismissed Morco and another policeman—only to be presented ten days later with a citizens' petition demanding Happy Jack's reinstatement. Momentarily chastened, the councilmen obliged. In the next few weeks they watched uneasily as police zeal escalated in the wake of this expression of public confidence. The number of arrests, invariably for drunk and disorderly conduct or for carrying deadly weapons, mounted steadily, with Morco being especially active. Between July 24 and the middle of August arrests totaled twenty-seven, or nearly three times the number for the same period of the previous year. The grand total for 1873 approached one hundred.[6]

On August 12 the council once again cut the police force by a man, although this time deferring carefully to

[5] Ellsworth *Reporter*, June 12, 26, July 3, 1873. For a uniquely forthright identification of the summer's opinion split on the law enforcement question see the Salina *Journal*, Sept. 4, 1873.

[6] Ellsworth *Reporter*, July 3, 1873; Ellsworth Council Record, pp. 90–91, 94, 96–97; Ellsworth Police Docket, *passim*.

the city marshal's recommendation. The marshal proved willing to dispense with John DeLong, the one member of the force known to enjoy any rapport with the Texans. Just two days later, with the feeling between police and transients running ever higher, Ellsworth's editor cautioned against an overly provocative display of six-shooters by the officers, but without apparent effect.[7] The following afternoon, August 15, Jack Morco intervened with relish in a quarrel between Ben Thompson and a gambler who owed Thompson money. Morco took the gambler's side, drawing his pistol on Thompson, who was at that moment unarmed. A few minutes later Ben and Billy Thompson appeared on the plaza ready to do battle. Sheriff Chauncey B. Whitney, an Ellsworth businessman, arrived on the scene as mediator. Whitney had succeeded in diverting the Thompsons toward a bar for a friendly drink when shooting suddenly broke out and he fell mortally wounded by a shotgun held in the unsteady hands of the inebriated Billy Thompson. As the sheriff lay bleeding on the sidewalk in front of Beebe's store, a number of Texans armed themselves to defend the Thompson brothers in an expected showdown with the police. But the officers demurred, much to Mayor Miller's disgust. He summarily discharged the three-man force and called his councilmen into session to appoint a new one.[8]

All summer long, under Jim Gore's leadership, the council had done what it could to mitigate police indiscretion. Now, with the public mood at a white heat, all but the bootmaker deserted Gore. The new majority demanded that the old police be rehired, excepting only the marshal (who had just that day been convicted on a

[7] Ellsworth Council Record, 97–98; Ellsworth *Reporter*, Aug. 14, 1873. In his reminiscences Ira Lloyd termed DeLong "a gambler and former policeman, who favored the Texans." Ibid., Aug. 8, 1957.

[8] Floyd Streeter's research was devoted in large measure to the details of this August 15 sequence of events. See *Prairie Trails and Cow Towns*, pp. 115–23.

drunk and disorderly charge). The majority also insisted that the force be beefed up again to four men. In this new situation Mayor Miller found himself allied with the two moderates. Possibly at Gore's suggestion, he nominated for marshal the recently discharged DeLong; the tough-liners disapproved, being willing to rehire DeLong as an underling but not as the officer in charge. Miller and the moderate minority wearily gave in. One of the other old policemen was named city marshal, Morco and DeLong rehired, and a new man, Ed Crawford, added.

A posse took the field, but Billy Thompson had flown, not to return until four years later, when he earned an acquittal. The reconstituted police force now mounted a campaign to rid the town of all undesirables, serving various gamblers and their friends with "white affidavits," as they were called, that in a few terse words ordered a recipient to leave town by the first train or suffer unpleas-ant consequences. Ben Thompson left; others refused to go but were not immediately molested. However much Miller and the council moderates deplored this show of inhospitality they were powerless to put a stop to it. In the midst of the turmoil Happy Jack Morco again laid the groundwork for violence by asserting that a white affi-davit had been issued for an especially popular Texan, Cad Pierce. On the afternoon of August 20 the angered Pierce accosted two other police officers in front of Beebe's store, demanding to know if Morco were correct. The answer was no, but during the verbal exchange Police-man Crawford lost his temper and killed Pierce, shooting him twice and then beating him over the head as he expired.

Once more the transients prepared for a showdown, voicing threats to burn Ellsworth to the ground. Ells-worthites hastily convened, resolved to rid the town once and for all of Texas gamblers, and organized themselves as vigilantes. Armed citizens patrolled the streets while others ransacked transients' hotel rooms in a search for an alleged cache of weapons. For the Texans this proved the final indignity. The next day, despite an editorial plea that bona fide cattlemen stay, a general exodus of transients began. A number of drovers evacuated their herds to Great Bend for shipment on the Santa Fe line. The rest agreed to remain at Ellsworth only if Morco and the other objectionables were removed as police officers.[9]

In the face of this profound economic threat sanity returned to Ellsworth. The message got through at last: the police force had caused more trouble than it had prevented. On August 22 a chagrined Ellsworthite tried to repair his town's severely damaged image by explaining the situation to readers of the Topeka *Commonwealth.* He was a tough-line advocate who blamed gambling and city council permissiveness for most of the trouble. But even he was now willing to admit that the police—especially Jack Morco—had also contributed importantly to the summer's violence. "Whenever any man or set of men," he observed,

> usurp more authority than has been given them, and act in a domineering and tyrannical manner, they should at once be displaced and others of cool, mature judgment put in the position. This is one of the complaints made of our police force and not without reason.
>
> . . . Many people think that one of the police lacks discretion and ought at once to know that we have not employed him to di[s]gracefully taunt everybody with his authority. He should be taught to do his duty without the use of abusive declarations; his words do not make him brave nor do they deter bad men from acts of violence. Hot words only make a "bad matter worse," and he

[9] Ellsworth Council Record, pp. 98–99; Ellsworth Police Docket, p. 198; Streeter: *Prairie Trails and Cow Towns*, pp. 126–31, 134–42; Ellsworth *Reporter*, Aug. 21, 1873; Ira Lloyd in ibid., Aug. 15, 1957; Junction City *Union*, Aug. 23, 1873; Topeka *Commonwealth*, Aug. 24, 27, 1873; Salina *Journal*, Sept. 4, 1873.

can do his duty without any such braggadocio and all will think better of him.

On August 27 the city councilmen met, discussed the law enforcement question at some length, and then acknowledged an altered public consensus by firing the old police. They appointed a local bartender as marshal, who in turn selected DeLong and a new man as his assistants. All three were known to be acceptable to the Texans.[1] News stories of impending civil violence at Ellsworth had by this time alarmed the Kansas governor, who dispatched his attorney general to look over the situation and see whether intervention by state authorities might be warranted. This official evidently reported that things seemed well in hand, the principal struggle now being to get the former lawmen to disarm.[2] Rather than submit, Jack Morco left town, but soon reappeared sporting a brace of ivory-handled six-shooters, loudly defying his "enemies." After several hours of impasse one of the new policemen confronted him directly, ordering him to surrender his pistols. Morco refused and was shot dead on the spot.

Quiet temporarily settled over Ellsworth, with law enforcement at last residing in firm but tactful hands. Many

[1] Topeka *Commonwealth*, Aug. 24, 1873; Ellsworth *Reporter*, Aug. 28, 1873; Ira Lloyd in ibid., Aug. 15, 1957; Ellsworth Council Record, pp. 102–03.

[2] Topeka *Commonwealth*, Aug. 23, 1873; C. A. Morris (secretary to governor) to Ellsworth Co. Attorney, Aug. 20, 1873, Governors' Letters, II, 181. Apparently upon his attorney general's advice, the governor did not intervene further than to issue a $500 reward for Billy Thompson. He also appointed to replace the deceased Sheriff Whitney the Ellsworth contractor-councilman, who evidently remained an unswerving hard-line advocate. Jim Gore protested this appointment, but without effect, since the governor assumed most Ellsworthites stood behind the new sheriff's mood. Junction City *Union*, Aug. 30, 1873; Salina *Journal*, Sept. 4, 1873; Thomas A. Osborn to Gore, Sept. 6, 1873, Governors' Letters, II, 221–22; Ellsworth *Reporter*, Sept. 4, 1873.

of the exiled gamblers drifted back into town without
interference. The deposed Ed Crawford had, like Morco,
left Ellsworth rather than disarm. On November 2 he returned. He shrugged off warnings that the Texans might
seek revenge for his brutal slaughter of Cad Pierce, and
five days later he too was dead, having been waylaid in a
local brothel thronged with transients. His killer was
never identified. Crawford's death ended the season's
mayhem.[3]

At great loss of pride and dignity, and possibly cattle
trade profits as well, Ellsworth's citizens had gained valuable insights into the mechanics of cattle town law enforcement. If 1873 offered any single lesson, it was that
the intricacies of repressing violence could not be entrusted to unfit personnel and an emotionally aroused
populace.

[5]

ON THE WHOLE, law enforcement efforts proved generally
effective, judging from the incidence of homicide. Many
legendary desperadoes and gunfighters sojourned in the
cattle towns at one time or another, but few participated
in slayings. Among those with clean records were such
famed killers as Clay Allison, Doc Holliday, and Ben
Thompson. The teen-aged gunman John Wesley Hardin
was responsible for only one verifiable cattle town homi-

[3] Salina *Journal*, Sept. 4, 1873; Ellsworth *Reporter*, Sept. 4, 11,
Nov. 13, 1873; Ira Lloyd in ibid., Aug. 15, 1957. On November 18 the
city council approved the appointment of Charley Brown, Morco's
killer, as city marshal, which proved a happy choice. Brown served
firmly but honorably until finally resigning with the council's approbation in mid-1875, the town's years as a cattle center having ended. See
Ellsworth Council Record, p. 108; Ellsworth *Reporter*, July 22, 1875.
Besides the Whitney, Pierce, Morco, and Crawford killings of 1873,
a fifth fatal shooting occurred that summer that evidently had no connection with the law enforcement situation. Ibid., July 31, Aug. 7, 14,
1873.

cide, apparently having fired through the wall of his hotel room one drunken night to silence a man snoring too loudly in the adjoining cubicle.[4] Nor did famous gunfighters serving as officers add much to the fatality statistics. As city marshal of Abilene in 1871, his only term as a cattle town lawman, the formidable Wild Bill Hickok killed just two men—one, a "special" policeman, by mistake.[5] Wyatt Earp, who served as an officer (but never actually as marshal) at both Wichita and Dodge City, may have mortally wounded one law violator, though he shared credit with another policeman for this single cattle town homicide.[6] The now equally renowned lawman William B. ("Bat") Masterson, at least according to contemporary sources, killed no one in or around Dodge, where he lived for several years.

With these celebrated personalities contributing far less than their supposed share, it is hardly surprising that the over-all homicide statistics are not particularly high. The table that follows is a compilation of all homicides— whether by police, resident citizens, or transients—for the periods in which each of the towns entertained the cattle trade. Only those killings that occurred in town have been counted, although fatalities in Abilene's and Ellsworth's suburban brothel districts are included because the communities attempted municipal control over

[4] Salina *Journal*, Aug. 10, 1871; Abilene *Chronicle*, Aug. 10, 17, 1871; E. C. Little: "A Son of the Border," *Everybody's Magazine*, IV (1901), 583; Thomas Ripley: *They Died with Their Boots On* (Garden City, N.Y., 1935), pp. 136–37.

[5] Abilene *Chronicle*, Oct. 12, 1871. For a close analysis of the literature concerning Hickok's term as city marshal at Abilene, its place in the "Hickok legend," and its curious relationship to fact see Robert Dykstra: "Wild Bill Hickok in Abilene," *Midcontinent American Studies Journal*, II (1961), 20–48. By far the best survey of Hickok's entire career is Joseph G. Rosa: *They Called Him Wild Bill: The Life and Adventures of James Butler Hickok* (Norman, Okla., 1964).

[6] Dodge City *Times*, July 27, Aug. 24, 1878; Dodge City *Globe*, July 30, Aug. 27, 1878.

CATTLE TOWN HOMICIDES

Towns	YEARS																TOTALS
	1870	1871	1872	1873	1874	1875	1876	1877	1878	1879	1880	1881	1882	1883	1884	1885	
Abilene	2	3	2														7
Ellsworth			1	5	0	0											6
Wichita		1	1	1	0	0											4
Dodge City							0?	0	5	2	1	1	0	3	2	1	15
Caldwell										2	2	3	1	2	2	1	13
TOTAL																	45

these areas. On the other hand, homicides in West Wichita were excluded from Wichita's figures since city authorities took not the slightest responsibility for enforcement in that independent trans-river community. The statistics commence with the first full shipping season in which each town existed as a municipality, except in the case of Caldwell, which gained organized status only in mid-1879 but attempted some law enforcement pending approval of an incorporation petition.

The sources for the statistics are the cattle town newspapers, of which continuous runs survive for all pertinent years but one.[7] For public relations purposes local editors sometimes chose to be circumspect about nonfatal affairs, making an adequate analysis of all lethal encounters impossible. But they inevitably succumbed to the newsworthiness of actual homicide, at which time public relations often went begging in the wake of hasty "extras" and reprinted regular editions, multiple copies of which citizens commonly bought to send to friends back East. Only when particularly useful or necessary have newspaper accounts been supplemented by other sources, secondary writings being in various degrees particularly unreliable.

As is evident, the number of homicides never topped five in any one cattle season year, and reached this figure only at Ellsworth in 1873 and at Dodge City five years later. In both instances, homicides may be said to have manifested "wave" dimensions, and were in fact thus con-

---

[7] Except for two issues the Dodge City paper for 1876 is no longer extant. According to a statement given by Wyatt Earp to his biographer, at Dodge in 1876 "There were some killings in personal quarrels, but none by peace officers." (Stuart N. Lake: *Wyatt Earp: Frontier Marshal* [Boston, 1931], p. 143.) Although Earp's testimony must always be treated with utmost caution, the uncharacteristically modest second half of his statement is probably correct. If there were no homicides by policemen then there were very possibly none by others, since law officers represented the numerically most important killers.

sidered by local residents. In at least six years no fatalities occurred at all. While not so significant in seasons of cattle trade decline as at Ellsworth in 1875 or at Wichita in 1875 and 1876, the zeroes recorded for two busy years at Dodge City seem particularly meaningful. The average number of homicides per cattle town trading season amounted to only 1.5 per year.

In the case of at least six of these killings—or well over 10 per cent—it is hard to identify any connection whatever with the existence of the cattle trade. Besides a Wichita insurance murder, and the murder of an Abilene tailor and the lynching of *his* murderer, already noted, these included the shootings of a Wichita hotel keeper resisting arrest on a federal warrant, that of one Wichita Negro by another, and that of a Caldwell housewife by her drunken husband.[8]

The majority of those involved in homicides, however, were indeed law officers, cowboys and drovers, or gamblers—the last a somewhat elastic category to accommodate four ex-lawmen without obvious means of support. Of homicide victims, nine were cowboys or drovers and nine were gamblers. Six were officers of the law. Aside from the non-cattle-trade killings mentioned above, victims included five townsmen with conventional occupations, three local rural settlers, two dance house proprietors, two miscellaneous visitors (one lawyer and a Pawnee Indian), and one female theatrical entertainer. The status of the remaining two victims is obscure.[9] Analyzed

[8] Eldorado *Times*, Mar. 3, 1871; Emporia *News*, Mar. 10, 1871; Wichita *Eagle*, July 19, 26, 1872; Caldwell *Journal*, June 5, 1884; Caldwell *Standard*, June 5, 1884.

[9] Documentation covering twenty-three cattle town homicides has not yet been cited in this chapter. Much of it relating to nineteen homicides is conveniently reproduced or summarized in Miller and Snell: *Why the West Was Wild*, pp. 33–35, 163–64, 166–70, 243–46, 273–76, 299–306, 351–52, 361–65, 459–72, 498–506, 512–13, 516–18, 567–68, 576–77, 612–13, 633–34. For the other four cases see Abilene *Chronicle*, Oct. 27, 1870; Dodge City *Times*, Nov. 20, Dec. 11,

in terms of perpetrators, sixteen cattle town homicides can be attributed to law officers, or citizens legitimately acting as such, twelve to cowboys or drovers, and eight to gamblers. The other nine homicides are distributed evenly among some of the categories already mentioned. These included two lynchings evidently carried out by cattle town residents rather than transients. Besides the episode at Abilene, a Caldwell gambler and bootlegger was hanged in somewhat mysterious circumstances to be discussed in another chapter.[1]

With the exception of killings by law officers and lynchings, the homicidal situations varied considerably. Seventeen apparently resulted from private quarrels, four were accidental or without discernible motive, two were committed by resisters of arrest, two avenged prior homicides, and two consisted of murders for profit. Homicidal disputes involving women, incidentally, exceeded by eight to one those mainly resulting from gambling disagreements. Of the six lawmen killed, interestingly enough, half met death in circumstances that must be termed accidental, although two of them—Ellsworth's Sheriff Whitney and the Abilene policeman killed by

---

1880; Dodge City *Globe*, Nov. 23, 1880, Jan. 25, 1881, Oct. 9, 1883; Caldwell *Journal*, Dec. 10, 1885; Caldwell *Free Press*, Dec. 12, 1885; Freeman: *Midnight and Noonday*, chap. xliii.

[1] In a notorious affair in late 1881 Caldwell nearly played host to another lynching, when J. S. Danford, the nonresident proprietor of Caldwell's private credit institution, the Merchants and Drovers Bank, in order to cover other outstanding debts covertly withdrew the bank's assets and fled town. Pursued by an angry posse of Caldwellites, he was captured at Wellington, brought back, threatened with bodily harm until he at last agreed to a settlement, and finally released. The episode caused comment in newspapers as far away as Chicago and Indianapolis, and the state authorities almost intervened. Danford later brought suit against his captors, as did his cashier, who had also been held for a time. The matter was finally compromised with Danford agreeing to pay back forty cents on the dollar. See Topeka *Commonwealth*, Nov. 29, 1881 ff.; Caldwell *Commercial*, Dec. 1, 1881 ff.; Caldwell *Post*, Dec. 1, 1881 ff.

Marshal Hickok—were attempting to help quell trouble when shot. Only two officers died attempting to make arrests; the other fell in a private quarrel.

Lest tradition be completely overthrown, let it be noted that gunshots were far and away the principal medium of death. But tradition also would have it that the cattle town homicide typically involved an exchange of shots—the so-called gunfight. Actually, though thirty-nine of the forty-five victims suffered fatal bullet or buckshot wounds, less than a third of them returned the fire. A good share of them were apparently not even armed.

Despite all the shooting it seems fair to conclude that the cattle town people largely succeeded in containing the lethal tendencies of their situation, despite the odds involved in suppressing violence while remaining hospitable to the Texas cattle trade. The collective adjustment demanded wisdom and finesse at all administrative levels, and wisdom and finesse were often at hand. Legend does the cattle town people a double injustice—falsely magnifying the periodic failures of their effort while altogether refusing to take account of its internal complexities.

IV

Preserving the
Cattle Trade

[1]

WHAT WE NOW TERM the "booster spirit" of the nine-teenth-century western town was a much more substantial activity than the frivolous conception of it that has come down to us. Newspapermen, frequently lured to the frontier by cash subsidies, thereafter labored conscientiously to make the most of their respective communities' prospects, defending them against detractors abroad, putting the best face on economic adversity, discreetly suppressing news of community divisiveness, advocating programs for local improvement, urging on citizens a mercantilist doctrine of "buying at home," and blatantly recommending their towns and constituent trade areas to prospective immigrants everywhere. All, in fact, was a matter of promotional routine.

Certainly one of the most important of the frontier editor's tasks was to keep local businessmen mobilized for collective action. Alternating the visions of a glowing community future with chilling images of community decay, editorial rhetoric teemed with metaphors of resolution ("Business men of Caldwell, to your posts! . . . Put your shoulder to the wheel, and roll the chariot of prosperity high up the incline till all the great Southwest can behold the gilded cart"), metaphors of vigilance ("There is no rest for a business man, more than a business city. No man can consider himself established, be his business ever so secure . . . ; no city can rest easy, content with what she has, some new Chicago would spring up and steal all her trade"), and metaphors of cohesion ("Let our leading men pull together with forecast wisdom and perfect harmony until energy and confidence shall have stamped permanency upon all that pertains to our young city").[1]

The cattle town people had special need of such inwardly directed propaganda, confronting as they did a unique problem for which few precedents existed outside the cattle town experience itself. As we have seen, each community triumphed over varying degrees of difficulty in becoming a full-fledged cattle trading center. Abilene, Ellsworth, and Dodge City sprang up beside the railroad line; the main concern of their citizens was to attract cattlemen to already available shipping facilities. Wichita and Caldwell had been purposely fixed on the established cattle trail; the problem here was attracting railroads. Yet, once having gained the proper conjunction of tracks and trail, townsfolk discovered that the struggle had only begun. Preserving the community's cattle trade, they found, was to be an annual effort requiring the expenditure of considerable sums of energy, influence, and money.

[2]

CATTLE DROVERS, to be sure, tended to repeat themselves in their yearly perambulations to the Kansas cattle towns. Adhering to a highly unstable business, individual cat-

---

[1] Caldwell *Post*, Apr. 20, 1882; Ellsworth *Reporter*, June 12, 1873; Wichita *Eagle*, June 28, 1872.

tlemen preferred to return to a familiar trading center where experience with the town, its outlying ranges, its businessmen, and its railroad agents helped mitigate apprehension about prices and dealers. Even so, especially in the first half of the cattle town era, *all* entrepreneurial groups connected with the trade remained mobile and capable of shifting to new shipping points according to changing conditions and advantages. Rural hostility greatly strengthened the menace of this persistent mobility. Farmers, fearing splenic fever and trampled crops, constantly threatened to close off the local commerce in range cattle by one means or another. As a result, the preservation of a town's cattle trade usually required a vigorous twofold effort both to attract and to protect it. All the cattle towns engaged in such efforts, and annual programs to preserve the cattle trade always constituted one of the most important community preoccupations.

Normally the routine varied from year to year and place to place only in its elaborateness. Shipping had usually closed down by November of each year, and the wholly alert cattle town business community did not pause long before starting preparations for the next season. A time of crucial importance was January through early March, when the state legislature met in Topeka.[2] Here the principal threat was a possible extension of the state's Texas cattle quarantine line beyond the town, which would effectively exclude the cattle trade from its immediate vicinity. In order to stifle such action, townsmen representing their respective counties sought influential positions in the legislature, especially on the Committee on Texas Cattle, the Committee on Inter-State Commerce, or whatever other legislative group was given initial jurisdiction over "deadline" bills. A delegation

---

[2] The Kansas legislature met annually through 1877, biennially thereafter.

might also be sent to Topeka to lobby on the cattle town's behalf.

Advertising constituted a second effort during the first months of any year. Letters from individuals extolled the advantages of either driving to or purchasing at the cattle town, depending on whether drovers or buyers were being solicited. These letters appeared in Texan and various midwestern newspapers, as well as in regional livestock journals. Visits to stock conventions also presented opportunities for exhorting customers to patronize the cattle center.

In April and May, as Texas drovers began moving their herds northward, more direct problems came under attack. If a new route was needed to skirt expanded agricultural settlements, hired agents might lay it out and mark it with signs or flags; if a route across a settled area was needed, agents negotiated with individual farmers for rights-of-way. Sometimes a herding ground adjacent to town had to be bargained for. Townsmen also frequently had to make arrangements to reimburse farmers for potential splenic·fever ravages and ruined field crops.

Normally in April a delegation descended the cattle trail, on the way tacking up printed circulars advertising the cattle town. It finally headquartered at some well-known point on the trail in Indian Territory or northern Texas, where, in directing drovers to the represented town, it often functioned in competition with agents of other cattle markets. Such delegations frequently stayed until June or July, or whenever the traffic slowed markedly after the big spring drive. Other representatives, meanwhile, might travel to Kansas City, St. Louis, Chicago, and other midwestern terminal markets to encourage the patronage of buyers.

Throughout the year, finally, a constant flow of publicity emanated from the cattle town. Editors and correspondents early in the season stressed the town's sucess as a cattle market the previous summer and its good potentialities for the coming year. Rival cattle centers were denigrated, emphasis given any specific bad report about such competitors, and any negative reports about the home community heatedly discounted. Favorable statements by visitors, particularly noting the town's hospitality, were called to drovers' attention and occasional groups of newspaper editors participating in railroad sponsored "excursions" were urged to advertise the town as a burgeoning cattle market.

[3]

CATTLE TRADE PRESERVATION PROGRAMS enjoyed a variety of possible sponsors. Promotional efforts by individual enterprisers constituted the most elementary alternative. Joseph G. McCoy's successful efforts of 1867 and 1868 in attracting drovers to Abilene and suppressing local rural hostility have already been discussed. Early in 1869, having recouped some of his financial losses through personal cattle sales and expecting a rebate contract with the Kansas Pacific Railway to accomplish complete solvency, he willingly spent some $2,000 lobbying at Springfield, Illinois, to modify a legislative proposal banning Texas cattle from that key consumer state. McCoy succeeded in having "wintered" longhorns exempted from the quarantine, proof of splenic fever immunity in every instance to be supplied by the county clerk at the place where the animals had been held over the winter. This requirement gave McCoy no trouble at Abilene; he simply bribed the local official to forge certificates for any purchaser who wanted to ship to or through Illinois. All in all, McCoy felt the Illinois legislature's action probably did as much good as harm, since its long debate over the proposed action served as gratuitous advertising both for Texas cattle and for Abilene.[3] That summer McCoy also was probably instrumental in establishing a measure for dealing with Dickinson County settlers who protested the importation of longhorns—an indemnifying bond in the amount of $20,000 to insure them against cattle damages.[4] But he himself was already overextended financially, and when the Kansas Pacific repudiated its contract with him in the winter of 1869–70, he was forced into insolvency and for a year virtually retired from the scene as a major cattle trade entrepreneur.[5]

In later years other individual cattle town businessmen emulated McCoy's example on grounds that what was good for the community was good for them. John H. Hood, merchant and banker of Caldwell, visited Texas just before the opening of Caldwell's first cattle shipping season. Writing from Fort Worth, he informed citizens of his efforts on their behalf. Concluded the town's editor: "Major Hood is leaving nothing wanting on his part to post the cattle men and induce them to make Caldwell their objective point." J. Ringolsky, a Leavenworth clothier who operated his Drovers Headquarters store at Ellsworth each cattle season, "will visit Texas during the winter," announced that community's editor

[3] Joseph G. McCoy: *Historic Sketches of the Cattle Trade of the West and Southwest*, ed. Ralph P. Bieber (Glendale, Calif., 1940), pp. 252–56 and notes. But according to a visitor in Abilene in 1869 the Illinois cattle quarantine was damaging in that it considerably delayed the start of the shipping season, and Kansas Pacific officials themselves complained that a severely constricted shipping season cut down on the numbers carried out by rail that year. Junction City *Union*, Aug. 7, 1869; Kansas Pacific Railway Co.: *Annual Report . . . 1869* (St. Louis, 1870), p. 9.

[4] Leavenworth *Times and Conservative*, June 25, 1869. Whether this was a bond filed with the state in compliance with the 1867 quarantine law, or only a local voluntary measure, remains obscure.

[5] For McCoy's own account of this difficulty see his *Historic Sketches*, pp. 249–52, 256–59, 271–80, together with Bieber's useful annotations.

late in 1873, "and will not lose an opportunity to speak a good word for Ellsworth." In 1881, Caldwell's large outfitting establishment, W. N. Hubbell and Company, stationed an experienced Texan on the cattle trail as a promotional agent for the town.[6]

Dodge City's leading merchant, Robert M. Wright, whose entrepreneurial venture has been described at some length, was one of the few individual cattle town businessmen so single-handedly involved in cattle trade preservation efforts to the extent of Joe McCoy before him. At the commencement of the 1877 season, Dodge City's first big shipping year, the town's editor announced that "Our citizens . . . do not believe in sending out runners and cappers" (derogatory terms for trail agents) to attract the cattle trade.[7] Throughout the era, with few exceptions, the community's program for retaining the cattle trade rested wholly on Wright's willing shoulders. His agents remained the only ones regularly employed on the trail, excepting those of his principal competitor, the York-Parker-Draper outfitting establishment. Wright's employee and later partner, Henry M. Beverley, for several seasons acted as Dodge City's winter publicity agent in Texas.[8] Wright himself often made personal visits to talk with drovers and dealers. In 1880 his miscellaneous expenses on behalf of Dodge included paying half the cost of a settlement-skirting trail marked out by farmers northwest of town for cattlemen who wished to take herds on to Nebraska or Wyoming. In the same year it was Wright's circular to Texas drovers that, while boosting the company's own facilities, assured cattlemen—in much the same tone and form of such promotional litera-

---

[6] Caldwell *Commercial*, May 6, 1880, Mar. 31, 1881; Ellsworth *Reporter*, Oct. 30, 1873; Caldwell *Post*, May 26, 1881.

[7] Dodge City *Times*, Mar. 24, 1877.

[8] See, for instance, Dodge City *Times*, Apr. 7, 1877, Feb. 8, Apr. 8, 1879. For examples of seasonal correspondence with Texas contacts, which must have been invaluable, see ibid., Jan. 26, Mar. 2, 9, 1878.

ture everywhere—that the entire area extended them welcome:

> We take pleasure in assuring you that there has not been, nor will there be any change in the present "dead line;" the trail as followed in years before, is free from interference, and the country south of Dodge City to the Texas line is almost entirely open and free from farmers and squatters; the prospects for water and abundant grass are better than for years past, while the drouth of last season has driven many of the itinerant farmers away, leaving a much larger scope open to the "through cattle" of 1880. The liberality with which cattle men treated the farmers during the past season has noticeably engendered a change of heart in the farmer, as experience has taught him that a plain showing of his grievance to the "boss" will bring him immediate settlement of his just claim.
>
> The interests of Dodge City (which comprises more than one half of the population of our large county) are with the Texas drive, and public sentiment will not allow the cattle-men to be hampered and harassed by the few farmers so inclined.[9]

It was also Bob Wright who, as Ford County's representative in the legislature, chaired the important house committees to which quarantine legislation in 1877, 1879, and 1881 was referred for action, and who thus proved extremely influential in preventing Dodge from being excluded as a market for Texas cattle in those crucial years.[1]

With their tremendous economic stake in the range cattle industry, the railroads serving principal cattle towns might have been expected to offer help in cattle trade preservation efforts. And so they did, as we will see in the cases of Ellsworth and Wichita, when competition

[9] Dodge City *Globe*, Oct. 29, 1878, Feb. 24, June 15, 22, 1880.

[1] Dodge City *Times*, Feb. 1, Mar. 15, 1879, Jan. 22, Mar. 10, 1881; Dodge City *Globe*, Feb. 11, 1879, Mar. 8, 1881; A. T. Andreas: *History of the State of Kansas* (Chicago, 1883), p. 1560.

between rival railroad companies provided sufficient impetus. But even then company assistance often did not seem very enthusiastically extended. As one Dodgeite wryly commented in 1877: "The only rival [cattle town] we fear is Ellis; but of course the action of citizens can have no weight—all depends upon the action of the two roads." Despite the competition of the Kansas Pacific at Ellis that season, the Santa Fe's monetary contribution for attracting the trade to Dodge totaled a mere $374. Railways did routinely serve the interests of the community by offering good stockyards and popular livestock agents, both of which assisted in increasing the general mood of community hospitality. As one cattle town observer reported:

> Everywhere you go you meet [J. H.] Phillips. Phillips is the A. T. & S. F. agent. He loads, brands and ships all the cattle, gives everybody a [free] pass that wants one (or talks him into not wanting one), knows everybody, is personally acquainted with every beef, bull, steer or cow between this place and the Rio Grande, can take a drink and is never busy.

Such an individual obviously proved an asset to the cattle town as well as to the railroad.[2]

But at all times a railroad's primary goal was maximum profits, and townsmen sometimes felt themselves to be at the mercy of various economic stratagems, especially freight rate manipulations. In the summer of 1880, for example, the Santa Fe at Caldwell and the Kansas City, Lawrence and Southern at nearby Hunnewell participated in a rate war that has already been described as part of Caldwell's early history. Shipping rates, normally $40 per carload, dropped to $10 at both places. Meanwhile, the Santa Fe retained the normal rate at Dodge,

[2] Hays City *Sentinel*, Mar. 28, 1877; Atchison, Topeka and Santa Fe Railroad Co.: *Annual Report . . . 1877* (Boston, 1877), p. 35; Dodge City *Times*, June 16, 1877.

which meant that for a time Dodge City was practically
shut out of the season's shipping. The end of the Caldwell-
Hunnewell competition that autumn finally "gives Dodge
City a chance," as an editor put it, for "one month of good
fall business." By and large, the summer had been a disaster for local businessmen.[3]

Even more important than shipping rates in the long
run were the railroads' land policies. As Joe McCoy discovered in the late 1860's when he asked the Kansas Pacific to reserve its land grant in western Dickinson
County as a local herding ground, real estate sales to
settlers took precedence over such cattle trade considerations.[4] When faced with a conflict of cattle shipping and
land profits, railroads typically wrote off the affected cattle town and began promoting new shipping centers farther down the line. In short, an impersonal railroad management could seldom be counted upon for voluntary and
extended assistance to a cattle trade preservation effort.

Local government was a third agency useful to the
cattle trade program. Indirect subsidies might resemble
the example at Ellsworth in the spring of 1875, when the
mayor and councilmen allowed Charley Brown, the city
marshal, to devote full time to work as the town's trail
representative without loss of pay.[5] But absolutely straightforward tax support of cattle trade programs, so far
as can be determined, occurred only at Wichita and
Caldwell, where a tradition of direct municipal aid to
private enterprise persisted strongly.[6] The Wichita expe-

[3] Dodge City *Times*, Aug. 21, 28, Sept. 18, 1880; Caldwell *Commercial*, Sept. 9, 16, 1880.

[4] McCoy: *Historic Sketches*, p. 259.

[5] Ellsworth Council Record, 1871–80 (microfilm copy, KSHS), pp.
175–76; Ellsworth *Reporter*, May 20, 27, June 3, 1875.

[6] In 1873, in *Commercial National Bank of Cleveland* v. *The City
of Iola*, the Kansas supreme court ruled taxation in aid of private enterprise to be unconstitutional. This decision had little effect, however,
since some latitude remained for the interpretation of the phrase
"private enterprise." Flour mills especially retained their attraction for

rience will presently be examined in some detail; that of
Caldwell may be dealt with briefly.

In early 1880, the town's first shipping season, Caldwell's city council appropriated $1,500 (businessmen had
requested $2,500) in response to a petition from the busi-
ness community urging an expenditure "to induce the
Texas cattle trade to Caldwell, and to properly advertise
said city as a cattle shipping point." Special circulars
were printed, two experienced men hired to work on the
trail, and the town advertised in Kansas City and St.
Louis newspapers. In 1881 the city council agreed to subsidize, at least partially, a new cattle trail to Caldwell
from Red River.[7] This proved to be an unrewarding expenditure, however, and enthusiasm for the direct employment of tax monies lapsed thereafter.

By far the most common community means for grap-
pling with the cattle trade preservation challenge, finally,
was the businessmen's ad hoc committee, often supplemented by special subscription funds drawn from the
citizenry at large. Filling the role of what in later years
would become the permanent board of trade or chamber
of commerce, such temporary groups in the cattle trade
era remained the normal instrument for handling all matters of general business community interest.

[4]

SEASONS WHEN CATTLE TOWNS competed were those in
which the various elements of their respective preserva-

public subsidies. (James Ernest Boyle: *The Financial History of
Kansas* [Madison, Wis., 1908], pp. 62–63.) For post-1873 tax support
of a mill at Wichita see Wichita Council Record, 1870–81 (microfilm
copy, KSHS), A, 380–81, B, 29; Wichita *Beacon*, Jan. 27, 1875. For
pro-subsidy opinion at Caldwell see the Caldwell *Post*, Nov. 3, 1881.
Caldwell often took its cue in such matters from the earlier experience
of Wichita, from which place the town had, in effect, been "colonized."

   [7] Caldwell *Post*, May 13, 20, 1880; Caldwell *Commercial*, May 20,
1880, Apr. 28, June 9, 16, 23, July 7, 1881.

tion efforts emerged most sharply into perspective. Every cattle town had its seasonal rivalries—if only to keep its collective hand in between real crises, one suspects—but that between Wichita and Ellsworth in the years 1871–74 represents a kind of apogee, stimulated as it was by the participation of competing railway companies.

Ellsworth's unsuccessful attempt to win a substantial portion of the shipping trade in 1869 and its subsequent quiescence were examined earlier, as was Wichita's defeat of the Park City effort to establish a Chisholm Trail cutoff in 1870 and 1871. Park City's challenge in 1871 actually was only a part of the strategy employed by the Kansas Pacific Railway that, if successful, would have permanently undermined Wichita's future as a cattle center. Wichitans rose to the occasion in magnificent style.

In early January 1871, Wichita's businessmen agreed to pay for all damages accruing to local settlers from the passage of Texas cattle through the county. Evidently in response to news that Arkansas City had employed an agent to divert the cattle trail to that community, they also hired a pair of men to ride down into Texas and advertise the regular route.[8] But the most important enemy, unknown to them at the moment, lay to the north rather than to the east.

The Kansas Pacific management, concerned that same year about impending shipping competition from the Santa Fe Railroad then approaching the cattle trail below Abilene, sought to divert all cattle traffic to its own new facilities at Brookville and Ellsworth. For the first time since their financial encouragement of Joe McCoy's project at Abilene, the company officers underwrote a substantial effort to retain the trade by wooing it west of the Santa Fe's grasp. Hiring Henry Shanklin, a former Wichita Indian agent familiar with southern Kansas and Indian Territory, the company sent him to stake out a

[8] Wichita *Vidette*, Dec. 29, 1870, Jan. 5, 12, Feb. 2, 1871.

Chisholm Trail cutoff. The new trail diverged from the established route at the Ninnescah River southwest of Wichita. Veering northwestward through Park City, it effectively bypassed both Wichita and the temporary Santa Fe terminus at Newton. Wichitans learned of this coup only as the first herd of longhorns proceeded up Shanklin's cutoff in late April. A hard-riding posse of citizens succeeded in diverting the herd back through Wichita by promising full payment for any damage to the animals, terms that subsequently amounted to only $15 for one steer that broke its neck fording the Arkansas River.

Having thus averted what they considered to be a very close call, but still faced with the Kansas Pacific threat, Wichitans met on May 13 to devise means to protect the established trail until such time as the Santa Fe tracks would arrive in town and fix Wichita as a shipping center beyond any doubt. Citizens elected a committee of seven prominent businessmen, who thereupon hired Wichita's newspaper editor to produce circulars advertising the town's hospitality and the advantages of the regular route. Riders posted these along the Chisholm Trail as far south as Red River. The city council, meanwhile, had begun spending what would eventually be a considerable sum of tax monies to retain the cattle trade, approving a recommendation "that Douglas Avenue be made as a thoroughfare for Texas Cattle en route through the city," the cost of which came to slightly more than $250.[9]

Expended sums, both private and public, rose measurably the following year. On May 6, 1872, as the approaching Santa Fe tracks and the closure of Abilene and Newton as cattle centers heralded their town's first shipping season, Wichitans conferred self-confidently about the cattle trade. A few days later several local merchants

[9] Wichita *Vidette*, Feb. 25, 1871; Wichita *Tribune*, May 4, 11, 18, June 1, 1871; Wichita *Eagle*, Feb. 28, 1884; Wichita Council Record, A, 57, 107, 109.

rode down the trail to welcome the first herds. On May 15 city councilmen empowered the mayor to appoint "some suitable person to work for the interests of Wichita on the Texas Cattle trail with a view to induce Cattle dealers to make this the shipping point for their herds."[1]

Up at Ellsworth, meanwhile, businessmen celebrating Abilene's relinquishment of the cattle trade hoped to capture it by obtaining the Drovers Cottage hotel. At the same time the Kansas Pacific prepared to spend something over $25,000 enlarging the local stockyard, which by midsummer was an intricate maze of fences and chutes covering thirty-three thousand square yards. As Wichitans toasted the arrival of the Santa Fe tracks, Ellsworthites received their first herds. On May 20 someone who had traveled down the Kansas Pacific line returned to Wichita and observed that Ellsworth intended to be a serious contender for the trade that year. This report spurred Wichitans to action. Joe McCoy, having recently moved to town from Abilene, met with the city council that evening, as did a prominent cattleman and banker, Thomas H. Stribling of San Antonio. Both volunteered advice on luring the bulk of the cattle trade. The councilmen then hired another Texas cattleman, James Bryden, to descend the Chisholm Trail and contact drovers, while a number of businessmen subsidized McCoy to travel north and east and advertise Wichita to cattle buyers.[2]

Early in June the Santa Fe finished constructing at Wichita the second largest stockyard on its line—an en-

[1] Wichita *Eagle*, May 3, 10, 24, 1872; Wichita Council Record, A, 174.

[2] Ellsworth *Reporter*, May 23, June 27, 1872; Kansas Pacific: *Annual Report . . . 1872* (St. Louis, 1873), p. 22; Wichita *Eagle*, Apr. 26, May 3, 24, 1872; Wichita Council Record, A, 174, 176; McCoy: *Historic Sketches*, p. 236. The city council later may also have hired a second man to work on the trail. See Wichita Council Record, A, 190.

closure slightly larger than even Ellsworth's—and it supplemented Wichita's promotional effort by purchasing the services of an experienced and talented trio to manage the yard and superintend shipping operations: the popular Texas cattleman Abel H. ("Shanghai") Pierce, together with Charles F. Gross and Samuel N. Hitt, both of whom had helped Joe McCoy establish the cattle trade at Abilene five years before. Pierce and Gross apparently spent part of their time on the trail contacting drovers.[3] Jim Bryden, Wichita's municipal agent, stationed himself at Caldwell until August, when he was discharged and paid a $400 fee. McCoy returned from his tour through Illinois, Iowa, and Nebraska in July. Just how much he earned is not certain; for some reason, he or his employers submitted all or part of his bill to the city council for payment, which that body, after some deliberation, declined to meet.[4]

A newspaper debate added a weekly punch to the cattle trade rivalry. The respective towns' two newly established editors—Wichita's Marshall M. Murdock and Ellsworth's George A. Atwood—assumed the main burden of the journalistic duel. In many respects these competing cattle town spokesmen possessed strikingly similar backgrounds. Both were men in their early thirties who had been born in the East, grew up in rural or small town circumstances, and who prepared for college but did not attend. Both served briefly in the Civil War, migrating west while still young men to settle initially in typical

[3] Gross to Edwards, Apr. 20, 1922, May 4, 1925, Edwards Papers; Wichita *Eagle*, May 17, 24, June 7, 28, July 19, 1872; Santa Fe: *Annual Report . . . 1873* (Boston, 1873), p. 15. A full-length biography—Chris Emmett: *Shanghai Pierce: A Fair Likeness* (Norman, Okla., 1953)—unfortunately contains almost no documentary reference to Pierce's long series of annual summer sojourns in Kansas.

[4] Wichita *Eagle*, June 14, July 12, Aug. 2, Sept. 19, 1872; Wichita Council Record, A, 211, 213, 228.

rural county seat towns—Murdock at Burlingame, Kansas, and Atwood at Adel, Iowa. Here each participated as a Republican in local politics, holding minor elective or appointive offices while editing a weekly newspaper. Murdock had already served two terms in the Kansas senate; Atwood cherished similar ambitions and would presently seek and win election to the house of representatives. Each man arrived in his respective cattle town just in time for the 1872 cattle season. Late in 1871 Murdock had received "a splendid offer" from James R. Mead and other Wichita notables to come and establish a Republican weekly. He promptly accepted, buying new materials in St. Louis, and published his first issue of the Wichita *Eagle* in April 1872. Atwood, for his part, was back East that winter evidently looking for new opportunities when his younger brother, an attorney, settled at Ellsworth. George shortly followed suit, purchasing the five-month-old Ellsworth *Reporter* from its original proprietor in May of the same year.[5]

The two young but experienced journalists soon locked horns. In June the Topeka *Commonwealth* carried a letter from "A Cattle Man" extolling the superior advantages to drovers of the Kansas Pacific Railway. The writer contended that a

> great point to be noted in favor of the Kansas Pacific grazing grounds over others is the fact that . . . no part of southern Kansas is adapted to hold Texas cattle any length of time (a thing very desirable with this particular trade) from the fact of their being wild and unruly, and easily stampeded by any degree of annoyance from flies and mosquitos, which prevail to an alarming extent this year in and about Wichita and adjacent points, seeking the trade,

[5] S. Lewis and Co.: *United States Biographical Dictionary: Kansas Volume* (Chicago, 1879), pp. 270–71; Wichita *Eagle*, May 6, 1875; Chapman Bros.: *Portrait and Biographical Album of Washington, Clay and Riley Counties* (Chicago, 1890), pp. 1132–34; Ellsworth *Reporter*, Feb. 22, May 23, 1872.

and which owe their increased number to the humid and sultry weather experienced there during this spring and summer.

In his issue of June 28 Marsh Murdock quoted this statement and unleashed upon it his aptitude for tart invective, labeling it an ingenuous "defense of the poor grazing grounds around Ellsworth." "If the lack of water and short grass are required to the well being of Texas cattle," he sneered, "then Ellsworth is the point." He also lashed the writer for falsely inflating the numbers of cattle already shipped from Ellsworth, asserting elsewhere that 90 per cent of the cattle driven to Wichita was bought by eastern purchasers and shipped out by rail, with only 10 per cent being sold (at reduced prices) to ranchers— "whilst just the reverse is the case at Ellsworth." He printed a cattleman's letter plumping for Wichita over its Kansas Pacific rival, and quoted Shanghai Pierce to the effect that Texans reported Ellsworth's range very short of moisture.

George Atwood, who had of course reprinted the letter from "A Cattle Man" with approval, professed surprise at the *Eagle*'s outburst. "It is hard to conceive," he mused darkly in his issue of July 11, "how that paper and that town should be so terribly down on Ellsworth, if this is such a miserably poor, worthless, barren country." He denied that a mere 10 per cent of Ellsworth's cattle was shipped east, suggesting that Murdock may have been misinformed by Joe McCoy, who—it was true—harbored a grudge against the Kansas Pacific. Atwood also took the occasion to observe, less correctly, that Ellsworth's stockyard was the largest in Kansas despite Wichita boasts. In the same issue he termed Ellsworth "the most orderly city on the border," blandly likening Wichita to Hays City and other notoriously violent towns where that summer "several have had their checks passed in, but here is order and law."

And so the war of words continued through the 1872 cattle season. Murdock took every opportunity to emphasize the dearth of moisture on the Ellsworth range. In early August, for instance, Atwood printed a letter from an Ellsworthite admitting earlier drought conditions but arguing that the local situation had now improved. Murdock countered simply by observing that the owners of two large herds had brought their animals back to the Wichita range from Ellsworth just that week, one of the reasons being scarcity of water. Indeed, as an interested Sedgwick County citizen observed in a letter to the *Eagle* in September, "the unfavorable weather reports from Ellsworth did more for us than anything else."[6] Certainly Marsh Murdock had done his utmost to publicize such reports, and therefore played a more or less influential role in establishing Wichita's victory in the shipping competition. When the season closed late in the year, Wichita proved far in the lead with 70,600 head shipped to Ellsworth's 40,161.[7]

Both communities implemented strenuous cattle trade programs in 1873. Wichita's efforts began early with an uninhibited expenditure of money. In January and February the city council spent $27.50 for five thousand promotional circulars addressed to drovers. Many of these went through the mails to Jim Bryden at Corpus Christi, who circulated them among the cattlemen in his area before the start of the spring drive. A newly formed board of trade financed a second batch of promotional circulars

[6] Ellsworth *Reporter*, Aug. 8, 1872; Wichita *Eagle*, Aug. 16, Sept. 19, 1872. The lack of moisture at Ellsworth was of course also publicized by other Wichita spokesmen. See, for example, the letter to the Topeka *Commonwealth* by Jim Bryden, the former Wichita employee, as reprinted in the Wichita *Eagle*, Nov. 24, 1872.

[7] Wichita *Eagle*, Jan. 23, 1873; Kansas Pacific; *Annual Report . . . 1873* (St. Louis, 1874), p. 18. Such comparative figures, while indicating relative cattle trading activity, do not embrace the herds driven on foot from Ellsworth, which activity always terminated a much greater portion of annual sales than at Wichita.

in March. The city council hired one Matt Shores to spend April and May, and longer if necessary, working on the trail. Shores was to receive $200 monthly, this amount to come from a citizens' subscription fund. The council also authorized its cattle trade committee to "advertise in two or three of the prominent papers of Texas." Fearing possible rural harassment of incoming herds now that settlement impinged on the west side of the county, the councilmen also moved to employ "some suitable person to interview the farmers in the vicinity of Wichita with a view to adjusting dif[f]iculties that may arise between the farmers and the Texas Cattle men." The individual selected for this important task, a farmer himself, in April obtained the signatures of 132 settlers along the route below Wichita, each of whom bound himself to sober arbitration of all damage claims.[8]

To the north, the men of Ellsworth also busied themselves. On April 3 they convened and formed a cattle trade committee, collecting a subscription fund with which they hired a local cattle raiser, Titus J. Buckbee, to work on the trail. Two weeks later the Kansas Pacific Railway contributed the services of three well-known stockmen. Leaving Ellsworth on April 16 under the leadership of William M. Cox, the road's general livestock agent, the party laid out a new trail down to Pond Creek in Indian Territory. Buckbee and two of the others then remained at that point as promotional representatives, handing out Kansas Pacific circulars showing passing drovers the new route to Ellsworth.[9]

On April 21 Wichitans learned of this expedition by

[8] Wichita Council Record, A, 262, 267–68, 289, 292; bill dated Feb. 19, 1873, in Wichita City Bills, 1872–73, microfilm copy, KSHS; contract dated Feb. 17, 1873, in Wichita Miscellaneous Papers, 1871–81, microfilm copy, KSHS; two multiple contracts dated 1873 in ibid.; Wichita *Eagle*, Mar. 20, 27, Apr. 17, 1873.

[9] Ellsworth *Reporter*, Apr. 17, 24, May 8, June 12, July 3, Sept. 4, 1873; Wichita *Eagle*, Apr. 17, 1873.

the Ellsworth promoters and, suddenly panicked, mounted a crash program of their own. Responding to a businessmen's petition, the Wichita city council met in emergency session with a large number of townsmen looking on. The meeting quickly dissolved into a general conclave. The council's cattle trade committee reported that only about $1,200 had been subscribed to the special fund authorized earlier. Those present thereupon acclaimed a resolution that whereas the Kansas Pacific was "making vigorous efforts to secure the Texas Cattle Trade," the city fathers should employ tax monies "to secure said trade to Wichita, not exceeding in amount four thousand dollars." They further urged the mayor to hire "two or more men" for promotion efforts on the trail. The assembled citizens also noted that the Santa Fe management had so far failed to aid in the struggle that year; the mayor and three prominent businessmen were delegated to travel immediately to Topeka and enlist its help. And while they were at it, they should also confer with Shanghai Pierce and various packers and buyers at Kansas City.[1]

The delegates' urgent visit to Santa Fe headquarters resulted in a special "Railroad Cattle Fund" of something over $2,000 contributed by the company.[2] Although the railway management subsequently hired a trail agent, Peyton Montgomery, the Wichita delegation used its new fund to get Pierce's signature on a contract whereby the renowned stockman agreed to use all his influence on Wichita's behalf and to "deter & hinder as far as possible the [cattle] trade from going to any other town." And, as requested, the city councilmen promptly loosed the municipal purse strings. They agreed to reimburse any

[1] Wichita Council Record, A, 291–94; Topeka *Commonwealth*, Apr. 30, May 4, 1873.
[2] Wichita *Eagle*, Apr. 22, 1875. The city council subsequently voted the mayor $250 as a reward for obtaining this lucrative contribution.

farmers suffering damages from Texas cattle and in July authorized a payment of $50 to a settler for a ravaged hay field—apparently the only such indemnity paid out. Another $50 went for advertising Wichita in the Chicago *Live Stock Journal*. The season's third batch of promotional circulars—five thousand signed by the mayor and his councilmen—were printed and mailed to all buyers who had frequented Wichita in 1872, as well as to northern and eastern buyers and dealers in general. In midseason the mayor and another businessman briefly toured the Middle West to promote Wichita among feeders as Joe McCoy had done the year before. All in all, Wichita spent about $4,000 to recruit the 1873 cattle trade, evidently including the $2,000 railroad contribution and the $1,200 solicited from citizens by the city council's cattle trade committee.[3]

As during the previous season, in 1873 the rivalry was also fought out on the public relations front. Ellsworth's letter writers, editor George Atwood, and journalistic partisans from other places argued that the countryside around Wichita was so settled by farmers as to pose a hazard to cattle drovers, in contrast to Ellsworth's own empty range. Wichita, as in 1872, played up its competitor's lack of water. With a slow market at both places, both Atwood and Murdock were able to report the transfer of waiting herds from one town to the other by dissatisfied drovers. During autumn's national financial panic, described elsewhere, shipping at last began in earnest. Although the final shipping figures do not include the more than 50,000 head driven on foot from Ellsworth during the season, the latter had again sent off far less by rail than had Wichita. The total for the entire year at Ells-

[3] Contracts dated Apr. 21, May 7, 1873, in Wichita Miscellaneous Papers; Wichita Council Record, A, 267–68, 316–17, 319, 342; bill dated July 9, 1873, in Wichita City Bills; Topeka *Commonwealth*, May 4, 1873; Wichita *Eagle*, May 22, June 26, 1873, Apr. 16, 1874.

worth was 30,540, while Wichita shipped something over 55,000 head from April through October 1873.[4]

Lulled by their resounding victory in the comparative shipping statistics, Wichitans' 1874 preservation effort did not get under way until well into spring. Townspeople once more were rudely jolted into action by a determined promotional effort in behalf of Ellsworth. Again, as it had since 1871, the Kansas Pacific Railway issued its annual *Guide Map of the Great Texas Cattle Trail* as a means of luring drovers from the shipping centers of rival railroads.[5] A 22-page pocket-sized booklet bound in incandescent yellow cardboard, the elaborate 1874 edition displayed illustrations adapted from Joe McCoy's *Historic Sketches*, then in process of publication. Its most important feature was a fold-out map, eighteen by twelve inches in size, pasted inside the back cover. This document boldly superimposed on an outline of Indian Territory and Kansas the "Ellsworth Cattle Trail," labeled "The Best and Shortest Cattle Trail from Texas." Although Wichita was nowhere mentioned specifically in the booklet's text, the map falsely indicated that Wichita lay something like forty miles inside the Kansas quarantine line, the crossing of which was warned against in bold-faced type on both back and front covers.[6] In addition, in April the Kansas Pacific hired a

[4] Ellsworth *Reporter*, Mar. 20, June 5, July 17, Aug. 14, 1873; Wichita *Eagle*, May 29, June 26, July 10, Oct. 9, Nov. 6, 1873; Kansas Pacific: *Annual Report 1873*, p. 18.

[5] Although the Library of Congress catalogue includes no reference to the Kansas Pacific guides, Wayne Gard's bibliography lists five editions (1871–75). Gard, however, specifically cites only the 1875 version. Floyd Benjamin Streeter somewhere consulted the 1872 and 1875 editions. (Gard: *The Chisholm Trail* [Norman, Okla., 1954], pp. 81, 190, 199, 274; Streeter: "Ellsworth as a Texas Cattle Market," *Kansas Historical Quarterly*, IV [1935], 395.) The Kansas State Historical Society possesses the 1874 edition, cited in the following note.

[6] Kansas Pacific Railway Co.: *Guide Map of the Great Texas Cattle Trail from Red River Crossing to the Old Reliable Kansas Pacific Rail-*

noted Texas cattleman, James Elliott, to act as the Ellsworth trail representative, while Ellsworth's businessmen collected a subscription of $1,000 to pay the influential Shanghai Pierce to act as their cattle trade recruiter. Pierce's employment lasted for six weeks, from early May through the middle of June.[7]

Wichitans hastily bestirred themselves in April, issuing their own annual circular to drovers. The Santa Fe Railroad again hired cattle dealer Peyton Montgomery as trail agent. The Wichita city council employed Jim Bryden, as in 1872, to serve alongside the company's man. These two joined the two Ellsworth representatives at Pond Creek in early May, where they contended over northbound Chisholm Trail traffic until it slacked off a month later—a small drive having resulted from the 1873 disaster. To supplement these efforts Wichitans secretly paid several drovers to bring their herds to Wichita as a means of encouraging others to follow suit. In May the city council marked out a new trail from Cowskin Creek to the Santa Fe's commodious new stockyard on the west side of the river, built on ground leased by the city, which was designed for temporarily holding herds when the pens at the railroad station were full. Paying out nearly $200 for ground and right-of-way leases, the council also spent at least another $146 to meet settlers' damage claims. Identifiable municipal expenditures for cattle trade recruitment in 1874 totaled something like $2,500. No evidence of the raising of any substantial private fund has survived.[8]

---

way (Kansas City, 1874). The fold-out map itself is reproduced in Robert W. Baughman: *Kansas in Maps* (Topeka, 1961), p. 80. Actually, the Kansas quarantine line had not been altered since 1872, and Wichita lay immediately adjacent to the free zone.

[7] Ellsworth *Reporter*, Apr. 16, 23, 30, June 18, 1874.

[8] Wichita *Eagle*, Apr. 23, 30, May 21, 1874, Apr. 22, 1875; Ellsworth *Reporter*, May 14, June 11, 1874; Wichita Council Record, A, 372–73, 381, B, 17; Wichita *Beacon*, Apr. 21, 1875; contract dated

The public relations conflict between Ellsworth and Wichita once more assumed its usual tenor. Wichita, while coping again with its own settler discontent directed against the cattle trade, could point to some considerable agitation at Ellsworth. For the third year in a row Wichita shipped more cattle than her main competitor; the figures amounted to 50,253 and 18,500 head respectively.[9] This season proved to be the last in which Ellsworth functioned as a cattle market.

The four years' competition over the Chisholm Trail trade saw certain differences in the preservation programs of Wichita and Ellsworth, due both to varying circumstances and to differing community attitudes. Saddled with a herd law—although its existence was for a time officially ignored—and a substantial rural immigration into that part of the county embracing both cattle trail and herding ground, Wichita's townspeople consistently employed money and energy to calm settler discontent. This necessarily remained a large part of their annual effort. In contrast, Ellsworth's outlying settlers were fewer, of much less political influence, and without herd law protection; townsmen simply ignored rural agitation. The other obvious difference was that Wichitans used tax monies generously to attract and protect the cattle trade, showing a tenacious determination to retain the profitable traffic as a kind of public enterprise.

May 13, 1874, in Wichita Miscellaneous Papers; two contracts dated May 19, 1874, in ibid.; Sante Fe, *Annual Report . . . 1874* (Boston, 1874), p. 19. The final figure is approximate, since no total cattle expenditure is listed in the published report for April 1874 through March 1875. Cattle trade expenditures during this twelve-month (and season-overlapping) period amounted to about $2,700—or 20.5 per cent of the city's total expenditures.

[9] Wichita *Eagle*, May 21, Dec. 3, 1874; Kansas Pacific: *Annual Report . . . 1874* (St. Louis, 1875), p. 14.

[5]

IN THE EIGHTIES the competition for the cattle trade lost most of its ferocity. After 1880, for one thing, the Santa Fe Railroad alone controlled the shipments at Dodge City, Caldwell, and Hunnewell, the three latter-day markets more or less dividing the Texas cattle trade in Kansas. No one of them was about to succeed in enlisting Santa Fe support in a competitive effort. Then, too, the Texas Panhandle and Indian Territory cattlemen who increasingly monopolized shipments at the cattle towns were much less subject to shifts of allegiance than the trail drivers of past years had been. In many cases these ranchers lived in close geographic and economic proximity either to Dodge City or to the almost interchangeable Caldwell and Hunnewell shipping facilities. The respective business communities of Dodge and Caldwell never lost their taste for competition, true enough, but the impetus seemed to be less a need to survive at the other's expense than a simple question of relative status—specifically, which of the two towns was to remain *the* great cattle market of the West in the eyes of the outside world. That their propaganda warfare concluded with a kind of adolescent attention-getting merely reflected the decline of the authentic competitive struggle characterizing the seventies. The famous Dodge City bullfight and Caldwell's compulsive response serve as the most revealing cases in point.

To Alonzo B. Webster went the approbation of his fellows for having conceived the original notion to celebrate the Fourth of July, 1884, with a "genuine Spanish bullfight"—presumably the first to be held on United States soil. The scheme occurred to this saloon keeper and ex-mayor of Dodge City in May of that year. Having examined the law books and claiming to find no statute forbidding such a thing, he seriously proposed it to his Front Street colleagues. Within an hour townsmen contributed $3,000 to implement the scheme, and the following day brought the balance of the $10,000 thought necessary for expenses. Announcements then went out to various leading Kansas newspapers, a device serving the dual purpose of proclaiming the unique festivities to be held at Dodge and eliciting expressions of editorial shock and dismay that only encouraged a wider interest in the project.

The enthusiastic Dodge City business community organized itself to push the plan to fulfillment, honoring Webster with the position of manager. Working through a Mexican attorney, Webster commandeered a troop of five part-time bullfighters from Chihuahua. A drover believed to be the first man to bring a herd of Texas cattle to Dodge was appointed to select the bulls. The promoters then constructed an amphitheater near town and arranged for associated entertainment. To the east, meanwhile, churchmen, reform editors, and other outraged spokesmen of respectability looked on in horror, hardly able to believe that a barbarous display heretofore associated with one of the least palatable features of Latin culture would actually take place in Kansas.

But take place it did. An estimated three to four thousand visitors turned up in Dodge City for the two-day spectacle. Although the attendance was smaller than the promoters had hoped, gate receipts evidently provided enough to defray their expenses. Most important in their view, the event attracted a special correspondent from the New York *Herald*, another from the St. Louis *Globe-Democrat*, and a third representing a number of Chicago newspapers. The national president of the American Society for the Prevention of Cruelty to Animals added to the excitement by vainly wiring Governor George W. Glick to stop the fight. As an unplanned climax to the ritual murder of the bulls, finally, a handsome gambler named Dave St. Clair shot and killed a young Texas drover in A. B. Webster's saloon. It was all too wonderfully wicked.[1]

A portion of Caldwell's business community reacted instantly upon learning of Dodge City's novel project. Editor Samuel Berry of the Caldwell *Standard* urged prompt action. "Caldwell," he insisted, "is not to be outdone by Dodge City or any other town that wears hair." Plans were already under way, he announced, for Caldwell's own bullfight that "if worked up and properly advertised . . . would draw like a circus." Under the supervision of a citizens' committee, grandstands were built and an arena enclosed. But Berry spoke too soon; many townsmen nursed doubts about the propriety of a bullfight. In the end the community's July Fourth festivities offered only conventional rodeo events. A considerable number of Caldwellites deserted their own town on the appointed day to witness the more pungent entertainment at Dodge. "Caldwell is way behind the times as a cattle town," a Dodge City editor taunted. "They didn't have any bull fight on the 4th."

Caldwell's businessmen, thus challenged, felt obligated to respond. Two months later Editor Berry announced his fellow townsmen's agreement to a Spanish bullfight for each day of the agricultural fair to be held at Caldwell in early October. The issue carrying this bold proclamation was Berry's last before going out of business as a local newspaperman. Further promotion fell to his rival, Tell Walton, editor of the Caldwell *Journal*. Walton, an original opponent of the scheme, reluctantly changed sides upon being convinced that the entrepre-

[1] Accounts of the Dodge City bullfight have appeared in many places. All derive from the original article by Kirke Mechem: "The Bull Fight at Dodge," *Kansas Historical Quarterly*, II (1933), 294–308. For the shooting by St. Clair, which occurred late in the evening after the second day's bullfight, see Nyle H. Miller and Joseph W. Snell (eds.): *Why the West Was Wild* (Topeka, 1963), pp. 476, 612–13.

neurial consensus favored it. He was promptly appointed secretary of the association charged with sponsorship.

Again the Kansas press reacted in a universally hostile fashion. Encouraged thereby, a number of Caldwell church-goers mobilized a week before the fair and pledged themselves "to use all legitimate means to prevent such a display of wickedness in our midst." The means they selected proved eminently fitting, and consisted of taking or sending to the newspaper editors of the region and the state an impassioned appeal for a press boycott. All newspaper publicity ceased abruptly. The spectacle indeed took place—but amid a virtual news blackout. Such was the effect of this ingenious turning of tables that the Caldwell affair to this day has escaped even the popularizers and the folklorists.

Apparently the only extant contemporary account of Caldwell's bullfight, a short note ventured by a dissident Wellington editor, dismissed it as "one of the tamest things of the season. The mad bulls that we heard so much about didn't have life enough to brush the flies off." Many years later an old-timer recalled that in truth the only excitement occurred when one of the enraged animals tried to jump the fence, tearing down a considerable section of it and causing spectators to disperse "in a mad scramble." Even Tell Walton, in printing a lengthy summary of fair events, dared not violate the publicity embargo. "The JOURNAL is through with the Spanish bull fight now," he observed cryptically, "and is ready to boost up that revival or any other enterprise that will benefit Caldwell, financially, morally or religiously."[2]

So ended the cattle town flirtation with a unique promotional device. It seems no coincidence that it hap-

[2] Caldwell *Standard*, June 19, 26, July 3, 24, Sept. 11, 1884; Caldwell *Journal*, Oct. 2, 16, 1884; Wellington *Wellingtonian*, Oct. 2, 1884; Wellington *Standard*, Oct. 4, 18, 1884; Caldwell News; *Golden Anniversary Edition* (Caldwell, 1937), p. 16.

pened at the very moment when the businessmen of Dodge and Caldwell—as other cattle town entrepreneurs before them—were losing their grip on the cattle trade, not through defeat in intercommunity rivalry but through external circumstances on which they could exert little effective influence.

V

The Rural Dimension

[1]

DESPITE THE COLLECTIVE COMMITMENT to range cattle as a general economic base, many cattle town people retained a vision of their communities as service centers for outlying farmers. Underneath all the rhetoric about the cattle trade and its promise of commercial profits and urban growth, the notion of an orthodox agricultural fate persisted. It was only natural that journalistic spokesmen for the cattle town people sometimes let this concept of the ultimate destiny escape into print.

"Our cattle trade is a big thing," a Caldwell editor reflected one day during his town's second shipping season, "and helps out wonderfully, but after all, for a steady business, and a continuous air of prosperity, a good, prosperous farming community is what every town in Kansas requires to make it grow steady and surely." Such occasional comments seemingly fused an emotional commitment to the country town ideal with a candid recognition that the cattle trade economy was only a transient phase of local development. "Some of our readers think we have a good thing in the Texas cattle trade," reflected George A. Atwood at the end of Ellsworth's first successful cattle season. "But," he warned,

> some of these morning[s] they will wake up and find the cattle and their keepers are departed. We want the cattle

trade two or three years longer, the town needs it and so does the county, but at the best we can only have it for a short time . . . "and what then?" That is the question. I will tell you what we want—we want farmers!

And even at Dodge City an ebullient editor could not refrain from fancying a prosperous agrarian future for the area. "Ten years from this time," he predicted, "Dodge City may be a city of 20,000 inhabitants, it may have all the business, wealth and airs of a city. These vast prairies will be thickly settled with rich farmers. There will be thrift, enterprise and luxury."

Yet the apparently typical cattle town businessman viewed the relatively impecunious frontier farmer with tepid interest. From saloonmen to hardware store owners they welcomed ruralites as a subsidiary clientele, but the day-to-day cash value represented by cattlemen, cowboys, and associated transients remained a potent argument that determined at least short-run commercial loyalties. "The grocery man can tell a stockman's trade from a granger['s]," quipped a spokesman for the cattle interest at Dodge, "in this way; If a stockman wants a jug of vinegar, he pays for both. If a granger wants the same, he wants to pay for the vinegar and have the 25¢ jug thrown in. A portion of the 25 cents will then be invested in crackers and cheese." Such anecdotes about the sturdy yeoman as a marginal consumer evidently reflected the sentiments of a good segment of any cattle town business community.[1]

Somewhat paradoxically, the advantages of the range cattle trade to local businessmen grew, rather than decreased, as trailing gave way to ranching in the last half of the era. This change measurably ironed out the summertime heights and wintertime depths inherent in an

---

[1] Caldwell *Commercial*, July 21, 1881; Ellsworth *Reporter*, Nov. 14, 1872; Dodge City *Times*, Feb. 23, 1878; Dodge City *Cowboy*, May 30, 1885.

economic dependence on the trail trade alone. Large-scale local stock raising originated in the practice of wintering Texas cattle, a commercial venture as old as the cattle town itself.[2] From the very first it was also an enterprise in which townsmen participated, since—in its pristine form, at least—it demanded no special skills, supervision, or substantial investment beyond the purchase price of the animals. Speculators, both urban and rural, customarily bought cheaply from the livestock remaining unsold in the cattle town markets late each autumn. Turned loose to forage for themselves, the cattle that managed to survive winter's rigors emerged thin in the spring, but rapidly fattened on the new prairie grasses in time for early summer sales. Such animals looked quite desirable in comparison to the gaunt longhorns just off the trail; in addition, they were no longer splenic fever carriers, which also increased their salability.

For some townsmen the winter speculation in cattle grew into an important annual venture. In the winter of 1874–75, for example, one of Wichita's largest capitalists, James R. Mead, grazed fifteen thousand head of cattle on a range in outlying Barber County. Twelve hundred of these were his own stock, purchased the previous autumn; he probably herded the remainder on shares. After about 1876, in addition to this standard enterprise, stock raising the year round with improved breeds developed on the vacant ranges lying beyond Dodge City and below Caldwell. At Dodge more and more established businessmen gravitated into full-fledged beef production. Among the most notable of the town's stock raisers, for example, were a tavern keeper, a delicatessen owner, and a boot-

---

[2] Due to lack of a good demand for Texas cattle in the terminal markets in the fall of 1867, many longhorns were bought by residents in and near Abilene for grazing over the winter. H. H. Hazlett to Samuel J. Crawford, Nov. 19, 1867, Governors' Correspondence (Livestock), KSHS; Junction City *Union*, Nov. 16, 1867.

181 · *The Rural Dimension*

maker.³ Caldwell, meanwhile, welcomed to its bosom the big Cherokee Strip ranchers, who moved their residences into town in order to partake of its social amenities. From 1880 onward these prosperous enterprisers heavily influenced the city's economic life, providing the impetus behind such diverse projects as a bank and a hotel.⁴ At both places, in any case, cattle and commercial interests solidly coalesced as never before.

For most of the period farmers on a cattle town's nearby prairies who desired, say, a herd law to protect their unfenced fields from the ravages of livestock tended to find themselves opposed by a united front of drover, local stockman, and town businessman.⁵ "The denizen of little Dodge City," reported a perceptive visitor of late 1877,

> declares with a great deal of confidence that the region round about the place is good for nothing for agricultural purposes. He says the seasons are too dry; that the country is good for nothing but grazing. The desire of his heart is the father of the statement. He is content with just what is, and he wants that to remain. He wants the Texas cattle drover and his associations and surroundings to be a presence and a heritage forever.

"Its business has grown up wholly upon its cattle interests," wrote another observer at Dodge a few years later, "and . . . the tilling of the soil is carefully discouraged as inimical to the interests of the cattle trade." Whether or not by design, such efforts discouraged rural settlement.

³ Wichita *Eagle*, Mar. 18, June 17, 1875; Dodge City *Times*, June 23, 1877; Dodge City *Globe*, Feb. 24, 1880.
⁴ See discussion in Chapter VI below.
⁵ Caldwell, of course, was a special case, in that its principal conflict with farmers took the form of defending its adjacent and tributary Indian Territory trails, grazing grounds, and ranches from militant "Boomers" who wanted to have that area opened for agricultural settlement. See Chapter VIII below.

An Ellsworth County resident deplored the attitude of those

> who sneer at the idea of the county's adaptation to agri-
> cultural pursuits; and when strangers, induced by the
> gratifying reports in the columns of the press in relation
> to our beautiful surroundings, come and determine for
> themselves how well the printed statements accord with
> the facts . . . and then are deliberately informed "that the
> country is not good for farming, but is very good for
> stock," no wonder they leave disgusted. . . . This "dog in
> the manger" policy, which has been characteristic of
> Ellsworth for years, must be discontinued.[6]

Caught between clashing economic interests, most
cattle town editors tried to reconcile the contenders until
the inevitable "natural" solution came to pass. While usually presenting themselves as the farmers' friend, their
first loyalties lay with their fellow townsfolk. Their primary efforts thus centered on encouraging local agriculture to accommodate itself to town interests, rather than
the other way around. This primarily meant transforming
the typical frontier farmer's predilection for staple crops.
Three main alternatives were proposed.

First, editors urged farmers to specialize in garden
and dairy products for the local transient market. A Caldwell editor, for example, suggested that "A market garden
near this city of three or four acres, properly attended to
would be worth more as a money making scheme than a
farm of 160 acres usually is by the common methods of
farming in the county."

Second, editors and other urban spokesmen solicited
rural attention to growing feed grains for drovers and
local stock raisers. A Dodge City journalist pictured the
result of such a perfected agricultural relationship as a
veritable utopia:

[6] Dodge City *Globe*, Jan. 1, 1878, May 31, 1881; Ellsworth *Reporter*, July 17, 1873.

No happier state of society could exist in this or in any other country, than to have one half of our people producing grain and farm products while the other half raised and bred stock. What a delightful equalization of interests this would be, we hope to see it exist in south-western Kansas.

Finally, farmers were encouraged to abandon cereals for livestock. "Farming or Stock-Raising?" asked Ellsworth's editor, and the answer was both: grow feed grain, serve it to cattle, then recognize a return from selling the fattened animals. Traditionalist resistance to this concept in the surrounding countryside finally moved a Caldwell editor to impatience:

> "The JOURNAL pays too much attention to the stock interest," is the complaint of some parties in our neighborhood who think the sale of a pint of peanuts is a first class business transaction. . . . The farmer, in this country, who combines all efforts to extract what he can from the soil without regard to proper feed and care of stock will not make his profession a success; and if he further carries his prejudice against stock so as to condemn everybody who says a word in favor of stock raising, he will, most assuredly, come out at the little end of the horn.

All cattle town spokesmen gladly documented personal examples to support their advice. For instance, a Dodge City correspondent revealed for the edification of local yeomen that "Wm. Britt after farming for four years, has come to the wise conclusion that stock raising pays better."[7]

[2]

FARMERS' REACTIONS to cattle town attitudes, as might be expected, varied somewhat. Not all farmers displayed

---

[7] Caldwell *Post*, Jan. 4, 1883; Dodge City *Globe*, June 25, 1878, Nov. 7, 1882; Ellsworth *Reporter*, Aug. 14, 1873; Caldwell *Journal*, Nov. 1, 1883.

hostility. Among them were men who had successfully adjusted to the transient-inflated cattle town market for products of the field.[8] Others no doubt felt as did the rural realist living near Wichita, who noted that a farmer's main profits came not from foodstuffs but from rising real estate values that increased in proportion to his property's proximity to the nearest large town. Rural citizens, he argued, should thus identify closely with Wichita's urban development. And not all rural antagonisms, of course, were directed townward. One strikingly class-conscious Ellsworth County settler, for example, saw the principal enemy as the countryside's "rich men" (rural stock raisers) who "care no more for the success of the poor man [the small farmer] than for the life of a troublesome flea." Nor did all conflicts in which farmers engaged fit a neat rural-urban polarity. The rural attempt to make a free public facility out of the hated Wichita toll bridge, for instance, while characterized by anti-town rhetoric, actually was long frustrated by "east side" farmers who did not need the structure.[9]

The general situation aside, a number of specific grievances emerged as persistent catalysts of rural irritation. Among these were the costs occasioned by cattle town felonies, district court prosecutions of which were financed by the county at large. These ran to considerable sums when they included sheriff's fees for returning escapees and boarding expenses for prisoners awaiting trial. Rural taxpayers understandably objected to bearing the financial burden of an abnormal crime rate caused by the cattle trade. "And the farmers had to pay for prosecuting

[8] See, for examples, a farmer's testimony in the Wichita *Eagle*, Nov. 27, 1873, and descriptions of the attitudes of the Lyon's Creek settlers toward the Abilene market in Abilene *Chronicle*, Nov. 13, 1876; J. B. Edwards: *Early Days in Abilene* (Abilene, 1940), p. 8.

[9] Wichita *Eagle*, Dec. 18, 1873; Ellsworth *Reporter*, June 12, 1873. For the Wichita bridge issue see discussion in Chapter VI below.

the criminals," was one Dickinson County settler's telling conclusion to a catalogue of Abilene wickedness.[1]

Another irritant was a pronounced cattle trade bias in the allocation of local credit. Drovers obtained bank loans at 4 per cent, complained a farmer near Wichita (and no one contradicted him), while farmers paid anywhere from 36 to 60 per cent per year. "The farmer," he continued, "can't borrow a dollar from the banks on his land or anything that is his except his note with undoubted security for thirty to ninety days, but the Texas [cattle] man can borrow ten thousand dollars on his individual note without indorsement."[2]

A third main source of rural antipathy was that funds drawn from the public for the general improvement, both tax monies and private subscriptions, usually went toward accommodating and encouraging the cattle trade instead of agriculture. This can be seen in the example that follows, which also demonstrates how specific rural-urban issues could quickly ignite eruptions of generalized animosity.

As recorded in a previous chapter, Ellsworth's business community in 1872 raised a subscription of $4,000 for subsidizing the erection of a hotel that it hoped would ensure the seasonal location there of the Texas cattle trade. A second proposed project, a public fund to underwrite a steam mill to service local agriculture, went begging.

That winter a farmer revived the mill project. Writing to the local newspaper under the pseudonym "Home In-

---

[1] Abilene *Chronicle*, Jan. 26, 1871.

[2] Wichita *Beacon*, Nov. 4, 1874. Similar specifics concerning rates paid by settlers near Wichita appear in ibid., Jan. 6, 1874; Wichita *Eagle*, Jan. 2, Nov. 23, 1873. For a comprehensive discussion of the frontier mortgage in the second half of the nineteenth century see Allan G. Bogue: *Money at Interest: The Farm Mortgage on the Middle Border* (Ithaca, N.Y., 1955).

terests," he called for a bond issue to finance the mill, which would not only encourage wheat raising within the county, he insisted, but would "bring money among us instead of allowing our merchants to gather up what money we have and send it east to support farmers and laborers who . . . have a surplus." At that moment the men of Ellsworth were busy promoting a bond levy for a second railroad through town, but one of them took time to put "Home Interests" in his place. Disguised as "Go To Work," he impatiently defended local merchants and counterattacked with an allegation that the county's farmers, with few exceptions, were simply indolent grumblers. "I wonder if Mr. 'Home Interest[s],' " he wrote, ". . . believes that anything could be done to make his farmer neighbors plant more wheat, don't he know that it takes WORK to sow, harrow and thrash the wheat. Don't he know that the farmers in Western Kansas as a class do not like to work?"

The original writer hotly retorted. He termed "Go To Work" and his fellow Ellsworthites mere "dry goods loafers." "Every day I go to town," he charged, "I see him with his feet perched upon a warm stove whiffing away at a dirty old pipe wondering why the tobacco burns out so soon, thus compelling him to do a little work to fill up the pipe." Some farmers, he admitted, were not laboring as hard as they might, but most were simply poor, which explained the lack of improvements on their holdings that "Go To Work" had observed. But if that gentleman and his fellows

who have nothing to do but to ha! ha! and crack jokes, would go to work themselves, and . . . improve the town as much even as these farmers do the country, they would be better employed, than wearing out the "underpinning" of their pantaloons while sucking away at that dirty pipe.

His urban opponent retaliated with a lengthy bill of particulars against "Home Interests" and his "legions of thriftless, shiftless, do-nothing neighbors." Farmers wouldn't raise wheat, he contended, because they would have to haul it to Salina to get it ground; they would rather buy bacon, lard, and corn meal than raise it; they wouldn't grow sorghum to make their own molasses because the store-bought product tasted better; if they broke an axe handle they would come to town and buy a new one rather than fashion one themselves; and so forth. "But if they will renounce their indolent habits," he loftily conceded, "I am in favor of the bonds to build the mill, for in that case I think it would be a good investment."

The enraged rural spokesman answered with a long missive again savagely critical of Ellsworth males, two thirds of whom he described as "drones on the body corporate"—loafing for a living or "just carrying on a little business as a cloak for their idleness."[3] After a couple more exchanges, however, Editor Atwood snuffed out this inelegant debate over relative rural-urban energy output, which had nevertheless provided a rare and startling glimpse into the underlying clash of attitudes.

One can surmise from the really vicious isolated comments occasionally reaching print that similar reciprocal sentiments circulated quite frequently. Several examples from Dodge City survive. "Damn the grangers," a citizen there reportedly exclaimed. "I wish it wouldn't rain this summer so that they would starve out." Some Dodge merchants, in fact, were quoted as saying they would "rather see the devil coming than a granger." The townsmen, charged a nearby rural editor, "never loose an opportunity to misrepresent and abuse the Granger as they call them, they have been frequently heard to wish 'that

[3] Ellsworth *Reporter*, Jan. 16, 23, 30, Feb. 6, 13, 1873.

the agriculturalists would be driven out of the County as they had no business here.[']" Far from desiring a prosperous surrounding farm community, he said, they "would rather the set[t]ler would sell ev[e]ry horse[,] cow[,] pig and chicken he has[,] spend the money with them, and then get out of the country." Farmers everywhere returned such compliments in kind. "There seems to be a good many of the farmers who continually keep crying down Wichita," revealed a settler near that place, "—'wishing she would sink,' and that she would 'bust up,' and a good many more as foolish and unmanly expressions."[4]

Farmers responded to a general sense of rejection by town dwellers with one of the few concrete weapons they had for wielding important power: county politics. Even when a minority in terms of numbers, they sometimes controlled the balance between urban factions contending for political dominance. The initiative, however, was frequently with the townsmen. In 1878, for example, Dodge City's uppermost clique retained its grasp on county offices by shrewdly gaining the endorsement of the rural Greenbacker element, outbidding its rivals for the easily manipulated rural German vote, and in general displaying a cynical affection, as an opposition editor put it, for "the 'dear farmer,' whom they have cursed and abused ever since those honest tillers of the soil have dared to settle on our lands."[5]

The difficulties inherent in any genuine amalgamation of rural-urban political action, on the other hand, appeared at Ellsworth in 1872. The town's business community had split along the lines of diverging city real estate interests, the specific issue being the location of a new courthouse. The less influential faction culled back-

[4] Dodge City *Globe*, Apr. 23, 1878; Spearville *Enterprise*, June 29, 1878; Spearville *News*, Feb. 14, 1880; Wichita *Eagle*, July 17, 1873.
[5] Dodge City *Globe*, Sept. 24, Nov. 5, 12, 1878.

ing from the rural populace and won the courthouse site. Infighting then spread into politics, each side seeking to undermine the other by gaining control of county offices. The recent victors enthusiastically cooperated with their newly won rural supporters to capture the Republican nominations, which resulted in a slate neatly shared by town and rural candidates. This success, in that normally Republican county, should have propelled the coalition ticket to easy victory at the polls. Yet it went down to defeat. Although Ellsworth's editor declined to comment on the outcome, the voting statistics reflect how fragile, in fact, had been the rural-urban experiment. Not one member of the amalgamation ticket gained office. The town's Republicans, it turned out, had failed to support rural members of the slate and the countrymen refused to vote for the townsmen. One farmer, for instance, carried nearly every rural precinct but captured a mere seven votes in Ellsworth. At the other extreme, a local business-man on the Republican ticket carried the town but lost heavily in every rural precinct. In short, rural-urban hostilities cut so deeply into the local social fabric that a temporary political alliance simply could not mend the gap.[6]

As another example, a straight rural-urban contest occurred at Wichita in 1873. The county's farmers, stirred by the Patrons of Husbandry movement, captured the Republican machinery of Sedgwick County that year and emerged victorious in an election battle with a Wichita ticket. As at Ellsworth in 1872, the local editor did not choose to analyze the outcome forthrightly, but the statistics betray the geographical split. The Wichita-dominated slate, with but two exceptions, carried the town handily as well as its principal suburb; it was thoroughly overwhelmed in large Republican margins

[6] Ellsworth *Reporter*, especially Dec. 28, 1871, June 20, Aug. 29, Sept. 5, Oct. 10, Nov. 14, 1872.

from the countryside. In at least one rural precinct, furthermore, many voters scratched the name of a Republican candidate from their ballots, as one farmer admitted, "for no other reason than that he lived in Wichita."[7]

[3]

THE TOWN-VERSUS-COUNTRY dimension of county political conflict left a somewhat blurred image as it emerged from the ministrations of cattle town editors, but contention rising out of the agricultural distress of 1874–75 and 1878–81 survives in more explicit form. The issue in both instances was the actual extent of rural destitution and the manner in which it was to be relieved.

The year 1874 was one of general rural catastrophe in Kansas. Midsummer's crops sagged under week after week of blazing sun, struggling restlessly against hot winds, drying and withering. When in early August the skies finally darkened they poured forth not rain but fluttering waves of Rocky Mountain locusts. Working their way across the state from northwest to southeast, the ravenous insects rapidly disposed of what harvest there would have been. Especially hard hit were recently and partially settled counties, where farmers found themselves least able to weather the rigors of natural disaster.[8]

For sensitive Kansans the old 1860–61 territorial emergency, when their pioneer destitute were saved from famine only through massive eastern charity, still rankled.[9] The current threat of widespread destitution, if grim, remained essentially a rural prospect. Those not directly or immediately affected tended to regard another

---

[7] Wichita *Eagle*, Aug. 7, Sept. 4, 18, Oct. 17, 23, Nov. 6, Dec. 11, 1873.

[8] Kansas State Board of Agriculture: *Annual Report . . . 1874* (Topeka, 1874), *passim*.

[9] George W. Glick: "The Drought of 1860," *Transactions of the Kansas State Historical Society*, IX (1905–06).

solicitation of out-of-state aid as far more disastrous than hard times on the farm. The testy booster fundamentalism of such minds recoiled at the lack of progress implied in again advertising the commonwealth's distress to stimulate outside help.[1]

Nevertheless, the Kansas legislature refused to extend material assistance in that recession year, in effect throwing the problem back to local authorities, who were offered only the unattractive expedient of county bond issues. Even the official Kansas Central Relief Committee, organized by Governor Thomas A. Osborn in November, was devised as much to counter bad out-of-state publicity as to administer charity and only reluctantly assumed other than passive aid distribution duties. Late that winter Congress finally provided federal assistance, but until then localities mainly had to cope as best they could with their own resources or what they could solicit elsewhere.[2]

Sedgwick County was one of the areas severely stricken. Wichita, its county seat, had come to welcome the flow of rural settlement as a replacement for the already declining cattle trade, trusting to the expenditure of substantial sums to reconcile the two interests. Now, in

[1] See the editorial from a Salina newspaper quoted approvingly in the Ellsworth *Reporter*, Nov. 19, 1874, for an example of proof that this attitude was not confined to the large urban centers in the northeast quarter of the state.

[2] For the original public relations concept behind the state relief committee see *House Journal*, 1875, pp. 289–90; "Address" (circular dated Nov. 20, 1874), Kansas Central Relief Committee Papers (Relief, 1874–75), KSHS.

There is no general account of the state's response to the 1874 crisis save that included in a survey of western crop disasters of the seventies in Gilbert C. Fite: *The Farmers' Frontier, 1865–1900* (New York, 1966), chap. iv. While solid enough on most matters, the author has clothed urban attitudes toward the rural destitute with an undifferentiated generosity that, at least in Kansas, it simply did not possess. Clearly his opinion research was deficient. For example, he quotes an October issue of the Wichita *Eagle* to support his picture of genuine urban humanitarianism; but as the present chapter will indicate, such a characterization of *Eagle* rhetoric is abundantly premature.

the autumn of 1874, some of the county's farmers who had the means to do so left to wait out the crisis back East. Most, however, stood fast by choice or force of circumstance, trusting to traditional rural pluck and hopes for a mild winter. Already worried about routine taxes, farmers strongly rejected two proposed bond levies for destitute aid, placing their faith instead in various voluntary township associations as a means for collective survival. These organizations, in turn, sponsored agents to solicit charity in the East, especially in neighborhoods from which many of their township's settlers had migrated not so long before.[3]

Still, with November's frigid gusts came a feeling in many rural breasts that their snug, comparatively well-off Wichita neighbors ought to initiate some help. "The question arises," wrote a farmer living out on the wind-whipped prairie west of town,

> what is to be done for the poor and destitute of this country? Let them . . . suck their thumbs as a generous lady said, or "let them starve and be damned" as a high toned gentleman in Wichita said last week? . . . A majority of those needing help have families of small children to support. One lady in Wichita said last week that they had no business to have a lot of young'uns to support. . . . But it is a fact, and it can't be got over.

The writer suggested that townspeople contribute $1,-400 or $1,500 for local relief, adding that Wichita businessmen had already garnered "thousands of dollars"

[3] Wichita *Eagle*, July 16, 1874 ff.; Wichita *Beacon*, Aug. 19, 1874 ff., Mar. 31, 1875. County authorities everywhere, apparently reflecting local opinion, utilized various legal reasonings in refusing to extend routine poor relief to the temporarily destitute. Whether aid by county warrant (the normal vehicle of poor relief) was to be forthcoming depended on interpretations officials gave statutes covering care of the poor and restrictions on the amount of taxation and warrant issuance. Kansas State Board of Agriculture: *Annual Report . . . 1875* (Topeka, 1875), p. 34; *Kansas Statutes*, 1868, pp. 294–95, 621.

from the countrymen's custom. Voluntary aid now would be no great sacrifice, he concluded, since it could be made up again by enormous cattle trade profits the following summer.[4]

Not all female Wichitans subscribed to the flinty feminine views quoted by this informant, and under the leadership of a prominent local matron of liberal and humanitarian inclinations a number of them had already reconstituted the Ladies' Aid Society of Wichita to prepare for the winter's needs. This group soon gained the support of interested Wichitans of both sexes, who in November met and endorsed it as a fund-raising and aid-distributing organization for all of Sedgwick County.[5]

Many countrymen, however, looked upon this town effort in their behalf with less than wholehearted enthusiasm. A potent factor impelling a jaundiced view from the country was the attitude displayed by perhaps the city's most important spokesman, Marshall M. Murdock of the Wichita *Eagle*, who was also his area's delegate to the state relief committee. Having backed the Grange-dominated Republican ticket in 1873, he had obtained a reputation as the farmer's friend. In the present crisis Murdock's journalistic rival, the editor of the Wichita *Beacon*, willingly expressed the rural viewpoint; but this fact only highlighted what many farmers felt to be Murdock's foul betrayal. Despite some initial ambivalence, Murdock had soon come round to the urban opinion that publicity was more to be feared than suffering. Early in the

[4] Wichita *Beacon*, Nov. 11, 1874.

[5] Wichita *Eagle*, Sept. 24, Nov. 5, 19, 1874; Wichita *Beacon*, Sept. 30, Nov. 4, 18, 1874. The guiding genius of the Ladies' Aid was Harriet Letcher Fisher, first cousin to General James A. Garfield. Her husband was Benjamin Fisher, a prosperous attorney whose proposal for a $13,000 system of town and county public works as a means of destitute relief was evidently deemed too radical a proposal for serious consideration. A. T. Andreas: *History of the State of Kansas* (Chicago, 1883), pp. 1395–96; Wichita *Beacon*, Oct. 28, 1874.

autumn he began to deflate alarming reports from the countryside. Only newcomers were really needy, he said, and in any case the solution to what ailed local farmers was the planting of less corn and more wheat. Murdock dismissed complainers as "lazy louts, dead beats and shirks," adding that "the quicker they sell their one hundred and sixty acres and 'pull out' the better it will be . . . for all concerned."

In November angered farmers of one township reported that Marsh Murdock's ill-advised statements had sabotaged their efforts to get out-of-state aid. Their agents in Indiana, they testified, had had to suspend operations because of a widely circulated copy of the *Eagle* that insisted no destitution existed in Sedgwick County and that all aid-seekers were imposters.[6] This attack precipitated Murdock's strongest retort. All this "whining" for charity, he raged, "is simply deplorably hurtful." Most of those who asked for aid, to his view, were "constitutional beggars" and those who,

> easily discouraged, expected that after their homesteads were secured the farming would attend to itself, without effort upon their part. . . . Such were satisfied to hold a claim, depend upon a little corn and potatoes—hoping for these even to grow spontaneous[ly]—and spend their time in loafing around, and drinking bad whisky and waiting for lands to take a rise.

In closing his lengthy tirade Murdock proclaimed on behalf of his fellow townsmen that "any action that tends to keep solid men from settling among us, or any talk that deters farmers of means and experience from coming to help us work out the true destinies of this broad valley," would be resisted.[7]

[6] Wichita *Eagle*, Sept. 17, 1874; Wichita *Beacon*, Nov. 18, 25, 1874.
[7] Wichita *Eagle*, Nov. 19, 1874. The state relief committee's plans for a December distribution of clothing to the Kansas destitute did not

In this last remark Murdock exposed the crux of the urban standpoint. As another Wichitan later explained to some perplexed Illinois residents who had received conflicting arguments from Sedgwick:

> The sentiment of the leading men of this county is divided on the question of soliciting aid from the east, and the reason of this is that . . . a great many who own property say that it will retard immigration, and they do not want the true condition of the "Great Arkansas Valley" known, for they say that "this valley has been advertised to the world as one of the best agricultural countries in existence, and if we go east to solicit aid to keep body and soul together, how can we ask people to immigrate here?"

No matter what Wichita objectors said, he observed, the grasshopper devastation had "left all in poor circumstances and nearly half of the people destitute."[8]

Statistics bore out this estimate. Sedgwick in 1874–75 contained at least five thousand rural residents. Of this number roughly two thousand, half of them children under fifteen, remained in need of food and/or clothing throughout the winter.[9] With perhaps two fifths, then, of

include distribution within the area (Sedgwick, Sumner, and Cowley counties) that Murdock represented on the committee. In a letter to Lieutenant Governor E. S. Stover, committee chairman, Murdock blamed the published report of the state board of agriculture for this oversight. Critics, however, subsequently revealed that Murdock himself was responsible by having assured the authorities that no destitution of consequence existed in his area. He did not dispute this charge. Driven to exasperation by visiting delegations of sufferers ("It will *set me crazy*," he wrote Stover), Murdock sought to retract his thoughtless act by means of a complicated subterfuge, but the upshot was that his area obtained only a token distribution. Murdock to Stover, Dec. 5, 1874, Governors' Correspondence (Relief); Wichita *Beacon*, Dec. 30, 1874, Jan. 27, Feb. 10, 1875.

[8] Wichita *Beacon*, Jan. 27, 1875.

[9] Board of Agriculture: *Annual Report 1874*, p. 199; ibid. *1875*, pp. 39, 403; *House Exec. Doc. No. 28*, 44 Cong., 1 sess., p. 8; Wichita *Eagle*, Mar. 25, 1875. The population of Wichita at this period was

the rural populace in serious straits, both the Wichita ladies and the various township organizations found themselves hard pressed to meet legitimate demands.

As a cheerless Christmas season approached a new factor was thrust into the already contentious relief situation—the Santa Fe Railroad announced free transportation for relief supplies addressed to county aid associations, provided each enjoyed formal endorsement by the respective county officers. This spurred farmers fearful of an impending Wichita monopoly on aid distribution to challenge the Wichitans for control. They sponsored a public meeting at which rural and urban factions contended for authority over the expected influx of railborne charity. Townsmen supported the Wichita Ladies' Aid Society, but the agriculturalists stubbornly proceeded to organize their own group. Thus emerged the Sedgwick County Aid Society. It was promptly boycotted by the Wichitans. The county commissioners wisely extended formal endorsement to both associations.[1]

The rural rank-and-file, meanwhile, grew ever more desperate. Increasingly they turned to occupational expedients—freighting supplies from Wichita to Indian Territory posts and reservations, collecting buffalo bones from the snow-swept prairies, hauling felled timber from the Walnut River, or simply moving into town to do odd jobs.[2] Because of the artificially inflated labor market, none of these efforts proved especially lucrative.

Henry H. Raymond, a young farmer living north of town, spent the winter freighting supplies at Dodge City.

---

about 2,400; in mid-March nearly three hundred of its own citizens were listed as needy, but probably many were rural sufferers who had taken shelter in town for the winter. See ibid.

[1] Wichita *Beacon*, Dec. 16, 30, 1874; Wichita *Eagle*, Dec. 17, 24, 1874, Jan. 7, 14, 1875.

[2] Wichita *Eagle*, Dec. 24, 1874; Wichita *Beacon*, Jan. 6, 20, Feb. 10, 1875.

His wife Sadie, a schoolteacher, was stoutly optimistic. "They had a meeting at my school house to organize an aid society," she wrote her absent husband at Christmas. "I guess nearly every family will come on the county. . . . I think a great many are asking for aid that might help themselves. If some of them would do as you and I are doing they would not need to make such a poor mouth." In early January the temperature dipped to subzero marks, one night to minus twenty degrees. "I tell you the cold weather pinches," Sadie confided to Henry in mid-month. ". . . The neighbors generally are accepting charity. I still report H. H. Raymond[']s family as not in a suffering condition. Was that not right?" Several lines later she admitted the worst: "I tell you Henry times are hard here. I had no idea it would be so bad. It is a good thing there is an aid society, if it were not for that I believe people would die."[3]

At this point all relief agencies found themselves running short on supplies, feed grain and fuel now having been added to other needs. Yet, supported by a few vocal rural eccentrics to whom Murdock lent the columns of the *Eagle*,[4] many Wichitans resisted further aid solicitations. Farmer spokesmen aired an appalling picture of rural suffering in letters to both Wichita papers,[5] and in

[3] Sadie Raymond to Henry Hubert Raymond, Dec. 18, 1874, Jan. 16, 1875, H. H. Raymond Papers, KSHS; Wichita *Beacon*, Jan. 20, Feb. 17, 1875.

[4] Wichita *Eagle*, Jan. 7, 28, 1875. The front page of the *Eagle* of February 4 even carried a crude satirical piece on the "Aid Business." Purporting to be a letter in which a young Wichitan seeks help from an Illinois uncle, it included absurd requests for all sorts of luxury items. Murdock playfully pretended that the "letter" had been "picked up by one of our business men on Main Street"; this, plus its date (January 11, 1875), suggests that it had been circulating within the local business community for some time before publication.

[5] Wichita *Eagle*, Jan. 14, 21, 1875; Wichita *Beacon*, Jan. 6, Feb. 3, 1875.

the face of continued urban insensitivity the Ladies' Aid officers addressed an open letter to the town. "It is *absolutely true* that there are families in the country," they argued,

> whose only safety from starvation lies in the charity of the people. *It is true* that stock in this county is dying for want of feed, . . . that women and children have no shoes and stockings, having their feet wrapped in rags, that families eighteen and twenty miles from timber have for their only fuel, *hay* [that is, needed livestock feed] and sunflower stalks. It is also true that many cabins have no floors, and their inmates at this inclement season place their beds upon the ground. To those who, like doubting Thomas will not believe, we propose to furnish transportation into the country and let them see for themselves. These statements are true and they cannot be contradicted by any who desire the truth to be known. As far as the injury to the country is concerned by the circulating of the truth, will it hurt the country as much to help these people in their need, as to let one man or woman die of cold or starvation?[6]

This vehement appeal broke through urban indifference, and at the end of January the women began weekly collections of food, clothing, and funds, and the distribution of supplies garnered locally and from the state relief committee. They countered criticism that some undeserving families had secured aid by requiring a destitution oath from those drawing supplies. With this the last vestiges of important rural suspicion vanished, and late in February, when the women's largess temporarily ran dry, the farmers' own aid society graciously extended them a quantity of meal and flour. Well might the ladies, as they closed out their operations in May, observe that "We have pursued our way, in regard to 'aid,' for the last eight months, not without many hindrances and much criti-

[6] Wichita *Beacon*, Jan. 27, 1875; Wichita *Eagle*, Jan. 28, 1875.

cism."[7] By this time even Marsh Murdock had fallen silent on the question of outside help. As county, city, and township relief agencies relinquished the torch to eleventh-hour federal intervention, the winter's turmoil at last subsided.[8]

[4]

DODGE CITY'S EXPERIENCE that same winter differed from Wichita's. With only a comparative handful of surrounding rural residents, the response of town-dominated Ford County was purely urban. In August 1874, only thirty members of the county's small farm population faced destitution, according to a local official. In November the number had reportedly risen to about 150. Having refused, however, even to put to a vote the question of relief bonds permitted by the recent special session of the legislature, townsmen bristled when the county destitution figures appeared in the state board of agriculture's annual report. At a mass meeting the statistics were angrily denounced as faulty, and it was insisted that only one local family stood in need of aid. Also rebuffing the federal government's offer of army surplus clothing, those assembled haughtily requested that it "be distributed to

[7] Wichita *Beacon*, Jan. 27, Feb. 3, 10, May 5, 1875; Wichita *Eagle*, Jan. 28, Feb. 4, 18, Mar. 4, 1875.

[8] Federal intervention consisted of the following actions: On November 12, 1874, President Grant authorized the War Department to issue army surplus clothing and blankets on the frontier. On January 25, 1875, Congress appropriated $30,000 to enable the Department of Agriculture to distribute free seed for spring planting. On February 10 Congress endorsed the clothing issue, and in addition authorized the distribution of army rations. At the same time, the only concrete aid finally offered by the Kansas legislature was an appropriation of $6,000 to pay freight on goods gathered by the state relief committee, plus a $5,000 gift for the same purpose to the executive committee of the state's Patrons of Husbandry organization. Fite: *Farmers' Frontier*, pp. 67, 69–71.

less favored localities." Merchant Robert M. Wright, the official aid representative for the area, forwarded a printed copy of the resolutions to the governor, and evidently turned a deaf ear to that executive's plea for reconsideration. "A more liberal class of men cannot be found than those which represent the business portion of this city," huffed Dodge City's editor, "and it is not likely that they will permit people to starve. They are amply able to feed their own poor, and will do it."[9]

Bob Wright and other ruggedly individualistic townsmen remained as leading members of the community when Ford County faced another test of attitudes toward rural relief in 1878–81. In 1877 a good 27.9 inches of rain fell in the county; in 1878 the figure dropped sharply to 18.0 inches; the following year it dipped to 15.4 inches; in 1880 it still measured only 18.1 inches.[1] Ford County's smaller watercourses, never very active, dried to dusty gullies and the earth under the withered buffalo grass proved rock-hard to the breaking plow. By the spring of 1879 the human effect of the long drought had also become evident.

As at Wichita five years earlier, a debate broke out between those openly acknowledging the rural disaster and those who, out of concern for the local image, felt it best to suppress any public discussion of it. When the Dodge City *Globe* printed a depressing picture of impending destitution as seen by the town's Methodist pastor, the rival Dodge City *Times*, reflecting a good segment of townside opinion, castigated both the reverend gentleman and his medium for "statements [that] have been extensively copied and commented upon by those

[9] Board of Agriculture: *Annual Report 1875*, pp. 22, 41; R. M. Wright to Thomas A. Osborn, Dec. 2, 1874, Governors' Correspondence (Relief); C. A. Morris (secretary to governor) to Wright, Dec. 8, 1874, Governors' Letters (KSHS), IV, 228; Osborn to Wright, Dec. 16, 1874, ibid., 245; Wichita *Eagle*, Dec. 17, 1874.
[1] Dodge City *Globe*, May 19, 1885.

newspapers unfavorable to this locality."[2] Thereafter the two publications carried on as had Wichita's *Beacon* and *Eagle* in 1874–75. The *Globe* contributed a sympathetic editorial voice and an opportunity for those so inclined to air personal expressions of concern. The *Times* editor, Nicholas B. Klaine, clung to an optimistic view that often bordered on outright falsifying. Klaine simultaneously urged settlers to maintain stiffer upper lips and to raise less wheat and more sheep—just as the unsympathetic Marsh Murdock had told desperate yeomen to turn from corn to wheat.

In the summer of 1879, with the state government unwilling to act and local bond levies for relief having been deemed unconstitutional, the town-dominated county administration determined to do what it could to head off an abhorred solicitation of aid from eastern localities. Santa Fe Railroad officials in Topeka were persuaded to furnish seed wheat at cost to all destitute settlers tributary to their line between Larned and Dodge. Ford County farmers thereafter could receive seed at about half the normal cost if it was bought at Dodge. Railroad officials hedged their generosity a good deal, however, by demanding cash on the barrelhead, the company's experience five years before with farmers' promissory notes having been an unhappy one.[3]

The 1879 wheat harvest looked increasingly doubtful as summer dwindled into autumn, and countrymen of the "east end" settlements convened in September to form the Ford County Aid Society, appointing agents to canvass in the eastern part of the state.[4] But as at Wichita in 1874, the town's womenfolk also formed a relief organization, the Dodge City Benevolent Society, to care for the needy

[2] Dodge City *Times*, May 24, 1879.

[3] Dodge City *Globe*, July 22, 29, Aug. 12, 1879; Spearville *News*, July 26, Aug. 2, 1879.

[4] Spearville *News*, Sept. 27, 1879 ff.; Dodge City *Globe*, Sept. 30, 1879 ff.; Dodge City *Times*, Oct. 4, 1879.

in town and those destitute families scattered over the west side of the county and in adjoining Meade County. Working as the Wichita ladies had through charity benefits and subscriptions papers, the association emphatically denied in January 1880 that it had ever sent any solicitations to, or accepted any aid from, parties outside the locality. Such a disclaimer seems to have been a necessary part of its effort.[5]

By the end of January matters had grown critical in the countryside. The remarks of T. E. Murphy, a regular *Globe* correspondent living in a rural neighborhood known as "Ryansville," illustrated the progressive deterioration of rural morale. "The farmers of Ryansville need no aid," Murphy declared in September 1879. In early November, however, he admitted that some of his neighbors were hungry, and he applauded the gratuitous distribution of a beef among them. "The hungry ones are sharpening their teeth in anticipation of the promised aid," Murphy remarked later that month, referring to an expected relief contribution from Topeka. In mid-December an edge of anger penetrated his dispatch. "Christmas comes but once a year, and when it comes it brings good cheer," he quoted sardonically.

> The author of the above line must have been figuring on a "big feed" when the day arrived on which the grand event occurred at Bethlehem. Not so, however, with the Grangers of Ford county. They expect nothing, for to be blunt about the matter, where in the devil are they going to get it[?] There has been aid promised frequently, but none has come.

Murphy visited Dodge City in January and told the *Globe*'s editor that a great number in his area desperately needed aid. Returning home from the flesh pots of Dodge

[5] Dodge City *Globe*, Nov. 18, 25, 1879; Dodge City *Times*, Jan. 24, 1880.

he reflected gloomily on the contrast between town and countryside:

"One half of the world don't know how the other half lives." The fellow who got that off spoke the truth, but somehow or other he didn't complete his sentence. He should have added, "nor do they care." At least such is the case in Ford county. In the east end of the county there is want, privation and suffering, and in the west [that is, at Dodge] there is waste, extravagance, dissipation and licentiousness. The money spent foolishly in the "Famous City" in one week would be sufficient to keep the poor of the county for the entire winter. But the good work goes on. Those who spend foolishly continue to do so and the hungry ones are still hungry.[6]

Mutual antipathy between Editor Klaine of the Dodge City *Times* and the restive rural citizenry finally crested in 1880. "A good deal of hypocritical gush has been indulged in by some people over cases of distress in the western part of Kansas," Klaine began in a lead editorial in January. The few cases of actual want, according to his interpretation, had been dealt with promptly by local charities. "The destitute bubble," he continued,

is sorely in need of pricking. The cry of distress has been used by certain philanthropically disposed persons to furnish a little buncombe at the expense of the charity of our own people, and a misrepresentation of the means at their command. . . .
A great wrong has been inflicted upon this section of the State, by the undue circulation given to the distressed condition of some of its people.

At a subsequent relief meeting an angry rural spokesman read this editorial aloud and obtained over one hundred

[6] Dodge City *Globe*, Sept. 16, Nov. 11, 25, Dec. 23, 1879, Jan. 20, Feb. 3, 1880. As in earlier quotes from Dodge City, the term "Grangers" simply means farmers, there being no Patrons of Husbandry organization in Ford County at this time.

signatures to a petition denouncing Klaine's effusion as "FALSE in the extreme, regardless of any motive he may have in making such statements." Elsewhere in the county separate gatherings of farm folk instructed committees to wait on the *Times* editor and demand that he retract comments that the county was abundantly able to care for its poor. On a Saturday these delegations descended upon Klaine's cluttered little office on Chestnut Street. Just what occurred has not survived, but Klaine remained grimly unimpressed. "The relief business is in a state of collapse in Ford county," his edition of that same day affirmed.

. . . As usual the actual needy were slighted, while those too proud to beg, and too lazy to work, have walked off with the stuff intended for the humble stricken families. A few who wish the cheap notoriety their labors in the cause will give, will hold on to the lingering corpse of destitution, hoping to keep their larder supplied until grass comes, when the aid business will vanish like a dream.[7]

The local county commissioners took a hand at last late in February 1880, and used Ford County's poor fund to buy 7,500 pounds of corn meal, 3,000 pounds of flour, and 500 pounds of bacon for destitute relief. After having long maintained that there was no substantial problem, Nicholas Klaine now viewed this massive effort as a wonderful vindication of his editorial position. "Who says Ford county is not able to take care of its poor?" he crowed. The ladies of the Dodge City Benevolent Society, denounced both by the skeptical Klaine and by east end settlers who felt slighted in the aid distribution, gladly took the occasion to disburse their remaining funds and goods and close down operations.[8]

[7] Dodge City *Times*, Jan. 24, Feb. 7, 14, 1880; Spearville *News*, Jan. 31, 1880; Dodge City *Globe*, Feb. 17, 24, 1880.
[8] Dodge City *Times*, Feb. 14, 28, 1880; Spearville *News*, Feb. 7, 1880; Dodge City *Globe*, Feb. 10, 17, 1880.

But as winter gave way to yet another dry spring, a new countywide relief organization moved to promote a fresh aid solicitation.[9] In mid-year a state aid society came to Ford's assistance. Once again the Santa Fe Railroad agreed to sell seed wheat at cost. The United States Congress then granted temporary leaves of absence to settlers proving up on government lands in western Kansas. In early 1881, finally, the state legislature established an official relief agency to handle frontier destitution.[1] With the arrival of bountiful rains in the spring of that year the bitter contention at last came to an end.

Just how extensive rural destitution in the county had been is difficult to assess. In mid-1880, after many of the estimated 250 settlers who ultimately fled the county had gone,[2] Ford held just over 3,000 residents, of which some 2,000 were rural dwellers.[3] At the same time 800 people were reported as destitute. Nicholas Klaine hotly disputed this figure, of course, and it may indeed have been somewhat lower.[4]

History, if only in the modest circumstances of human response, had repeated itself. Given the constellation of issues, it is not surprising that the accumulated social atmosphere at all the cattle towns remained one of rural-urban tension. How much the situation in this respect

[9] Dodge City *Globe*, Apr. 27, 1880; Dodge City *Times*, May 1, 1880.

[1] Dodge City *Globe*, June 8, July 6, Aug. 24, 1880, Mar. 29, 1881; *U.S. Statutes*, XXI, 543–44; *Laws of Kansas*, 1881, pp. 249–53.

[2] According to W. F. Petillon in an interview with a Chicago *Times* reporter, "The drouth has driven away nearly two hundred and fifty residents of the county, many of whom have returned to the East." Quoted in Dodge City *Globe*, Feb. 15, 1881.

[3] Kansas State Board of Agriculture: *Second Biennial Report . . . 1879–80* (Topeka, 1881), p. 519. The board in this report included no treatment of the situation in the western part of the state, as it had done earlier for the disaster of 1874–75.

[4] Dodge City *Globe*, Aug. 17, 31, 1880; Dodge City *Times*, Sept. 11, 1880.

was unique, and how much only something endemic in town-country relationships everywhere in the nation, is hard to say. In any event, at every cattle town rural animosity became a part of nearly all aspects of community life. Growing in influence as settlement intruded upon the surrounding hinterlands, farmers increasingly menaced the commerce to which each cattle trading center had entrusted its immediate economic fate.

1. Joseph G. McCoy,
Abilene livestock dealer.

2. Theodore C. Henry,
Abilene land agent.

3. William ("Dutch Bill")
Greiffenstein, Wichita
town promoter.

4. Robert M. Wright,
Dodge City merchant.

5. Alonzo B. Webster,
Dodge City merchant.

6. Marshall M. Murdock,
Wichita editor.

7. *Abilene, September 1867, looking east from Mud Creek. In the background rises the new Drovers Cottage hotel. At right stands one of the log structures making up the early settlement.*

8. *Closer view, two or three years later. Beyond the hotel sprawls the stockyard.*

9. Smoky Hill Crossing, October 1867, where the military road met the river near the newly platted Ellsworth.

10. Ellsworth, late 1872. At the right stands the Drovers Cottage, moved from Abilene that spring.

11. Wichita, 1870, looking north along Main Street from Douglas Avenue.

12. Same view about five years later. At right looms the "Eagle Block" business building. The New York Store was a dry goods and clothing emporium.

13. Bird's-eye view of Wichita, late 1873, when the town contained two thousand or more permanent residents.

14. Dodge City's Front Street, September 1872. The outside staircase identifies Bob Wright's mercantile house before it was rebuilt in brick.

15. Bird's-eye view of Dodge City, June 1882. Resident population: twelve hundred.

16. Caldwell in the mid-1880's, a view from the south edge of town.

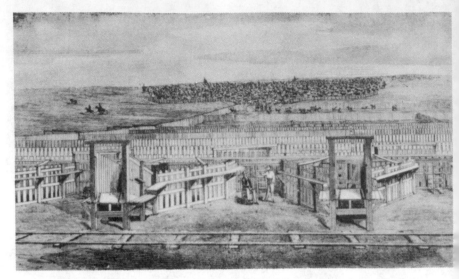

17. *The Ellsworth stockyard, built in 1869 and enlarged in 1872.*

18. *Wichita's railway depot in the mid-1870's. Charles Marsh, whose coal dispensary stands at right, served as local business manager for the Santa Fe line.*

19. Ellsworth's Drovers Cottage. The hotel enclosed a dining room, saloon, and about seventy-five upstairs bedroms.

20. The Southwestern Hotel, built at Caldwell in 1883. It contained a second-floor "ladies' parlor" and thirty-eight rooms.

21. *How the well-dressed cowhand may have looked after visiting a cattle town clothier. Three Dodge City businessmen pose as cowboys, about 1885.*

22. *Interior of a Dodge City dance house, originally built as the Varieties Theatre in 1878. George Masterson, brother of the famous Bat Masterson, tends bar.*

23. *Rare photo of cowboys camped near a cattle town. This group lounges on the Cherokee Strip below Caldwell in the mid-1880's.*

24. *A Dodge City prostitute, known only as "Squirrel Tooth Alice." Note the pet squirrel in her lap.*

25. *Bob Wright's brick store, Dodge City, about 1883. Two doors to the right stands the popular Long Branch Saloon.*

26. *Wichita's controversial Douglas Avenue bridge, built over the Arkansas River cattle ford in 1872 at a cost of $28,000.*

27. *Interior of the Stock Exchange Bank of Caldwell, established in 1881 by a group of Cherokee Strip cattlemen.*

28. *A second "south end" project: Caldwell's giant civic auditorium —the so-called opera house—built in 1884.*

29. *John Mueller's boot shop, as it appeared in the early 1870's on Ellsworth's South Main Street.*

30. *Mueller's Dodge City home, built in 1881 of locally quarried gray stone. An editor called it "the finest residence in the West, . . . a credit to the town and a monument to the enterprise of the owner."*

31. *After the cattle trade left Ellsworth, Mueller shifted operations to Dodge City. Here, in April 1879, his shop stands on Front Street opposite the railroad depot.*

32. *Frederick C. Zimmermann's store, Dodge City, about 1875. Zimmermann, with flourishing whiskers, grasps the hand of a fidgety child.*

33. *Zimmermann's home, built in the late 1870's. An editor described this as one of the "several fine residences" that "have made the Western part of the city the most attractive and picturesque view of our entire surroundings."*

34. *Interior of Zimmermann's store, 1885. Again the proud proprietor stands at right.*

35. *Two very early cattle town homes. The house at left, the first frame dwelling in Abilene, was built by T. C. Henry in 1868. In 1872 he put up the slightly more decorative house on the right.*

36. *Southeast outskirts of Dodge City in the mid-1880's. In the background lie the Santa Fe rail yards.*

37. *A farm of the late cattle town era: the Samuel Burrell homestead, with sod farmhouse, twelve miles southwest of Dodge City.*

38. *Midsummer scene at the F. M. Sumpter farm northwest of Caldwell in the 1880's.*

39. Vear P. Wilson, Abilene editor.

40. William B. ("Bat") Masterson, Dodge City lawman and politician.

41. Nicholas B. Klaine, Dodge City editor.

42. Daniel M. Frost, Dodge City editor.

43. Albert M. Colson, Caldwell livestock dealer.

44. David B. Long, Ellsworth County dairy farmer.

VI

The Politics of Factionalism

[1]

"WHEN WE LOCATED in Ellsworth we supposed, this being a new town, that there was no dissension or rivalry between people." So reflected George A. Atwood, a recently transplanted New Englander who had thought that in starting life anew on the Kansas frontier one escaped the petty social animosities of the typical country town. Well, he'd been wrong and he now admitted it, listing a few of the things that divided his fellow citizens. "All of which is too bad," Atwood concluded, still shaken by the revelation. His reassurances were not especially convincing: "Let us never despair. We are all in favor of 'long horns.' We all want a big city. After a little the jealousies of the present will be forgotten in the endeavor of each to do his most to build up Ellsworth."

It must indeed have seemed strange to thoughtful observers that in cattle towns struggling against both internal and external enemies—lawless elements within and economic rivals and rural dissidents without—local energies were not entirely consumed by constructive civic effort. The assumption that frontier townsmen should be too busy to allow themselves the luxury of social conflict made sense. But conspicuous common efforts by no means fully disguised simultaneous internecine strife. The author of a relatively sophisticated cattle town memoir, whose illusions at least did not embrace the psychological characteristics of his former fellow citizens, held conflicts to be

inevitable in all new towns. The scuffling for footholds, the reaching out for the real money afloat, the strifes between sections of communities over locations of civil utilities, the political squabbles in city and county, all gave opportunities for open or silent antagonisms. . . . While everybody was publicly expected to look out hospitably for the largest number, the largest number seemed by some . . . to be Number One.[1]

Whether personal antipathy led to factionalism or factionalism to personal antipathy is of course a moot question, since the two forms of conflict complement one another in a social situation. Individual animosities flourished, reflected in the virulent personal gossip that occasionally reached public print and in the angry blows that sometimes fell. At the same time, factionalism both created and exacerbated such antipathies. Group associations gave antagonists much greater scope for action—in union there being not only strength but courage. Sheer factionalism goes far toward explaining the mysterious intricacies of local political warfare, about which cattle town editors in most cases expressed such fragmentary, guarded, or designedly untruthful insights, and concerning which, as in no comparable instance, the historian's understanding is gained through exceptionally painstaking attention to documentary nuance and detail. But the result is exposure of one of the most important threads running through the cattle town experience.

[1] Ellsworth *Reporter*, Aug. 29, 1872; Stuart Henry: *Conquering Our Great American Plains* (New York, 1930), pp. 299–300.

[2]

EASILY THE MOST PRIMITIVE form of factionalism was the joining together of "old settlers" against later arrivals. In such cases the concept of a prerogative bestowed by sheer seniority played a commanding role. While pioneer townsmen normally displayed an early date of arrival with pride, the idea of a privilege conferred by such a thing possesses rustic overtones and may not have been taken very seriously by town dwellers. According to a cattle town editor with several years' experience on the frontier, who was willing to express some opinions on what he felt was a general problem, this type of factional coalescence encompassed the lowest form of pioneer ele-ment—"a certain class, who, owing, in many instances, to lack of thrift or means, in old localities, are forced to emigrate a little in advance of others." Such characters, he charged, infested town and countryside throughout Kansas, illogically claiming a monopoly on public office. "We have known people to be in a locality two weeks before others, who were in advance of them in every other way," he continued, and yet the former "claimed a p[r]erogative on the plea of 'I am an older citizen and set[t]ler than you are.' . . . Every public movement must have its 'old citizen' to the exclusion of the new comer, whose brains are at a discount."[2]

The question of old versus new citizens did not appear to reach any particular political test at the cattle towns, since many members of the first wave of westward set-tlement simply withdrew from the scene as newcomers moved in. Such, for example, was the case with Charles H. Thompson and Timothy Hersey, the original proprie-tor and original settler, respectively, of Abilene. By the autumn of 1870 Thompson had retired to a stock farm

[2] Wichita *Vidette*, Dec. 22, 1870.

and apparently sought to exert no further influence in local affairs, while Hersey, a classically restless border type, had located a claim farther west.[3]

[3]

FACTIONALISM THAT DID FIND expression in politics always indicated just how far local society would allow such a blatantly "irrational" aspect of the social process to go. Caldwell's political experience in the years from 1881 through 1884 reveals, at least at this level, a conscious repression of the clique instinct.

Although the seeds of local factionalism had been germinating for some time, it was the influx of ranchers into Caldwell in the early eighties that precipitated their flowering. By 1881 the town had become an informal headquarters for Cherokee Strip cattlemen, and they increasingly established permanent residences there. Opportunity for their children to attend school was a major reason. Indeed, Caldwellites footed the expenses of a new brick schoolhouse and a good teaching staff in 1881–82 partly for the purpose of enticing the stockmen to relocate there.[4] In October 1881, a number of these cattlemen pooled their resources and, with the assistance of a financier from nearby Wellington, established Caldwell's Stock Exchange Bank.[5]

[3] Junction City *Union*, Oct. 1, 1870; J. B. Edwards: *Early Days in Abilene* (Abilene, 1940), p. 5. For some colorful testimony to the fact that Thompson and Hersey had for several previous years been very influential in local affairs, however, see the Detroit *Western News*, Feb. 11, 1870.

[4] Caldwell *Post*, Aug. 18, 1881, Jan. 26, June 22, July 27, Sept. 7, 1882.

[5] Caldwell *Post*, Oct. 27, 1881; Caldwell *Commercial*, Oct. 27, Nov. 17, 1881; A. T. Andreas: *History of the State of Kansas* (Chicago, 1883), p. 1503. For the continuing predominance of cattlemen among the Stock Exchange Bank's stockholders and directors, see especially the lists in the Caldwell *Commercial*, Nov. 9, 1882, Jan. 4, 1883.

More important than having established a somewhat exclusive credit facility for themselves was the fact that the stock raisers constructed their bank at the extreme south end of the recognized business district. This lent a new impetus to what was already a growing competition between the townsmen inhabiting Main Street business sites north of Fifth Street (now Central Avenue), and those who had located to the south of it—not on original townsite ground but on the downtown addition platted by the nonresident speculator, Charles H. Stone, in 1879.[6] That the embattled area was only some three linear blocks in extent made it no less an axis of contention, competition over downtown real estate values lending itself admirably to factional polarization. The whole question, to simplify the matter in Caldwell's case, was which end of Main Street would form the prime nucleus of urban growth. Most of the resident Cherokee Strip cattlemen, the most important of whom maintained an association with the Stock Exchange Bank, added their wealth and influence to the ranks of the "south-enders." Early in 1882, four months after the stockmen's bank opened for business, the north end businessmen organized their own credit institution, the Caldwell Savings Bank. As proof that business location rather than vocational calling was the foremost variable in the rivalry, the new institution listed among its nine charter directors at least four cattlemen, two of them Cherokee Strip stock raisers.[7]

[6] Sumner Co. Plats (Register of Deeds Office, Wellington), I, 39, II, 5, 29. The first hint of sectional competition on Main Street appears in the Caldwell *Post*, Sept. 29, 1881, before the establishment of the stockmen's bank, and clearly demonstrates that the cattlemen only intruded (though importantly) into an existing situation.

[7] Caldwell *Post*, Mar. 30, 1882; Andreas: *History of Kansas*, p. 1503.

THE CATTLE TOWNS · 212

In March 1883, the annual cattlemen's convention held at Caldwell underscored the town's need for a good hotel. Apparently the south-enders first began talk of organizing a company to finance one, but within a week the north-enders had banded together to sponsor a hotel at their own end of Main. Thus Caldwell soon boasted two elegant three-story brick hotels: the south end's Leland— fifty bedrooms, a commodious dining hall, second-floor ladies' and gentlemen's parlors that provided a broad view of the Indian Territory skyline—and the north end's Southwestern with thirty-eight rooms and other accommodations similar to the Leland's.[8]

Competing banks in 1882, competing hotels in 1883. In 1884 the south-enders organized a stock company to build an "opera house"—that is, a civic auditorium— without which no town with metropolitan pretensions could hope to be taken seriously. A few of the more volatile north-enders immediately announced plans to build a rival opera house.[9] Economic sanity prevailed over factional rivalry, however, and only the first project actually came to fruition.

Caldwell's businessmen dissipated the potential political impact of their contention in a most remarkable manner. This was somewhat easier to do at Caldwell than at the other cattle towns, since Caldwellites did not possess the seat of county government and therefore could not manipulate county politics to any great extent—a situation that discouraged any notion of carrying their competition into the annual November warfare. There remained only that other channel of political opportunity, the election of a mayor and city councilmen each spring. Factional conflict, thus restricted, was compromised at

[8] Caldwell *Post*, Mar. 8, 15, 22, 1883; Caldwell *Commercial*, Mar. 15, 22, 1883. For good descriptions of these two facilities see Caldwell *Journal*, Apr. 3, 1884; Caldwell *Standard*, Aug. 21, 1884; Caldwell *Oklahoma War-Chief*, June 18, 1885.

[9] Caldwell *Standard*, Feb. 7, 1884; Caldwell *Journal*, Feb. 7, 1884.

the municipal level. For four years following the advent of sharp Main Street rivalry in late 1881, the business community annually met in caucus and carefully apportioned the town's major elective offices between the two Main Street cliques. Since the result nevertheless represented a more or less undemocratic determination of elections, local editors never forthrightly discussed the arrangement. But identifiable sectional loyalties of chosen personnel reveal its existence.

Albert M. Colson was elected without opposition to terms as mayor in 1882 and 1883. This well-liked young man, an early settler of the area, was in all respects a satisfactory compromise candidate. Colson was on the one hand a cattleman and on the other hand a charter director of the Caldwell Savings Bank, president of the north end's hotel corporation, and later manager of its hotel.[1] However acceptable he might be to the stock raisers composing the hard core of the south end faction, Colson maintained a prime loyalty to the northerners. South-enders thus demanded and received a one-man preponderance on the five-man council in 1882. This body, as finally constituted, included two ranchers and a grocer and farm implement dealer as south end representatives. A stock-raising farmer and an outfitting store manager served for the north end. By the election of 1883 the outfitter had moved from town; his place was allotted to a north end bookstore owner.[2] (Appointive offices

---

[1] For general biographical data on Colson see Andreas: *History of Kansas*, p. 1503; Chapman Bros.: *Portrait and Biographical Album of Sumner County* (Chicago, 1890), pp. 201–02; G. D. Freeman: *Midnight and Noonday, or the Incidental History of Southern Kansas* (Caldwell, 1892), pp. 400–02.

[2] Caldwell *Post*, Mar. 23, 1882; Caldwell *Commercial*, Apr. 6, 1882, Apr. 5, 1883. In most instances, loyalties of the councilmen can be determined by whether or not their names appear as stockholders or directors of either bank (ibid., Nov. 17, 1881, Nov. 9, 1882, Jan. 11, 1883; Caldwell *Post*, Mar. 30, 1882), or directors of the Southwestern Hotel (Caldwell *Commercial*, Mar. 15, 1883). The list

were filled on a nonpartisan, merit basis.) When the city fathers decided to build a new city hall early in 1884, they carefully located the structure just off Main at Fifth Avenue, yet another demonstration of geographic balance in government.[3]

A bipartisan slate of candidates was offered to voters a third time in 1884, but the *modus vivendi* then threatened to break down. After Colson's two terms in office some of the south-enders wanted the mayorship to come their way. Also, one of the two new choices for councilman, Dr. W. A. Noble, while an otherwise respected north end physician, had gotten drunk the year before and shot and seriously wounded an inoffensive bartender. Noble failed to receive a totally favorable consensus probably for this reason. In the election both he and Colson were soundly defeated. The entente had begun to crumble, but it managed to survive one more season. In 1885 a businessmen's caucus again devised a balanced ticket, but the Main Street factional compromise no longer remained the most critical factor.[4] As we shall see in the following chapter, moral reform had injected itself into local politics, and secular factionalism, as a community issue, faded into relative insignificance.

[4]

IF CALDWELL'S EXPERIENCE with the clique impulse could be called a study in political inhibition, that of Dodge City in the late seventies illustrates the other extreme,

---

of directors and stockholders of the successful opera house (Caldwell *Journal*, Feb. 7, 1884) represents a bipartisan membership, and is thus not a good index.

[3] Caldwell *Journal*, Jan. 3, June 5, 1884.

[4] Caldwell *Post*, Mar. 29, 1883; Caldwell *Commercial*, Mar. 29, 1883; Caldwell *Standard*, Mar. 27, Apr. 3, 10, 1884; Caldwell *Journal*, Apr. 10, 1884, Apr. 2, 1885.

with factional conflict pervading both municipal and county politics. The origins of the Dodge factions are mysterious, and they do not seem to have been structured according to any rational criteria. In a sense, the factional dispute was simply between a political "establishment" on the one hand and a group of dissident "outs" on the other. And yet the long-run impermanency of the incumbent group's entrenchment justifies an analysis in terms of cliques.

The dominant party was known to its opponents as "the Gang," an appellation soon taken up in all good humor by the incumbents themselves. The Gang drew much of its power as a political instrument from its support by Robert M. Wright, a man whose enormous local influence stemmed from the widespread personal loyalties he commanded in the community. This prosperous merchant, whose name has already appeared several times in these pages, was not a visibly active member of the Gang. But the Gang deferred to him whenever Wright chose to intervene in any particular situation, and apparently his intervention was always decisive. Until late in the cattle trade era, when his view of the prohibition crisis demanded that he personally assume the responsibilities of mayor, Wright normally held himself aloof from formal municipal politicking.

At this level the Gang invested ongoing leadership in its perennial choice for mayor, James H. ("Dog") Kelley. A slightly built, rather unkempt man with a receding chin, heavily lidded eyes, a handlebar mustache, and nape-length hair, Kelley was an immigrant boy now in his thirties, a former Confederate soldier who had also served on the Plains with Custer. In August 1872, he and a partner, Peter L. Beatty, moved a frame building down from Hays City to the corner of Front Street and First Avenue, where they opened the popular Beatty and Kelley Res-

THE CATTLE TOWNS · 216

taurant. A disapproving newcomer to Dodge described Kelley as a feisty, "flannel mouthed Irishman" who regularly kept a mistress. Besides women, his extrapolitical enthusiasms were fine hunting dogs—hence the colorful sobriquet—and fisticuffs. In a personal encounter in 1878 Kelley handled a young cattleman so severely that the victim tried to assassinate him by firing into his sleeping quarters one evening, only to kill a pretty theatrical entertainer by mistake.[5]

Kelley commanded the rank-and-file support enjoyed by the Gang. Prominent within this constituency was a considerable remnant of the old frontier element with backgrounds similar to Kelley's—buffalo hunters, teamsters, ex-cavalrymen, and other so-called border characters. A few of these, like the law-enforcing Masterson brothers, lent themselves to comparatively useful roles in the community. Others were no more than semi-professional gamblers or in some cases mere alcoholic hangers-on. Bob Wright, having a rugged frontiersman's background himself, obviously identified emotionally with this group, which constituted a kind of informal men's club. He never genuinely repudiated its dubious political influence, and looked upon its routine pursuits with tolerant amusement.[6]

Finally, some important Gang members, such as lawyer Michael W. Sutton and the *Times* editor, Nicholas B. Klaine, seem to have been sheer opportunists—relative

[5] F. A. Hobble: "Dodge City Pioneers and Buffalo Hunters" (typescript, KSHS), pp. 1–2; Dodge City *Democrat*, June 19, 1903; Robert M. Wright: *Dodge City: The Cowboy Capital* (Wichita, 1913), pp. 82–85, 174; Nyle H. Miller and Joseph W. Snell (eds.): *Why the West Was Wild* (Topeka, 1963), pp. 311, 351–52, 361–63.

[6] See Wright: *Dodge City*, especially chaps. xi–xvi. As Wright makes clear, the primary collective activity of the clique (beside indulging in wine, women, and cards) was perpetrating elaborate practical jokes on "greenhorns" and other easy targets. Many of its antics as narrated by Wright can be verified in the columns of the Dodge City newspapers.

latecomers to the scene who "joined the Gang," as the phrase went, simply as a means of hitching their immediate political ambitions to the then dominant faction. Both men, however, contributed important services to the clique, Klaine acting as its mouthpiece and Sutton providing its legal counsel and being one of its shrewdest politickers, especially at the county level.[7]

The Gang's opposition never possessed a contemporary designation. Associated with this faction was George M. Hoover, Dodge City's big liquor wholesaler. The factional polarity of Hoover and Bob Wright suggests that a personal conflict between them might account for local alignments, but such does not seem to have been the case. No personal animosity between them can be detected in the record, and Hoover's involvement with the anti-Gang element seems almost episodic. The opposition's continuing leadership, rather more centralized than that of the Gang, devolved largely upon lawyer and *Globe* editor Daniel M. Frost.[8]

[7] Reminisced Bob Wright of Sutton (Wright: *Dodge City*, p. 308): "He and the writer ran on the same ticket, and were always elected by overwhelming majorities. He was behind me, as adviser, in all my deals and undertaking[s]." Wright and Sutton actually became bitter political enemies in the 1880's, but Wright's statement here not only is based on a subsequent rapprochement (ibid., p. 309), but is in spirit accurate for the late seventies.

[8] For the best single (though not inclusive) index to the rank-and-file composition of the Frost faction by late 1877, see the list of those supporting George Hoover's candidacy for county commissioner in Dodge City *Times*, Oct. 13, 1877. This can be usefully compared to the list of Gangsmen supporting George B. Cox in ibid., Oct. 20, 1877. Some Frostites were apparently persons formerly associated with the Gang who by 1876–77 had somehow become *persona non grata* to the establishment. Dan Frost, for example, had served as Ford County's representative in the state legislature in 1876. A few years later the *Times* editor (Apr. 10, 1880) asserted that the Gang had once "elected Frost to the Legislature." Bob Wright, in the following county caucus, received the Gang's nomination for state representative, Frost no longer enjoying its favor.

Real estate location apparently had little influence on Dodge City factionalism.[9] Nor did the question of old versus new settlers apply. The only strongly differentiating group characteristics that impress themselves on the investigator are that the Gang embraced most of the rowdy frontier types described above, while the Frost faction numbered the local German-Americans among its adherents.

From its earliest days Dodge City harbored a small nucleus of German-born residents who seem to have been more than a little ethnically sensitive.[1] Merchants Frederick C. Zimmermann and Morris Collar probably were their two most important leaders.[2] Collar, at least, was vividly outspoken in his hostility to the incumbent faction.[3] Without openly breaking with the establishment until late in 1877, the local "Dutch" long seem to have attracted the Gang's dislike. While one can only surmise, it is possible that the preponderance of border characters within the Gang largely contributed this attitude to its consensus. The grounds for this mild antipathy were certainly neither the Germans' traditional liberalism toward

[9] The only detectable attempt by a member of the Frost faction to gain his group's support on a question of real estate failed miserably. In this case it involved the location of a new schoolhouse. The choice actually was made on grounds of suitability, and was supported by members of both cliques. Dodge City *Times*, Apr. 26, May 10, 17, 1879; Dodge City *Globe*, May 13, 1879.

[1] See, for example, the letter of Samuel Galland, German-born hotelman, in the Dodge City *Times*, Feb. 1, 1879.

[2] For biographical sketches of Zimmermann see Andreas: *History of Kansas*, p. 1562; S. Lewis and Co.: *United States Biographical Dictionary: Kansas Volume* (Chicago, 1879), pp. 516–17. For his being a recognized leader of the local Germans see the Dodge City *Times*, Dec. 22, 1877. Detailed information on Collar is lacking, but he, too, was an early resident. Dodge City *Globe*, Apr. 14, 1885; Dodge City *Democrat*, June 19, 1903.

[3] See Collar's vitriolic letters about local government in Spearville *Enterprise*, June 29, 1878; Yates Center *News*, Sept. 9, 1880. The second letter was printed anonymously, but Collar's authorship is identified in the Dodge City *Globe*, Sept. 14, 1880.

the use of alcoholic beverages, nor—from such indifferent churchgoers as the Gang rank-and-file—their religious preferences. At base, in all probability, was merely a mocking disesteem for a collection of conspicuous "foreigners."[4]

P. L. Beatty, Kelley's business partner, was Dodge City's charter mayor, holding office through its first winter as a municipality. The details of the town's first political contest, when George Hoover won the mayorship in April 1876, are lost. Possibly factionalism was held in abeyance and nonpartisan support extended to one slate of candidates as a general mandate for sanctions against unbridled lawlessness.[5]

Less guesswork is required for subsequent city elections. In 1877 some businessmen devised a bipartisan slate in the Caldwell manner, suggesting Hoover for re-election as mayor and apportioning city council seats three to two in favor of the Gang. But the Gang refused to adhere to any such gentlemanly division of political spoils. In a grimly contested election Jim Kelley became mayor and the Gang won a majority on the council as well. Dan Frost himself, however, was granted the position of police judge and, perhaps in return for some German-

[4] Clear-cut evidence of ethnic scorn is difficult to find; editors usually did not choose willingly to give such a locally explosive attitude publicity (but see letter cited in footnote 1 above). Wright's own sentiments seem somewhat ambiguous at first glance. He describes himself as having been an admirer of the young Dominican missionary Felix P. Swemberg, who, as an Alsatian, was instrumental in locating Germans in Kansas. (Wright: *Dodge City*, pp. 161–62.) But also see his terming W. F. Petillon a "foreigner," and his alleged attitude toward the Germans of rural Ford County in the Dodge City *Globe*, Oct. 19, 1880.

[5] In the absence of any other source see Stuart Lake: *Wyatt Earp, Frontier Marshal* (New York, 1931), pp. 140–41, as further embellished by Stanley Vestal: *Queen of Cowtowns: Dodge City* (New York, 1952), pp. 96–98. For the resulting composition of the city administration, which contained adherents of both factions, see Dodge City *Times*, Oct. 14, 1876.

American support, the victors re-appointed one of them, Lawrence E. Deger, as city marshal.[6]

By the end of that year factional conflict had grown considerably more important. In an intricate exchange of personal animosities Kelley obtained the replacement of Deger with a Gang adherent. Unsuccessful attempts also were made to force Judge Frost's resignation from office. Although the infighting then grew even more bitter, the 1878 city elections only demonstrated how complete was the Gang domination. Kelley won re-election and all other offices went to men of similar loyalty. In the spring of 1879, except for Morris Collar's acquisition of a council seat, the Gang triumphed again. In 1880, though at last facing opposition within his own clique, Kelley won a fourth term as mayor.[7] From 1878 through the spring of 1880 this clique controlled city hall without much formal opposition at the polls from the Frost group, which apparently saw no chance of winning in the face of Kelley's command of a voting bloc that invariably included transients casting illegal ballots.

Unable to gain any major victories on the municipal scene, the Frost faction found itself equally frustrated in county politics. From the day of its birth in empty Ford County, the town had controlled the courthouse. Even after a measure of rural settlement had come to the east end, townsmen continued to dominate by gerrymandering election districts so as to give the town two representatives on the three-man board of county commissioners. From 1873 through 1875 citizens possibly de-

[6] Dodge City *Times*, Mar. 31, Apr. 7, 1877. Deger was native-born, but his parents were apparently German-speaking immigrants from Switzerland. See U.S. Manuscript Census, 1880: Kansas (microfilm copy, KSHS), Ford Co., Dodge Twp. "North of Arkansas River," p. 2.

[7] Dodge City *Times*, Nov. 24, Dec. 8, 1877, Apr. 6, 1878, Apr. 12, 1879, Apr. 3, 10, 1880; Dodge City *Globe*, Mar. 12, Apr. 2, 1878, Apr. 8, 1879, Mar. 9, 16, 30, Apr. 6, 13, 1880.

cided the apportionment of political offices in general caucuses, with elections mere formalities. In the first county election on which we possess any details, that of November 1876, an attempt was made to effect such a compromise. Representatives of both cliques met in October to devise a ticket that would divide the nominations between them. The Gangsmen at the meeting, evidently outnumbering their opponents, made a fight of it and the resulting slate, except for two relatively unimportant positions, was composed completely of Gang adherents. This ticket gained office without a single loss.[8]

A year later, in 1877, with one of Dodge City's county commissioner posts up for renewal, the Frost faction proposed George Hoover as a candidate, and their opponents promptly nominated hotelman George B. Cox. The factions then agreed that the remaining elective posts were to be apportioned in caucus. The Frostites should have known better. Once again Gangsmen dominated the meeting and for all but the least important positions selected their own members. In the ensuing election virtually the entire caucus slate won office.[9]

The winter of 1877–78 witnessed the beginning of a substantial influx of farmers into northeast Ford County. These immigrants included a considerable body of Germans, partially stimulated by Fred Zimmermann, Morris Collar, Larry Deger, and other Dodge City "Dutchmen" organized as the German Immigration Society of Ford County. By spring, at the new town of Spearville, the Santa Fe Railroad's land agent was already busy, there

[8] Dodge City *Times*, Oct. 14, 1876. For the election results one must consult the list of county officers in the next surviving issue of the *Times*, that of Mar. 24, 1877. The offices of coroner and superintendent of public instruction do not seem to have been subject to factional contention. These were two posts demanding some degree of objective professional expertise, often being filled by bipartisan nominees.

[9] Dodge City *Times*, Oct. 13, 20, Nov. 3, 10, 1877.

being no more unclaimed government real estate within ten to fifteen miles.[1] By summer the influx threatened to promote a political as well as demographic change. The Frostites immediately grasped at this immigration boom as an opportunity to gain the upper hand against their enemies. In June the first politicking began as Morris Collar wrote to the newly established Spearville newspaper that the Gang leaders already were "preparing the medicine for the people of Ford county." "By people," he explained, "they mean that portion of the population of Ford county who have come to stay, the actual settler. The farmers are cursed daily by that part of the population who have not come to stay . . . but I hope the way affairs are run now will not last forever."

In October the Frost faction's most important spokesmen suddenly converged on Spearville and met at the local schoolhouse with political leaders from the east end. Opening the caucus, lawyer Harry E. Gryden examined the political situation in Ford County in a half-hour speech, stating, as a reporter paraphrased his words, that "the time had been when Dodge City considered Ford county a part and portion of the city, but that now some of the citizens had 'tumbled' to the fact that there were people outside of its sacred walls whose opinions in choosing our county officers should be consulted." This, he concluded, was why he and his friends had come. From the meeting emerged a "People's Ticket," with Dodge City's Richard W. Evans for state representative, Dan Frost for county attorney, and three rural citizens proposed for posts of lesser importance.[2]

The alliance was short-lived, however, since the Frost forces had slighted Spearville's political sachem, a devout

[1] Dodge City *Times*, Dec. 15, 22, 1877; Dodge City *Globe*, Jan. 22, Apr. 2, 1878.
[2] Spearville *Enterprise*, June 29, 1878; Spearville *News*, Oct. 12, 19, 1878; Dodge City *Globe*, Oct. 15, 22, 1878.

Greenbacker. The Gang, consequently posing as partisans of his cause, maneuvered the east end leaders into abandoning the Frost slate for an "Independent Ticket" controlled by themselves. In the general politicking both the declared candidates for representative, Dick Evans and Bob Wright, promised farmers a legislative extension of the Texas cattle quarantine line into Ford County, and the rest of the campaign degenerated into hand-shaking forays among the east-enders.[3] If the Frostites assumed they had the rural German vote sewed up, they reckoned without the influence peddled by a German-American editor imported by the Gang from an adjoining county, or Bob Wright's liberal expenditures for food and drink.[4] The Gang won heavy majorities in all precincts except Hazelwood northwest of Dodge. Settlers there were angry at the political incumbents for refusing to include them in a distribution of state firearms allocated to Ford during the Indian panic of September 1878.[5]

Bob Wright, re-elected as representative, proved as good as his word in obtaining an extension of the "deadline" to protect local farmers.[6] But there was to be no resting upon laurels: a new issue arose in 1879—the ques-

[3] Dodge City *Globe*, Oct. 22, 29, Nov. 12, 1878; Dodge City *Times*, Oct. 26, Nov. 2, 1878; Spearville *News*, Oct. 26, 1878.

[4] Dodge City *Times*, Nov. 9, 1878. Angry allegations concerning the usefulness of liquor were invariably made by losing sides in local elections, but see in this case the relatively specific charge by Spearville's "Ajax" in the Dodge City *Globe*, Nov. 19, 1878, and W. F. Petillon's letter two years later in ibid., Oct. 19, 1880.

[5] Dodge City *Globe*, Nov. 12, 1878. The Frostites, however, won a victory soon after when, in a conflict between the sheriff and the county commissioners, the Gang's George Cox resigned from the board. In a subsequent vote by the two remaining board members and the county clerk the Frost faction's George Hoover was selected to replace Cox, the county clerk for some reason abandoning his Gang allegiance to support Hoover. See ibid., Mar. 18, Apr. 8, Aug. 5, 1879.

[6] Dodge City *Globe*, Feb. 11, Mar. 18, Apr. 22, 1879; Dodge City *Times*, Mar. 22, 1879. The new quarantine line did not affect Dodge City's access to the cattle trail, of course.

tion of destitute relief for rural sufferers, as discussed in the last chapter. Although some members of both Dodge factions busied themselves in efforts to mitigate the rural plight, it was probably the sympathetic tone of Frost's *Globe* as against the hostile Gang organ, the *Times*, that turned the balance toward the Frostites. As in the previous year both sides sponsored caucuses, and again a "People's Ticket" opposed an "Independent Ticket" at the polls. Once again rural types stood as candidates for the less important posts on both. This time, however, the anti-Gang forces triumphed.[7]

Extracurricular encounters that soon followed included an unpraiseworthy effort by William B. ("Bat") Masterson, the Gangsman serving as sheriff, to dispatch both Dan Frost and Fred Zimmermann to the federal penitentiary.[8] The primary strategy of the Gang, however, was to transform their clique into a county Republican Party, since it began to be obvious as early as mid-1878 that their most important adherents held to this partisan position, while many of the Frost leaders were Democrats.[9] Besides, most of the rural newcomers seemed to be Republicans, and 1880 was to be a presidential election year, making a local victory via a Republican label that much more certain.

The main stumbling block to this Gang plan was that Dan Frost, Fred Zimmermann, Morris Collar, Dick Evans, and others of the Frost persuasion also claimed to be Republicans. In March 1880, both factions sent delegations to the Republican county convention, each clique

[7] Dodge City *Times*, Oct. 11, 18, 25, 1879; Dodge City *Globe*, Oct. 14, 21, Nov. 4, 11, 1879; Spearville *News*, Oct. 18, 1879.

[8] Dodge City *Times*, July 19, Sept. 20, Dec. 6, 1879, Jan. 17, Feb. 21, 1880; Dodge City *Globe*, Dec. 2, 23, 1879, Jan. 13, Feb. 17, Apr. 13, 20, 1880, Nov. 6, 1883.

[9] See the names of delegates selected at Republican and Democratic county conventions in Dodge City *Globe*, Aug. 6, 13, 27, 1878; Dodge City *Times*, Aug. 31, 1878.

acquiring one seat on the new central committee by virtue of a compromise arrangement. In October the party met in a nominating convention at which the devised slate represented another *modus vivendi* between Dodge City's factions—at the expense of the once-courted rural electorate, now numerically depleted by the effect of the long drought. Dissident Republicans, Democrats, and the Spearville Greenbackers tried to capitalize on the rural sectionalism aroused by Dodge City domination but could not agree on a single ticket. The regular Republican slate triumphed at the polls, therefore, by virtue of a split opposition vote.[1] Factional compromise had prolonged Dodge City's political hegemony in Ford County for one more year, but the emergence of prohibition as an issue was promptly to throw all into confusion again. In the years that followed neither uncomplicated secular factionalism nor national political partisanship was to provide the key to local alignments and conflicts.

[5]

DODGE CITY was unique in being able to manipulate county politics almost at will as an adjunct of its internal factionalism. The situation at Ellsworth, on the other hand, illustrates how a rural electorate, once aroused, might win a commanding role in a contention of town cliques. In that the general evolution at all the cattle towns was from less to more rural political power, Ellsworth's example represents a slightly more advanced evolution over that of Dodge in the interaction of urban factions and rural voters. Although briefly mentioned earlier, the following episode seems worth considering in more detail.

Ellsworth's citizens decided in 1871 that they must

[1] Dodge City *Globe*, Mar. 23, Oct. 19, 26, 1880; Dodge City *Times*, Mar. 27, Oct. 23, 30, 1880.

have the prestige an imposing new courthouse could confer. In October of that year, therefore, at the instigation of townsmen, Ellsworth County citizens voted on the question of issuing courthouse bonds. Despite an overwhelming opposition from farmers, who evidently saw the proposition as unnecessarily enhancing the town's circumstances, almost unanimous approval in Ellsworth itself tipped the scales in the bonds' favor. Rural citizens immediately petitioned the board of county commissioners to restrain issuance of the bonds. The townsmen countered by acquiring approval for a new vote on the matter, but the countrymen frustrated this by obtaining a court injunction.[2] In January 1872, Ellsworthites again sought a new election, and in March, with the injunction dissolved, the town-dominated board of county commissioners scheduled the election for April. In the balloting the bond proposition carried by a slim majority of twenty-one votes.[3]

By late 1871 two Illinois capitalists had assumed the proprietorship of the Ellsworth townsite. These gentlemen were nonresidents, but many of the community's original businessmen, such as grocer Ira W. Phelps and dry goods merchant Perry Hodgden, either held stock in the company or had purchased town lots from it. For some time the company had reserved a block on which a permanent courthouse might be built; this site was already referred to locally as the "courthouse square." People with properties adjacent to the square anticipated a

[2] Ellsworth Co. Commissioners Journal, 1867–87 (transcript, KSHS), pp. 132, 134, 136, 138. The Journal lists only the fact that the bonds carried Ellsworth Township, so perhaps the injunction mentioned in ibid., p. 146, kept all but Ellsworth voters from the polls.

[3] Ellsworth Commissioners Journal, pp. 146, 150, 157; Ellsworth *Reporter*, Mar. 14, Apr. 4, 1872. The local editor tried both to conceal and suppress contention over the bonds by stating that they "were carried by a large majority, and . . . those opposed will hardly carry the question any further."

sharp rise in real estate values once the new public building was erected in their midst.

If the county's rural citizens could not frustrate the courthouse bonds, they could at least destroy their use as a blatant vehicle for land speculation by the town's oldest businessmen. The one purely rural member of the county board introduced the notion of an alternate location for the new courthouse, suggesting that it be built on Main Street. When in later years the county would need a still larger structure, he argued, the old property could be profitably sold as a business site. The idea appealed to merchant Arthur Larkin, whose loyalties did not lie with the town company. After confidential negotiations between Larkin and the commissioners, one of whom happened to be Larkin's business partner, the board in June accepted his donation of two North Main Street lots as a site for the new structure.[4]

When the news leaked out, the stunned promoters of the old location—as well as some who thought the square more appropriate from an esthetic viewpoint than the new downtown site—converged on the county commissioners with a fifty-signature petition urging them to retract their decision. Those with real estate interests near the new site then sprang to Larkin's defense. Many of the town's newer business and professional men, who possibly had felt themselves excluded from the old and established entrepreneurial group, joined this faction. But the most powerful support came from disgruntled countrymen. When in turn the Larkin adherents produced petitions carrying a total of 139 signatures, perhaps 90 per cent were those of rural residents.[5] The board declared

[4] Ellsworth *Reporter*, Dec. 14, 1871 ff. (Ellsworth Town Co. ad), June 20, 1872.

[5] Ellsworth *Reporter*, June 13, 20, 1872. In its minutes, printed in the June 20 issue, the board recognized petitions with a total of 139 names attached. For the same issue of the paper, Larkin submitted to the editor one petition with 160 names. Presumably Larkin's list in-

an intention to adhere to its decision. The courthouse square leaders obtained a temporary injunction to keep the bonds from being issued, but a hearing upheld the commissioners. Thereupon the board commenced a suit for wrongful suing of the injunction.[6]

Further details on the legal maneuvering are lacking, but the larger factionalism spilled noisily over into county politics, resulting finally in a Republican slate equally shared by Larkin partisans and farmers. This ticket opposed a slate dominated by the old courthouse square proponents. As the preceding chapter showed, this Republican coalition, despite its bright prospects, sank in defeat because it could not overcome the mutual rural-urban antagonisms that increasingly divided the county's electorate. Confronted by this potent hostility from the hinterlands, townsmen closed ranks again—closed enough, at least, so that never again in the cattle trade years would factional conflict seriously impair a solid front against the countrymen in county politics. If the farmers had helped precipitate the factionalism of 1872 they were also instrumental in stifling it again.

[6]

BY FAR the most spectacular contention between real estate cliques occurred at Wichita. "Wichita was organized by two opposing forces," admitted a citizen in late 1875,

cluded all the signatures on the board's petitions, and then some. A systematic check of the 160 names against the 1870 manuscript census for Ellsworth County reveals only 40 positive correlations; however, the structure of Larkin's list suggests that only the first 15 to 18 were town residents and the remaining 142 to 145 rural citizens. Prominent among the signatories was David B. Long, a rural leader who had been active in petitioning against the courthouse bonds in October 1871. See Ellsworth Commissioners Journal, p. 134.

[6] Ellsworth *Reporter*, June 27, Aug. 1, 1872; Andreas: *History of Kansas*, p. 1275.

"and a contest has been going on ever since."[7] Such was indeed the case, and it stemmed from the city's beginnings as a townsite divided between the holdings of David S. Munger and William Greiffenstein. At first what buildings the town contained stood on the Munger site— two rows of shacks facing each other across a wide segment of the cattle trail named North Main Street. A few blocks south of this embryo business district, where the Chisholm Trail emerged from the Arkansas River, Bill Greiffenstein laid out an east-west thoroughfare he named Douglas Avenue. A short distance from the riverbank, at the right-angle intersection of Douglas and Main, Greiffenstein envisioned the heart of his own urban development. The Munger site enjoyed a head start, but to entice further growth his way Greiffenstein refused to be undersold by the owners of North Main Street lots. He circulated extremely attractive offers to prospective businessmen and soon began giving lots free to any who promised to build on them—a practice promptly imitated by his North Main competition, though probably not as liberally. Douglas Avenue soon took the lead as a built-up sector. In August the town's newly acquired newspaper editor proclaimed "Dutch Bill" the true founder of the community.[8]

Backed as he was by wealthy nonresident remnants of the old Wichita Town Company, Munger was not a man to give in easily. He was soon relegated to the ranks, however, by more powerful economic leaders with property interests on North Main Street—such men as William C. Woodman, private banker and land speculator, and James C. Fraker, president of Wichita's First National Bank. Both Woodman's and Fraker's institutions

---

[7] Wichita *Eagle*, Dec. 2, 1875.
[8] C. J. Roe to A. F. Horner, July 2, 1870, Horner Papers, KSHS; Topeka *Commonwealth*, May 10, 27, 1870; Wichita *Eagle*, Oct. 24, Dec. 12, 1872, Jan. 16, 1873; Wichita *Vidette*, Aug. 13, 1870.

graced Main Street. But Douglas Avenue possessed its own
credit facility in the Wichita Savings Bank, as well as its
influential businessmen allied to Greiffenstein. Soon the
Greiffenstein clique was known as the "Douglas Avenue
crowd," as opposed to the "north-enders." In later years
the northern faction also came to be called the "Occidental
crowd," from the name of its hotel-office building headquarters.[9]

Public-spirited Wichitans, perceiving the importance
of community solidarity, usually pretended that the factional conflict did not exist. "Unaffected by any personal
interests, the sole object of her citizens has been to build
up a model town," lied a spokesman to a Kansas City
newspaper. "In all local elections politics are entirely
ignored." The last sentence, at least, was technically correct. Its implication was false. As a Greiffenstein partisan
explained some years later:

> Politics did not count much. . . . To establish and maintain
> the supremacy of Douglas avenue was more than politics;
> it was a religious faith, and its promises to its votaries
> were not of any spiritual condition or location after death,
> but it was victory over the north end and high prices for
> Douglas avenue lots when the battle was over.[1]

In this spirited conflict over downtown real estate
values all public facilities represented fair game for the
side clever enough to capture them. Originally, as in the
case of Ellsworth's courthouse, a rational basis underlay

[9] An uninhibited brief account of the Main-Douglas conflict, lacking
only dates, is that by Kos Harris in O. H. Bentley (ed.): *History of
Wichita and Sedgwick County* (Chicago, 1910), I, 139–41, 144,
181–86, 236–41, 268–71. Harris did not himself arrive in Wichita
until 1874 (see his ad in the *Eagle*, Apr. 16, 1874 ff.) and, he admits,
was not received into the Douglas inner circle until after the death of
James McCulloch that autumn. But Harris most likely learned many
earlier details from conversation within the Greiffenstein clique.
[1] Wichita *Tribune*, Oct. 5, 1871; Bentley: *History of Wichita*, I,
237.

this activity, since a close proximity of public buildings made for higher land values. At Wichita, however, it often degenerated into mere factional tests of wits. The post office, which did not yet have its own special building, was an example. Originally this important amenity stood on North Main Street. In late 1872 the Douglas men induced the postmaster to transfer his operations to Greiffenstein's new brick office building, the Eagle Block, located at the strategic intersection of Douglas and Main. Two years later, with a fresh postmaster at the helm, the north-enders lured the institution to quarters in their massive new Occidental Hotel on the corner of Main and Second Avenue. Lest strife get wholly out of hand, Marshall M. Murdock of the *Eagle* — a civic-minded neutral even though he made his editorial headquarters in Greiffenstein's building—reluctantly accepted the postmastership. He wisely located the postal facility at a midway point.[2] Soon afterwards, however, the north-enders concocted a scheme by which W. C. Woodman would give the post office space in his new brick building on upper Main while his north end colleagues contributed the rent. Murdock readily agreed to this thrifty arrangement, despite the disappointment of the Douglas crowd. By this time the peripatetic post office had become a tired joke, and it finally lost its fascination as an object of contention.[3]

The bitter dissension between factions kept Wichitans

[2] Wichita *Eagle*, Dec. 5, 1872, Dec. 10, 1874, Jan. 28, Feb. 11, 1875; Andreas: *History of Kansas*, p. 1391: Wichita *Beacon*, Nov. 25, Dec. 9, 1874; Bentley: *History of Wichita*, I, 139, 186–87. Besides Murdock, a few other community leaders were factional neutrals. Lawyer H. C. Sluss, who had close friends on both sides, was one. James R. Mead and Charles F. Gilbert are also to be included in this group; as large real estate speculators, they were neutralized by land holdings and/or business interests on both Main and Douglas. Ibid., I, 144, 182–83, 236.

[3] Wichita *Beacon*, Sept. 15, 1875; Bentley: *History of Wichita*, I, 237.

from uniting long enough to locate a permanent court-house. Temporarily housed, therefore, like the post office, the seat of county government wandered to and fro according to changing factional fortunes. In 1872, with a Douglas partisan serving as the Wichita representative on the board of county commissioners, the Greiffenstein clique won the governmental rooms even though under-bid by the north-enders on the amount of rent. Two years later the Douglas men lowered the rent to zero but were unable to keep the county offices from slipping away to the Occidental Hotel. Although Greiffenstein's clique then took the case to court, the governmental facilities remained on Main. When Fraker's north end bank went under in 1876, owing the county a large deposit, it was taken over and used as a courthouse for several years, the businessmen of Wichita still being unable to close ranks for the purpose of promoting a permanent structure.[4]

The principal medium of Wichita factional conflict, despite the implication of these examples, was essentially economic rather than political. Even so, as at Dodge City and Ellsworth, the rural populace often played an intervening role. This was never more clear than when the Main-Douglas rivalry turned to the question of bridging the Arkansas River at Wichita.

One of Bill Greiffenstein's early projects was a bridge over the cattle ford at the west end of Douglas Avenue that would ensure the value of the street and thus of his own property values. In August 1870, Greiffenstein and some allies formed a company to build a Douglas Avenue bridge. The association apparently attempted to obtain public aid by way of a county bond levy, but even with its president sitting as chairman of the board of county

[4] Sedgwick Co. Commissioners Journal, 1870–74 (transcript, KSHS), pp. 103, 108, 147; Wichita *Beacon*, Dec. 16, 1874, Apr. 28, June 16, 1875; Wichita *Eagle*, Feb. 11, 25, Mar. 11, 1875; Bentley: *History of Wichita*, I, 140–41.

commissioners the Douglas project was not among those on which a bond vote was authorized. A year later, therefore, the Douglas clique formed a second company and succeeded in placing $15,000 in bridge bonds on the ballot in a township election. Probably due to the fact that the structure was to be a toll bridge, as well as to the opposition of north-enders, citizens turned down the proposal.

Greiffenstein promptly organized a new company to finance a toll bridge with private capital alone. The lack of official funds forced him to broaden the base of his project, and he accepted suburban residents as stockholders and also some North Main businessmen.[5] The new bridge—a thousand-foot span fixed in place with stone abutments and tubular iron piers resting on pile foundations—opened for traffic in July 1872. Providing a much-improved crossing for trail herds, a large source of summer tolls, its income from the date of opening through November totaled upwards of $10,000—or one third of the original capital investment. Stockholders expressed confidence that the structure would pay for itself the coming year.[6]

Simultaneously, farmers living west of the Arkansas River, whose traffic of course contributed to the bridge receipts, began to complain. It cost a west-sider fifty cents to haul his produce across the bridge into Wichita and another twenty-five to return. Early in the year one such farmer called for county purchase of the facility in order to liberate it from tolls or, failing that, the building

[5] Wichita *Vidette*, Aug. 13, 25, 1870; Sedgwick Commissioners Journal, p. 8; Wichita *Tribune*, Aug. 31, Sept. 7, 14, Nov. 3, 1871. Kos Harris makes much of Greiffenstein's sagacity in promoting north end defections by allowing some of them to buy into the bridge project (Bentley: *History of Wichita*, I, 182, 236); but, as surmised here, this seems rather to have been forced on the Douglas Avenue leader.

[6] Wichita *Eagle*, June 14, Sept. 13, Oct. 24, 1872, Jan. 16, Apr. 24, 1873.

of a free bridge. As 1873 wore on the protests mounted. "We pay for the bridge every year," complained a westsider, "yet you of the town own it." Unless something was done, he warned, the farmers in his area would retaliate by organizing cooperative buying and selling on the Patrons of Husbandry pattern. Expressing hostile views toward monopolies, letters to the Wichita *Eagle* demanded that the county commissioners order a reduction of the tolls. Marsh Murdock eventually felt obliged to observe that the board possessed no such authority.[7]

That autumn petitioners pestered the county commissioners for another vote on bridges, this time to include a provision to purchase the Douglas span for $25,000. As far as some west-siders were concerned, however, the Wichitans themselves should buy it and make it free. The idea of paying so much for the bridge was probably anathema to most rural dwellers, especially to those living east of the river, and the commissioners refused to submit the proposal to a public vote.

The west-side farmers would not back down. A petition circulated in February 1874, demanding bonds up to $20,000 in amount to bridge the Little Arkansas River above Wichita, and either to build a second span paralleling the Wichita toll bridge or else to buy the toll bridge "at a fair valuation . . . and make it a free bridge." Critics immediately denounced this proposition as a creature of the Wichita Bridge Company, a design to obtain an inflated price for its own property. Thereupon a group of influential farmers submitted an open letter to a Wichita contractor, requesting bids on four proposed bridges around the county, including one at Wichita. This report seemed to verify the notion of bridge company skulduggery. Alarmed that the board was about to receive the suspect petition favorably, rural delegates from all over the county descended on Wichita for the commissioners'

[7] Wichita *Eagle*, Jan. 2, July 31, Aug. 21, Oct. 3, 17, 23, 1873.

meeting of March 2, 1874. Those in attendance spent the afternoon debating the issue, and the board finally agreed to submit to the voters the question of $55,000 in bonds for five bridges in the county. Each of these was to be separately approved but with the proviso that if any one of them failed, all would fail.[8]

Rural critics bitterly assailed the proposal for the Wichita bridge, which allowed $20,000 for either a new structure or purchase of the present one. In the southern part of the county agitators spoke of a "Wichita swindle," and, as anticipated, rural sectionalism proved rife all over Sedgwick County, neighborhoods naturally wanting their own bridges built but begrudging tax increases to build those of others. Finally a few west-side farmers admitted that even they preferred high bridge tolls to a tax increase. An eleventh-hour letter to the *Eagle*, signed by Wichitans from both ends of the business district, urged townsmen to forget "all little local strife and jealousy" and vote yes on the bridge bonds. Perhaps this manifesto from the town decisively killed the proposition in rural Sedgwick. All of the bridge bonds, in any event, failed at the ballot box.[9]

In a complex series of factional maneuvers during the winter of 1874–75 the bridge issue finally approached a resolution. That the repeated defeat of efforts to free the Douglas Avenue structure might work to their own advantage finally dawned on the businessmen of the north end. In the fall of 1874 they decided to bridge the flow upstream at Central Avenue, an alternative they had avoided to date because it meant spanning the Little Arkansas River as well as the Arkansas proper. Nevertheless, a free crossing there would definitely draw traffic away from Douglas to the enhancement of their own dis-

[8] Wichita *Eagle*, Sept. 25, Oct. 9, 23, 1873, Feb. 19, 26, Mar. 5, 12, 1874.

[9] Wichita *Eagle*, Mar. 19, 26, Apr. 2, 9, 16, 1874.

trict. The rural-dominated county board approved their petition for a $1,500 subsidy, but, in an effective playing off of the two factions, also authorized a $1,000 donation to the Wichita Bridge Company should it remove the tolls from the Douglas Avenue span. The west-side farmer would get his free bridge one way or another, and at a bargain.[1]

Early in 1875 both cliques sought to obtain bridge appropriations from the Wichita city council but, with that body divided fairly evenly between Main and Douglas adherents, their propositions checkmated one another. A fortnight later James M. Steele, a shrewd Douglas partisan on the council, proposed a compromise whereby the north end's Little Arkansas span—the one actually within city limits—would be given $1,000 and double that amount would go to purchase the Douglas bridge. This also lost. In March, Steele tried again: $500 in cash to the Little Arkansas span upon its completion and $2,000 in city warrants for the Douglas structure. This measure succeeded by a unanimous vote. Unfortunately, the Wichita Bridge Company proved not entirely responsive to Douglas Avenue discipline and voted to reject both county and city offers. In midsummer, however, a number of Douglas businessmen raised $800, used this subscription to acquire a ten-month lease of the bridge, and opened it to free traffic.

The advent of free crossings at both Douglas and Central avenues in 1875 by no means ended the factional conflict over bridges. By September the hasty construction of the upstream spans had betrayed itself: the north end's facility was reported to be in such flimsy shape as to be unusable. Then in November Jim Steele won election as Wichita's representative to the board of county commissioners. "Jim, pursuant to his implied promises," re-

[1] Wichita *Eagle*, Dec. 17, 1874; Andreas: *History of Kansas*, p. 1390.

called the Douglas crowd's historian, "proceeded to tear down the Central avenue bridge 'eye-sore' and distribute it to the various townships in the county, thereby restoring to Douglas avenue its natural trade and offsetting the rage of the north end by the solidification [behind itself] of the agricultural classes who obtained bridges without higher taxes."[2]

[7]

How SUCH FACTIONAL CONFLICTS are to be related to the question of "democracy" at the cattle towns largely depends on how one chooses to define this term. If a broad participation in public issues is selected as the overriding criterion, it then seems fair to say that political factionalism was at least democracy's handmaiden. Certainly the reverse was true: when factionalism *failed* to enter politics popular decision-making suffered.

Democratic forms, imposed by law on the local scene, were no doubt always implicitly threatened at places like the cattle towns where the entrepreneurial consensus so dominated. But business community factionalism often provided the critical leavening. When townsmen polarized into cliques, and cliques became political combatants, partisan appeals to the widest possible franchise could seldom be avoided. Factional conflict helped keep the citizens at large politically mobilized, even though the issues it brought forward were not always "rational" ones. It offered a continuing challenge to any political establishment and denied the formation of any single power structure. And it allowed—even encouraged—participation in local decision-making by rural electorates

---

[2] Wichita Council Record, 1870–81 (microfilm copy, KSHS), B, 30–32, 34–35; Wichita *Eagle*, Feb. 11, Mar. 11, Apr. 8, July 22, 1875; Wichita *Beacon*, Apr. 14, July 28, Sept. 22, 1875; Bentley: *History of Wichita*, I, 140.

and their representatives. That the greatest good for the greatest number did not regularly triumph does not deny democracy's existence; it only emphasizes the difficulties of attempting to determine by any means whatsoever just what that amounted to.

VII

The Politics of Reform

[1]

TIME WOULD ERASE the obvious social evils in their
midst, "respectable" cattle town people felt sure; the
sheer increase in permanent population would necessarily
bring with it a proportionate growth in influence of a
"better class of citizen." This belief in the inevitability of
moral progress, however, was tested at the cattle towns
by more than mere routine human weakness and deprav-
ity. Those who defined the business community consensus
viewed the brothel, the dance house, the gaming room,
and the saloon as necessary adjuncts to the cattle trade.
Moral betterment, for all its inevitability, was actively
resisted and openly defied on every hand.

It was probably as much immorality's unashamed
challenge as it was the desire for both general and specific social improvements that moved the cattle town
reformers—self-conscious instruments of nineteenth-century progress—to agitate for change. Beginning modestly
in terms both of stated aims and popular support, their
efforts increasingly cut across the prevailing patterns of
local political conflict.

[2]

IF EARLY CATTLE TOWN REFORMERS expected municipal organization to overcome the deficiencies to which they ob-

jected, they were soon disabused of the notion. Community incorporation was strictly an entrepreneurial device imposed to do little more than counteract violence. As we have seen, the next step of those who sparked the establishment of formal law enforcement machinery was to extend to prostitution and gambling a form of official recognition through regular tax assessments. The illegal professions did not take kindly to this discrimination. When taxation was introduced at Dodge City, for example, furious prostitutes convened and voted to fight city hall, hiring for the purpose two local attorneys—who no doubt advised the girls of the amusing illogic in their appeal to legal redress. At Ellsworth the gamblers' angry response to taxation helped precipitate the violence of 1873.[1] It seems doubtful that respectable citizens gained much comfort either from this resistance or the knowledge that sin was more than "paying its way," as it was commonly put. To such men and women municipal recognition was a backward step whereby immorality simply bribed local government for permission to exist in contradiction of the law.

In roughly the first half of the cattle trade period, secular factionalism dominated local politics exclusively almost everywhere. It is clear that moral reformers enjoyed few opportunities to participate, as such, in the various machinations of contending cliques. There were, true enough, economic leaders whose personal piety nourished radical moral sentiments, but such men were not generally expected to intrude these predilections into either business or politics. Other such men presumably played down their personal attitudes in order to mesh better with the dominant political and economic apparatus. "There were severe things to endure," recalled Nicholas B. Klaine, Dodge City's editor-politician and a late-

[1] Dodge City *Times*, Aug. 10, Sept. 7, 1878. For the Ellsworth episode see Chapter III above.

blooming reformer, referring to the bleak years before a moralist consensus emerged in his town, ". . . because there appeared no mode of redress—because the valor lay in bowing to the inevitable."[2]

That bowing to "inevitable" progress took more courage than could be mustered by many cattle town people was evident to many, if not most, of the clergymen called to minister to townspeople's spiritual needs. Few of them in turn cared to press moral reform issues from the pulpit, or so the surviving evidence would indicate, until such time as they could count on something approaching a favorable popular response. Cattle town churchgoers apparently were subjected to as many sermons condemning public opinion as those condemning specific wickedness in their midst. In 1873, for example, during a brief and somewhat mysterious flurry of moral agitation at Wichita, the town's Presbyterian pastor dared to speak strongly against Wichita's chief evils, even criticizing the "fallacious arguments," as a reporter paraphrased his sermon, "that the city is dependent on these vices for a revenue, as also that by them the Texas trade is drawn to the place." The "only effectual" remedy, the pastor concluded, would be a new reform consensus. Exactly a year later, sadly enough, he could as yet see no compelling general interest in eradicating even local prostitution, and he left it at that. In 1878 the new Methodist pastor at Dodge City respectfully informed his congregation that putting all the blame for professional sin on public officials was sheer hypocrisy. "The officers are always glad to do what you want them to do," he argued; "the law is enforced as you desire it. Officers are simply exponents of public opinion."[3] He might have said much the same of

[2] Dodge City *Times*, Jan. 4, 1883.
[3] Wichita *Eagle*, July 10, 1873; Wichita *Beacon*, July 29, 1874; Dodge City *Times*, Dec. 7, 1878.

himself and his fellow clergymen, who could lead only at such time as their listeners were prepared to follow.

[3]

THESE EXPRESSIONS of despair about a deficient moral consensus emphasize the fact that cattle town people normally did not divide into two camps, pro and con, on the reform question. Reform opinion was instead distributed along a spectrum of attitudes marked by degrees of difference on how far any program of immediate social improvement should be carried. Three general positions can be grouped on this scale without doing them injustice: minimum, moderate, and radical.

Townsmen who might be called adherents of the minimum position resisted any substantial change in the old free-wheeling frontier tone of local society. Introducing city government, they seemed to feel, was quite enough of a concession to civilization. By the cattle trade era such types had become true reactionaries in a social sense. A moderate reform editor at Dodge City pictured the residue of this element that dated from the town's earliest years:

There is a class, still a large one . . . which looks with horror upon the approach of manners, customs and ideas tending to drive out the "frontier" character[is]tics of Dodge. To them, to live in the "wickedest city in the west" is a source of pride. They look with profound contempt upon a town whose police officers are not walking arsenals. They look back with regret to the time when "a drink was a quarter and a cigar two bits." They are not such bad fellows after all; but they do not long for a quiet life. They are not so many as they were. Some have lately felt the cordon of grangers pressing upon them and they have flitted; some to [Las] Vegas, some to Silver Cliff, and some to Leadville.

Still we have enough left among us to be an influence,

and we now ask them if it will not be better to bow to the inevitable and begin at once to "shape our ends" toward subsiding into the perhaps ignominious, but certainly peaceful and prosperous position of an interior Kansas city.[4]

When such men held political power, local government tended to embody very much the character of its reigning personalities. That they were constitutionally incapable of viewing moral reform with approval goes without saying.

The second, or moderate, position is less easily delimited. The "*semi* moral party," one Ellsworth businessman playfully called himself and his fellow moderates.[5] At best, the moderate position provided no definite formula for social change and included no mandate for general moral reform. Its guiding ethic clearly was a traditional American businessman's definition of social reform— hesitant, ultimately rationalized in economic terms, limited to specific responses for specific exigencies.

The special situation in which the cattle town businessman found himself dictated a pragmatic approach. On the one hand, he remained sensitive to the argument that his best economic interests demanded local facilities for gaming, whoring, and heavy drinking in order to hold the cattle trade. On the other hand, public opinion abroad was always to be respected. Outsiders unanimously condemned homicide; therefore governments had been instituted among the cattle town people and violence, so far as possible, had been suppressed. But lesser sin, in that unlike homicide it served a functional purpose, constituted a problem of different magnitude.

A complicating factor here was that observers from outside by no means presented a solid front toward cattle town wickedness. Many of them, who had expected to

[4] Dodge City *Globe*, Mar. 18, 1879.
[5] Ellsworth *Reporter*, Mar. 5, 1874.

find something straight out of Hogarth, commented favorably on the cattle town scene. Others, their judgments less conditioned by moral relativity, condemned it in the harshest terms. Cattle town newspapers, publishing visitors' statements clipped from other journals to fulfill a ravenous local curiosity about outside opinion, were in one sense simply running dialogues on the morality question. Local editors, of course, congratulated or damned the writers according to their expressed impressions. One standard editorial retort to critics was that the cattle town people disdained hypocrisy: "Every one is honest in Ellsworth; there are no back parlor gambling rooms, no backroom bars, no sanctimonious sinners." Or: "There is no concealment [in Dodge City], and that is why loose things and unruly acts appear so flagrant."[6] But such attempts to convert manifest immorality into a social virtue hardly proved satisfactory over the long run.

The moderate reformer defined his position largely by outside opinions, conflicting though they might be at times, and when he acted he did so against those facets of local sin most shocking to visiting observers. Targets for moderate reform thus tended to include not prostitution, but rather its overt manifestation, the dance house, not professional gambling as such but "front room" games. Moderate reformers could also be moved to oppose dishonest gambling and confidence games, since the practitioners of these related arts preyed almost exclusively upon visitors. In every case, however, moderates responded promptly to spectacular outbreaks of violence, which suggested that self-government itself had failed.[7] "Good order" remained their social goal, but as applied to

[6] Ellsworth *Reporter*, Feb. 26, 1874; Dodge City *Times*, Mar. 16, 1878.
[7] See the comments from Dodge City about two such occurrences at Caldwell in Dodge City *Times*, Apr. 20, June 29, 1882.

local immorality the term was synonymous with the *appearance* of good order.

Rarely did the moderate feel justified in challenging the political *status quo* directly with reform in mind unless one important prerequisite existed: the incumbent administration could be accused of financial irresponsibility. Wichita's and Ellsworth's abolition of gambling, Caldwell's response to a serious law enforcement lapse, Dodge City's actions against confidence gamesmanship, Abilene's against prostitution—all these relatively powerful pre-prohibition reform movements, as we shall have occasion to see, were accompanied by allegations of fiscal irregularity at city hall. Though perhaps employed mainly as a political shibboleth in these instances, this particular criticism clearly reinforces an entrepreneurial interpretation of moderate reform.

The third position, that of the radical in the reform spectrum, embraced those who desired the total eradication of sinful elements in local society. Its partisans might applaud an institution of moderate reforms—the imposition of "some restraint, some respect, and some show of decency in the illegitimate and unlawful affairs," as Nicholas Klaine put it.[8] But they actually had more far-reaching things in mind. "The *praying womans temperance movement*," the Ellsworth wit already quoted termed this position. Indeed, its initial impulse appeared to be a conventional alliance of evangelical, feminist, antiliquor idealism.[9]

[8] Dodge City *Times*, Mar. 22, 1882. Such a statement reveals that radical reformers also were motivated at least partially by outside opinion; their commitment to an absolute moral position, however, is what set them apart from the moderates.

[9] Ellsworth *Reporter*, Mar. 5, 1874. According to the attorney general of Kansas, who met with the Dodge City prohibitionists in 1885, "The backbone of the temperance element of the city are the ladies . . . and I found their views to be much more practical and sensible than

Those legendary pillars of frontier moral uplift, aroused housewives, proved of little collective influence during the early years. In 1871 over one hundred Abilene ladies petitioned their city council to abolish local brothels. The petition was ignored. A similar document signed by seventy-four female Wichitans met the same fate the following summer. Outside the sphere of organized charitable efforts, mobilized women were unwelcome intruders into the administration of public affairs. Toward the end of the cattle trade era Samuel Berry, the abrasive Caldwell lawyer and editor, vividly expressed what evidently remained the prevalent feeling in many male minds about female reformers. "The *men* of Caldwell can transact her business," sneered Berry, "and they don't really need any assistance."[1] As an illustration of a successful reform action in the years before state prohibition, a petition of 1873 that apparently effected the closing of Wichita's variety theater on Sunday nights carried the names of 131 signatories, none of them women.[2]

The feminine influence, as one might expect, increased according to the increasing proportion of wives and married men in the local population. The gradual

those of many of the men." (Topeka *Capital*, July 11, 1885.) Though males usually staffed the highest executive posts in cattle town prohibition groups, it seems likely that, as at Dodge, women formed the bulk of the rank-and-file. For a comprehensive analysis of this unique female involvement in the prohibition reform of post-Civil War America see Joseph R. Gusfield: *Symbolic Crusade: Status Politics and the American Temperance Movement* (Urbana, Ill., 1963), especially chap. iv.

[1] Abilene Council Record, 1870–76 (microfilm copy, KSHS), p. 67; Abilene *Chronicle*, June 1, 1871; Wichita Council Record, 1870–81 (microfilm copy, KSHS), A, 210; Wichita *Eagle*, July 19, 1872; undated petition misfiled as the final document for 1873 in Wichita Miscellaneous Papers, 1871–81, microfilm copy, KSHS; Caldwell *Standard*, June 12, 1884.

[2] Petition dated 1873, in Wichita Miscellaneous Papers. The relationship of this petition to the brief reformist outburst of July 1873 is unclear. See footnote 9 below.

TABLE 1 The Changing Age-Sex Composition of Three Cattle Towns
(Shaded areas, 1880 and 1885, indicate married population)

domestication of cattle town society can be seen with the aid of "population pyramids" constructed for Wichita, Dodge City, and Caldwell in the cattle trade period (Table 1). The peculiar deck-gun profile of the early years in each case reflects a population heavily dominated by males in their twenties and thirties—bachelor communities, as it were. But in each case the trend was also toward the classic triangular configuration as family groups gradually infiltrated the demographic structure.[3]

A second apparently important population change that accompanied the emergence of radical reform at the cattle towns, although not once mentioned as such in the narrative sources, was the shifting ethnic composition of the cattle town people. Table 2 illustrates this factor in the "decision-making" or voting population—that is, the white males of over twenty years of age—at the same three places: Wichita, Dodge, and Caldwell.[4] It is at once apparent that ethnic change was not altogether pronounced except at Dodge, where the span of years measured

[3] The data for the tables in this chapter were compiled from U.S. Manuscript Census, 1870: Kansas (KSHS), Sedgwick Co., Wichita Twp.; Kansas Manuscript Census, 1875 (KSHS): Sedgwick Co., City of Wichita; ibid., Ford Co., Dodge Twp., pp. 1–21; U.S. Manuscript Census, 1880: Kansas (microfilm copy, KSHS), Ford Co., City of Dodge City; ibid., Sumner Co., City of Caldwell; Kansas Manuscript Census, 1885 (KSHS): Ford Co., City of Dodge City (minus transient irrigation ditch workers, pp. 66 ff.); ibid., Sumner Co., City of Caldwell. To contrast the population pyramids of Table 1 with that for the entire state in 1880 see C. D. Clark and Roy L. Roberts: *People of Kansas: A Demographic and Sociological Study* (Topeka, 1936), p. 98.

[4] In isolating voters from the general population in order to highlight the (geographically defined) ethnic basis of politics, I indicate my debt to the lead provided by George H. Daniels's pioneering article: "Immigrant Vote in the 1860 Election: The Case of Iowa," *Mid-America*, XLIV (1962), 146–62. The U.S. regions designated in the tables of this chapter are defined as follows: New England—states lying east or northeast of New York; Middle Atlantic States—New York, New Jersey, Pennsylvania; Middle West—Ohio, Indiana, Illinois, Iowa, Michigan, Wisconsin, Minnesota; South—the slave states of 1860; West —all remaining states and territories.

TABLE 2

THE CHANGING ETHNIC COMPOSITION
OF THE VOTING POPULATION

WICHITA

	1870 No.	1870 %	1875 No.	1875 %
Native-Born	272	78.2	723	82.2
New England	30	8.6	50	5.7
Middle Atlantic States	81	23.3	194	22.0
Middle West	112	32.2	321	36.5
South	48	13.8	146	16.6
West	1	0.3	12	1.4
Foreign-Born	76	21.8	157	17.8
Ireland	21	6.1	30	3.3
Germany	13	3.7	64	7.3
Great Britain	18	5.2	28	3.2
Canada	19	5.4	13	1.5
Other	5	1.4	22	2.5
TOTALS	348		880	

DODGE CITY

	1875 No.	1875 %	1880 No.	1880 %	1885 No.	1885 %
Native-Born	321	69.9	358	82.9	416	80.2
New England	31	6.7	25	5.8	21	4.0
Middle Atlantic States	78	17.0	86	20.0	85	16.4
Middle West	99	21.6	141	32.6	229	44.1
South	106	23.1	95	22.0	74	14.3
West	7	1.5	11	2.5	7	1.4
Foreign-Born	138	30.1	74	17.1	103	19.8
Ireland	64	14.0	12	2.8	18	3.5
Germany	17	3.7	23	5.3	30	5.8
Great Britain	29	6.3	12	2.8	25	4.8
Canada	12	2.6	13	3.0	8	1.5
Other	16	3.5	14	3.2	22	4.2
TOTALS	459		432		519	

CALDWELL

	1880		1885	
	No.	%	No.	%
Native-Born	385	88.3	564	88.8
New England	20	4.6	16	2.5
Middle Atlantic States	75	17.2	102	16.1
Middle West	204	46.8	264	41.6
South	80	18.3	168	26.4
West	6	1.4	14	2.2
Foreign-Born	51	11.7	71	11.2
Ireland	6	1.4	12	1.9
Germany	16	3.7	14	2.2
Great Britain	10	2.3	18	2.9
Canada	9	2.0	16	2.5
Other	10	2.3	11	1.7
TOTALS	436		635	

constitutes a full decade. The sharpest change was the increase of midwestern-born voters (22.5 percentage points), which accounts for a second statistically important change: the 10.3 percentage point increase in native-born voters. One would also expect the marked decline, both in absolute and relative terms, of Irish-born and southern-born voters (10.5 and 8.8 percentage points respectively) to have favored the success of moral reform in frontier Dodge City. Prohibition in particular usually encountered stiff resistance from immigrants, especially non-Protestants, as well as from older southern-born Americans, because of its close associations with nativism, Protestantism, and the Republican Party.

It is unfortunate that ethnic analysis of specific reform groups is made all but impossible by the failure of cattle town newspapers and other surviving materials to identify rank-and-file members. For example, the names of male prohibitionists of voting age culled from the Dodge

251 · *The Politics of Reform*

TABLE 3

ETHNIC COMPOSITION:
DODGE CITY REFORMERS AND THEIR OPPONENTS

| | PROHIBITIONISTS | | ANTI-PROHIBITIONISTS | |
	No.	%	No.	%
Native-Born	28	93.3	23	71.9
New England	5	16.7	–	
Middle Atlantic States	8	26.6	5	15.6
Middle West	13	43.3	6	18.8
South	2	6.7	12	37.5
West	–		–	
Foreign-Born	2	6.7	9	28.1
Ireland	–		1	3.1
Germany	2	6.7	3	9.5
Great Britain	–		2	6.2
Canada	–		1	3.1
Other	–		2	6.2
TOTALS	30		32	

City newspapers of 1882–84, and whose personal characteristics appear in the manuscript census for either 1880 or 1885, number only thirty. Still, a comparison of these men against an 1884 list of self-identified anti-prohibitionists at Dodge, thirty-two of whose characteristics are similarly a matter of record, is revealing (Table 3).[5]

Although the quantities represented by the tabulated

[5] The names of Dodge City prohibitionists were compiled from the following lists: I.O.G.T. officers, the 1884 "Holy Water" municipal ticket, K.S.T.U. contributors, the committee on arrangements for the A. B. Campbell visit, and the Dave Mather bondsmen. (Dodge City *Globe*, June 6, Aug. 15, 1882, Mar. 18, 1884; Dodge City *Times*, Feb. 28, May 15, Aug. 21, 1884.) For the anti-prohibitionists see the list of petitioners against the Campbell visit in the Dodge City *Democrat*, May 10, 1884.

TABLE 4

ETHNIC COMPOSITION: CALDWELL REFORMERS

	No.	%
Native-Born	75	92.6
New England	3	3.7
Middle Atlantic States	21	25.9
Middle West	38	46.9
South	13	16.1
West	–	
Foreign-Born	6	7.4
Ireland	–	
Germany	2	2.5
Great Britain	3	3.7
Canada	1	1.2
Other	–	
TOTAL	81	

figures are so small as to preclude much confidence in their percentage relationships, those for the Dodge prohibitionists are supported by similar results with the only extensive index of cattle town radical reformers that survives—a list of signatories to a Law and Order League statement issued at Caldwell in 1885, eighty-one of whose characteristics are found in the 1885 census. The collective ethnic makeup of the listed reformers (Table 4) closely resembles that of the Dodge City prohibitionists.[6]

Radical reform at the cattle towns was distinctly a native-born movement, voters of native birth being present in reform groups at both Dodge and Caldwell in greater percentages than their representation in the total population; and just the opposite was true of foreign-born

[6] Names compiled from separate listings of the signers of the Law and Order League resolutions. Caldwell *Journal*, Dec. 24, 1885; Caldwell *Free Press*, Dec. 26, 1885.

voters. The ethnic constitution of Dodge City's anti-prohibitionist element, which included a foreign-born percentage greater than the foreign-born percentage at large, supports this observation. It also seems clear that American-born voters from northern states tended to comprise the principal support of radical reform, while southern-born voters were inclined to join the foreign-born in opposition to it. But in the cases of both Dodge and Caldwell, the ethnic shifts taking place in the general decision-making population—with the single exception of a declining New England influence—worked in favor of the reformers. This, together with the increasing feminine influence, indeed made radical reform the wave of the future.

[4]

THE NOTION that a temperance movement might have any appreciable impact on the cattle towns must have seemed to many citizens ludicrously utopian. Radical reformers of the early years did well if they could make an impression on those "derivative" moral evils, gambling and prostitution. But the sudden flowering of prohibition sentiment in Kansas in the late 1870's, the popular ratification of a prohibitory amendment to the state's constitution in November 1880, followed by a legislative imposition of total abstinence on May 1, 1881—these rapid-fire events transformed the dreams of cattle town radicals into incipient realities.[7]

In the sense that the internal logic of cattle town moral reform pointed toward prohibition, this social solution can be thought of as its ultimate goal. But until the triumph of the prohibitory amendment, cattle town anti-liquor sentiment more or less remained underground, nor-

---

[7] For an incisive account of the legal triumph of prohibition in Kansas see Ernest Hurst Cherrington *et al.* (eds.): *Standard Encyclopedia of the Alcohol Problem* (Westerville, Ohio, 1926), III, 1429–32, 1438.

mally considered something too volatile for full public exposure. Only after 1880 did reform discourse become absolutely straightforward over liquor. At Wichita, Ellsworth, and Abilene in the early and middle seventies the nature and effectiveness of pre-prohibition moral reform can be seen.

Wichita, in its cattle trading years, played host to no discernible temperance movement. Yet moderate reforms proceeded apace, constantly modified by a sophisticated restraint. By late 1872 the city fathers had forced all local dance houses across the Arkansas River to the independent suburb of West Wichita, where they remained in appropriate proximity to cattle trade transients but where the mischief they caused could occur without Wichita proper technically having to bear the onus.[8] The somewhat mysterious reform outburst of 1873 resulted only in the enforcement of Sunday closing for all businesses.[9] The major target of Wichita moral reform was gambling, and apparently the most influential leader of the attack— until he went to jail for violating the National Bank Act— was a prominent financier and former Methodist preacher,

[8] Wichita *Eagle*, June 28, 1872; Wichita Council Record, A, 223, 232–33. The low homicide rate at Wichita (see table, Chapter III above) can be accredited in large measure to this unique precaution. The prevailing administrative philosophy at the other cattle towns was that dance houses should be located within city limits to facilitate police supervision.

[9] The episode began on July 6 with coordinated denunciations of local wickedness (including "Sabbath desecration") from the town's Presbyterian, Methodist, and Baptist pulpits, followed by reform resolutions passed by the respective congregations. That day, for a change, all business places were closed. On July 7 the mayor said he intended to make Sunday closing permanent, and the city council passed an ordinance to this effect. On July 12 virtually the entire business community volunteered "to do duty as Police in this City one Night in a Week without compensation." The local editor refused to give details, but a visitor afterward reported: "An attempt has been recently made to cleanse the city from prostitutes and gamblers." Wichita *Eagle*, July 3, 10, 17, 1873; petition dated July 12, 1873, in Wichita Miscellaneous Papers; Emporia *News*, July 18, 1873.

James C. Fraker.[1] In 1872, 1873, and 1874, the authorities temporarily closed all gambling places in town, but for purposes other than permanent social reform.[2]

Early in 1875 Wichita's three Protestant clergymen jointly preached their annual religious revival. Attendance was large, boosted by hard-pressed farm families living in town during the 1874–75 rural emergency, and unusually enthusiastic. Extending well into February, the protracted revival aided a popular revulsion against local wickedness just in time for spring's city election. In March an open letter from a grimly aroused Wichitan couched standard moderate reform catch phrases in rhetoric that disclosed a chilling undercurrent of religious fanaticism. "The status, social and political, of this city," the writer maintained,

> . . . must certainly define in the mind of every honorable man, the side to which he instinctively belongs. The ear is a deceptive organ, the eye is not to be eluded. *We have all seen*, and by that light we are called upon soon to declare by sacred ballot, whether we stand on the side of anarchy, murder and pillage, or upon the side of government, security and order. To smother truth any longer is dangerous, and ceases in any event to be a virtue. . . . It is written "He that is not with me is against me[.]" So in this ballot it will be recorded, and so shall the sower reap his harvest.

This new moralist fervor, its potency reinforced by a charge of municipal fiscal irregularity, resulted in a successful political assault on the incumbent mayor, liquor dealer James G. Hope.[3]

[1] For Fraker's business career in Wichita see George L. Anderson: "From Cattle to Wheat: The Impact of Agricultural Developments on Banking in Early Wichita," *Agricultural History*, XXXIII (1959), 3–15.

[2] Wichita Council Record, A, 247; Wichita *Eagle*, Dec. 12, 1872, Aug. 14, 1873, July 30, 1874; Wichita *Beacon*, July 29, Aug. 5, 1874.

[3] Wichita *Beacon*, Jan. 6, Feb. 3, Mar. 3, 1875; Wichita Council Record, B, 41; Wichita *Eagle*, Apr. 22, 1875. The economic arguments

The new mayor, George E. Harris, despite his status as a saloon owner, proved sensitive to the city's increasingly militant reform temper. That summer his councilmen banned prostitutes and then dancing from the local beer garden, though drawing the line at permanently abolishing all gambling facilities as demanded in a petition signed by forty-four men. Anti-gambling feeling remained high, however, and in 1875 visitors noted a greatly reduced incidence of gambling over previous years —a change no doubt due more to the cattle trade's decline than to reform agitation. In February 1876, Mayor Harris approvingly reported to his council that for the first time in its brief history the city harbored not a single gambling house. Henceforth, he insisted, Wichita should legally disallow gaming as a positive moral evil no longer to be tolerated—on cattle trade, municipal revenue, or any other grounds. The council's radical reformers, led by James Fraker, outvoted their moderate colleagues to put Harris's proposal into legislation, subsequently extending the injunction to prostitution as well as gambling.

This reform success proved short-lived. In the following city election Jim Hope won back the mayorship, apparently in a popular reaction to the radical drift of Harris's administration, and Hope immediately reopened the question. Fraker and his fellow council radicals fought resolutely, defeating those moderates who would tolerate gambling behind closed doors. But they saw their ban on prostitution revoked.[4] The cattle trade era closed at Wichita without any attempt whatsoever having been made to circumscribe the vending of liquor.

Ellsworth's experience with violence in 1873 reflected

---

used against the Hope administration focused on municipal expenditures to promote the cattle trade.

[4] Wichita Council Record, B, 64, 70, 74, 92–94, 109, 113; Wichita *Beacon*, Aug. 4, 1875, Sept. 20, 1876 (city financial report); Wichita *Eagle*, July 15, Aug. 26, 1875, Feb. 24, 1876; petition dated Sept. 1, 1875, in Wichita Miscellaneous Papers.

the influence of some popular temperance sentiment. The tough-line position on law enforcement examined in a previous chapter included overtones of a moral reform impulse. The dismal results of popular meddling in law enforcement that homicidal summer did little to dampen this impulse. Moral reformers, while perhaps not entirely avoiding responsibility for having urged an improper choice of peace officers, laid the major blame on the incumbent city administration and on gamblers and saloon keepers. "One thing is certain," asserted the town's editor in contemplating the next cattle season: "gambling must not be allowed and the number of saloons licensed must be limited and licenses issued to none but responsible men." This feeling seemed to prevail as the 1874 municipal election approached. Critics ensured the effectiveness of the consensus by introducing suspicions of financial mismanagement at city hall.

Although neither of the men whose names emerged as reform candidates for mayor became serious contenders, voters turned out the old chief executive and all but one of his councilmen. The new council slashed municipal salaries, abolished gambling, and raised the tavern license fee to its legal maximum—$500.[5] But other than making a special effort to close down places dispensing liquor without licenses, this reform administration took no further action against saloons. As at Wichita, prostitution continued unmolested, the public remaining insufficiently aroused over this particular moral shortcoming.[6]

Of the five major Kansas cattle towns, only Abilene

---

[5] Ellsworth *Reporter*, Oct. 9, Nov. 13, 1873, Feb. 26, Mar. 5, 12, 19, 26, Apr. 16, 23, 30, 1874; Ellsworth Council Record, 1871–80 (microfilm copy, KSHS), pp. 123–24. For a discussion of the high license fee as a temperance device see Cherrington: *Standard Encyclopedia*, IV, 1540–47.

[6] A writer in the Ellsworth *Reporter*, May 3, 1874, for instance, condemns local prostitutes and dance houses, but does not ask that they be banished.

produced any substantial prohibition movement during the seventies. But its rather powerful effect foreshadowed what was later to occur at Dodge City and Caldwell. In late 1870 an undisclosed number of Abilene citizens formed a local chapter of the Independent Order of Good Templars. This nationwide organization, then experiencing a period of phenomenal growth, required of its votaries not only belief in a divinely posited prohibitionism but a militant propagation of the faith as well.[7] Radical reform at Abilene also gained strength through the services of two vociferous propagandists—Vear P. Wilson, Universalist preacher and editor of the town's newspaper, and the Reverend W. B. Christopher, a Congregational pastor and lately an editor of a Chicago prohibitionist journal. Both arrived in Abilene as leaders of "colonies" of rural settlers, thus enjoying readymade reform constituencies. Each man had a talent for speaking out against sin in furious invective. The only important difference between them was that Wilson, a theological liberal who also nourished political ambitions, was publicly willing to espouse only the temperate use of alcohol, while Christopher openly stood for uncompromising abstinence.[8]

Although Editor Wilson declined to print details, initially being extremely reticent toward social controversy, it seems clear that as the 1871 city election approached local prohibition enthusiasts began pressing for a $500 liquor license fee. It also seems that they rationalized their program, for the benefit of less radical voters, as a means of providing enough municipal revenue to make

[7] Abilene *Chronicle*, Dec. 15, 1870, Jan. 5, 1871. For an excellent short history of the I.O.G.T. see Cherrington: *Standard Encyclopedia*, III, 1332–41.

[8] The essential biographical facts on Wilson can be found in Joseph G. McCoy: *Historic Sketches of the Cattle Trade of the West and Southwest*, ed. Ralph P. Bieber (Glendale, Calif., 1940), p. 293 *n*. For data on Christopher see Abilene *Chronicle*, Feb. 16, Mar. 2, 23, May 25, July 13, 1871; Adolph Roenigk (ed.): *Pioneer History of Kansas* (Denver, 1933), pp. 33–34.

general business taxes unnecessary. As finally assembled, the new city council contained only one doctrinaire moral reformer—S. A. Burroughs, an attorney. Elected as mayor was Joseph G. McCoy.[9]

McCoy clashed immediately with Councilman Burroughs. Favoring strict municipal economy to justify his argument that a high liquor tax could accommodate all public expenses, Burroughs balked at a conventional salary scale for city officers that McCoy introduced. The others passed it over Burroughs's objections. The council then split on the liquor license question. Only Burroughs espoused the punitive legal maximum; two councilmen favored a moderate $200 fee urged by McCoy; the remaining councilmen, Samuel Carpenter and Lucius Boudinot, evidently in deference to local saloon keepers, pressed for the legal minimum of $100. After contriving to have Burroughs absent from the meeting of May 1, McCoy and his partisans passed the $200 fee, the mayor's ballot breaking a tie vote. Carpenter and Boudinot thereupon resigned, then won back their seats in a special election that united prohibitionists and saloonmen against the $200 license on grounds that its only purpose was to provide "high" municipal salaries. Making only minor adjustments in other fiscal matters, however, the reconstituted council passed the minimal $100 license fee. Whereupon McCoy's supporters, in turn, resigned.[1]

At this point a fresh reform issue—prostitution—arose

[9] Abilene *Chronicle*, Sept. 14, 1871, Feb. 15, 1872 ff. (I.O.G.T. notice); Salina *Journal*, Nov. 23, 1871. McCoy had been in virtual retirement since 1869 because of insolvency brought about by his failure to collect cattle-carrying fees owed him by the Kansas Pacific. In March 1871 he finally won a district court suit against the railroad and also an appeal in the July term of the state supreme court. (*Kansas Reports*, VIII, 538–45.) McCoy probably returned to public life at this moment in order to defend the cattle trade from its local critics. The letter signed "Ibex" in the Abilene *Chronicle*, Feb. 2, 1871, a vigorous defense of the trade, is very much in McCoy's prose style.

[1] Abilene Council Record, pp. 58–59, 61–64, 66; Abilene *Chronicle*, May 4, 18, 25, June 1, 1871.

to complicate political alignments even further. In the spring of 1871 the prostitutes who annually served the cattle trade returned to Abilene in greater numbers than ever before. Respectable ladies of the town received polite treatment from the Texans when venturing into the business district to do their shopping; but the brilliantly garbed whores who paraded Texas Street, often in tipsy condition, were sometimes insulting. To aggravate matters, a new brothel stood practically next door to the schoolhouse. On May 27 incensed townswomen presented an anti-prostitution petition to the city council, but, as noted earlier, without immediate effect. In June the two individuals who won the newly vacated council seats did so by promising to take action against local brothels. Again, having supported these candidates, reformers gained only disappointment. Burroughs remained the single radical member of the council. The reaction to the issue by the other four members was merely to approve a moderate solution proposed earlier by Mayor McCoy: instituting the illegal tax on whores as well as gamblers, removing all brothels to a segregated tract on the outskirts of town, and hiring two extra policemen to keep order in the new district.[2]

This innovation proved to be Joe McCoy's last substantial contribution to Abilene city government. His recklessly overbearing adminstrative style had effectively alienated his councilmen, and he stood none too high in the esteem of the business community because he had foolishly violated a principle governing good public relations with the world outside. During the council meet-

[2] C. F. Gross to J. B. Edwards, Apr. 13, 1922, Edwards Papers, KSHS; Stuart Henry: *Conquering Our Great American Plains* (New York, 1930), pp. 277–78; Abilene Council Record, pp. 67–71; Abilene *Chronicle*, June 1, 15, 1871; Abilene Ordinances, 1869–74 (microfilm copy, KSHS), p. 56. The brothel district consisted of forty acres leased by the city in Fisher's Addition to Abilene. Roenigk: *Pioneer History of Kansas*, p. 38.

ing at which Carpenter and Boudinot had resigned, Burroughs also withdrew from the council chamber, collapsing the quorum. Marshal Hickok was ordered to bring him back, but no sooner had he done so than Burroughs bolted again. This time Hickok carried Burroughs in on his shoulder and stood guard while the council transacted further business. Next day McCoy took the train to Topeka, where he commissioned the noted artist Henry Worrall to get up a comic drawing of the incident. This was then photographed and copies informally advertised for distribution in the Topeka *Commonwealth*. V. P. Wilson furiously charged McCoy with sending prints "all over the country to be hawked about and laughed at as a standing disgrace to his own town."

McCoy abdicated his effectiveness as mayor with this act. Without much support from any quarter, he now became a convenient scapegoat. Correctly labeling the brothel solution as McCoy's suggestion, Editor Wilson blamed him exclusively for the failure to eradicate prostitution. Eventually he even implied that McCoy supported local vice because of his own depraved lusts, printing a letter accusing the mayor of regularly patronizing the brothel district. "On last Saturday night," charged the anonymous writer,

> he was seen there with two harlots at once on his lap, one on each knee. I suppose that in this way he is trying to carry out his plan of making houses of ill-fame "respectable." Why don't the city council have enough backbone to turn out such a worse than beastly mayor? Every respectable citizen must despise such conduct.[3]

Wilson made only oblique negative references to other officials, perhaps hoping to wean them from sup-

[3] Abilene Council Record, p. 64; Topeka *Commonwealth*, May 10, 11, 1871; Nyle H. Miller and Joseph W. Snell (eds.): *Why the West Was Wild* (Topeka, 1963), p. 237; Abilene *Chronicle*, May 18, July 27, 1871.

porting the brothel scheme. But the council majority refused to give ground. On August 2, encouraged by Wilson's editorial drumfire, a delegation of citizens presented petitions demanding an end to prostitution and discharge of the two policemen supervising the red-light district. As the councilmen demurred, the city attorney independently instituted legal action against the brothels. Having promised brothel keepers immunity from such action, however, the council majority now increased the general property tax levy "in order to meet and pay all damages and expenses that may be incurred by said keepers" from the city attorney's activity. Wilson diverted his attention momentarily from McCoy to castigate the two councilmen who had introduced this proposal. Early in September the council finally dismissed two police officers and closed down the town's dance house. But they stoutly resisted the abolition of routine prostitution.[4]

Meanwhile the reform campaign crested as Wilson and the Reverend Mr. Christopher expounded ever more militantly on prostitution and gambling and wickedness at city hall. Behind this vituperative barrage the assault moved forward against that ultimate social shortcoming —liquor. One citizen, apparently the local Lutheran pastor, cautioned against placing more faith in "pro[hi]-bitory enactments" than in divine grace, but the agitation mounted. Early in October, after a drama performance of *Ten Nights in a Barroom*, Good Templar membership stood at over seventy; at the end of November it topped one hundred. Transients had cleared the brothel district for parts east by then, the cattle season having ended.[5]

But the moral crusaders surrendered none of their

[4] Abilene Council Record, pp. 83, 86–87, 90; Abilene *Chronicle*, Aug. 24, Sept. 7, 14, Oct. 5, Nov. 2, 1871.

[5] Abilene *Chronicle*, Sept. 14, 28, Oct. 5, Nov. 16, 30, 1871. Abilene's remaining two policemen were discharged on November 27, as was Marshal Hickok on December 13. Abilene Council Record, pp. 105, 107–08.

momentum. In January 1872, they brought the inevitable charge of financial mismanagement against the incumbent administration. One election slate that spring embraced the four anti-radical members of the old council; the other consisted of various businessmen. Although not as radical a group as Wilson would have liked, the latter were at least moderates more compatible with local radicalism than their opponents. In spite of months of reformist propaganda, however, the race was close, the businessmen's ticket barely capturing all the council seats and losing the mayorship to former councilman Sam Carpenter. Without further ado the new council voted a $500 liquor license. Carpenter—still the saloon keepers' friend —vetoed it. The council then passed it over his veto.[6] Since the cattle trade did not return in any appreciable substance that year, no new test of prostitution and gambling reform occurred.

The experiences of Wichita, Ellsworth, and Abilene in the 1870's included moral reform movements of varying effectiveness. While reform was partially successful in all cases, it was also true that at each town reformers made important headway only when the cattle trade was on its way out. In early 1876 Wichitans faced what looked to be their last cattle-shipping summer; the same was true for Ellsworth in early 1874; and, as we shall see in the next chapter, in early 1872 a substantial number of citizens in and near Abilene already had asked Texas cattlemen not to return. To some extent the community hostility implicit in local reform legislation may have helped discourage the cattle trade's return in those years, just as the critics of reform always predicted. But we shall see that much more powerful discouragement than this had risen in other sectors. It seems correct to say that at Wichita, Ellsworth, and Abilene moral reform vigor increased in

[6] Abilene *Chronicle*, Jan. 11, 25, Mar. 21, 28, Apr. 4, 18, May 2, 1872.

direct proportion to the public's perception of an imminent demise of cattle trading. On the other hand, the reform experiences of Dodge City and Caldwell—especially after 1880 and state prohibition—provide glimpses of more prolonged and socially volatile confrontations of moral and economic commitments.

[5]

IN THE SUMMER of 1878 an observant visitor to Dodge City noted that the town "has already a strong element opposed to cattle coming there to be shipped" owing to the moral vices connected with the Texas cattle trade.[7] A pre-prohibition reform movement had indeed arisen there, an underlying stimulant being (as in the above cases) the prospect of a cattle trade decline in the face of an expected rural immigration boom. But secular factionalism also played an important role.

As detailed earlier, the clique known as the Gang ruled the governmental affairs of Dodge and surrounding Ford County in the late seventies. On the question of social reform, this political establishment was emphatically reactionary, as exemplified by its wheel-horse at the municipal level, Mayor James H. Kelley.[8] A combination of factors drew the opponents of the incumbent Gang to reform. In 1877–78 local German-Americans sponsored colonies of immigrant Germans for settlement in the Ford County hinterlands. The ruling establishment remained committed to the cattle trade nevertheless, since a general rural immigration and cattle trading were recognized as mutually exclusive. A second determining factor was the criminal activity engaged in by certain Gang elements. The clique's rank-and-file, it will be recalled, embraced a semi-

[7] Dodge City *Times*, June 8, 1878.
[8] For an inclusive moral critique of Kelley and his official cohorts see the letter by a newly arrived resident reprinted in Miller and Snell: *Why the West Was Wild*, pp. 311–12.

transient leisure group. That its members occasionally descended from orthodox gambling to rigged games, con games, and even stickups as a means of livelihood was not only known to the incumbent Kelley administration, but officially tolerated. Many victims of the more elaborate robberies were prospective rural settlers, "land agent" being a featured camouflage for sharpers who knew, as an editor observed, "that the unsuspecting stranger can be more readily caught on land than most anything else."[9] Such nefarious activities, together with Dodge City's bad moral odor abroad, made it exceedingly difficult for immigration promoters to create the proper aura of community hospitality.

The gambler types allied to the reigning political clique headquartered at Dodge in order to be close to the cattle trade. Therefore moral reformers soon merged anti-administration, anti-crime, and anti-cattle arguments into one general criticism of the establishment. But as long as they included hostility to the cattle trade in their critique, local businessmen remained totally insensitive to their pleas for social improvement. For a time the reformers possessed a good financial argument—the high cost of law enforcement. This ploy lost considerable persuasiveness, however, after the business community pressured Mayor Kelley into imposing tax assessments on gamblers and whores. The reformers thereafter concentrated on the issue of official complicity in crime, airing their grievances in the columns of the Dodge City *Globe*, a newspaper initially financed by the local German-American leader Frederick C. Zimmermann, a gunsmith and hardware merchant. Its editor, Daniel M. Frost, was the sachem of the anti-Gang faction.[1]

[9] Dodge City *Times*, Dec. 15, 22, 29, 1877, Jan. 12, 1878; Dodge City *Globe*, Jan. 22, Feb. 12, Mar. 12, Sept. 10, 1878.
[1] Spearville *Enterprise*, July 27, 1878; Dodge City *Times*, Aug. 3, 10, 17, Sept. 7, 1878, Nov. 1, 1883.

In the autumn of 1878 two local confidence men posing as realtors were thrown into jail to await trial for having fleeced a naïve home seeker. Sheriff Bat Masterson promptly allowed the pair to escape custody. Outraged reformers tried to get Ford County's commissioners to convene a grand jury investigation of the incident. But the Gang also controlled the board. County Attorney Michael W. Sutton, the establishment's strategist, apparently argued that "necessary" prostitution and gambling would stand in jeopardy if fifteen good men and true, drawn from the county at large, met to discuss Dodge City's civic shortcomings. The proposal died.[2]

Throughout the next year, 1879, Dan Frost's *Globe* criticized the Kelley administration's do-nothing attitude toward confidence gamesmanship, but with crops and rural immigration alike dried up by the year's drought, the cattle trade won a new lease on life. Straightforward moral reform rose again only with the passage of state prohibition, and after a moderate reform movement had upset the old political alignments.

As the end of Jim Kelley's third term in office approached, the city's business community—including Robert M. Wright—decided the time was ripe for a change, belatedly condemning the mayor's extravagance and general lack of businesslike procedures in municipal finance. In March 1880, a number of townsmen both from within the clique and from outside it proposed a respected druggist for mayor. This nonpartisan endorsement made the

[2] Dodge City *Times*, Sept. 14, 21, 1878; Dodge City *Globe*, Sept. 17, 24, 1878. For local reasoning against a grand jury see the Dodge City *Times*, July 20, Aug. 10, 1878. Specific objections aside, the lack of grand jury usage at the cattle towns is also to be laid to a general distaste for the "star chamber" aspect of this investigative device. See comments in Caldwell *Commercial*, Sept. 7, 1882; Caldwell *Journal*, Dec. 4, 1884. For the general anti-grand jury movement in the nineteenth century see Richard D. Younger: *The People's Panel: The Grand Jury in the United States* (Providence, 1963), chaps. v, ix.

druggist's election seem a sure thing. But on election day Kelley quietly rallied his rank-and-file adherents and rushed them to the polls early enough for their appointment as poll watchers and election judges, ensuring an unmolested casting of illegal ballots. He thereby gained a fourth term at the head of a hand-picked city council.[3]

This *coup d'état* alienated Kelley's remaining support in the business community. The influential Mike Sutton deserted the Gang banner and led the new anti-Kelley consensus in a continuing assessment of administration fiscal irregularity. Late that summer the old issue of official complicity in crime added another fillip to moderate reform's momentum when a party of local confidence operators brazenly robbed two young Colorado-bound sightseers from Yates Center, bilking them of their money, supplies, wagon, team, and harness in an elaborate series of masquerades. Dodge City's crusty old German-American physician turned hotelman, Dr. Samuel Galland, helped the victims file a complaint, but Kelley's city attorney refused to act on it. The incident resulted in strident headlines in the Yates Center newspaper: "DODGE CITY. A DEN OF THIEVES AND CUT THROATS. THE WHOLE TOWN IN LEAGUE TO ROB THE UNWARY STRANGER." Published letters from Dr. Galland and Morris Collar supported the featured allegation. "It must not be understood that we have no good citizens here," Galland explained, "for such is not the case, but the facts . . . are that the city is in the hands of the aiders and abetters of such schemers, and the city attorney has been making brags that he gets $50.00 per week for not prosecuting the gamblers." Collar's angry statement was even more devastating to the city's public relations: "What you have said about Dodge City is correct only you have not said half enough. . . . I have lived in Dodge over eight years and cannot get away, for the reason

[3] Dodge City *Globe*, Mar. 9, 16, 30, Apr. 6, 13, June 8, 1880; Dodge City *Times*, Apr. 10, 1880.

that property is not saleable. Can you blame anyone for not wanting to buy property in a place where people, especially strangers, are not safe of their life and property?"⁴

At year's end the approval of statewide prohibition threatened the liquor license revenues making up Dodge City's main income. This and a current municipal debt of some $3,000 sealed Jim Kelley's fate. In the spring of 1881 businessmen nominated Alonzo B. Webster for mayor. Webster, a dark-haired, dark-eyed man whose mustache and trim goatee lent a determined forward thrust to his jaw, possessed credentials for Dodge City leadership that were as good as any man's. A tough former cavalryman who had been on the Plains since the Civil War and who had apparently once killed a man in a gunfight at Hays City, Webster had lived in Dodge since that first summer of 1872. He first operated a dry goods store and later branched out into groceries, but since 1878 had followed the lumber business exclusively. In factional politics he had long been associated with the Frost clique. Though his election in no wise promised the immediate local triumph of prohibition (within two years he himself would abandon lumber for the saloon business), moral reformers applauded his candidacy as a step in the right direction. A strong-arm committee at the polls kept non-resident Kelley supporters from voting, which assured Webster's virtually unanimous victory.

The new mayor's first official act was to warn all "thieves, thugs, confidence men, and persons without visible means of support" that their presence would no longer be tolerated. His likeminded councilmen obligingly armed him with a new ordinance respecting vagrants. The first test came just a few days later when ex-

⁴ Dodge City *Globe*, July 27, Aug. 24, Sept. 14, 1880; Yates Center *News*, July 29, Aug. 19, Sept. 9, 1880. The letters by Galland and Collar were printed anonymously in ibid., September 9, but identified in the *Globe*, September 14. While the *Globe* commented on Galland's letter, neither Dodge editor dared reprint either letter in its entirety.

269 · *The Politics of Reform*

city marshal James Masterson wired his brother Bat—
then at Tombstone, Arizona—to come and help him resolve a feud with a business partner. At high noon Bat
stepped off the train at Dodge and immediately precipitated a gun battle on Front Street. No one fell dead, but a
great deal of lead whirled indiscriminately through the
business district. Mayor Webster headed up an impromptu posse that forced the Masterson brothers and
two gambler friends to leave town. Three weeks later
Webster ordered the police into dapper blue uniforms in
a further effort to regularize local law enforcement. His
fiscal reforms included re-establishment of the fines on
whores and gamblers, which had been allowed to lapse,
and introduction of similar assessments on the now illegal
saloons. By the end of his first term Webster's moderate
reform version of good order had proved so popular with
the taxpayers that he was re-elected without opposition.

The Webster regime's negative attitude toward radical reform remained clear. But the prohibition issue soon
emerged at the county level. It seems fair to say that, at
least in terms of leadership, Dodge City remained pre-
dominantly "wet" while the surrounding rural area grew
increasingly "dry." In the fall election of 1881, the prime
contention was over the position of sheriff—the actual
issue being a rigid or a lax enforcement of the prohibitory
law by that officer. In Ford County a heavy turnout, for a
contest in which no national party lines were drawn,
voted back into the sheriff's office a wet whose main support came from the town.[5]

The following month John P. St. John, the state's
prohibitionist chief executive, singled out several Kansas

[5] Miller and Snell: *Why the West Was Wild*, pp. 191, 353; Dodge
City *Messenger*, Feb. 26, 1874 (ad); Dodge City *Democrat*, June 19,
1903; Dodge City *Times*, Apr. 7, 1877, Feb. 16, Apr. 20, 1878, Mar.
31, Apr. 7, 14, 21, 28, May 26, Sept. 15, 29, Oct. 27, Nov. 17, 1881,
Mar. 16, 30, 1882; Dodge City *Globe*, Mar. 8, 29, Apr. 5, 12, 19, May
3, 10, 31, Oct. 4, 18, Nov. 8, 15, 1881, Mar. 21, Apr. 4, 1882.

communities, one of them Dodge City, as targets for special prohibition enforcement efforts by state authorities. County Attorney Mike Sutton predicted little success for anything he himself could do. "I shall probably take no action in the matter," he candidly admitted to a reporter, "because every officer in the county whose duty it will be to help me enforce the law are themselves openly and avowedly against its enforcement, and can furnish me no aid, and I know I have no moral backing."[6]

Indeed, the relative impotence of citizens professing radical sentiments was seen in the council elections accompanying Webster's return to office in April 1882. A printed circular alleged that two council incumbents from 1881 favored "suppressing gambling and prostitution," and voters consequently turned one of them out. The following month, however, an officer of the Kansas lodge of the Good Templars organized a chapter in Dodge City. Even as Nicholas Klaine of the *Times* reasoned that "men who have come to Dodge to engage in secular pursuits will [hardly] lay them aside to take the lead in reform measures that will abate their profits," the presidency of the local Templars fell to Robert E. Rice. Twenty-nine years old and a devout Virginia-born Methodist, Rice happened at the same time to be one of the area's leading manufacturers of fancy California saddles for the ranch trade of southwest Kansas, Indian Territory, and the Texas Panhandle. Though he catered to cattlemen, Rice made many of his sales through the mail, so the rhetoric concerning "necessary" sin as a means of preserving the cattle trade at Dodge may not have touched him appreciably. The same lack of *local* cattle trade depend-

[6] Dodge City *Globe*, Dec. 13, 1881. The other communities cited with Dodge were Atchison, Leavenworth, Topeka, Kansas City (Kansas), and Wyandotte—all large centers in the northeast corner of the state. Dodgeites' anger at being singled out was obviously tinged with pleasure at being linked with such distinguished urban company.

ence seems to have characterized the other nonclerical types listed as Good Templar officers. By August the chapter's membership had climbed to forty-five, and the resumption of a strong rural immigration into the county gave prohibitionists new hope.[7]

In 1883 a serious falling out occurred among the moderate reform businessmen who had deposed the Kelley regime, which briefly allowed Dodge City's growing number of radical reformers an abnormal amount of leverage in municipal affairs. The trouble stemmed from a business rivalry between Mayor Webster and the partnership of William H. Harris, a prosperous cattleman and banker, and Luke L. Short, a gambler and gunfighter. For more than a year Webster and Harris owned adjoining saloons on Front Street. In February 1883, Short bought into Harris's establishment. Somehow this transformed the business rivalry into downright bad feeling, and the bad feeling spilled over into politics.[8]

After two years as mayor, Webster did not choose to run again in 1883. His personal choice for a successor was Lawrence E. Deger, a bulky second-generation German-American who worked as a freight company agent; Deger was also a bitter enemy of the old Jim Kelley machine, having once been fired by Kelley from the position of marshal. Webster and other moderate reformers expected the recommendation of Deger to be decisive. But what was intended to be a general business community caucus turned out to be sparsely attended. Instead of Deger, the

[7] Dodge City *Globe*, Apr. 4, June 6, Aug. 15, 1882; Dodge City *Times*, June 1, 1882; Kansas Manuscript Census, 1885: Dodge City, p. 39. For the orientation of Rice's entrepreneurship see especially the Dodge City *Globe*, Apr. 26 (with ad), Aug. 16, 1881, July 25, 1882.

[8] Dodge City *Globe*, Feb. 6, 1883. Not to be discounted as an additional factor turning Webster against Harris and Short was their role in an incident whereby a notorious confidence man escaped justice in February 1883. Dodge City *Times*, Sept. 28, 1882; Dodge City *Globe*, Feb. 20, Oct. 30, 1883; Topeka *Capital*, May 18, 1883; Topeka *Commonwealth*, May 20, 1883.

minority element present nominated Webster's business rival, W. H. Harris.[9]

Two days later those who felt that Harris's candidacy menaced the reign of law and order initiated by Webster—and they included Bob Wright—met at the courthouse to organize an opposition slate. Having endorsed a two-years' war on vagrants and confidence men, the moderates wrote off any important support from the old Gang rank-and-file still in town. But with Deger at the head of the slate, they could count on the German vote. For additional backing they turned to the moral reformers, who already favored Webster's tested moderate reformism over what Harris seemed to promise. In return for their active support, the radicals were able to extract some large concessions. Prostitution, while not to be abolished, would be stripped of its egregious trappings: whores were to be banned from saloons, no new dance houses would be permitted to open, and in return for a monopoly in the 1883 cattle season the one existing dance house would close down on November 1. Radicals may also have been promised that Deger would act against gambling.[1] Not least in importance, two of their number were included on the proposed city council. In a bitter election, in which a goodly number of railroad section hands apparently cast illegal ballots, the Deger slate gained office.[2]

On April 28, two days after the new policy banning prostitutes from saloons took effect, W. H. Harris and Luke

[9] Dodge City *Globe*, Mar. 20, July 31, 1883.

[1] That a formal pre-election agreement was struck with the moral reformers remains a conjecture, but see indicative remarks in Topeka *Capital*, May 12, 18, 1883; Dodge City *Times*, Nov. 15, 1883; Dodge City *Globe*, Nov. 20, 1883.

[2] Dodge City *Globe*, Mar. 20, Apr. 3, 1883. Railroaders' voting is described in Kansas City *Times*, May 10, 1883; Topeka *Capital*, May 12, 1883. For a brief but revealing reminiscence about this election by Nicholas Klaine see the Dodge City *Globe-Republican*, Nov. 7, 1895.

Short unwisely defied it. When the policy was enforced against them but not against A. B. Webster or the dance house proprietors, they charged the city fathers with discrimination. The events that followed are now known as the "Dodge City War," an episode that provoked headlines in the Kansas press for several weeks and even got coverage in New York and Chicago newspapers.[3]

On the night of April 28–29 Luke Short exchanged gunshots with a policeman and was promptly arrested. Soon afterwards a vigilance committee led by Mayor Deger and the city's peace officers took Short from jail and ordered him to leave town. He did so, but was soon venting his legitimate complaints about denial of due process to Governor George W. Glick and the urban press. He vowed to return backed by force if need be, a threat that stimulated panicky appeals from Dodge City for state militia to defend the town. On May 17 the governor's adjutant general, Thomas Moonlight, negotiated a settlement: Short could return for ten days to close out his affairs at Dodge without fear of official molestation. Luke Short contemptuously rejected this solution. At the end of the month a group of his gunfighting pals, including Bat Masterson and Wyatt Earp, descended on Dodge to prepare their comrade's return. Short himself then appeared. For a few nervous days in early June the community teetered on the brink of violence, but General Moonlight mediated a new settlement. Short stayed in town, a second dance house opened up, and everything was as before the spring election.[4]

[3] Most of the newspaper materials relating to the action described in this and the paragraph that follows have been reprinted in Miller and Snell: *Why the West Was Wild*, pp. 519–65.

[4] On June 4, at the height of the excitement, Mayor Deger closed down all gambling in retaliation for the failure of Short's gunfighting partisans to leave town. The council sustained his act. A few days later, however, the gamblers threatened that if gambling remained suppressed they would bring suit to cause enforcement of the pro-

Having suffered grievously from internal social tension and damning publicity abroad, Dodge City's business community was fed up with moral reform. In August, when the radicals suggested abolishing gambling, businessmen convened and firmly denounced any additional meddling with the *status quo*. Citizens then learned that the Santa Fe Railroad's top officials had been upset by the unflattering limelight focused on one of "their" towns and wanted permanent moral reforms carried through. Otherwise, they said, the company would revoke Dodge's status as a division terminus and major cattle shipping point and defer substantial additional facilities scheduled for construction there. Bob Wright and other alarmed business leaders sped to Topeka to negotiate, returning with full information on the company's demands. These proved to be less revolutionary than first feared: the closing of all places of business and entertainment on Sundays, the banning of music even in dance houses, and the restriction of gambling to back rooms.

The injunctions dictated by the railroad were violated as soon as the heat was off, but moral reform gained momentum in the Dodge City War—if only because the experience greatly emboldened and solidified local radicals. Illustrating the new reformist *élan*, Nicholas Klaine and Mike Sutton, both important opinion leaders, defected openly to the prohibitionists. The two men were close friends. Both had been born near New York City; both had served in the Union army. There the outward similarities ended. Klaine was forty-five years old in 1884, of slender build, with a hooked nose, intense pale eyes,

hibitory and Sunday closing laws. Gambling was therefore allowed to resume behind closed doors. (Dodge City *Globe*, June 5, 12, 1883; Dodge City *Times*, June 7, 14, 1883; Topeka *Commonwealth*, June 9, 1883.) Before disbanding, Short and his supporters posed for a group photograph that they playfully labeled "The Dodge City Peace Commission." Miller and Snell: *Why the West Was Wild*, pp. 354–55.

and an astringent personality, a man completely without humor and given to a kind of grim philosophizing. Sutton, on the other hand, was thirty-six and a beefy, enormously mustached fellow, wily but also congenial and outgoing. For five years both had lived in the village of Warrensburg, Missouri, where Klaine edited the local newspaper and dabbled successfully in politics while Sutton farmed and studied for the bar. In 1872 Sutton migrated to Kansas and finally settled in Dodge in 1876. Late the next year Klaine followed, possibly at Sutton's instigation, and bought the Dodge City *Times* from its founder.[5]

Their decision to join forces with the Dodge City radicals appears to have been made jointly and for a similar motive—the desire to remain politically up to date as Republicans in what was no longer a solidly Democratic Ford County.[6] Republicanism had been accruing strength rapidly as a result of new immigration into the county, while at the same time the prohibitionist movement had captured the upper echelons of the Kansas Republican Party. Embracing prohibition reform now seemed imperative for any man aspiring to Republican Party leadership at any level.[7] In Ford County, however, Dodge City wets

[5] Dodge City *Globe*, Aug. 14, 28, Sept. 4, 1883; Dodge City *Times*, Aug. 16, 23, 30, Sept. 6, 1883; A. T. Andreas: *History of the State of Kansas* (Chicago, 1883), pp. 1561–62.

[6] In 1876 Ford was the only county in Kansas to give a majority to the Democratic presidential candidate. In 1878 it returned majorities for the Democratic candidates for governor and Congress. In 1880 it went for Garfield by the slimmest of margins, although the wet sentiment of many Republicans is disclosed in the county's rejection of the prohibitionist Republican gubernatorial candidate, John P. St. John. Also, the prohibitory amendment failed in Ford by a vote of 488 to 125. In 1882 the Democratic gubernatorial candidate won both town and rural precincts in what was obviously another bipartisan wet vote. Dodge City *Globe*, Sept. 3, Nov. 12, 1878, Nov. 2, 16, 1880, Nov. 14, 1882.

[7] See especially Klaine's prediction in the Dodge City *Times*, Nov. 15, 1883. But the county election of 1884 would prove that prohibition's conquest of even local Republicans still had a long way to go.

like Dan Frost and Bob Wright retained control of the party machinery. As spokesmen of the growing dry wing of the party, Klaine and Sutton hoped to usurp leadership by transforming Ford's Republicans into a militant group willing to make liquor consumption a partisan issue.

Back in the autumn of 1882 Klaine had editorialized for more stringent enforcement of the prohibitory law. In 1883 he and Sutton strongly backed Deger's candidacy for mayor. That September they unsuccessfully tried to wrest the leadership of the county central committee from Dan Frost. (The subsequent county election was once again a nonpartisan contest, this time between residual secular factions from the spring's conflict.) By early 1884 Klaine's newspaper blatantly served as a prohibition organ in opposition to Frost's *Globe*, which continued to speak for Republican wets. Local wets of the Democratic persuasion had their own sheet by this date, the Dodge City *Democrat*.

Drys and wets locked horns in politics for the first time in the municipal election of 1884, causing a new polarization of voters. A. B. Webster labeled the prohibitionists "unprincipled, damned hypocrites," and led most of the town's moderate reform businessmen into an alliance with their old enemies of the Kelley-Harris axis. Local German-Americans, mainly anti-prohibitionist moderates, also were forced by the alternatives to follow Webster's suit. Of the important German leaders only Dr. Galland—a believer, as he put it, "in the unalienable right of a man to govern his own stomach"—joined the radicals, but solely because the new anti-prohibitionist alliance included men unwilling to discountenance pros-

---

Ford rejected the prohibition-committed Republican gubernatorial candidate, but gave margins to the Republican nominees for every other state office and for Congress. It also favored the Republican presidential candidate. It went Democratic (that is, wet) for state representative and state senator, as well as for nearly every county office. Dodge City *Globe*, Nov. 11, 1884.

titution, of which Galland was a passionate foe. The political realignment thus saw the old coalition of moderates and radicals, which had long stood for "law and order," dissolve into a "liberal" amalgamation of moderate and minimum reformers against the isolated prohibitionists. The subsequent city election featured a liberal slate with liquor wholesaler George M. Hoover for mayor and Jim Kelley as a council candidate. It defeated its dry opponents by a resounding 4.5-to-1 majority. "The city election," Nicholas Klaine conceded, "would indicate that the people of Dodge were not ready for reform."

Nevertheless, the same liberal-prohibitionist polarity characterized autumn's county election. The Klaine-Sutton faction succeeded in turning the Republican nominating convention over to rural Republicans, a maneuver that resulted in a dry slate. Its opposition was a Democratic slate to which wet Republicans gave their support. Again, in a particularly vitriolic political exchange, the wets kept their hold on the county offices.[8]

Whipped in open combat, prohibitionists had more luck with sniping tactics. That spring a dangerous but soft-spoken gambler and ex-policeman named David ("Mysterious Dave") Mather became co-owner of the Opera House Saloon on Front Street, which he and his partner intended to turn into a dance house. Such a den of iniquity was not to be tolerated on Dodge City's principal thoroughfare; the city council immediately passed an ordinance outlawing dance houses. The injunction was used against Mather and his partner, but not against the

[8] Dodge City *Times*, Nov. 16, 1882, Oct. 11, 18, 1883, Feb. 14, Apr. 10, Oct. 9, 30, 1884; Dodge City *Democrat*, Feb. 23, Mar. 8, 15, 22, Oct. 11, 1884; Dodge City *Globe*, Sept. 11, 18, Oct. 9, 16, Nov. 13, 20, 1883, Mar. 18, Apr. 1, 8, 15, Oct. 7, 14, Nov. 11, 1884. This election featured the emergence of Bat Masterson as a journalist, a career he followed professionally in later life. For a facsimile reproduction of his slanderously anti-reform newspaper, of which an election edition was the only one to appear, see Miller and Snell: *Why the West Was Wild*, pp. 357–60.

more geographically remote dance house owned by Assistant City Marshal Thomas Nixon. Possibly out of spite, the Opera House Saloon then began retailing beer for five cents per glass, undercutting the going rate of two glasses for a quarter. Their competitors, including Tom Nixon, pressured the local beer wholesalers and thereby dried up the supply to the Opera House Saloon. Bad blood simmered between Mather and Nixon. On July 18 the assistant marshal took an ineffectual shot at Mather and claimed self-defense. Three nights later Mysterious Dave pumped four shots into Nixon and killed him. Upon Mather's arrest Mike Sutton sprang to his aid as head defense counsel. Nicholas Klaine and other radicals furnished Mysterious Dave's bond, evidently feeling that he was to be rewarded for having spread confusion among the saloonmen and ridding Dodge of a major anti-reform militant. Although patently guilty of first degree murder, Mather won an acquittal.[9]

On February 18, 1885, the state's legislators strengthened the prohibitory law. One key improvement allowed a private citizen to bring a permanent injunction against saloons without recourse to local officials, and in such cases any lawyer employed by the plaintiff could act in lieu of the county attorney. Shaken by this new enforcement provision, some of Dodge City's most prosperous liquor dealers, Mayor Hoover among them, abandoned the business to those willing either to operate illegally or as licensed druggists legally dispensing liquor in small amounts for "medicinal purposes."

The spring election witnessed a return to former political alignments on the liquor issue, the ideological polarization of 1884 being deemed too fraught with potential

[9] Dodge City *Democrat*, May 24, 31, July 19, 1884; Dodge City *Globe*, May 27, July 22, Aug. 5, 1884; Dodge City *Times*, May 29, June 12, Aug. 21, 1884, Jan. 8, 1885; Dodge City *Cowboy*, July 26, Aug. 23, 1884; Topeka *Commonwealth*, Aug. 3, 1884.

violence by at least a minority of the prohibitionists. Of the two most important tickets put into the field, one was a "law and order" coalition of moderates and radicals. The other, a "liberal" ticket, more or less resembled the Gang slates of old, offering Bob Wright for mayor with Hoover, Kelley, and W. H. Harris included as council candidates. The liberals triumphed easily, the majority of voters no longer being in the mood for compromise. Under Wright's permissive eye Dodge welcomed what would be its last cattle trading season. "The town is beginning to fill up with cowboys and stockmen," it was observed late in May. "The saloons, gambling halls and dance halls are in full blast again."[1]

From then till the end of the year, however, feeling between liberals and prohibitionists escalated dangerously. An unavailing radical effort to institute district court proceedings against the saloonmen had raised tempers on both sides to the boiling point when in June an organizer for the Kansas State Temperance Union, Albert Griffin, delivered a prohibition address to a standing-room-only crowd at the town's new Methodist church. The anti-saloon reception was much more enthusiastic than Griffin had expected. He left to speak at Garden City, but returned on June 24 to preside over the founding of a local K.S.T.U. chapter with some sixty charter members. The next day Griffin filed injunction papers against Dodge City's liquor sellers, only to have the county attorney refuse to act on them. He promptly left for Topeka, where he urged Attorney General S. B. Bradford to go back with him to see justice done at Dodge. Bradford instead appointed a deputy to represent him. Griffin and the deputy arrived at Dodge on June 29. That evening they found themselves besieged in Sam Gal-

---

[1] *Compiled Laws of Kansas*, 1885, pp. 382–90; Dodge City *Democrat*, Feb. 21, 28, Mar. 7, 31, Apr. 4, 1885; Dodge City *Globe*, Mar. 3, 10, 17, Apr. 7, 1885; Dodge City *Times*, Mar. 19, 1885; Dodge City *Cowboy*, May 30, 1885.

land's hotel by a threatening crowd. Many of those assembled outside happened to be construction workers employed on a large irrigation project north of town. Temporarily idle because of rain, they were on the street because the saloon keepers had shut down in response to Griffin's visit. The mob manhandled Galland and a few other prohibitionists who appeared on the scene, but was probably more vocally menacing than actually bent on a lynching. After a harrowing night, the two visitors fled town on an eastbound train.[2]

Griffin hysterically begged Governor John A. Martin to send the militia into Dodge. But a confidential report to the governor from Jeremiah C. Strang, the district court judge for Dodge City's area, urged restraint. The town, Strang insisted,

> is in a transition state and will come all right soon of itself.
>
> The [Texas cattle] quarantine law passed last winter is quietly working out the salvation of Dodge City. The festive cowboy is already becoming conspicuous by his absence in Dodge, and ere long he will be seen & heard there, in his glory, no more forever. The cowboy gone the gamblers and prostitutes will find their occupations gone, and, from necessity, must follow. The bulk of the saloons will then die out because there will be no sufficient support left, and the temperance people can close the rest as easily as they could in any other city in Kansas.

Attorney General Bradford visited Dodge to learn the facts firsthand and agreed almost word for word with Judge Strang's assessment.[3]

But a second incident that autumn renewed the state authorities' concern about Dodge City. In late October

---

[2] See especially Dodge City *Cowboy*, June 27, July 4, 1885; Topeka *Commonwealth*, July 2, 4, 1885; Dodge City *Globe*, July 7, 1885.

[3] J. C. Strang to John A. Martin, July 5, 1885, Governors' Correspondence (General), KSHS; Topeka *Capital*, July 11, 1885.

the officers of Edwards County filed a complaint against a gambler who then fled across the county line to Dodge City. An Edwards deputy sheriff followed and arrested him in Dodge, but—as reported to Governor Martin—a mob surrounded the deputy and forced him to leave town without his prisoner. Martin threatened to intervene, only to discover finally that the mob consisted of one man— Bat Masterson. But in the course of his long-distance investigation the exasperated governor implored Mayor Wright to clean up the town once and for all. "The fact is," he complained,

> ... the condition of affairs in Dodge, instead of improving, as I had hoped, seems to be growing worse. I hear, every now and then, of robberies committed on innocent strangers, who have come to Kansas to seek homes. Visitors inform me that the saloons are increasing, not only in numbers, but in depravity; and that thieves, desperadoes, gamblers and criminals generally, are multiplying. It is also alleged that these lawless characters dominate in the city; that they have terrorized all the better elements of society; that they openly and defiantly flaunt their viciousness and depravity; and that they appear to think there is no power or authority that can reach or punish them. . . .
>
> Sooner or later, you know that Dodge must reform or perish. Why not reform it now? Why cannot all decent citizens of Dodge unite in a determined effort to make Dodge an orderly, peac[e]able, decent and prosperous city?

Bob Wright's reply only revealed how little unity of purpose there could be between Dodge City's liberals and its reformers. "Governor," he wrote, barely restraining his anger,

> you have been imposed upon by a lot of soreheads of this Town. This gang only consists of about a dozen who breed all the trouble here & continually keep things in hot

water, they are public disturbers & agitators & are a curse to any community—who want every one to think & do as they say—who if they cant rule want to ruin, who do not hesitate to lie & prevaricate to gain their selfish ends, who pretend to be Moralists but are wolves in sheeps clothing, in short who are hypocrites of the deepest & darkest kind. Such even is M. W. Sutton[,] N. B. Klaine . . . & a few others of this kind. There are only one or two of this whole bunch who own a dollars worth of property here & if they cant have things their own way, they abuse Dodge City & its surroundings in the vilest manner & say worse things about it, than Dodge's worst outside enemy can or dare say. It is a dirty bird that befouls its own nest & that is the case with these hypocrites. I know them & I know well their dirty black hearts, which never beat with a single generous thought for their fellow man. Sutton is a good lawyer & I admire his ability, but I know his motives. He pretends to be a great temperance man & he drinks more whiskey in a week than I do in a year. Now Governor these are the men who have caught your ear & I assure you I have not pictured them half as mean & contemptible as they really are.

Wright concluded by almost wistfully assuring Governor Martin that reform would come in its own good time:

You must recol[l]ect that our situation is dif[f]erent from that of other Towns in the Eastern part of the State, which have always enjoyed the benefits of churches, schools & other civilizing influences. We have always been a frontier Town, where the wild & reckless sons of the Plains have congregated, their influences are still felt here, but we are rapidly overcoming them, let us alone & we will work out our own salvation in due season. I flatter myself that I know how to handle the boys, they cannot be driven. . . . Please do not borrow trouble Governor about the conduct or management of Dodge City.[4]

[4] The incident of the absconding gambler did not make the local newspapers, but see especially Martin to P. F. Sughrue, Governors' Letters (KSHS), LXII, 123–26; Martin to Robert McCanse, ibid.,

Even as Wright penned these words the results of the 1885 county election became known, causing yet another official inquiry from Topeka. Back in September the wet and dry factions of the local Republican Party had tried to compromise on a regular Republican slate, but failed. Therefore the wets of both parties fused in support of a "People's Ticket" to oppose a prohibitionist "Independent Ticket." The wet candidates won by virtue of an enormous Dodge Precinct majority. The reformers cried fraud, stating that they were kept from voting by organized intimidation while at the same time the polls had been shamelessly stuffed with anti-prohibition ballots. On November 24 they filed suit in the state supreme court to throw out the Dodge Precinct ballots and thus reverse the outcome.[5] On the same day, Attorney General Bradford arrived to close down the saloons, but found them to have suspended business. Mayor Wright somehow convinced him that they would stay closed, and at the same time ordered the closing of the local dance house. Bradford left town again on November 26, but the very next day the saloons resumed operations as quasi drugstores.

Late that night, November 27–28, a fire of unknown origin broke out in the Junction Saloon and leveled the Front Street buildings between First Avenue and Bridge Street, destroying several saloons as well as Bob Wright's brick store. Rumor immediately blamed the prohibitionists. At four o'clock that morning Wright fired three shots

---

298–300; Sughrue to Martin, Oct. 31, 1885, Governors' Correspondence (General); McCanse to Martin, Nov. 9, 1885, ibid. For the quoted exchange between governor and mayor see Martin to R. M. Wright, Governors' Letters, LXII, 127–37; Wright to Martin, Nov. 5, 1885, Governors' Correspondence (General).

[5] Dodge City *Times*, Sept. 17, Oct. 8, Nov. 5, 12, Dec. 3, 17, 1885; Dodge City *Cowboy*, Oct. 10, 17, Nov. 7, 1885; Dodge City *Globe*, Dec. 1, 8, 1885. The suit was not heard until 1887. Then, after over a thousand pages of testimony had been taken, the court decided in favor of the defendants. *Kansas Reports*, XXXVI, 225–36.

into Mike Sutton's house. Later, in separate conferences with the governor, Sutton maintained that the mayor's act was a misdirected attempt at vengeance, while Wright himself claimed that he had been on hand to protect Sutton and his family from more potent damage and had fired ineffectively at a prowler. As legal action impended on this episode, flames spreading from a Chestnut Street whorehouse on the night of December 8–9 leveled yet another city block.

Lest the true pitch of Dodge City's internecine strife give a *coup de grâce* to what little remained of the town's good name abroad, none of its editors dared speculate in print about incendiarism. Since matters could only get better at this point, cool heads on both sides finally prevailed, signaling a general revulsion against Bob Wright's version of city management. In March 1886, a petition signed by 227 businessmen—saloonmen and prohibitionists included—asked that A. B. Webster assume the post of mayor and bring stability back to the community. "The boys," as Wright had fondly termed them, made one last effort to assert themselves as Bat Masterson incongruously filed complaints against all the liquor dealers in an attempt to blackmail them into opposing Webster's candidacy. Webster triumphed anyway. District court prosecutions of Masterson's complaints resulted in hung juries, but as a moderate reform concession Mayor Webster ordered all saloons closed, front and back, on Sundays.[6]

The conflict over prohibition enforcement survived the cattle trade by several years. As many had predicted, however, the end of its era brought an end to con-

[6] See especially Martin to J. C. Strang, Governors' Letters, LXIII, 267–76; B. F. Milton to S. B. Bradford, Feb. 13, 1886, Attorney Generals' Correspondence, KSHS; M. W. Sutton to Bradford, Mar. 10, 1886, ibid.; A. J. Abbott to Bradford, Mar. 30, 1886, ibid.; Topeka *Capital*, Nov. 28, 1885; Dodge City *Democrat*, Nov. 28, Dec. 12, 19, 1885, Mar. 13, Apr. 17, 1886; Dodge City *Globe*, Dec. 1, 15, 1885, Mar. 9, 16, 1886; Medicine Lodge *Cresset*, Dec. 17, 1885.

spicuous wickedness at Dodge—the dance house, the gambling facility, the overt saloon. In the final analysis, successful moral reform proved less a matter of evangelical or political agitation than of those impersonal forces of demographic and economic change.

[6]

CALDWELL'S REFORM experience under the prohibitory law was uniquely shaped by the fact that its citizens did not control or even appreciably influence the composition and functioning of their county government. In the first years of state prohibition this did not seem particularly important. In 1881 and 1882 the county attorney descended from Wellington and raided Caldwell's saloons, but after finding convictions difficult to obtain gave up the effort as unrewarding.[7] In the long run, as we shall see, pressure from the county seat proved of considerable assistance to Caldwell's radicals.

Internal community efforts toward moral reform, meanwhile, were sporadic and of limited effect. As early as June 1880, the town had a temperance association; by October of that year the group claimed a membership of about one hundred. Women probably comprised most of this seemingly inflated figure, although enough adult males of the temperance persuasion lived in town to give the prohibitory amendment a surprising forty-five majority there.[8] Caldwell's city fathers dismissed this victory as a fluke, and continued to tolerate saloons as necessary to both the cattle trade and the municipal treasury.

Occasionally they wavered. On Saturday, December 17, 1881, a protracted gun battle between townsmen and

[7] Caldwell *Commercial*, Mar. 24, July 28, Aug. 18, 1881, Feb. 9, 16, 1882; Caldwell *Post*, Aug. 25, Sept. 8, 22, 1881.

[8] Caldwell *Post*, June 17, Oct. 21, 1880; Caldwell *Commercial*, June 17, Aug. 19, Oct. 28, Nov. 4, 1880.

a party of carousing cowboys killed a popular saloon keeper and former mayor. Over Sunday incensed residents placed the blame on the various illegal entertainment facilities, urging prompt official action against them. On Monday, Caldwell's councilmen accordingly met and passed ordinances outlawing saloons, professional gambling, and prostitution. The next week the police judge ordered a number of whores out of town, and an angry delegation of citizens forced the owner of the dance house to close up shop.

This brief "moral spasm," as an editor described it, lasted only through the Christmas season, during which time the anti-reformers got up a "numerously signed" petition demanding repeal of the interdict on professional sin. A saloon keeper presented this petition at the next meeting of the council, together with a verbal argument that liquor had played no part in the recent trouble. More importantly, the council also heard remarks by George W. Reilly, the prosperous owner of a brick business block housing a casino in one of its upper rooms. As reported by a somewhat hostile editor, Reilly maintained that

> the ordinances passed were a detriment to the city. As a direct result of their enforcement, trade had fallen off, and people would soon begin to leave the city. He insisted that the people and the city were losing money by not permitting the saloons to run. He drew a gloomy picture of the future if the saloons were kept closed, and endeavored to paint in glowing colors the *material* prosperity which would come to the town if it only had a few open places where one could get his regular dose of bug juice. He could show, he said[,] where the whisky business was conducted in a gentlemanly way and to the benefit of the city, by . . . some of the best men in the state, and referred to Dodge City as a model town.

This powerful appeal to entrepreneurial considerations had no prompt effect; through January the councilmen

hesitated. On February 2 they finally bowed both to protests and personal threats and repealed the offending injunctions. Caldwell's entertainment business resumed normal operations.

In April local businessmen caucused and replaced the
old mayor with Albert M. Colson, and the old council
with a group of men who stood for pure and simple good
order rather than moral reform, their aim being tougher
law enforcement and a heavier levy on the protected but
illegal professions. The resulting improvement seemed so
marked that in 1883 the business community re-elected
Colson and his councilmen to second terms. Colson's
regime thus corresponded to that of A. B. Webster at
Dodge City.[9]

Late in 1884 a sustained moral reform movement finally stirred Caldwell. That December the wife of a visiting prohibition lecturer organized a local chapter of the
Women's Christian Temperance Union, which three
months later boasted a membership of "over thirty."
When Caldwell's saloons suspended operations soon
after, the W.C.T.U. organizer claimed credit. In fact,
however, the credit belonged to an undercover agent
from the county seat who caused the prosecution of three
local saloonmen; the others, a dozen or so, simply closed
down temporarily in precautionary response. A month
later, under the considerably stiffened enforcement statute just passed by the legislature, County Attorney John
A. Murray, a young anti-liquor zealot, struck again. The
heat was on at last. "The open saloon is a thing of the
past," reckoned one Caldwell editor. Its local replacement
was the "blind tiger"—a covert liquor dispensary featur-

[9] Caldwell *Commercial*, Dec. 30, 1880, Jan. 6, 1881, Jan. 5, Feb. 2,
9, 1882, Apr. 5, 1883; Caldwell *Post*, Jan. 6, Dec. 22, 1881, Feb. 9,
Apr. 6, 1882. After the Colson administration took charge, it raised
the fines on all the town's illegal businesses. (Ibid., May 4, 1882;
Caldwell *Commercial*, June 8, 1882.) For Colson's "get tough" law
enforcement philosophy see the Caldwell *Post*, Dec. 7, 1882.

ing a low window with revolving tray where cash and bottles could change hands without buyer or seller being able to identify each other. As at Dodge City, increased enforcement pressures also prompted the more substantial saloon keepers to abandon the trade to less respectable operators willing to risk legal exigencies.

For the first time in the town's history its prohibitionists formally moved into politics in April 1885, entering a moral reform municipal ticket. Businessmen countered with a slate of candidates headed by George Reilly. The newly established Caldwell *Free Press*, edited by Enos Blair, a devout Quaker and uncompromising foe of drink, supported the prohibition effort; but in a heated contest the Reilly ticket triumphed.[1]

On July 20 an important incident again mobilized both the radicals and their opponents. The county authorities arrested two Caldwell gamblers and whisky peddlers, Frank Noyes and Dave Sharp, spiriting them off to Wellington for trial. Both pleaded guilty and languished behind bars for thirty days. During the night of August 30–31, closely following their release, Editor Blair's house went up in flames at the hands of unknown incendiaries. Blair himself barely escaped with his life. Through September and October his narrowly averted fate served as a standing threat to any potential prohibition informers. Then, in early November, County Attorney Murray dispatched a deputy sheriff and an assistant to Caldwell to gather evidence on the elusive blind tiger operators. The two officers hung about town one evening, and the next day made an arrest. They marched their sullen prisoner to the railroad depot for return to Wellington, only to be prevented from leaving by an armed

[1] Caldwell *Journal*, Dec. 18, 1884, Feb. 5, 12, 19, 26, Mar. 12, 19, 26, Apr. 2, 9, 16, 1885; Chapman Bros.: *Portrait and Biographical Album of Sumner County* (Chicago, 1890), pp. 375–76. The first issue of the *Free Press* emerged just before the election, but the surviving run of the publication dates only from September.

mob that besieged them in the baggage room until the morning train had left. Mayor Reilly wisely intervened, dispersing the crowd and having the prisoner locked in the city jail to await the sheriff's arrival on the evening train. But the reconstituted mob descended on the calaboose and released the prisoner. The sheriff accordingly arrested eighteen Caldwellites, including Noyes and Sharp, seven of whom were subsequently convicted in district court for unlawful assembly.

Late in the year, as this court action pended and as County Attorney Murray stepped up his campaign against Caldwell's blind tigers, liberal resistance grew increasingly militant. On December 3 the *Free Press* foreman received a threatening letter, and the next night another letter advised him to get out of town. A few days later a third letter identified itself as a final warning. William Lee, a young Caldwellite who had helped the sheriff make the unlawful assembly arrests a month before, received a similar threat.[2]

The tension stretched restraints to the breaking point. At one o'clock in the morning of December 8 a group of men posing as law officers from Wellington awakened Frank Noyes at the cottage he shared with his mistress and marched him off into the frigid night. At dawn his body was found at the stockyard, dangling stiffly from a crossbeam in the pelting sleet that prefaced the winter's first snow. A note protruding from one pocket—addressed "To House Burners" and signed "Vigilance Committee" —advised Dave Sharp and six other whisky sellers to "take warning."[3]

[2] Caldwell *Journal*, July 23, 30, Sept. 3, Nov. 12, Dec. 3, 10, 1885, Feb. 18, 1886; Caldwell *Free Press*, Nov. 7, Dec. 12, 1885; Wellington *Press*, Feb. 11, 18, May 6, 1886.

[3] See especially Wellington *Press*, Dec. 10, 17, 1885; Caldwell *Journal*, Dec. 10, 1885; Wellington *Standard*, Dec. 11, 1885; G. D. Freeman: *Midnight and Noonday, or the Incidental History of Southern Kansas* (Caldwell, 1892), chap. xliii.

Noyes's mistress claimed to have recognized two members of the lynching party, one of them a hard-bitten frontiersman turned prohibitionist. In a hearing at Wellington, however, her identifications failed to stand up, the impression being that she changed her story in response to threats. With that, all prosecution efforts came to a halt. Local public opinion was divided over possible guilt. Many took the evidence at face value, holding that Noyes had been lynched by a fanatical prohibitionist minority in retaliation for the burning of Enos Blair's house and to frighten other blind tiger operators into submission. "The charge that the hanging was done by prohibitionists does not seem to us to have the least bit of sustaining evidence," a Caldwell editor protested, "as the men in this city who are recognized as ultra in that matter are men that no sane person would ever accuse of hanging a fellow-man." A second hypothesis had it that Noyes planned to turn state's evidence on his fellow liquor dealers, but county officials knew of no such scheme. "Others think Noyes was in possession of secrets which co-criminals concluded was dangerous to allow him to retain," the deputy county attorney privately informed Governor Martin in answer to a request for particulars; "however we do not know."[4]

[4] Wellington *Press*, Dec. 17, 24, 31, 1885; Caldwell *Free Press*, Dec. 19, 1885; Caldwell *Journal*, Dec. 24, 1885; C. Everest Elwood to John A. Martin, Dec. 23, 1885, Governors' Correspondence (Criminal Records), KSHS. Caldwell has never yielded the identities of the killers, although the dominant assumption is that the responsible parties were some "border elements" among the local prohibitionists. A longtime Caldwell editor, David D. Leahy, who happened to meet the lynching party that night but who implies that he recognized no one, reminisced that after Blair's house burned down "Noyes was . . . lynched for the supposed offense." And as Blair's own grandson testified: "Sentiment by the law abiding element began to get so strong that someone had to be hung, so Frank Noyes was the goat." Caldwell *News: Golden Anniversary Edition* (Caldwell, 1937), p. 32; undated news articles in "Sumner County Clippings" (scrapbook, KSHS), II, 50, IV, 117.

Caldwell's city council reacted impartially to the clash of theories, unanimously voting rewards for the arrest and conviction of Noyes's killers, the burners of Blair's house, and the writers of the threatening letters to the *Free Press* foreman and Will Lee. All blind tigers meanwhile suspended business, citizens kept their shotguns and rifles close at hand, and a volunteer police force patrolled the streets by night. A day or two before Christmas, with the Wellington hearing having ended inconclusively, some 130 male Caldwellites met and formed a local Law and Order League—the name being currently in vogue among urban groups throughout the nation seeking governmental fealty to reform laws, especially those restricting the liquor traffic. The most important of the new Caldwell association's militant resolves was that "we demand of the Mayor and all the city and county officers the enforcement of all state and city laws by which the city may be rid of all gamblers, vagrants and prostitutes."[5]

Critics of moral reform, angered by the League's ultimatum, talked of organizing in resistance. Civil war threatened over Christmas. On December 28, following a general call, some three to four hundred Caldwellites gathered at the opera house to resolve the community crisis. "The prohibition element was confined to one side of the house," according to a colorful reminiscence, "and the liberals to the other. There was not a man in the vast audience, and everybody was there, who did not have from one to three revolvers concealed about him and hades was expected every moment." After leaders of both persuasions had acknowledged the need for social unity, those in attendance passed resolutions approving the municipal rewards and requesting that similar rewards be issued

[5] Caldwell Council Record, 1884–91 (microfilm copy, KSHS), pp. 93–94; Caldwell *Journal*, Dec. 10, 17, 24, 1885; Wellington *Press*, Dec. 17, 1885; Wellington *Standard*, Dec. 18, 1885; Caldwell *Free Press*, Dec. 26, 1885; Cherrington: *Standard Encyclopedia*, IV, 1512–13.

by county and state officials. While condemning all voluntary associations that tended "to divide the citizens of Caldwell into factions calculated to damage or injure the local, legal, or commercial interests of the 'Queen city' of the border, her citizens or society," the assembly endorsed the Law and Order League's principle aim: the enforcement of all laws on the statute books. Before breaking up, the citizens appointed a committee to collect private reward money to be added to that posted by the city.[6]

Within a week the special committee had gathered $1,500, but neither this fund nor the official rewards brought forth the names of any guilty parties. In accordance with the assembly's wishes, the city councilmen gave notice that all ordinances would be strictly enforced. Local prostitutes were hailed to court and the year ended, Enos Blair noted happily, "without a saloon or open gambling den" in town. But the long-sought millennium was not really at hand, as the rapid breakup of December's reform consensus demonstrated. Instead of disbanding as expected, the Law and Order League tried to consolidate its gains by throwing the moderates out of city hall in the spring of 1886, but went down in total defeat.[7]

As at Dodge City, radical agitation continued long after trail driving had ended, although never again would Caldwell resemble the wide-open cattle trading center of old. Cattle town reformers everywhere had learned that winning even a modest degree of social perfection was no mean accomplishment.

[6] Caldwell *News*, Oct. 29, 1896; Caldwell *Journal*, Dec. 31, 1885; Wellington *Standard*, Jan. 1, 1886; Caldwell *Free Press*, Jan. 2, 1886.
[7] Caldwell Council Record, pp. 96–97; Wellington *Press*, Dec. 31, 1885; Caldwell *Free Press*, Jan. 2, Apr. 10, 1886; Caldwell *Journal*, Jan. 7, Mar. 25, Apr. 1, 8, 1886.

VIII

The Cattle Town Besieged

[1]

O N A SPRING DAY in 1872 two short but meaningful
items appeared in a cattle town newspaper, one
following the other in a proximity not intended to display
the irony actually conveyed:

> There is little or no doubt that Wichita will be the
> important shipping point for the Texas cattle trade the
> coming season. Already several large herds are being pas-
> tured sixty and a hundred miles south of us waiting until
> vegetation becomes more advanced before venturing this
> far north.

> Settlers are pouring in from the north and east—home-
> steaders. The great majority come in wagons, bringing
> along their cattle, horses, farming implements and house-
> hold furniture, and accompanied by their families. Home-
> steaders are the men who make and develop a new coun-
> try.[1]

Each of the cattle towns in turn felt the force of these
utterly irreconcilable economic interests here so innocently juxtaposed. And one by one, each finally submitted

[1] Wichita *Eagle*, Apr. 12, 1872.

to the farmer at the expense of the commerce in range cattle. The result in every case may have been inevitable, but the agricultural victory did not come easily. Abilene, which had been the first of the important Kansas cattle centers, was also the first to succumb.

[2]

THE YEAR 1870 proved to be more than just another cattle shipping season to Abilene. At last rural settlement on a large scale was under way in surrounding Dickinson County. By mid-season an estimated sixteen hundred new citizens had arrived in the county, boosting its total population to slightly over three thousand. At least two thirds of these were farm folk who increasingly overflowed onto the hitherto empty upland grazing grounds.[2]

The beginnings of cattle trading at Abilene are rightly ascribed to Joseph G. McCoy; its end was also probably more nearly the work of a few influential individuals than would be the case elsewhere. However one tries to avoid invoking a conspiracy thesis, the evidence indicates that a small number of real estate dealers provided a militant nucleus of leadership for the anti-cattle trade movement, without which an immigration onslaught alone would surely not have succeeded with such striking dispatch.

Foremost among these land agents was Theodore C. Henry, the young man who in early 1868 had helped draft the resolution at Humbarger's Ford that pretended to reflect a countywide consensus favoring the Texas cattle trade. The heir of a prosperous, recently deceased New York State farmer, Henry had exhausted his patrimony as an unsuccessful cotton grower in Alabama immediately following the war. He then drifted up to Springfield, Illinois, to read law in the office of Joe McCoy's

2 Abilene *Chronicle*, May 19, 1870, Jan. 5, 1871; "List of Population by Counties" (typescript, KSHS), Dickinson Co. section.

attorney, but late in 1867, at McCoy's urging, he migrated out to Abilene. Henry spent his first winter writing advertising copy for a local land speculator, then bought into a partnership with James B. Shane, the agent for some 200,000 acres of Dickinson real estate opened to settlement by the Kansas Pacific Railway. A partially disabled war veteran, Jim Shane managed the accounts while Henry did the actual selling. "Henry was right in his element," recalled one informant, "it was *His* chance. I presume he was responsible for more farm sales in 1868–69 & 70 & 71 than all the others combined. Henry was a Hustler."[3] The firm of Shane and Henry, Real Estate Brokers, also included a secret partner, probably S. A. Burroughs, the prohibitionist lawyer mentioned in the preceding chapter. All three sought political office, by which frontier businessmen commonly enhanced their economic potential. In 1870 Henry and Shane sat on Abilene's village council, with Henry as provisional mayor. Henry served as county register of deeds in 1870–71, Shane as county treasurer. Burroughs filled the post of county attorney in 1871–72, also serving on the Abilene city council in 1871.[4]

A second real estate agency, the National Union Land

[3] C. F. Gross to J. B. Edwards, Apr. 13, May 29, 1922, Edwards Papers, KSHS; Junction City *Union*, Apr. 11, 1868; Lawrence *Tribune*, June 23, 1868; Abilene *Gazette*, Feb. 25, 1881; T. C. Henry: *An Address to the Old Settlers Re-Union at Enterprise, Kansas, October 9, 1902* (n.p., n.d.), p. 1; T. C. Henry: "The Story of a Fenceless Winter-Wheat Field," *Transactions of the Kansas State Historical Society*, IX (1905–06), 502 *n.*, 503; Stuart Henry: *Conquering Our Great American Plains* (New York, 1930), pp. viii–ix.

[4] Shane was Henry's overt partner, but Henry mentions *two* partners, both two-term county officers, in his "Story of a Wheat Field," 503. All evidence points to Burroughs as the third (secret) partner. Henry purchased Shane's interest in the firm in June 1872 and in the spring of 1873 bought out his competitors. Burroughs retired to a farm in June 1873, which suggests that he, too, had sold out, as Henry states. Abilene *Chronicle*, June 20, 1872, Apr. 3, 1873; Enterprise *Gazette*, May 19, 1876.

Office, embraced another important group of land agents. Jacob Augustine, a temporarily out-of-pocket midwestern capitalist, had visited Abilene in June 1869, and caught Joe McCoy—then in economic eclipse—in a selling mood. From McCoy and a fellow developer, Augustine bought both the original townsite and a subdivision on thirty days' time. Back in Ohio he contacted young C. H. Lebold, who agreed to furnish the necessary capital in exchange for a half-interest in the acquisition. Late in 1869 these two opened for business, Lebold serving as resident agent; Augustine did not settle permanently in Abilene until two years later.[5] For a time Vear P. Wilson—preacher, *Chronicle* editor, and sponsor of the rural "Buckeye Colony"— was an overt member of the firm and may have been a secret partner from the start.[6] Lebold and Wilson also held public office, the former as a member of the village council in 1870, the latter as county probate judge in 1871.

Henry's and Lebold's land offices remained the most important in Abilene. While some observers identified a neat division of interest between the two firms—Henry concentrating on rural acreage, Lebold on town lots— their respective newspaper advertisements displayed a generous overlap of farm sales. Both firms thus looked to a countryside cleared of Texas cattle as an inducement to rural immigration and resultant land profits.[7] In addition,

[5] Joseph G. McCoy: *Historic Sketches of the Cattle Trade of the West and Southwest*, ed. Ralph P. Bieber (Glendale, Calif., 1940), pp. 64, 292; Adolph Roenigk (ed.): *Pioneer History of Kansas* (Denver, 1933), pp. 32–33; S. Lewis and Co.: *United States Biographical Dictionary: Kansas Volume* (Chicago, 1879), pp. 658–59; Junction City *Union*, Dec. 11, 1869; Abilene *Gazette*, Feb. 25, 1881.

[6] See the agency's advertisement in the Abilene *Chronicle*, Nov. 3, 1870, through May 4, 1871.

[7] For the most specific division-of-interest statement see Gross to Edwards, Mar. 31, 1925, Edwards Papers. For Lebold's specialization in town lots see Topeka *Commonwealth*, May 19, 1870; *U.S. Biographical Dictionary*, p. 658. For evidence that this was not an exclusion preoccupation see (besides his lists of farms for sale) the editorial

Henry may already have conceived the idea for his mammoth "fenceless winter wheat field" operation near Abilene. Barbed wire had not yet come on the market; the costs of enclosing such a large acreage stoutly enough (with posts and boards or smooth wire) would have been prohibitive. Henry's plan therefore required passage of a herd law, obliging livestock owners to herd their animals and making fencing unnecessary. But since Texas drovers would surely be the most persistent offenders, an even more ideal expedient was to close the county to the cattle trade. Giving the main address at the first Dickinson County fair in October 1870, Henry demanded a herd law and also ventured the first public suggestion that the cattle trade should go. He made his point crystal clear. "When the time comes that these thousands and hundreds of thousands of cattle that are annually pouring in upon us," he declared,

> retard the development of our county by deterring its settlement and cultivation—rather than contributing to its advancement, as perhaps they have done heretofore, then their presence should no longer be encouraged or tolerated here. Possibly I am mistaken, but my conviction is, that that time is very near at hand.

In January 1871, an anonymous writer to the Abilene *Chronicle*, purporting to be one of the county's oldest settlers, in effect endorsed T. C. Henry's contention. He maintained that Abilene's cattle trade benefited only a minority of actual residents while causing increased taxation for law enforcement as well as contributing "demoralizing influences." Editor Wilson cautiously opened his columns to a limited number of replies. "The citizens of Dickinson county who are becoming enriched by the cattle trade," declared a defender, "pray for its continuance."

blurb in his behalf in the Abilene *Chronicle*, Dec. 15, 1870, and his ad in ibid., Feb. 16, 1871 ff., which reveals that his firm had become an agent for the local Kansas Pacific Railway lands.

The original critic promptly rebutted, reiterating that most of the profits of the trade went to nonresidents and claiming that Abilene's major return was a reputation as "the meanest hole in the State." He demanded that a herd law, which would seriously discourage the Texas cattle trade from returning to Dickinson County, be put to a vote in the spring, predicting a three-to-one majority in favor.[8] More communications followed, but with excitement rapidly rising Wilson clamped the lid on the controversial dialogue.

As recently provided for by the state legislature, citizens voted in a herd law plebiscite in April 1871, an event unattended by fanfare in the *Chronicle*. The prediction of decisive approval proved grossly inaccurate. The herd law lost by a 123-vote margin, carrying only four of the county's fourteen precincts. But due primarily to the heavy majorities at Abilene's bitterly jealous sister settlements, Detroit and Solomon City, the proposed measure captured nearly 41 per cent of the ballots. The new upland settlers of Buckeye and Upper Chapman Creek precincts went heavily against the trade, their unfenced prairie claims being especially vulnerable to longhorn depredations.[9]

Though the portent of the vote must have been obvious, Wilson did not yet identify enough of a consensus to justify criticizing the cattle trade as such. In the summer months that followed he brutally hammered at Joe McCoy, the father of Abilene's cattle trade, and vice, its supposedly

[8] Henry: "Story of a Wheat Field," 503–06; Abilene *Chronicle*, Nov. 10, 1870, Jan. 12, 19, 26, 1871.

[9] *Laws of Kansas*, 1871, pp. 208–11; Dickinson Co. Commissioners Journal, 1861–83 (microfilm copy, KSHS), pp. 157–64. The Journal mistakenly records defeat of the law by only sixty-six votes. Wilson printed the text of the herd law in the Abilene *Chronicle* of March 23, but his only comment on the vote was: "From what we can learn the herd law was defeated on last Tuesday, in this county." Ibid., Apr. 6, 1871.

indispensable concomitant. This implicit linking of social immorality with Texas cattle evidently impressed Wilson's readers, and by autumn the point had been made.[1]

The details of events in the six weeks after defeat of the proposed herd law are not entirely clear but can be reconstructed with reasonable certainty. Cattle trade opponents in Dickinson County mobilized and forced a showdown. Besides Abilene's realtors, the most militant of them were not those embattled upland settlers but rather the farmers closely surrounding Abilene, many of whom had turned to raising domestic cattle in response to the burgeoning prices of the previous year and whose foremost concern was splenic fever. In Grant Township, which held the county seat, only the pro-cattle trade votes of the town itself had swung the margin against the herd law. Now these angry ruralites, organizing as the Dickinson County Farmers' Protective Association, evidently threatened to take vigilante action against the first incoming herds. Somehow T. C. Henry and his fellow anti-cattle enthusiasts among the townsmen induced Abilene's business community to negotiate.[2]

The farmers consented to be peaceable during the coming cattle season. The price exacted from the Abilene businessmen was an agreement signed May 15, 1871, by representatives of both the farmers' association and the town. The document specified that only wintered Texas cattle could be driven over the lands of any association member without prior written consent. It defined a trail

[1] An exception to this circumspection occurred in July when, in a postscript to his report on the state of county finances, J. B. Shane stated that but for "thousands of dollars . . . thrown away" on criminal prosecutions the county would have been $6,000 ahead. To which Wilson commented: "Here is a fact for the tax-payer to ponder.— Nearly every one of the criminals was a non-resident, and only in the county for temporary purposes." Abilene *Chronicle*, July 27, 1871.

[2] Unfortunately, the issues of the *Chronicle* that may have contained details on the beginnings of the farmers' organization are no longer extant.

and grazing ground for incoming herds, all right-of-way easements to be purchased by the townsmen. It also established a $5,000 fund to be raised by the business community, out of which splenic fever losses would be paid to association members (nothing was said about trampled fields). A three-man arbitration committee was to disburse this fund, and if the provisions of the agreement were not obeyed the money would revert to the farmers' association. Finally, the contract specified that the Texas cattle trade would continue in Dickinson County after March 1, 1872, only with the expressed consent of the association.

Realtors Henry and Lebold signed on behalf of the town, thereby revealing their roles in its inception. Also signing was an Abilene city councilman—a lumberyard owner—who thus gave the agreement a semi-official flavor. An Abilene farm equipment dealer signed for the association, as did two farmers, one of them the very prosperous James Bell, who lived on the outskirts of town. The arbitration committee comprised T. C. Henry, Jim Bell, and an Abilene liveryman. If those with economic interests oriented toward the farmers were thought to have sold out their fellow townsmen, Wilson allowed no such criticism into the columns of his newspaper. The $5,000 fund was promptly subscribed, businessmen giving their promissory notes to fall due in four months. The arbitration committee began hearings the first week in June, and by mid-month had already ruled on over $4,000 worth of legitimate splenic fever claims.[3]

This essentially local agreement, however, did nothing immediate for farmers farther out in the hinterlands, who had to fend for themselves. The settlers on Upper Chapman Creek, for instance, passed a militant anti-cattle trade resolution in May to forestall grazing depredations. The settlers of two other rural townships, in the

[3] Abilene *Chronicle*, May 18, 25, June 1, 8, 15, July 13, 1871.

absence of a county herd law, sought relief in a local option substitute, a statute of 1868 providing that three fifths of a township's electors could require the county commissioners to impose a "night herd law" on the township. Forcing cattlemen to keep their animals under restraint during the hours of darkness, when many depredations normally occurred, settlers deemed this the next best thing to a full herd law.[4]

Texas cattle literally inundated Dickinson County that season, a situation aggravated by poor market prices that forced drovers to pasture their herds longer than anticipated. Although not publicized in the *Chronicle*, several individual accounts of the summer's cattle depredations have survived. One farmer and his wife, having settled in the northern part of the county that spring, put in a small corn crop but the longhorns held on vacant lands nearby trampled it into the ground. "No fence would stop them," recalled their daughter. Any momentary negligence on the part of herders invited disaster, as when a cowboy and his partner discovered the herd they were guarding had broken into a patch of young corn, had pawed and trampled it badly, and had crushed twenty chickens to death. Aggravating this negligence was the deliberate orneriness of many Texans. When a member of the Buckeye Colony intercepted some longhorns approaching his claim he requested the two cowboys in attendance to guide them around his forty-acre meadow. The cowboys advised him "to go to hell," and insolently bedded the herd down right in the meadow, causing the settler serious loss as hay was a valuable crop.

Bloodshed was narrowly averted a number of times. William S. Brewer, farming near the south border of Dickinson County, attempted to head off some longhorns hungrily approaching his patch of sod corn. He asked the

---

[4] Abilene *Chronicle*, June 8, 15, July 27, 1871; *Kansas Statutes*, 1868, pp. 1001–02.

herd boss to divert them. "Oh, certainly, certainly," the Texan mumbled, riding on and paying no attention. Brewer lost his temper and ran for a rifle, but some Mexican cowboys he had befriended grasped what was about to happen and intercepted the cattle. Elsewhere in the county S. L. Graham had a small field of corn planted, but the Texans paid no mind to either his fence or his warnings. When he protested destruction of his crop too vehemently they threatened to burn him out. Finally the owner of a nearby herd rode over and said he was going to kill Graham. Though unarmed, Graham moved in close as the other started to draw his revolver. But then the Texan relented and said he would spare Graham because he was a husband and father. More serious was the incident at Jacob Schopp's claim. Schopp also had a few acres of corn that were one day invaded and nearly destroyed by a herd of longhorns and Texas cow-ponies. The angered settler captured two of the ponies and held them in lieu of damages. A platoon of cowboys threatened his life, but Schopp and a friend held them off at gunpoint, daring them to draw. The Texans finally paid Schopp $50 and commended his grit.[5]

Mounting splenic fever losses among domestic live-stock further increased rural hostility that summer. Several aggrieved farmers hailed drovers into court—with the same negative results that characterized such legal action throughout the cattle trade era in Kansas.[6]

Called together for the first time since spring, the

[5] Abilene *Reflector*, Nov. 20, 1953; J. Marvin Hunter (ed.): *The Trail Drivers of Texas* (2nd edn.; Nashville, Tenn., 1925), p. 436; "Dickinson County Historical Sketches" (typescript, KSHS), I, 60, II, 170; Chapman *Advertiser*, May 12, 1932; Abilene *Democrat*, July 12, 1901.

[6] Abilene *Chronicle*, Sept. 14, 1871. For a summary of the difficulties in attempting to gain convictions under the successive quarantine laws even after they had been toughened, see James Humphrey: "The Administration of George W. Glick," *Transactions of the Kansas State Historical Society*, IX (1905–06), 406.

Farmers' Protective Association met in September 1871 and made elaborate preparations to transform the group into a true countywide organization. Spokesmen urged every school district to send three delegates to an October convention with the object of taking action against the cattle trade—"to resist every effort put forth for its continuation in our county, feeling that it impedes the development of our agricultural resources, and brings nothing but taxation and crime upon us."

S. A. Burroughs and T. C. Henry were the most active speakers at October's meeting. Burroughs introduced a successful resolution that the 1867 quarantine law be enforced, and dwelt vociferously on the evils arising from the cattle trade. Henry introduced a second successful motion that a committee be appointed "to prepare resolutions and present a plan of organization which shall embrace the whole county and concentrate the opposition to this trade, and make it most efficient and powerful." Burroughs won appointment to the five-man group. A third successful resolution called for a committee to gather statistics on the total agricultural losses resulting from the season's cattle trade. Burroughs, Henry, and Jim Bell were selected as the Abilene subcommittee. In November the association met again and completed its plans. Three days later the organization's arbitration committee issued a report on the Abilene splenic fever fund. Many businessmen had refused to make good on their notes given in May. Of the $5,000 pledged, the committee could only collect some $3,100, leaving many legitimate claims only partially paid.

The cattle season had closed by this date. It had been a desultory one in terms of prices, though nearly fifty thousand head were shipped from Abilene and perhaps three times that number moved out on foot. The season had been a busy one for merchants but the hearts of the anti-cattle leaders remained unmoved. The protective association met for the last time on January 27, 1872, having invited to membership "All who are opposed to the continuance of the great curse of the county, the Texas cattle trade and its concomitants." It was probably at this meeting that T. C. Henry unveiled his famous manifesto that then appeared in the *Chronicle* of February 8. The product of over a year's maneuvering on his part, it read as follows:

> Circular.—We the undersigned members of the Farmers' Protective Association and Officers and Citizens of Dickinson county, Kansas, most respectfully request all who have contemplated driving Texas Cattle to Abilene the coming season to seek some other point for shipment, as the inhabitants of Dickinson will no longer submit to the evils of the trade.

The names of fifty-two male citizens followed, the first three being those of Henry, Burroughs, and Jim Shane. In three subsequent issues Wilson repeated the item over a growing list of signatures and under the explicit heading, "TO CATTLE DROVERS." Henry emphasized the message by mailing copies to various Texas newspapers. In its final printing a total of 366 names followed those of all the county officers, extending an entire newspaper column. The list probably did not include all of the signers, since according to Henry a majority of the county's voters had actually appended their signatures.[7]

Dickinson's representative to the 1872 legislature was a country miller who had presided over the anti-cattle trade meeting of October. The miller carried his constituency's message to Topeka. The legislature amended the

[7] Abilene *Chronicle*, Sept. 28, Nov. 2, Dec. 14, 1871, Jan. 25, Feb. 1, 8, 15, 22, Mar. 14, 1872; T. C. Henry: "Thomas James Smith of Abilene," *Transactions of the Kansas State Historical Society*, IX (1905–06), 532. Henry probably exaggerated the proportion of citizens actually signing; however, the *Chronicle* appears to have carried only part of the final list of names—that is, as much of it as would fill one column.

old 1867 quarantine law, tightening up its regulatory specifications and effectively rebuking those who had ignored the law as unconstitutional. It unequivocally fixed the limit for summer importation of Texas cattle some forty miles west of Abilene.

Yet a third formal action serving to discourage the Texas cattle trade emerged that spring. A new herd law measure passed by the 1872 legislature brusquely repealed all conflicting statutes and provided that county boards could declare a herd law in effect without the necessity of petitions or plebiscites. With the names of all three Dickinson commissioners planted beneath the anti-cattle manifesto, there seemed little doubt that a herd law was in store. In March the commissioners imposed the measure, but generously agreed to let the citizens at large ratify or reverse their act. In April over a thousand voters, or nearly the entire county electorate, cast ballots on the herd law, sustaining the measure by a vote of 780 to 314.

Only the three precincts of Union Township, in the Lyon's Creek watershed, returned a margin against it. "The herd law," a resident of that area wrote a few years later, "was ordered in force by the board of county commissioners, much to the annoyance and against the wish of the settlers on Lyon's Creek." These probably were farmers who had successfully adjusted to the cattle trade's consumer demand. The rather strong pro-cattle vote on Turkey Creek and Lower Chapman Creek may also reflect this factor. The three population centers of the county all went heavily against the trade; the total town vote, in fact, was almost three to one against it, whereas the rural total was something less than 2.5 to 1. While the strong margins at Detroit and Solomon City can be taken as primarily anti-Abilene votes, the margin at Abilene itself (118 to 85) reflects an ascendancy of the reformist conviction that a vote against the Texas cattle trade was a vote for social morality and governmental thrift.[8]

Some wintered Texas stock was shipped from Abilene in 1872, but the previous season had been Abilene's last as a cattle town.[9] In early July a Leavenworth journalist, possibly after having talked with the bitter Joe McCoy, lightly lamented the town's metamorphosis. "Its glory has departed from it, and so have the cattle," he observed,

> and the streets that were once filled with life and animation, are growing up with grass. The principal business street is almost entirely deserted, and over two-thirds of the business houses are closed. All this has resulted from the action of a few farmers and some real estate men, who last year formed what was called a "Farmers' Association" for the purpose of driving the cattle trade away, thinking to profit thereby. Last year everything a farmer could raise was cash, and at a good figure; to-day, two bunches of radishes and a peck of beans, at starvation prices, will glut the market. So much for policy.[1]

[8] *Laws of Kansas*, 1872, pp. 384–85, 387–91; Abilene *Chronicle*, Oct. 13, 1876; Dickinson Commissioners Journal, pp. 202, 206–14.

[9] For cattle shipping at Abilene in 1872 see the Abilene *Chronicle*, Oct. 17, 31, 1872. A Dickinson County farmer, Eli George, grazed a herd of nonwintered Texas cattle on the public domain in the northwest corner of the county until July 1872, when the settlers of that area organized and forced him to remove the offending animals. This apparently ended quarantine violations in Dickinson. Ibid., May 2 (ad), Aug. 8, 1872; Abilene *Reflector-Chronicle*, Nov. 20, 1953.

[1] McCoy echoed this analysis a year or so later, charging that the cattle trade "was driven away by the schemes and concerted actions of a trio of office seekers . . . affiliated with certain county officers, . . . [who] formed a ring, or clique, which, with consummate presumption, undertook to manipulate all public matters, even assuming to dictate who should and who should not have public offices, or in any manner have ought to say about matters of a public nature." (McCoy: *Historic Sketches*, pp. 292–94.) T. C. Henry, who claimed authorship of the anti-cattle circular, adds credence to McCoy's charge in summarizing his own Abilene career: "I purchased quite a tract of land, adjoining the town . . . [and] became a farmer. . . . I soon 'caught on,' however. Within two years I captured a county office and became a real-estate broker. My two partners were both county officers, and all together, in-

V. P. Wilson replied that despite the cost in trade, morality had triumphed. "Business is not as brisk as it used to be during the cattle season," he confessed, "—but the citizens have the satisfaction of knowing that 'hell is more than sixty miles away.' "[2] The reference was to Ellsworth. Cattle town moral reformers and rural dissidents would never again coalesce so decisively, and never again would farmers obtain such important urban assistance against the cattle trade. The rural siege of Ellsworth was a case in point.

[3]

NOT UNTIL AFTER 1875 did Ellsworth County experience an immigration boom to match that of Dickinson in 1870–71. And meanwhile, an important domestic livestock industry had developed on the empty prairies of the county.[3]

---

cluding some deputyships, we held about four-fifths of what there was of them in sight. Having successfully organized what the envious termed 'the court-house ring,' we gained a second term. Meantime I was steadily adding to my land holdings. By 1872 I had bought out my partners and my competitors, gaining practically a monopoly of the real-estate business in Dickinson county." Henry: "Story of a Wheat Field," 503.

It seems worth noting that Stuart Henry's description of his older brother's role in these events is cloaked in romanticism and is not to be trusted. James C. Malin effectively demolishes his contention that T. C. Henry, in an heroic effort to save Dickinson County from "impending bankruptcy," covertly introduced winter wheat into Kansas. Stuart Henry: *Conquering Our Great American Plains*, pp. 306–07; Malin: *Winter Wheat in the Golden Belt of Kansas* (Lawrence, Kan., 1944), pp. 35–36.

[2] Abilene *Chronicle*, May 30, 1872. For Wilson's extended retort to the Leavenworth *Commercial* piece—in the same vein as this brief quote—see his issue of July 18, 1872.

[3] "List of Population by Counties," Ellsworth Co. section. For brief descriptions of the county's large resident stockmen of the early period see Robert Dykstra: "Ellsworth, 1869–1875: The Rise and Fall of a Kansas Cowtown," *Kansas Historical Quarterly*, XXVII (1961), 162–64.

Excepting a few who ranged no Texas stock, the county's resident cattlemen closed ranks with the business community of the town to protect the commerce in longhorns.

As discussed in Chapter I, the Ellsworth County board of commissioners—dominated by stock raisers and businessmen—refused to impose a herd law in 1872 in spite of a good deal of agitation for it. That autumn, after several confrontations between unfenced fields and Texas herds, the issue rose once again. In late September, their crops harvested and stored, farmers convened at the courthouse in Ellsworth to organize a countywide protective association. Initiators of the action appear to have been two newcomers, the Reverend A. Essick, a Presbyterian clergyman who was also a prominent stock raiser, and W. M. King, a prosperous livestock breeder already on record as a critic of those who let their animals run free to commit depredations. The group voted to petition the county board for a herd law. The flavor of the gathering is captured in the motto concluding the secretary's report: *"Protection we want. Protection we must have!"*[4]

In October the group, still an informal one, met again. Those on hand postponed the presentation of herd law petitions and scheduled a third meeting to consider forming a county agricultural society. This may have reflected an attempt to direct the group to less militant pursuits. In any case, it disbanded, perhaps having broken up over the question of objectives. Two months later Ellsworth's newspaper editor, George A. Atwood, noted that the Reverend Mr. Essick now believed in wintering Texas cattle, evidently in the standard way, so despised by conventional farmers, of turning animals loose to forage. The following spring Essick was specifically branded an antiprotectionist.

[4] Ellsworth *Reporter*, Oct. 10, 1872. For King's attitude toward those who allowed their cattle to range free, see his sarcastic notice in ibid., May 2, 1872.

Others who had earlier spoken in favor of protection for farmers also switched sides. In March 1872, the Reverend Levi Sternberg and David B. Long, both dairy farmers, had been chosen officers of a local protective association in Empire Township. At that time Sternberg declared farming and stock raising to be totally incompatible. A year later he had become a big cattleman himself and president of the Stock Growers Association of Kansas. As for Dave Long, he too seems to have reappraised his position by 1873. "This county," he asserted in a letter to Atwood's newspaper, "is a stock county, and not an *Agricultural county*. When you cripple the stock interest, you cripple the *true interest* and *wealth* of the county." So much for any consistent leadership.

Prior to 1873 most anti-cattle trade agitation came from southeast of Ellsworth, where rural settlement lay thickest. In 1872, however, a considerable number of farmers began moving into the county's northwest corner near the town of Wilson. A year later the Wilson area was clearly the seat of a campaign seeking not just herd law protection but total exclusion of the cattle trade from Ellsworth County. Early in 1873 its residents met with farmers from adjoining Russell County and petitioned their representatives in the legislature to extend the Texas cattle quarantine line beyond both counties.

Though in vain, the winter's agitation was a disturbing portent of the future. In the spring of 1873 George Atwood tucked a timely slogan among the news items: "Ellsworth county farmers will not fight the Texas Cattle." Variations on this theme seemed to promise that repetition would make it so. But angry voices from the hinterlands promptly renewed demands for the herd law. It became clear in May that without it settlers could hope for little satisfaction from local courts. A farmer swore out a complaint against two Texas trail drivers who had allowed their cattle to invade his claim, but no grounds were found for prosecution. The judge dismissed the case at the request of the Ellsworth lawyer serving as county attorney.[5]

In June a letter from a young dirt farmer, J. W. Ingersoll, bitterly attacked what the writer termed the county's "rich men," like the Reverend Mr. Essick, who owned anywhere from seventy-five to four hundred head. These stock raisers, said Ingersoll, treated the rights of the small farmer with contempt, "and it is just such men that make a herd law necessary." "The rights of the laboring men," he argued, "must be protected by our laws and respected by capital."[6] This rural class consciousness, an interesting harbinger of Populist rhetoric, drew forth no similar effusions. In fact, many other small operators were following the lead of those about whom Ingersoll complained. One of them spoke the minds of settlers like himself who had been converted from protectionism to the opposite view. His principal argument was that a herd law would frighten away the Texas cattle trade, leaving local farmers with greatly reduced numbers of consumers to supply. It would also scare off the big domestic stockmen who paid most of the taxes. Anyway, he claimed, Ellsworth County farmers could do worse than become cattle raisers themselves. Many new arrivals to the county agreed, abandoning plans for conventional agriculture in favor of stock. The Faris brothers, for example, arrived in 1872 and took up homestead claims on Clear Creek. They

[5] Ellsworth *Reporter*, Mar. 14, Oct. 17, Dec. 19, 1872, Jan. 23, Feb. 13, 20, May 8, June 12, 1873; Topeka *Commonwealth*, June 4, 1873.

[6] Ellsworth *Reporter*, June 12, 1873. In view of his argument, Ingersoll's personal data is of some interest. In 1870 he gave his age to the census-taker as twenty-eight, his birthplace as New York, his occupation as farmer, his dependents as a wife and two children. He estimated the value of his real estate holdings at a modest $200. He offered no estimate of his personal estate. U.S. Manuscript Census, 1870: Kansas (microfilm copy, KSHS), Ellsworth Co., second section, p. 4.

presently became so absorbed in managing their small
but growing herds, which they grazed on the public
domain, that they allowed their claims to revert back to
the government.[7]

Although Editor Atwood supplied no details, two
different farmers' organizations were now active, perhaps
reflecting the polarity of rural opinion on the herd law.
One was the old Farmers Protective Association of Empire Township, in the county's southeast quarter, which
met as late as May 31, 1873, "to arrange for better protection from the ravages of Texas cattle." The other, the
Ellsworth Farmers' Independent Association, continued
active near Ellsworth and met in June and again in October of that year at the home of a farmer who also worked
as a contractor. In 1873 he was building the town's new
schoolhouse, and it seems unlikely that he would have
antagonized Ellsworthites by advocating the herd law.
The only other member of the group on record was a one-
legged war veteran who came to Ellsworth County as a
farmer but who opened a watch-repair shop in Ellsworth
in 1874.[8] He also seems an unlikely protectionist agi-
tator.

In October, as the county elections approached, those
favoring a herd law sought candidates for county commissioner who would work for the measure. Thirty-three
farmers of the eastern electoral district met to select a
protectionist candidate to oppose the incumbent from
their area, the anti-protection stock raiser Jacob C. Howard.
Dave Long tried to inject a note of compromise into the
proceedings by suggesting that the group ask for a herd
law only for the summer months, but just one other person
displayed a compromising mood. Those attending nomi-

[7] Ellsworth *Reporter*, June 26, 1873; Lewis Publishing Co.: *A Bio-
graphical History of Central Kansas* (New York, 1902), I, 630;
Ellsworth *Messenger*, Sept. 15, 1955.
    [8] Ellsworth *Reporter*, Dec. 14, 1871 ff. (ad), May 29, June 12,
Aug. 7, Sept. 18, Oct. 9, 1873, Nov. 19, 1874.

nated a strict protectionist. On the same day the protectionists of the western district selected Leonard Knox as their
candidate.

George Atwood meanwhile observed truthfully that
"There are many farmers who have no stock but who
hope to have some, that oppose a herd law, and there are
some farmers who own good sized herds who favor the
law." The editor himself opposed protection, and he gave
over almost the entire front page of an October issue to
an anti-herd law article. Composed by Henry Inman, a retired army officer living in Ellsworth, this piece simply
elaborated on the premise that the herd law was "obnoxious to the very principles of justice and of right." Then, a
week before the crucial county election, the paper carried
a letter from a stockman who wasted no compliments on
protectionists. "We have all the wealth and respectability
of the county on our side," he asserted, "and what does
their side consist of?" The writer himself provided an
answer:

> A few sore heads who couldn't get office on our side and
> have gone over so as to be first in position and honors,
> even if it is among vagabonds and paupers, and the major-
> ity are composed of poor worthless grubber[s] of the
> ground, who have a little truck patch, or a few acres of
> corn and no fence, or a mere pretense for a fence, so as to
> collect damages from their neighbors. . . . All that is nec-
> essary for the cattle men to do, is to hire all their poor
> neighbors a few days before election, and keep them away
> from the hungry office seekers, who try to make them
> believe that the herd law will benefit them, in order to get
> their votes.

But the election went off quietly. J. C. Howard defeated
the herd law advocate in the eastern district, maintaining
his position on the board. Leonard Knox ran unopposed
in the west. In Ellsworth's district an incumbent saloon

keeper retained his seat.[9] With the county board still two to one against protection, a herd law was not to be.

The issue was bound to rise again in 1874, exacerbated by the spring's new influx of farmers. The eastern half of the county, Editor Atwood noted early in the year, was "settling up quite fast." In a letter that same month Dave Long called attention to the county's southern tier of townships, into which wheat growers from adjacent Rice County had begun to overflow. Once again Long about-faced on the question of agriculture versus stock raising, now urging that a flour mill be built to accommodate these newcomers. He observed that Ellsworth had only one or two seasons left as a cattle town and its businessmen might as well face it. "It is high time our attention was turned to something," he concluded, "that will be of permanent and lasting benefit to the county."

The state legislature, meanwhile, forced upon citizens yet another variable in the cattle trade question. In March it approved an act that seemed tailor-made for local protectionists. In counties like Ellsworth, where the commissioners refused to exercise their power to impose herd laws, two thirds of the electorate now could require them to do so by petition. The measure also increased the penalty. Under the old law owners of straying animals were subject only to damages; the new statute made it a misdemeanor punishable by fine.[1]

Doubtless encouraged but uncertain whether they could muster enough signatures for a countywide herd law, Empire Township's settlers drummed up support for a night herd law. Probably the reason why this measure had not been resorted to earlier was that many considered the act on which it was based to have been voided by the 1872 herd law statute. These farmers, however, were desperate. They

[9] Ellsworth *Reporter*, Oct. 9, 16, 30, Nov. 6, 13, 1873.
[1] Ellsworth *Reporter*, Feb. 5, 19, 1874; *Laws of Kansas*, 1874, pp. 203–04.

presented their petition to the board, only to have it declared five or six names short of the requisite three fifths of the township electorate.[2]

Undaunted, Empire farmers met again in April to consider a herd law campaign under the new provisions. Near Wilson, at the opposite end of the county, farmers also demanded a countywide herd law. And near Ellsworth itself farmers led by W. M. King met and resolved to prosecute any Texas drover bringing his longhorns across the Smoky Hill River in their vicinity. Late in the summer Leonard Knox, the protectionist county commissioner from the western district, resigned from office. His successor was to be picked in the November elections. The name of a clergyman holding protectionist views was put forth by the settlers in and around Wilson. The preacher faced no opposition. "We all know what we want," declared a supporter, "and let us be in earnest to get it. We want a herd law twelve months in the year; we want the dead line moved from where it now is far enough west so that we shall not be troubled with Texas cattle crossing our country."[3]

The portents were all bad. Ellsworth's cattle shipping had tailed off steadily since 1872 as opportunistic drovers increasingly sought rival cattle markets. In June 1874, George Atwood talked at length with various Texans who told him that Ellsworth could expect its cattle trade to peter out in the next year or two as railroads pushed into Texas itself and drained the state of all surplus stock. Also, agricultural settlement along the Arkansas River to the south of Ellsworth County threatened to choke off the cattle trail. Emphasizing this dismal reading of the fu-

[2] Ellsworth *Reporter*, Mar. 19, Apr. 16, 1874. Apparently the 1868 act in part providing for night herd laws, though still on the books, was in many quarters considered repealed. See *Compiled Laws of Kansas*, 1879, p. 921 *n.* and marginal gloss opposite the first section of Art. 1.

[3] Ellsworth *Reporter*, Mar. 12, 26, Apr. 16, May 14, Oct. 29, 1874.

ture, livestock sold at bottom prices in town that season—
a depressing failure to drovers, to domestic stock raisers
who had wintered longhorns, and to those Ellsworthites
whose living depended on serving cattle trade transients.[4]
The economic argument in favor of Texas cattle had waned
considerably.

Drought, prairie fires, and grasshoppers devastated
the harvest in Ellsworth County as they did elsewhere in
the state that summer, forcing so many farmers to move
out that by the following year the county's population was
sharply reduced. Some townsmen undoubtedly welcomed
this crop disaster as the salvation of the Texas cattle
trade. But with the loss of that industry already a fore-
gone conclusion, the more astute businessmen in the community resigned themselves to the inevitable.

That autumn they made hesitant overtures to the distressed farmers. George Atwood, who had sold his newspaper in order to run for state representative, began the
rapprochement by explaining away his previous anti-
protection stand. He declared himself in favor of a herd
law, but a better one than that provided by the act of
1874. "Let the impracticable law of last winter be re-
modeled," he wrote, "so that the two great interests, farming and stock-raising, may both prosper, and our county
will increase in wealth and population." Having neatly
straddled the issue, Atwood gained the necessary majority.

The newspaper's new editor, Henry Inman, also
shamelessly reversed his earlier position to reflect the new
consensus. In December he observed cheerfully that the
herd law movement "is assuming a shape in this county
that promises protection to our much abused farmers, at
last." Even the local business community was giving way,
he admitted:

---

[4] Ellsworth *Reporter*, June 11, 1874; Hunter: *Trail Drivers of
Texas*, pp. 128–29.

At last a majority of the people of Ellsworth county, including our leading merchants, have opened their eyes to the fact, that the basis of our wealth, and prosperity, lies in the proper advancement of our agricultural interests. . . . In a word, a new era is to dawn upon Ellsworth county, we are to become revolutionized in a measure, and the grandest feature in the changes that are to take place, is that, town and country—farmer and merchant, are firmly supporting each other in this matter. . . . The *Bete Noir* that has been the means of estranging the two classes in advancing the real interests of the county is the "Herd Law" question. . . . With a judicious herd law there need be no conflict of interests. . . . Let us have a herd law by all means![5]

In January 1875, the protectionists publicly warned the county commissioners that herd law petitions were circulating. The commissioners received the documents on March 10, but put off considering them. On March 23 they reluctantly ordered a herd law into effect beginning May 1.[6]

The campaign was not quite over, however. Despite the crippling herd law Ellsworth's businessmen sought to eke out one last cattle shipping season. Editor Inman asked farmers not to bite the urban hands that had graciously signed their herd law petitions, but the unresponsive militants near Wilson repeated their demand that the cattle trade be immediately excluded from the county. In February they met with counterparts from Russell County and vainly instructed their legislative representatives to press for removal of the quarantine line farther west. They soon reconvened to form the Farmer's Protective Union, an organization designed "to enforce the laws, and protect our-

[5] Charles J. Lyon: *Compendious History of Ellsworth County* (Ellsworth, 1879), p. 41; Ellsworth *Reporter*, July 30, Aug. 6, Oct. 29, Dec. 3, 10, 1874.
[6] Ellsworth *Reporter*, Jan. 28, Feb. 11, 18, 25, Mar. 25, 1875.

selves against the encroachments of herds of stock of every kind."

Ellsworth meanwhile gathered itself to recruit the cattle drive. The newspaper carried the entire text of the 1874 herd law to make incoming drovers aware of its every provision. By the middle of May some herds had arrived in the county and Ellsworth's city marshal, detailed as a trail guide, was attempting to steer them clear of the Wilson area. Late that month Inman revealed that a local businessman owned the only land on the Arkansas River over which drovers could pass on their way to Ellsworth, every other property owner along the stream refusing them a right-of-way. Herd law or no herd law, rural settlement to the south was rapidly strangling the flow.[7]

Inman's observation was notice that Ellsworth's cattle trade was dying hard, but dying all the same. Thereafter editorial optimism dwindled to a pathetic silence on the subject. In August, finally, an obscurely placed item innocently entitled "Fall Trade" announced the end of another cattle town. "We predict an excellent trade in Ellsworth this fall," declared Inman,

and the logic of the thing is, that all the money to be spent will remain among ourselves. We are happy in the fact that the days of the Texas trade is numbered among the things that were. Of all the hundreds of thousands of dollars that changed hands during the years of that erratic traffic, we fail to see where it has benefited one man in the county whose determination it was to make his home among us. We have a herd law, and we have proved the richness of our soil, and our wonderful pastoral possibilities beyond a peradventure, and all that remains for us to do is to encourage a healthful immigration, devote our

[7] Ellsworth *Reporter*, Jan. 28, Feb. 25, Mar. 11, Apr. 8, 15, 22, May 20, 27, 1875.

energies to wool growing, graded stock, and small grain, and we shall soon find ourselves second to no county in the state in wealth and importance.[8]

Deserted by the Texas cattle trade despite a valiant effort to lure it back for just one more season, Ellsworth's farewell was a peevish declaration of independence.

[4]

BEGINNING IN 1872 the cattle traffic on the Chisholm Trail proper had to rein in at Wichita because of that year's new quarantine line, and only those Sedgwick County farmers thinly scattered over the prairies on the west side of the Arkansas River faced difficulties with incoming herds. In addition, Sedgwick's board of commissioners placed their county under the 1872 herd law immediately after its passage by the legislature, an action that apparently took town dwellers by surprise; no discernible debate accompanied its imposition. Those worried about its potential effect on the cattle trade reacted by privately maintaining that its passage had not been accomplished in strictly legal fashion.[9] Farmers' failure to obtain court judgments against the owners of straying herds during a period of costly depredations attending the shipping panic of 1873 seemed to verify this notion.[1]

A year later new anti-cattle trade effusions began to flow from rural pens. William S. White, a west side settler who was later to become a Wichita journalist, sparked the most interesting exchange on the subject. Writing under the pseudonym "Agricola," White argued that the cattle trade profited almost no one, even the drovers hav-

[8] Ellsworth *Reporter*, Aug. 5, 1875. See also the retrospective editorial denigrations of the cattle trade in ibid., Sept. 28, 1876; Lyon: *Compendious History*, p. 10.
[9] See Chapter I above.
[1] Wichita *Eagle*, June 11, 1874.

ing "suffered heavily" in the business. The only direct taxes resulting from the trade were those assessed against farmers who wintered Texas cattle, and he maintained (not very convincingly) that "legitimate" stock raising suffered thereby. White concluded by doubting the value of the cattle trade to urban growth. "I suppose this will seem," he wrote,

> to a loyal citizen of Wichita, as a direct thrust at the vital cause of her prosperity; but I am inclined to think that it would not be difficult to prove that she has fed and waxed fat upon the losses of her trade, rather than upon her profits; that her prosperity is fictitious, her growth ephemeral and her future dark, unless she build on some surer foundation than this unnatural foreign commerce.

One Wichitan wryly suggested dumping White and his fellow rural critics into the river, but another writer countered with a sophisticated cattle trade defense. Effectively challenging White's other arguments, he expressed astonishment that anyone would seriously question the cattle trade profits accruing to enterprise of all kinds, including local agriculture. "The suppression or restriction of this trade could result in no benefit to farmers who are producers, the requirements of the cattle trade being in every sense of the term consumptive," he insisted. "And when the cattle trade has to remove west—which it evidently will do—then and not till then will its loss be felt by our merchants, mechanics, and the always dependent laboring classes."

White struck back. Conceding some earlier arguments and simply repeating others, he felt obliged to expand on his criticism of the cattle town economic base. "I willingly acknowledge some individual and local benefits, for it is a 'blast from hell' that blows no one any good," he wrote. "I admit some towns built up like magic. National and Savings Banks with bloated presidents and fat directors (in a bold holding way,) grocery houses, hotels, eating houses, dance houses etc. flourish. And all jingle along the cattle trail as merry as a marriage bell." The superficiality of his critique was betrayed by the fact that all he could muster to contradict his opponent's image of cattle town prosperity was cheap scare-talk: "If we look again we will see *ruins* of towns that once swelled like the frog in the fable, with a sense of their importance and the grandeur of their future."

Less than four months later, however, the effects of the 1874 agricultural disaster had appeared. White—under his own name this time to mask his abrupt about-face—now cautioned all citizens to cooperate in preserving the cattle trade. "It is unnecessary to enumerate the advantages of the trade to Wichita," he argued.

> There can hardly be two opinions, as to that. To us farmers, living in the southern part of the county, it furnishes a market for everything we raise, at prices 25 to 100 per cent better than Wichita; gives employment to teams and men in various ways, supplies us with fresh beef during the whole summer and fall at from 2 cents to nothing a pound. . . .
> Beyond any former period in our history we need the trade this year.[2]

The Patrons of Husbandry movement had swept Sedgwick County in 1873–74. Late in 1874 west side Grangers took advantage of their collective affiliation to press more effectively for protection from Texas cattle ravages. On Christmas Eve the members of the Ninnescah Grange met

[2] Wichita *Beacon*, Oct. 14, 21, Nov. 4, 1874, Feb. 17, 1875; Wichita *Eagle*, Oct. 22, 1874. White, by 1875 working as a printer for the *Beacon*, assumed the editorship of the newspaper in November of that year. In the issue of Feb. 9, 1876, he again urged that the cattle trade be induced to stay at Wichita. For a biographical study of him during this period see James C. Malin: "William Sutton White, Swedenborgian Publicist: Part One," *Kansas Historical Quarterly*, XXIV (1958), 426–57.

and resolved to use all peaceable means at their command to eradicate "this curse in our midst," imploring fellow Grangers and Sedgwick farmers generally to join them in demanding that the state legislature move the quarantine line farther west. Acknowledging Wichita's stake in the cattle trade, they urged the quarantine of only the settled part of Sedgwick behind the outside edge of Range Three West. They also asked that Wichitans survey a direct right-of-way from the grazing grounds to the stockyard, "and that cattle in transit be strictly confined to said drive or trail."

In January 1875, the Ninnescah petitions began to circulate, and one by one the other chapters endorsed them: on January 20 the east side Rockford Grange, ten days later the grange in Delano Township opposite Wichita, on February 1 and 2 the Lincoln and Attica granges. The chapter in Waco Township followed suit on February 13. Soon quarantine line petitions with over four hundred signatures traveled to Topeka, to be received by the Wichita druggist who represented Sedgwick County in the legislature and also served as chairman of its Committee on Texas Cattle. Similar petitions went forward from the farmers of adjoining Sumner County.

Responding to this pressure, the Texas cattle committee reported a bill moving the deadline past the settlements in Sedgwick, although allowing an inlet by which Wichita could receive longhorns for shipment. Also to Wichitans' benefit it barred both Ellsworth and Great Bend from any possible access to the cattle trail. Unfortunately, this bill, expected to receive last-minute approval, was stolen from the docket clerk's desk on the day before adjournment and it was then too late to get up a duplicate. Disappointed Wichitans laid the blame to a Kansas Pacific Railway agent, or some other partisan of one of the cattle towns to be quarantined.[3]

[3] Wichita *Eagle*, Jan. 7, Feb. 4, 11, 18, 25, Mar. 11, 1875; Wichita *Beacon*, Jan. 20, Feb. 17, 1875.

In March 1875, a cattleman wrote from Texas that despite the cattle town competition "if Wichita will make an effort like she has done heretofore, she will secure the greater portion of the cattle" driven that season. Evidently the Kansas Pacific had been publicizing the rural agitation near Wichita. Many Texans, the writer revealed, "fear [that] this opposition on the part of the settlers will be the means of throwing their herding grounds too far from the railroad, and also make it inconvenient to show buyers their cattle." Responding posthaste to this news, Wichita's mayor and council financed the printing of an appropriate advertising circular. "As the Kansas legislature has just adjourned without any action in regard to the cattle trade," it read, "we hasten to inform cattle drovers (as a contrary impression has been conveyed) that the way is open, and you are cordially invited to make the drive here."[4] They also hired a cattleman, Gus A. Wills, to travel down to Fort Worth and vicinity and spend two months dispelling apprehensions. Wills was to pay his own expenses out of his $400 fee; the council tendered him half of this amount in advance and apparently secured him free railroad passes.[5]

On March 1, the city council also leased seventy-five acres on the west side of the river as a potential holding ground for cattle herds awaiting shipment, for which it paid a sum of $50 for the year. No move was made toward obtaining a right-of-way as requested by the Ninnescah Grangers. Later that month the settlers of three west side townships met and resolved that because of the theft of the quarantine bill at the recent legislative session, "it becomes our duty to defend our God-given

[4] Wichita *Beacon*, Mar. 24, 31, 1875; Wichita *Eagle*, Mar. 25, 1875. The Santa Fe also issued a circular encouraging Texans to drive to Wichita, Great Bend, "and other shipping points" on its route. Ibid., Apr. 29, 1875.
[5] Wichita Council Record, 1870–81 (microfilm copy, KSHS), B, 36–37; Wichita *Beacon*, Mar. 24, 1875.

rights by all honorable means in our power." They called for a general conclave of west-siders to consider measures for mutual protection from Texas cattle. As apprehensive Wichitans watched, the meeting convened on April 17 with representatives from ten townships attending. The farmers resolved to use force if necessary to make drovers graze their herds beyond Range Three West, but approved the idea of a right-of-way into Wichita and obligingly established a committee to confer with the city administration for the purpose of securing such a route.

Four days later a newly elected Wichita mayor and council met and appointed a committee, headed by the mayor himself, to complete right-of-way negotiations and thereafter superintend the season's cattle trade. The committee promptly convened a special meeting of the full council that approved the employment of a man to lay out the required trail, his fee not to exceed $40. Next the committee invited the west side representatives to meet with it on May 1 to approve an acceptable route. The gathering proved an amicable affair, and a week later the cattle committee and three rural delegates signed a formal contract. The cattle committee would urge drovers to hold their cattle beyond the settled area; the farmers would see that longhorns passed unmolested over the trail. Three "disinterested" farmers agreed to act as arbiters of any damage claims. Late that month the new access route was laid out. It diverged from the Chisholm Trail near the forks of the Ninnescah, extending some twenty-four miles in length. Farmers had been generous in allowing water privileges as well as rights-of-way.[6]

Wichita was the one cattle town always more than willing to dip into municipal coffers to preserve its cattle

[6] Lease dated Mar. 1, 1875, in Wichita Miscellaneous Papers, 1871–81, microfilm copy, KSHS; Wichita Council Record, B, 45–47; Wichita *Eagle*, Apr. 8, 29, May 6, 13, 27, 1875; Wichita *Beacon*, May 26, 1875.

trade. But objections to this practice now began to be heard, particularly since in the recent city election rumors had circulated that the incumbent mayor, James G. Hope, had profited personally from funds expended on behalf of the trade. Although his council exonerated him, this criticism and a broader argument against the entrepreneurial use of tax monies were evidently potent factors in Hope's defeat for re-election.[7] Critics thereafter seized every opportunity to obstruct the cattle trade's access to public funds.

Early in May, Gus Wills wrote from Fort Worth to tell the city council that he had spent his advance "and am compelled to draw on you for $75.00 which please protect." At a council meeting considering Wills's predicament, Wichita's new city attorney advised that the municipality had no legal power to subsidize the cattle trade or any other commercial enterprise. The council majority ignored this statement of fact. Over the objections of moral and fiscal reformer James C. Fraker and one other councilman of that persuasion, the council allowed Wills $100 on account. The two dissidents then stalked angrily from the council chamber, after which the equally angry remaining members considered abolishing the position of city attorney. Two weeks later the councilmen appropriated $1,000 to be used in reimbursing damages to farmers along the right-of-way and for otherwise protecting the cattle trade that season.[8]

Despite Wills's efforts and the arrangement with west

[7] Wichita Council Record, B, 41; Wichita *Beacon*, Apr. 21, 1875; Wichita *Eagle*, Apr. 22, 1875. Grist for Hope's critics was the fact that no quarterly statement of city finances had appeared recently. But as the council pointed out (in ibid.), this was "for the reason that we did not wish drovers and others to know that some of them had been paid for using their influence to induce cattlemen to stop their herds here."

[8] G. A. Wills to Wichita mayor and council, Apr. 29, 1875, in Wichita Miscellaneous Papers; Wichita Council Record, B, 53, 57; Wichita *Beacon*, May 26, June 9, 1875.

side farmers, Texas cattle arrived at Wichita in greatly reduced numbers compared to the previous year. Accusing Gus Wills of having been an unfaithful agent, the city fathers withheld the remainder of his fee. Councilmen hired one William T. Jewett as his replacement on the trail, paying him $100 as an advance on a $200 fee. To no avail. What a Wichita editor euphemistically called a "temporary lull in the cattle trade" in June and July proved so profound that many members of a visiting editorial party referred to the town as a "former" cattle center. On August 4, having disbursed probably some $500 on the cattle trade (not counting right-of-way and damage payments), the city council reluctantly closed the lid on further expenditures. As another indication that the cattle season had proved a failure, the councilmen relieved all policemen save one from duty.[9]

In 1875 and 1876 Sedgwick's farmers finally resolved the vexatious herd law question. Early in 1875 the local district court judge decided a cattle trespass case that demonstrated once and for all that the herd law as imposed by the county board in 1872 was useless, its passage having been improperly accomplished. On March 11, 1875, therefore, the farmer-dominated county board abruptly repassed the measure. A few months later a west side settler termed the new provision, like the old, merely a snare and a delusion. "The hungry lawyers of Wichita are whispering in the ears of cattle men that the law is worthless," he charged,

> and thus encouraging recklessness on their part, and most farmers in this county are aware that they had just about as well draw stakes and leave the country at once, as ask protection at its hands. . . . Judge Campbell [of the Sedg-

[9] Wichita *Beacon*, June 9, July 28, 1875; M. B. Loyd to Wichita mayor and council, June 30, 1875, in Wichita Miscellaneous Papers; Wichita *Eagle*, July 15, 22, 1875; Wichita Council Record, B, 66–67.

wick County district court] told a lawyer in town the other day, that the people couldn't make such a darned law.

In the face of a veto by the local legal establishment, he said, west-siders had no alternative but the pinch-penny redresses handed out by the Wichita cattle trail committee.

Within the next two weeks petitions requesting imposition of the more stringent 1874 herd law began circulating. In September petitioners presented their documents to the county commissioners, who found them some four hundred names short of the required number. With the impending demise of Wichita's cattle trade now obvious, both the town's editors gracefully endorsed the proposed herd law. In December the commissioners ordered the county clerk to "procure blank herd-law petitions and distribute the same throughout the county." These returned with signatures in the proper proportion, and on February 7, 1876, the board ordered the new herd law into effect. Lest diehards remain skeptical, in April the county attorney publicly certified that the law as passed was indeed legal.[1]

Although wheat production had already shown itself to be an adequate replacement for Wichita's declining cattle trade, many Wichitans refused to relinquish it without a fight. In January 1876, the mayor urged a gathering of determined citizens to give prompt attention to a bill then pending in the legislature that would remove the quarantine line a hundred miles west. The Santa Fe's general livestock agent also spoke, promising that the railroad would concentrate the entire shipping of its line at Wichita if townsmen could get the bill defeated. He also asked them to acquire a west side right-of-way again that

[1] Wichita *Eagle*, Feb. 25, Mar. 18, July 1, Sept. 2, 16, Dec. 30, 1875, Feb. 17, 1876; Wichita *Beacon*, July 14, Nov. 10, 1875, Apr. 12, 1876.

season. Interested Wichitans sprang into action. Though failing to prevent passage of the quarantine bill, their representative managed to have the new deadline removed only to the west edge of Sedgwick County, thereby preserving Wichita's access to the cattle trail.

Since the new statute barred Great Bend from the cattle town rivalry, some Wichitans viewed it as a victory. Others, however, cast jaundiced glances at the prospect of city funds for a new right-of-way. "Many of the citizens are quite indifferent," wrote a correspondent from Wichita, "claiming the tax to be in excess of all benefit to be derived." Indeed, when Bill Jewett applied for the $100 balance due him for service on the cattle trail during the previous summer, Councilman Fraker was able to muster a majority of three against payment, the remaining council members simply abstaining. But after 124 townsmen forwarded a petition urging acquisition of a right-of-way the council footed the $395 bill.[2] Businessmen themselves subsidized the agent who rode down the trail that spring to work against representatives from Dodge City and Ellis. Despite these expenditures, farmers along the new access route proved hostile and the cattle town competition too great. From July 1 through the end of the year Wichita shipped only 12,380 head.[3]

In early 1877 the legislature passed yet another deadline measure, moving it west beyond Comanche County. Some influential Wichitans would not acknowledge that the end of the cattle trade was finally at hand. Once again Wichita's mayor called for an energetic re-

[2] Wichita *Beacon*, Jan. 26, Apr. 5, 26, 1876; *Laws of Kansas*, 1876, pp. 316–17; Wichita Council Record, B, 100, 105–06, 111–12, 117; bill of William T. Jewett, Apr. 7, 1876, in Wichita Miscellaneous Papers; four undated petitions to Wichita mayor and council, in ibid.; Charles W. Hill to Wichita mayor and council, Apr. 14, 1876, in ibid.

[3] Wichita Council Record, B, 121; Wichita *Beacon*, May 10, 31, 1876, Jan. 17, 1877. During the same period Wichita shipped out over twice as many carloads of wheat as cattle (1,420 as against 619).

cruitment effort. Brandishing a letter from the Santa Fe management in support of his enthusiasm, he declared that if west side settlers would allow forty or fifty thousand head through to the city "it would be of great benefit to our business men." A motion to open a right-of-way carried the council, and for the last time the mayor appointed a cattle trail committee. The railroad, however, realistically decided to concentrate its cattle shipping at Dodge that season, expending funds specifically for the purpose. At their meeting of May 14, 1877, Wichita's councilmen glumly listened to a letter—apparently from the railroad company announcing this decision—and "after some consideration in the matter" disbanded the cattle trail committee.

As might have been expected, the relatively sophisticated Wichita press issued no defensive or recriminatory denunciation of the cattle trade once it had passed from the scene. Townsmen rested secure in the knowledge that nothing had been left undone to exploit this resource as long as humanly possible, and it was gracefully relinquished. When Peyton Montgomery, a prominent cattleman, visited town briefly that spring before going on to make his summer's headquarters at Ellis, the *Eagle* reported—with just a touch of nostalgia—that "Mr. Montgomery says cattle men throughout the Lone Star State speak highly of Wichita and their experience here when she was the shipping point."[4]

[5]

THE SAME 1876 quarantine legislation that signaled the close of Wichita as a cattle trading center proved to be

---

[4] *Laws of Kansas*, 1877, pp. 241–43; Wichita Council Record, B, 174, 176–77, 183; Wichita *Beacon*, Apr. 11, 1877; Atchison, Topeka and Santa Fe Railroad Co.: *Annual Report . . . 1877* (Boston, 1877), p. 35; Wichita *Eagle*, Apr. 26, 1877.

the making of Dodge City, which (until the emergence of Caldwell) would monopolize cattle shipping on the Santa Fe line. To the north, for a few seasons after Ellsworth's capitulation, the Kansas Pacific shipped Texas cattle from Ellis until conceding the contest—at least in Kansas—to the Santa Fe.

But rural agitation for westward extension of the quarantine line started almost immediately near Dodge. Late in 1876 the farmers who had recently settled Ford County's northeast corner called for protection from longhorn ravages while disclaiming any hostility toward the new cattle town nearby. Early the next year, as noted above, the legislature approved another deadline extension, but the new limit simply retraced the earlier one along the eastern edge of the county. Apparently the residents of the rural "east end" thereupon negotiated an informal deadline to protect their section, which the county surveyor located for them in the spring of 1877. As this expedient probably did not prove very satisfactory, it was not implemented the following season.[5]

In the summer of 1878 rural immigration promised to assume major proportions in Ford County, giving rise to new appeals for quarantine line extension. A correspondent to no less a newspaper than the New York *Times* predicted that "a very strong petition" for moving the deadline would go to the legislature from Ford in 1879. Settlers also began organizing support for a herd law. "It will not take long until Dodge City is what Newton is," observed one townsman, comparing his community with that short-lived cattle center, "and Ford county what Harvey, Sedgwick or Dickinson counties are."[6]

[5] Dodge City *Times*, Oct. 14, 1876, Mar. 24, Apr. 7, 1877. A correspondent from the east end wrote that August: "The farmers [here] have not been bothered to any great extent by Texas cattle, although they have no dead line or herd law." Ibid., Aug. 18, 1877.
[6] Dodge City *Times*, July 6, 1878; Spearville *News*, Aug. 31, 1878. Petitions asking for the 1874 herd law circulated through the fall and

So it appeared. In the fall elections of 1878, the first in which the rural vote played any serious role, both candidates for legislative representative endorsed quarantine protection for the east-enders. In 1879, with the victor, Robert M. Wright, supporting the proposal while simultaneously serving as chairman of the Committee on Texas Cattle, the legislature extended the quarantine line into the county. The new limit enclosed only the agricultural northeast corner, leaving the remainder as a grazing ground for incoming herds.[7]

As described, the influx of rural settlers slowed abruptly in reaction to the drought of 1878–81, and would not resume a sustained ascendancy until late 1882. By the end of the second dry year Dodge City's businessmen realized that the prolonged disaster was giving their cattle trade a new lease on life. Bob Wright's 1880 circular to Texas drovers straightforwardly emphasized the significance of this natural phenomenon. "The drouth of last season has driven many of the itinerant farmers away," it explained, "leaving a much larger scope open to the 'through cattle' of 1880."[8]

During this drought period, local rural pressure for quarantine line legislation remained understandably weak, and the men who served as representatives at Topeka were able to stifle all proposed changes that would have sealed the town off from the cattle trade. In 1881, Bob

---

went to the county commissioners in February 1879, but were found to be short of the required number of signatures. Another petition circulated late in 1879, but probably foundered on settlers' knowledge that a two-thirds majority of the county electorate, given the resistance at Dodge, would prove impossible to obtain. Dodge City *Globe*, Aug. 27, 1878; Dodge City *Times*, Aug. 31, Sept. 21, 1878, Jan. 11, Feb. 15, 1879; Spearville *News*, Oct. 19, 1878, Feb. 22, Dec. 20, 1879.

[7] Dodge City *Globe*, Oct. 22, 1878, Apr. 22, 1879; Dodge City *Times*, Oct. 26, 1878, Mar. 22, 1879; *Laws of Kansas*, 1879, pp. 345–46.

[8] See Chapter V above; Dodge City *Globe*, Feb. 24, 1880.

Wright, again chairman of the committee to which cattle trade questions were referred, defeated an effort to close the entire state against summer importation of longhorns. In 1883, George M. Hoover, Wright's successor, gained the crucial committee post. Under Hoover's supervision the new quarantine line of that year continued to exempt Ford County from protection. In the special legislative session of March 1884, called primarily to cope with an outbreak of hoof-and-mouth disease in Kansas, the quarantine line was not altered.[9]

With conventional agriculture in a decline, local farmers—as elsewhere in Kansas and the West in these years—turned to sheep raising. The sheep boom hit Ford County in the fall of 1880 and extended through 1881.[1] The spring of 1882, however, opened on a dead wool market. This effectively killed local interest. In midsummer perhaps the foremost sheep raising outfit in the area, Tarbox Brothers of Meade County, sold out their sheep and turned instead to cattle.[2]

The Tarboxes' decision reflected a new positive attitude toward cattle as well as a negative attitude toward sheep. Regional cattle raising had gradually gathered momentum in the years since Dodge became a shipping center. As early as 1876 Texas cattlemen began locating

---

[9] Dodge City *Times*, Feb. 24, Mar. 10, 1881, Jan. 25, 1883; Dodge City *Globe*, Mar. 1, 8, 1881, Jan. 23, 1883; *Laws of Kansas*, 1881, pp. 292–94; ibid., 1883, pp. 218–19; ibid., Spec. Sess., 1884 (bound with 1885 vol.), pp. 15–16; Humphrey, "Administration of George W. Glick," 404–05. In the winter of 1882–83, east end settlers did manage to gain a dubious measure of protection. In November 1882, Wheatland Township farmers obtained a night herd law, as did those of Spearville Township in January 1883. Dodge City *Globe*, Nov. 14, 1882, Jan. 9, 1883.

[1] Editor Klaine of the Dodge City *Times* was especially enthusiastic in urging sheep on his rural readers. During 1880–81 seemingly every issue of the *Times* carried something on sheep culture. For representative rhetoric see his issues of Jan. 17, Dec. 4, 1880, May 26, 1881.

[2] Dodge City *Globe*, Aug. 22, 1882.

ranches on the empty ranges west and south of town. Two years later editor Nicholas B. Klaine declared that a dull shipping season, supposedly portending an end to the trail trade, "in nowise affects the fortunes of Dodge City. The cattle trade of this town, in a measure, is being localized, by the establishment of cattle camps and ranches on the broad plain. This insures a permanency and establishes a local trade that will meet with no fluctuations." In November 1878, Daniel M. Frost's *Globe* was the first newspaper in the state to carry a continuing display of live-stock brands for the benefit of tributary ranchers. A month later Klaine's *Times* followed suit.[3]

In 1882 the demand for range cattle mounted for the second season in a row, and maximum beef prices in the Chicago market proved the best since 1870.[4] The "beef bonanza" struck Ford County and its outlying areas in a big way. Brief mention has already been made of Dodge City tradesmen entering the cattle business. Some Dodge-ites, like bootmaker John Mueller, had been engaged in subsidiary stock raising for years, but those succumbing for the first time to the speculative craze included such persons as merchants George Hoover and Herman J. Fringer, who together invested some $20,000 in an im-proved herd of eight hundred head. Merchant Jacob Col-lar, as another example, agreed to sell his half-interest in his herd in August 1882, but at the end of the year instead sold his store in favor of dealing exclusively in cattle. Jake's brother Morris, after having championed Ford's

[3] Dodge City *Times*, Oct. 14, 1876, Aug. 31, Dec. 21, 1878; Dodge City *Globe*, Nov. 19, 1878.

[4] Ernest Staples Osgood: *The Day of the Cattleman* (Minneapolis, 1929), p. 95. The high Chicago price, of course, did not mean that all beef animals were moving to terminal markets, but does reflect the fact that buyers everywhere—including western ranchers themselves—were paying high prices. The literature on the economics of the cattle boom of the eighties is vast, but for good short treatments see ibid., especially chap. iv; Louis Pelzer: *The Cattlemen's Frontier* (Glendale, Calif., 1936), especially pp. 119–50.

agricultural settlement since the days of the old German Immigration Society, now also abandoned his mercantile business in favor of livestock. Other businessmen and ranchers even talked grandly of forming cattle corporations and pools.[5]

With cattle shipments in 1882 more than double those of 1881, and retail sales of one Dodge merchant up 55 and 90 per cent in June and July respectively over the same months of the previous season, citizens naturally identified prosperity with the cattle boom. "The ranch business, so called, furnishes the bulk of trade to Dodge City," remarked Nicholas Klaine in the spring of 1883. "The business of paramount importance will be the ranch trade. To cultivate that trade, will be the object of the business men of this city."

In April 1883, Dodge City's resident livestock speculators joined with the ranchers of the multi-county area south and west of Dodge to form the Western Kansas Cattle Growers' Association. The organization thereafter maintained its headquarters in Bob Wright's store, holding its annual conventions at Dodge.[6] This tighter binding of the local business community to the ranch industry further weakened the town's hitherto unswerving loyalty to the conventional cattle drive from Texas, since the operations of ranch and trail grew increasingly incompatible.

Everywhere on the western ranges in the early eighties the demand for cattle shipped in from the East soared as ranchers sought to improve their herds with young breeding stock and stock steers. But the dread splenic fever continued to be as mysteriously lethal a destroyer of domestic cattle as in the years immediately following the

[5] Dodge City *Globe*, Mar. 21, 28, Aug. 8, 1882; Dodge City *Times*, Mar. 23, 30, Dec. 7, 1882, Jan. 11, 1883.

[6] Dodge City *Times*, Aug. 3, 1882, May 10, 1883; Dodge City *Globe*, Jan. 16, 30, Apr. 17, 24, 1883.

Civil War. Cattle raisers of the central Plains increasingly looked to the federal government for a solution to their dilemma. In the spring of 1884 Congress finally passed a bill creating a Bureau of Animal Industry within the Department of Agriculture, headed by a commissioner empowered to prohibit the interstate transportation of diseased stock. Originating in the need to cope with pleuropneumonia in cattle intended for European markets, under the powerful impetus of the Wyoming stock growers the bill was made to cover splenic fever as well. But the Senators from Texas, mulishly insisting that the disease existed only in the northern imagination, succeeded in having "the so-called splenetic or Texas fever" specifically exempted from the operations of the act.[7]

Meanwhile, meeting at Dodge City in its second annual convention, the Western Kansas Cattle Growers' Association called for an end to the summer importation of through Texas cattle into the state. "We have spent years of care and labor," the assembled stock raisers argued through their executive committee's report, "and have expended thousands of dollars in the purchase of high grade and thoroughbred bulls, to bring our herds to their present high degree of improvement, by which very improvement they are rendered more susceptible to the contraction of disease." On the other hand, they claimed, "The business of driving Texas cattle northward is now confined to hardly more than a score of men, and these few men claim to make but a small margin of profit on the purchase and driving of their cattle to be sold in this and other northern markets." The entire state, they exhorted, must be quarantined against southern stock.

Those Dodge businessmen unwilling to relinquish the trail trade apparently kept their sentiments to themselves. But their actions betrayed them. When the southern

[7] *U.S. Statutes*, XXIII, 31–33; Osgood: *Day of the Cattleman*, pp. 164–73.

Texas stock raisers sent a representative to Dodge to negotiate rights-of-way through western Kansas, Bob Wright
and others gave him valuable assistance. And when in late
June the drovers convened at the Ford County courthouse
to discuss matters of mutual interest, Wright and Dan
Frost willingly accepted appointments to a committee
formed to investigate depredations against herds passing
through Indian Territory.

July's cattle prices slumped badly and fell even further when splenic fever broke out among improved herds
in the stockyards at Kansas City, St. Louis, and Chicago.
The state of Illinois threatened to embargo all cattle
shipped from Kansas, and drastic action seemed imperative. On August 13, 1884, at the urging of alarmed livestock firms, stockyard companies, and railroad manage-
ments, Governor George W. Glick of Kansas summarily
quarantined his state against further imports of through
cattle for the remainder of the season. An estimated
300,600 head had already been driven to Dodge by the
cutoff date. Now Sheriff Patrick F. Sughrue, in charge not
only of Ford County but also of those unorganized southwestern counties attached to Ford for legal and administrative purposes, waged virtually a single-handed campaign on the Western Trail below Dodge, turning back
suspect herds and their hard-bitten trail crews at the Kansas border. For this dangerous work Pat Sughrue earned
Glick's personal congratulations in September.[8]

The battle between drovers and ranchers comprised
only one phase of that season's conflict, however. The
resurgence of rural immigration, against which there was
no legal redress, directly challenged the ranchers—these
enterprisers being merely squatters on the public domain. From 1882 to 1884 Ford County's population nearly

[8] Dodge City *Globe*, Apr. 8, May 6, 13, 20, July 1, 1884; Humphrey:
"Administration of George W. Glick," 406; Dodge City *Cowboy*, Aug.
23, 1884; Dodge City *Democrat*, Sept. 27, 1884.

doubled. During the latter year immigrants liberally infiltrated the county, rapidly overspreading the cattle ranges
below and beyond Dodge.[9]

That summer of 1884 two of Dodge City's four newspaper editors mounted an energetic campaign to defend
the outlying ranch industry. In July, Dan Frost brought
out a new and enlarged version of his weekly sheet,
changing its full title to the *Globe Live Stock Journal.*
Joining him in explicitly serving the local stock-raising
interest was the *Kansas Cowboy*, a weekly originally published in Ness County until that area had been overrun
with settlers. Its editor was Samuel S. Prouty, a veteran
journalist whose fierce visage, rakishly topped by a Texas
hat, graced the masthead of his lively publication. Both
newspapers sought to stem the agricultural tide then
swirling about Dodge. Prouty far outstripped Frost in
this effort. He warned new farmers that the season's good
rainfall was delusive and exceptional. Stock raising, he
emphasized, provided rural inhabitants with the only sure
future in western Kansas.[1] But words could not stop the
flood. "The man looking for government land continues to
arrive daily," Frost pensively confessed in November. "The
frontier line long ago moved west of here and we are getting
to be 'settled up.' "

Coincident with the agricultural influx came the decline of the local beef boom. "There are not so many men

[9] "List of Population by Counties," Ford Co. section; Dodge City
Globe, June 24, Oct. 7, Nov. 4, Dec. 23, 1884; Dodge City *Times*, Sept.
18, 1884.

[1] Dodge City *Globe*, July 15, 1884 ff.; Dodge City *Cowboy*, June
28, 1884 ff. Prouty printed anti-agriculture propaganda generated both
by himself and by contributors (see especially ibid., July 5, Aug. 23,
1884). He also devoted space to the old argument, used by cattle trade
defenders since Joe McCoy's first days at Abilene, that farmers should
grow garden produce and feed grain rather than the popular staple
crops (see, for example, ibid., Aug. 30, 1884). For his expected negative attitude toward the herd law see ibid., June 28, 1884.

wanting to engage in the cattle business now, as there has been for the past three or four years," wrote Frost at the end of 1884. Heretofore, he said, there had been "a regular craze among almost all classes of men to engage in some way in the cattle business." This impulse had fast diminished as the market price of beef plummeted from its 1882 zenith:

> We have met a dozen or more men lately who were in the cattle business a few years ago, that have sold out and are back at their old business or calling whatever that may be, others who didn't make anything the past year are a little bit sick, and could be induced to sell without much bonus.[2]

Low prices aside, the decreasing availability of empty range land forced many out of stock raising. Men who had invested heavily now faced unattractive alternatives: sell out their animals at ruinously low prices in the Dodge City market or seek new pastures farther west and south ahead of the inexorable agricultural advance. By the end of 1884 many of the largest ranchers of southwest Kansas had been forced to take refuge on the so-called Neutral Strip, the narrow neck of federal land lying between the Kansas line and the Texas Panhandle.

That winter some 160,000 head of cattle, mostly belonging to Kansas owners, grazed on the Strip. In January 1885, four southwest Kansas stock raisers representing these interests, including Ford County's new legislative representative, conferred in Topeka with Governor Glick. Reversing the stand of the 1884 Dodge City stockmen's convention, the four opposed quarantining the state against through Texas stock. Any such measure would turn the Neutral Strip into one vast holding ground for southern cattle awaiting legal winter entry into Kansas,

[2] Dodge City *Globe*, Nov. 11, Dec. 16, 1884.

and their massed proximity to the improved herds now there would prove absolutely murderous.[3]

A month later, however, the legislature took up debate on a bill to do just that. This was bad enough, but as originally introduced the proposed law placed a summertime embargo on *all* cattle from below the Kansas line. Kansas cattlemen with livestock in the Neutral Strip, the Texas Panhandle, and Indian Territory reacted strenuously, and the act as passed barred only cattle originating in central and southern Texas, where splenic fever was truly endemic and which served as the source of each year's northern infection. "The Texas cattle quarantine law passed the legislature," announced Nicholas Klaine. "No more Texas cattle to Dodge City." What he meant was that the through trade, the traditional trail drive into Kansas from Texas proper—the cattle trade in its pristine form—had ended.

South Texas drovers soon revealed an intention to drive anyhow, and if necessary to pasture their herds below the Kansas line until permitted to enter in December. Neutral Strip and Panhandle ranchers saw the splenic fever nightmare beginning to take definite shape. Lest the cattle trade escape them entirely that year, Dodge City's businessmen provided these ranchers with an avenue of escape. In March 1885, they met "to consider the question of opening a stock trail from Dodge City to the southern line of the state." A subscription paper circulated, and interested citizens formed a trail committee headed by Bob Wright, Dan Frost, and a local jeweler. The committee secured a tortuous right-of-way through the agricultural settlements, hired a trail guide, and issued a declaration of responsibility for all damages to growing crops adjoining the route. For the last time cir-

---

[3] Dodge City *Times*, Jan. 8, 1885. The new legislative representative, a former trail driver turned Ford County rancher, at this time owned some twenty thousand head. Dodge City *Democrat*, Feb. 28, 1885.

culars advised cattlemen that Dodge City would ship range stock.[4] But by June uncooperative farmers along the trail had instituted trespass actions against incoming herds.[5] Added to this harassment, cattlemen reaching Dodge found they could unload their animals only at desperation prices in a buyer's market. "All are aware of the fact that thorough-bred stock never was sold as low as at the present time," Frost commented in August, "while on range stock no prices can be quoted unless a good large range, with plenty of water can be secured with them."[6]

Of course few such ranges were then to be had. If the 1884 immigration had wreaked havoc, the even greater influx of 1885 administered a final mopping up. Everywhere ranchers fled before the onrush of newcomers. Settlers that spring overran the range of Chalkley M. Beeson, one of Dodge City's most dedicated businessmen-ranchers, forcing him to hire a fenced Neutral Strip range for twenty cents per head per month. Understandably, he searched elsewhere for a vacant haven, but in vain. Patrick Ryan, perhaps Ford's oldest permanent rural resident, evacuated his herd to the nether end of Finney County and turned to conventional farming on his old homestead. J. M. Day resigned himself to selling most of his twenty thousand head and dropping the balance into Indian Territory. The Beverley Brothers planned to follow suit. Bob Wright chose to send the bulk of his five

[4] *Laws of Kansas*, 1885, pp. 308–11; Dodge City *Globe*, Feb. 3, 10, Mar. 31, Apr. 28, June 16, July 14, 1885; Dodge City *Cowboy*, Feb. 14, 1885; Dodge City *Times*, Mar. 12, 1885; Dodge City *Democrat*, Mar. 7, June 6, 1885.

[5] Dodge City *Globe*, June 9, 30, July 28, 1885. As usual, successful legal action against cattlemen proved impossible to obtain. See petition from thirty-one Ford settlers to John A. Martin, June 19, 1885, Attorney Generals' Correspondence, KSHS; Martin to S. B. Bradford, June 25, 1885, ibid.

[6] Dodge City *Globe*, Aug. 4, 1885. See also Frost's joyless year-end summary, Jan. 26, 1886. Dodge shipped 42,171 head that last season. Ibid., Dec. 1, 1885.

thousand head to northwest Colorado. A number of others partially occupying Kansas ranges planned to move wholly into the Territory or the Neutral Strip. "Yes," agreed Dan Frost in December 1885, "our ranges have passed into history."[7]

With mixed feelings the citizens of Dodge City capitulated to agriculture in 1885. "The business men of the town complain a little of hard times and the Kansas quarantine law," reported a visiting editor in June.[8] Local moral reformers, on the other hand, expended few regrets on the end of an era, seeing in its passing the simultaneous departure of "whisky selling, gambling and prostitution," as Nicholas Klaine put it. The respective editors of the livestock-oriented *Globe* and *Cowboy* tossed desperate barbs as they gave way to the inevitable. "Cattlemen will just keep quiet until a dry year," predicted Frost in April, "when they can buy just as big ranches as they want, that is if history repeats herself, and we think she do." A few weeks later Sam Prouty scornfully denigrated the "granger trade" in terms long familiar to Dodge City readers. As late as September 1885, in fact, a visiting editor was told by "a prominent merchant of Dodge" that the town's business community "did not wish to bother with the cheap trade of the rural districts."[9]

But the truly awesome momentum of the summer's population inflow weakened, ruptured, and then abruptly

[7] Dodge City *Cowboy*, June 20, 27, Aug. 29, Sept. 19, 1885; Dodge City *Globe*, June 30, Dec. 1, 1885; Dodge City *Times*, July 30, 1885.
[8] Dodge City *Globe*, June 23, 1885. The commercial allurements of the through cattle trade remained such that many Dodgeites, including editors Prouty and Frost, rushed to invest in town lots or open businesses at Trail City, Colorado, which for a time hoped to fall heir to the cattle trade. Dodge City *Times*, Aug. 20, 1885; Dodge City *Cowboy*, Aug. 22, Sept. 26, 1885; Dodge City *Globe*, Aug. 25, Sept. 15, Oct. 6, 1885.
[9] Dodge City *Times*, Mar. 5, 1885; Dodge City *Globe*, Apr. 14, 1885; Dodge City *Cowboy*, May 30, 1885; Cimarron *Herald*, Sept. 24, 1885.

swept aside all rhetorical barriers. Amid the debris, editors Frost and Prouty began the painful but necessary task of reordering their economic thinking from cattle to crops. "Farmers are the producers that supply our tables," Frost conceded in August, "and there is no class of people that the world would rather see prosper than the farmer. . . . Good times on the farms mean good times in town." Once he put his mind to it, Prouty proved even more emphatic. "All of the public land [hereabouts] will soon be occupied," he observed in September, "and towns which have an assured future, like Dodge City, will keep pace with the growth of the country." "We have always been grangers out here and have always said that this was an agricultural country," he fibbed shamelessly a month later. He soon amplified his new attitude. "We believe," he wrote, "that the farmer has come here to stay and that he will be fully justified in staying. Western Kansas is now blooming and booming, and although occasional discouragements to the people are liable to occur, on the whole success and prosperity will attend those who possess manliness and pluck." Finally, on the closing day of October 1885, Prouty issued a thoughtful editorial in which he utilized his long acquaintance with the cattle trade in Kansas to stress the brighter side of its passing. "The experience of all cattle towns," he wrote,

is that their growth has been held in check during the period when they depended upon the cattle traffic for support. The country surrounding could not be developed while it was being held for stock ranges. Abilene, Wichita, Newton, Ellsworth and Great Bend have all been cattle towns. They all supposed they would be ruined when the cattle trails departed from them. They were mistaken. Those towns all shot ahead with amazing rapidity when the cattle business left them. Dodge city has been for the past ten years an exclusive cattle town. The cattle traffic made money for its citizens but it did not make a town. It was a question whether the country would ever warrant the making of a respectable town here. The rains of the past three years, the assurance that the soil of the country is susceptible of successful cultivation, the recent absorption of the public domain by settlers, the removal of the cattle trail and the rapidly disappearing cowboy, have now thoroughly convinced our people that a permanent commercial metropolis at this point is demanded by the needs of the country.[1]

Cold comfort, perhaps, but with no happy alternative in sight Dodge City surrendered to the logic of its economic fate.

[6]

CALDWELL'S EXPERIENCE in the eighties proved similar to Dodge City's in that it involved a three-way conflict between drovers, ranchers, and farmers. But with Sumner County having been thrown well within the zone forbidden to summer imports of Texas cattle by the quarantine legislation of 1877 and being long favored with a herd law and a steady immigration of farmers, no large-scale range cattle industry developed within the county itself. As previously discussed, the ranching subsidiary to Caldwell occurred across the state line in the Indian Territory's Cherokee Outlet, an elongated area universally referred to as the "Cherokee Strip."

This territory originally had been deeded to the Cherokee Indians, but soon after the Civil War the Cherokees in turn had given the United States government the right to locate other tribes there. A few non-Cherokees had established themselves in the eastern end of the Strip. The remaining ground, still vacant, lay across the top of Indian Territory, some six million acres of prime grazing

---

[1] Dodge City *Globe*, Aug. 18, 1885; Dodge City *Cowboy*, Sept. 5, Oct. 3, 24, 31, 1885.

land. Although it belonged to the Cherokees, they could not legally settle there themselves, and since it was separated from their main reservation it was of no use for pasturing their own livestock. The empty tract, bisected by the Chisholm Trail, soon became an important area for grazing Texas trail herds, and by the mid-1870's numerous cattlemen had informally pre-empted large sections of the Strip.[2]

Toward the end of the decade the Cherokees put pressure on these rancher-squatters to pay annual "grazing taxes" for the use of the land. The cattlemen considered them confiscatory. In 1879 the Secretary of the Interior at last ruled that only those who had remitted the proper fees would be allowed to remain. Some of them, at least, thereupon paid up. But pressure from Washington was again required in 1880. Now inured to federal threats, the ranchers proved most elusive, and late that year the Cherokees wisely reduced the tax. At a convention at Caldwell in early 1881 the Cherokee Strip stockmen protested that even the new rates were too high, but also recommended their payment. Of some two hundred men holding cattle on the tract, only about forty had complied with the measure by summer or shown any disposition to do so. A threat by the Cherokee's Indian agent to call in military aid did not mature—as the delinquent majority had suspected.[3]

In the spring of 1882 the Cherokee Strip ranchers for a fourth year running received an ultimatum. But more

---

[2] For a good summary on Cherokee Strip ranching in the late nineteenth century see Edward Everett Dale: *The Range Cattle Industry* (Norman, Okla., 1930), pp. 146–55. For additional details on the period 1879–86 one may consult *Senate Exec. Doc. No. 54*, 48 Cong., 1 sess., IV; *Senate Exec. Doc. No. 17*, 48 Cong., 2 sess., I; *Senate Rep. No. 1278*, 49 Cong., 1 sess., VIII.

[3] Caldwell *Post*, June 19, July 10, 1879, June 30, 1881; Caldwell *Commercial*, May 13, June 10, Aug. 5, 12, 19, Sept. 16, Oct. 7, 21, Dec. 23, 1880, Mar. 13, July 21, Aug. 18, 1881.

potent pressures were also brought to bear. The Cherokees begged Congress to purchase the land and give it over to formal settlement, since the tribe could obtain no important financial return from the cattlemen. For its part, the federal government displayed an increasing inclination to ban stock raisers from the controversial Cheyenne and Arapaho tract lying southwest of the Strip, something that threatened to be a precedent. Finally, the fantastic rise of beef prices that season contributed a positive impulse. The more forward-looking ranchers paid their grazing taxes and enclosed their ranges with cheap barbed wire fencing now on the market. By the end of the year the entire Cherokee Strip had been apportioned among taxpaying stockmen. "The facts are," a Caldwell editor responded to a November inquiry, "that there is not a vacant location suitable for a cow ranch on the Cherokee Strip, and it is useless for any one to look for one."[4]

In March 1883, having met annually at Caldwell since 1880, the Cherokee Strip ranchers convened again and formed themselves into a corporation chartered as the Cherokee Strip Live Stock Association, with headquarters at Caldwell.[5] Chartered organization offered several advantages, the most immediate being an opportunity to contract formally with the Cherokees for a collective lease of the Strip. Such an arrangement had recently been consummated between a group of ranchers

[4] Caldwell *Post*, Mar. 23, 30, Aug. 3, 31, Sept. 21, Nov. 16, 1882. During the winter of 1882–83 complaints arising from the enclosure of some small ranges by a large cattle company brought the fencing situation to the attention of the federal government, and the Secretary of the Interior ordered all fences removed. He then reversed himself, however, with the understanding that the ranchers were to obtain a formal leasing agreement from the Cherokees. Dale: *Range Cattle Industry*, pp. 148–49.

[5] Caldwell *Commercial*, Mar. 8, 1883; Caldwell *Post*, Mar. 15, 1883. The charter and bylaws of the association may be found in *Senate Exec. Doc. 17*, I, 149–50.

and the Cheyenne and Arapaho tribes, the Secretary of the Interior posing no objection to the contract.[6] All boded well in the minds of the Cherokee Strip cattlemen for a similar agreement. In early May, the chief of the Cherokees called his national council into special session to consider leasing the Strip. Probably through some substantial bribes, the C.S.L.S.A. lobbyists acquired a lease to the entire tract for a five-year period at an annual rent of $100,000. The association's jubilant officers then ordered the Strip surveyed and divided into something over one hundred ranges, each in turn being leased for five years to the individual or firm occupying it for a semi-annual rent of 1¼ cents per acre.[7]

The significance of the new arrangement did not go unnoticed in town. "The advantages of this lease to Caldwell will be immense," remarked an editor,

> because it gives an assurance of a steady and profitable business. Having an assurance that they will not be disturbed for the next five years, many of the stock men will make their homes in our city, and with their wealth and influence contribute largely toward making it one of the most substantial towns in the West.[8]

Despite this rosy view of the future, some in Caldwell demurred. They objected to the idea of adjacent Indian Territory as a permanent pasture in the foreseeable half decade. Instead they sought to identify the town with the

[6] Dale: *Range Cattle Industry*, pp. 139–41. As Dale explains, the Secretary of the Interior in effect declared that his department, while not extending official endorsement to such leases, would accept them as valid so long as they did not cause mischief. This policy, of course, also governed the subsequent Cherokee Strip arrangement.

[7] See especially Caldwell *Post*, May 10, 1883; Caldwell *Journal*, May 24, 31, July 12, 1883; Dale: *Range Cattle Industry*, pp. 150–52. A congressional investigation of alleged bribery in connection with the winning of the lease failed to prove the charge, but Dale thinks it was probably true. Ibid., p. 152 *n*.

[8] Caldwell *Journal*, May 24, 1883.

growingly militant "Boomer" movement that aimed to open the Territory to agricultural settlement. In such an eventuality, these citizens reasoned, their border city would become a combined debarking point and commercial entrepôt for the great population invasion. Kansans had long cast hungry eyes on the "permanent" tribal reserve to their south, and in the late seventies this interest took an organized form. It was the lush central tract below the Cherokee Strip known as "Oklahoma" that attracted most of the excitement and on which the Boomer attention remained fixed. A colonization movement flourished briefly at Independence, Kansas, in 1879 until dispersed by a presidential proclamation and a threat of force. Thereafter leadership fell to an enigmatic war veteran, ex-legislator, and unsuccessful Kansas farmer, David L. Payne.

At Wichita in late 1879 Payne organized his famous Oklahoma Colony, with himself as president. Among the other charter officers was William B. Hutchison, a long-time Wichita newspaperman. Word of the organization and its purpose reached Caldwell in January 1880. "The watchword is 'On to Oklahoma via Caldwell,' " the town's editor exulted. Two weeks later citizens learned that petitions asking Congress to open the Territory to settlement were making the rounds. "Send one to Caldwell if you want signers," the editor urged. As if such unrestrained journalistic enthusiasm were not enough, Will Hutchison himself arrived in town that spring to establish the Caldwell *Commercial*, which of course joined its rival in endorsing Payne's project.[9]

Refusing to be dissuaded by a new presidential veto,

---

[9] Carl Coke Rister: *Land Hunger: David L. Payne and the Oklahoma Boomers* (Norman, Okla., 1942), pp. 36–52; Caldwell *Post*, Jan. 22, Feb. 5, 1880. Hutchison, strangely (or shrewdly) enough, maintained a detached attitude toward the movement in his publication. See, for instance, the Caldwell *Commercial*, May 13, June 10, Nov. 25, 1880.

in April 1880 Dave Payne crossed into the Territory from Arkansas City with a small advance party. They eluded all military patrols and surveyed a townsite deep in the Oklahoma tract. Two weeks later the army marched them out again. Payne returned to Wichita a hero. With another group he penetrated Oklahoma a second time in July, but once again fell victim to army vigilance. That autumn, as subscribing membership in his organization swelled rapidly, he resolved to move southward again with a full complement of settlers. In early December some two hundred Boomers gathered at Arkansas City for the invasion. Detachments of cavalry deployed along the Territory line prevented them from crossing. For a time the colonizers jockeyed for position. Then, on December 14, they broke camp near Hunnewell and advanced on Caldwell, where citizens ushered them into town in a gay cavalcade complete with brass band. No sooner had the Boomers set up camp on nearby Bluff Creek than it became clear that most were as poor in pocket as they were in land, being unable to replenish depleted supplies. At Christmas some sympathetic Caldwellites gave them food and forage, but discouraged Boomers began trickling away, bound for the various places from which they had come. On December 28, finally, Dave Payne advised them all to disperse and await a more propitious moment for acquiring Oklahoma.

Seeing Payne's raggle-taggle army at close quarters for two weeks had effectively disenchanted many Caldwell businessmen, few of whose cash boxes proved weightier for the experience. "The merchants here are to a man for the opening [of Indian Territory]," a correspondent to a Kansas City newspaper had written from Caldwell on December 22. "They to day subscribed over a thousand dollars in provisions to aid the colony." In response the editor of the Caldwell *Post* dryly suggested that the enthusiastic missive could do with some revision.

Local merchants, he advised, "are decidedly against opening the territory for settlement [and] instead of subscribing one thousand dollars worth of provisions to aid the Colony, from the best information we can get thirty-five dollars will cover all that has been subscribed."[1] Not until 1882 did Payne's Oklahoma project regain its momentum, and during the interim the Caldwell consensus remained distinctly cool toward it.

With the Boomers temporarily out of the picture, Caldwellites increasingly committed themselves to Cherokee Strip ranching as a sustained source of community livelihood. At the same time, the growing incompatibility of ranching and the annual drive of cattle from southern Texas became apparent. As early as March 1881 the Cherokee Strip ranchers, now grading up their herds with improved cattle, asked the Cherokee national council to require all drovers to use a segregated holding ground they had laid out for southern cattle awaiting sale at Caldwell or Hunnewell. In their 1882 convention the ranchers reaffirmed this resolution of the previous year and, while deciding not to press the matter through the Cherokee authorities, published the limits of the holding ground and urged drovers to comply. The enclosure of the Cherokee Strip ranges in the latter half of that year posed a direct threat to the through drive. Several ranchers had encroached on the holding ground, and some Caldwell businessmen expressed concern that the established trails through the Strip might also fall victim to fencing.[2] Throughout the 1883 and 1884 seasons this remained a potent threat.

The 1885 act closing all Kansas to summer importation of southern cattle did not abolish the through trade at Caldwell, since to all intents and purposes the town did

[1] Rister: *Land Hunger*, chaps. v–vii; Caldwell *Post*, Dec. 30, 1880.
[2] Caldwell *Commercial*, Mar. 17, 1881, Nov. 23, 1882; Caldwell *Post*, Mar. 9, Nov. 16, Dec. 21, 1882.

not lie within the state. But at the annual spring meeting of the Cherokee Strip ranchers a Santa Fe Railroad spokesman disclosed that the road and its affiliates would ship through cattle from neither Caldwell nor Hunnewell. The splenic fever danger to improved stock carried by the company simply posed too great a risk.[3] The ranchers themselves vacillated, at first approving, then going on record as opposing, a northern drive of southern cattle. But resolution of the dilemma was out of their hands. When the determined southern drovers headed up the trail toward Caldwell again that spring they encountered more difficulty getting out of their own state than even that experienced by those attempting to push through the Panhandle for Dodge City. "The facts are," noted a Caldwell editor, "that Texas men have so fenced up the lands in Texas along the old routes of travel, that it is almost impossible for the Southern or Central Texas herds to reach the north line of that country at a point where the Caldwell trail can be successfully used."[4] As at Dodge, therefore, the Texas cattle trade died in the spring of 1885.

A resurgent Boomer movement, powerfully challenging the Indian Territory ranching operations, had by this date captured Caldwell's attention. Though he remained relatively inactive during 1881, Dave Payne had by no means surrendered his project. In the spring of 1882 he led a wagon train into Oklahoma from Hunnewell and, undaunted by the usual result, tried again in August. In January 1883 the Boomers mustered once more. A group of Caldwell businessmen issued a bid for the general rendezvous site, but Payne and his lieutenants were hostile because of their bad press there; they chose Arkansas

[3] Caldwell *Journal*, Mar. 26, 1885. Even though splenic fever was specifically excluded from the operations of the 1884 animal industry law, the railroad companies evidently feared prosecution under its provisions. See observations to this effect in ibid., Feb. 26, Apr. 9, 1885.

[4] Caldwell *Journal*, Mar. 26, Apr. 30, June 11, 1885.

City instead. In February the colonizers penetrated Oklahoma and were again thrown out. Payne then turned all field operations over to the colony's vice-president, William L. Couch, who led abortive thrusts later in 1883 and again early the following year.

The alarm of those Caldwellites loyal to the cattle trade reached its zenith in June 1884, when Payne personally led a new invasion—this time to a site within the Cherokee Strip, five miles south of Hunnewell on the Texas cattle holding ground. There, early that month, Payne established a townsite, "Rock Falls," and from this spot the land-hungry avalanche spread out in every direction. The commander of the hopelessly outnumbered cavalrymen attempting to shield the area soon reported that the Boomers had overrun it to a depth of some forty-five miles below the Kansas line. On July 1, President Arthur formally warned all intruders that they faced expulsion by military force. Payne's followers stood their ground, and armed conflict impended between them and the Cherokee Strip ranchers on whose ranges they were rapidly encroaching. In early August, finally, the cavalry rode forth to disperse the settlers, now estimated at some two thousand souls. To everyone's surprise, the soldiers accomplished the task without bloodshed.[5]

Boomer resolution only soared to new heights. That November, while planning yet another thrust into the Territory, Dave Payne died suddenly in a Wellington hotel. His crusade rolled on without him. Two weeks later, under the leadership of Bill Couch, three hundred

[5] Rister: *Land Hunger*, chaps. ix–xiv; Caldwell *Commercial*, Jan. 11, 1883; Caldwell *Post*, Jan. 11, 1883. Payne's 1884 invasion prompted more than alarm in Caldwell. For a week or two in June, Caldwellites entertained notions that a permanent military post was to be established in their area, and they did their best to lure the facility to Caldwell. The (temporary) camp was instead located well inside the Strip. Caldwell *Standard*, June 12, 19, July 17, 1884; Caldwell *Journal*, June 19, 1884.

Boomers invaded Oklahoma, pledging to resist by force all removal efforts. At the end of January 1885, however, the army brought them out once again.[6]

An important result of this dramatic civil disobedience was an increase in regional and national interest in the Oklahoma movement. Despite its repeated local defeats, it appeared that the movement might well succeed if widespread public sympathy was any criterion. Not surprisingly, many Caldwellites succumbed to the movement's new impetus. The Boomer program, to be sure, menaced the cattle trade that had heretofore enhanced their town economically. But declining cattle prices, the rapid deterioration of the trail trade, and the possible removal of Cherokee Strip ranchers under the aegis of the new Democratic administration in Washington all portended ill for any further dependence on the cattle trade as an economic base.

Caldwell's first general expression of attitude change since 1880's disillusioning Christmas occurred in February 1885; some four hundred citizens convened at the opera house in support of opening Oklahoma to settlement. Speakers, including the influential George W. Reilly, urged the Boomers to make Caldwell their headquarters for spring's anticipated invasion. As a concrete demonstration of faith in the movement, some Caldwellites formed a local chapter of colonizers. Bill Couch designated Arkansas City for the rendezvous, but Caldwell's support did not falter. A slate of Oklahoma enthusiasts even entered the lists in the subsequent municipal election. Political contention over prohibition reform took precedence over everything else at the polls, although the wet choice for mayor, George Reilly, was also the Boomer favorite. Reilly easily won the post.[7]

[6] Rister: *Land Hunger*, pp. 178–93.

[7] Arkansas City *Oklahoma Chief*, Mar. 3, 1885; Caldwell *Journal*, Mar. 5, 26, Apr. 2, 9, 1885.

Caldwellites then tried again to attract the headquarters of the movement, capitalizing on the colonizers' growing dissatisfaction with the hospitality at Arkansas City. In late April local businessmen dispatched two emissaries, $600 in cash, and an invitation for the Boomers to relocate. Couch and his lieutenants accepted. In May the would-be Oklahomans, numbering about two hundred, arrived and arranged their tents and wagons near the stockyard east of town. Caldwellites welcomed them with speechmaking and all the trimmings. "Three rousing cheers were given for the Oklahoma Colonists," reported the editor of the Boomers' own newspaper, who could not resist an ironic aside: "(At the Cattle Kings' headquarters.)"[8]

In June this journal, militantly retitled the *Oklahoma War-Chief*, also migrated from Arkansas City. Its editor promptly cemented relationships with the movement's new hosts by recommending that all prospective colonists travel light and buy their essentials at Caldwell. "There is hardly anything used by settlers that cannot be purchased in the city of Caldwell at saving prices," he advised—music to the ears of a business community becalmed in a dull cattle season. Local real estate and general mercantile promise also earned notice. For the "speculator and capitalist" the editor's message was emphatic:

> Go to Caldwell, invest in real estate, in merchandise, manufactory, the lumber and stock trade, as no better field for speculation in the near future offers itself in the west or south. Caldwell must soon be the great supply city of a vast area of newly settled country that will extend more than one hundred miles south and many miles east and west.[9]

[8] Charles A. Siringo: *Riata and Spurs* (rev. edn.; Boston, 1927), pp. 116–17; Arkansas City *Oklahoma Chief*, Apr. 30, May 7, 14, 1885; Caldwell *Journal*, May 7, 14, 1885.

[9] Caldwell *Oklahoma War-Chief*, June 18, Aug. 6, 1885.

The Boomer leaders had hoped for a change in federal policy respecting Indian Territory with the installation of Grover Cleveland's administration. But on March 13, 1885, the new President notified all present or potential intruders on "the Oklahoma lands" that removal would be by military force if necessary. The Secretary of the Interior, however, personally informed Bill Couch that the removal policy would apply to ranchers as well as to agricultural squatters.

This consolation proved short-lived. Weeks passed, and no action against cattlemen occurred anywhere in the Territory. In June a Senate subcommittee arrived in Caldwell and took considerable testimony from Couch about the squatting stock raisers, but no effort to oust them resulted. The *War-Chief's* editor finally grew so vitriolic in his denunciations of the administration that in July federal authorities arrested and confined him for a month on charges—not subsequently pressed—of "seditious conspiracy and inciting insurrection." Late that same month Boomers took brief comfort from the U.S. Attorney General's opinion that Indian Territory grazing leases had no legal validity—but in reality this no more than affirmed the assumptions underlying the Interior Department's hands-off policy of the past two years.[1]

In July, President Cleveland suddenly ordered ranchers off the Cheyenne-Arapaho tract. Again the Boomers applauded, seeing this as a precedent for all territorial cattlemen. In fact, however, the administration had intervened only because the Indians seemed about to take the warpath against the ranchers on their lands. In December the Secretary of the Interior confirmed that as long as relations between the Cherokee Strip ranchers and the Cherokees remained amicable he had no plans to interfere with the leasing arrangement there. Cleveland's

[1] Rister: *Land Hunger*, pp. 193–99; Caldwell *Journal*, Mar. 19, Aug. 6, 1885; Caldwell *Oklahoma War-Chief*, Aug. 6, 1885.

August proclamation ordering the removal of all fencing on the public domain was equally ineffective in clearing cattlemen from Indian Territory.[2]

In the face of repeated disappointments, Couch concluded that his movement must mount yet another invasion of the Territory or fall apart. On October 22, therefore, the colonists' wagons moved south on the old Chisholm Trail. Captured and brought north again in November, the Boomers vented their frustration on the Cherokee Strip ranchers, starting vast prairie fires that destroyed many cattle ranges along the line of march. This spitework, combined with the movement's decreasing vigor, turned Caldwellites decisively against the Boomers a second time. They were not welcomed back to town. Not until 1889 would they appear again in Caldwell for the famous rush into Oklahoma, followed by that into the Cherokee Strip itself four years later.[3]

In early 1886 the men of Caldwell confronted an uncertain future. They would enjoy the diminishing trade provided by their tributary ranches until such time as the Strip fell to permanent settlement. But dependence on local agriculture definitely seemed their destiny. They faced the prospect without appreciable flinching. And in contemplating the old Texas cattle trade—the unique enterprise that had structured the experience of every cattle town since Abilene's heyday—their spokesmen betrayed no identifiable regrets for having once entertained it in their midst.

[2] Dale: *Range Cattle Industry*, pp. 142, 144; Caldwell *Journal*, July 30, Aug. 13, Dec. 31, 1885; Caldwell *Oklahoma War-Chief*, Aug. 6, 13, 20, Oct. 8, 1885.
[3] Caldwell *Journal*, Nov. 19, 1885; Wichita *Eagle*, Nov. 25, 1885; Rister: *Land Hunger*, pp. 199–200, chap. xvii.

CONCLUSION

History and the Cattle Town Experience

[1]

IN THE 1950's the citizens of Abilene, Wichita, and Dodge City capitalized on the emergence of "adult western" movie and television drama and put together collections of frontier structures to reproduce the cattle town past for the tourist trade. "Old Abilene" now overspreads a small plot on the southeast edge of town, an incongruous neighbor to the grim battle-monument architecture of the Eisenhower Presidential Library. "Cowtown Wichita," a more ambitious project, occupies a corner of Wichita's city park, where each summer, in a kind of unintended whimsy, young Girl Scouts serve as tourist guides. Dodge City's "Front Street Replica" nestles within an excavation that was once the bald south slope of Boot Hill. On the crest above is a mockup graveyard with comic headboards. In such reconstructions is the cattle town heritage tangibly, if not quite plausibly, enshrined.

Visitors who turn from these attractions discover few genuine remnants of the pioneer past. At Abilene, Ellsworth, and Dodge the main business thoroughfares no longer overlook the railroad tracks. At Wichita the historic juncture of Main and Douglas is now but one of many busy downtown intersections. The Caldwell of today, on the other hand, is no larger than when the Texas cattle trade left it in 1885. Its business district remains much as it was then, though the wooden facades are gone, replaced by brick and stone. From the end of Main Street one can still gaze southward across Fall and Bluff creeks to the prairie skyline where Oklahoma begins. Only here is a sense impression of the cattle town authentically recapturable.

[2]

WHAT, IN THE FINAL ANALYSIS, was the relationship of the Texas cattle trade to the successful town-building impulse? This is not a question easily or definitively answered. How a citizen judged whether the cattle trade had properly contributed to local prosperity and growth depended on his partisan viewpoint—that is, whether he was social reformer, farmer, or pure-and-simple businessman. It seems clear that the dominant consensus at the cattle town was nearly always that of its business community. At least until special circumstances intervened, this consensus consistently endorsed the cattle trade, and for good reasons. At the average frontier community the only substantial influx of capital came in the pockets of new settlers, or in the form of taxes on railroads and nonresident landholders. In light of this fact, not even the most lukewarm townsman could deny that the cattle trade's transients comprised an unusual resource. Buttressing this entrepreneurial endorsement was the feeling, even as far west as Dodge, that conventional agriculture would be the ultimate community economic base. Cattle trade profits were therefore to be made while the making was good; the future would take care of itself.

What profited business profited all, businessmen reasoned. The cattle trade thus represented "progress" despite its attendant social evils. Moral reformers, however, denied this one-dimensional analysis, introducing an alternate approach to town-building that placed an immediate premium on social quality. Those who regarded moral uplift as a threat to the current economic situation —to say nothing of a congenial style of life—strongly resisted this reasoning. The general economic consensus gave way to its critics reluctantly, if at all. When they could, reformers cleverly employed economic arguments against cattle trade sin, but these arguments made little headway so long as local municipal finances waxed fat on illegal tax assessments and police court proceeds. Sin was easy to condone when it not only could be considered a prop to prosperity but also "paid its own way," as the saying went.

That the cattle town's flirtation with the cattle trade could last but a few years at best also failed to cheer the impatient rural settler. Farmers, when they publicly reflected at all on the town's development, begged its citizens to abandon range cattle and orient themselves to local agriculture. Some farmers, true enough, exploited the cattle town market for feed grain and garden, dairy, and poultry produce. But whether or not farmers should (or could) have adjusted permanently to this market was merely an academic question, since the cattle trade required that large areas of potential farmland remain fallow as pasture—a requirement not to be countenanced for long by incoming settlers intent on cultivating staple crops for national and international markets. Farmers as well as social reformers, therefore, demanded that the cattle town business community redefine its idea of the town-building process. In the long run, neither the premises nor the goals of local progress proved to be universal or absolute conceptions.

Even today any kind of sophisticated measurement of the cattle trade's impact on community growth is difficult. Local population, for example, rose during the era, but to differentiate that induced by the cattle trade from that which was merely routine is impossible. Abilene's population expanded from a handful of families in 1867 to between five and six hundred residents in mid-1870.[1] Immigration continued strongly thereafter, and early in 1871 Vear P. Wilson claimed nearly one thousand citizens for the town, repeating this estimate a year later. In 1874, however, Abilene's population stood at only about seven hundred.[2] Wilson's top figure is not to be trusted literally, but probably the number of residents did peak in 1871, the town's last full cattle trading year, falling off again thereafter. Ellsworth appears to have experienced a similar demographic evolution. In July 1870 it contained approximately four hundred and fifty citizens. In the spring of 1874 its population was estimated at six hundred. A year later, with the cattle trade in decline, Ellsworth's population had fallen to around five hundred.[3] Apparently the same lapse in population increase occurred with the end of cattle trading at Dodge City and Caldwell, each of which contained some two thousand residents at the close of the era.[4]

[1] In the 1870 census Abilene is not differentiated from surrounding Grant Township. By excluding those listed as farmers and members of farm families, one obtains the total of 525 residents. But presumably a number of farm families lived in Abilene itself during this period of rural influx. U.S. Manuscript Census, 1870: Kansas (microfilm copy, KSHS), Dickinson Co., Grant Twp., pp. 1–6, 8–12, 17–22.

[2] Abilene *Chronicle*, Jan. 5, 1871, Mar. 14, 1872; Kansas State Board of Agriculture: *Annual Report . . . 1874* (Topeka, 1874), p. 122.

[3] U.S. Manuscript Census, 1870: Kansas, Ellsworth Co., City of Ellsworth; Board of Agriculture: *Annual Report 1874*, p. 142; Kansas Manuscript Census, 1875 (KSHS), Ellsworth Co., Ellsworth Twp., pp. 1–13. In the 1875 census Ellsworth is not differentiated from its township, but seems to have been enumerated in the very first pages, making the extraction of town dwellers a simple matter.

[4] Kansas Manuscript Census, 1885 (KSHS), Ford Co., City of Dodge. By eliminating a number of transient irrigation ditch workers (pp. 66 ff.), one obtains a total population, as of March 1885, of

In all four cases a business recession accompanied the loss of the cattle trade, but this too is difficult to assess. Dodge, for example, in the words of Robert M. Wright, "at one fell swoop was reduced to extreme poverty, almost want. . . . For ten long years [after 1885], Dodge City was suspended in reverses." The end of cattle trading was only one influential factor, however. Almost simultaneously new railroads intervened between the town and extreme southwest Kansas and the Texas Panhandle, completely undercutting Dodge City's overland freighting business. In addition, the temporary financial straits of the Santa Fe Railroad sharply curtailed operations at the Dodge divisional facilities, reducing their importance as an economic asset.[5]

The only one of the five major cattle towns destined for metropolitan status was Wichita, which by 1960 had gained a population of 254,698.[6] Its growth was well under way in the cattle trading years. Wichita acquired at least 2,000 citizens in its first two years of formal existence, becoming a city of the second class even before it shipped any livestock. The increase for the next few years proved a good deal more modest, but with a population of some 2,500 in 1875 Wichita rated as the eighth largest city in Kansas.[7]

1,402. A year later Dodge was made a city of the second class on order of the governor, proof having been furnished that it contained at least two thousand citizens. (Dodge City *Times*, Mar. 11, 1886.) Caldwell's population in March 1885 totaled 1,972. Kansas Manuscript Census, 1885, Sumner Co., City of Caldwell.

[5] Robert M. Wright: *Dodge City: The Cowboy Capital* (Wichita, 1913), pp. 327–28.

[6] U.S. Bureau of the Census: *United States Census of Population, 1960: Kansas, Number of Inhabitants* (Washington, D.C., 1961), p. 28. The 1960 populations of the other former cattle towns were, in descending order, as follows: Dodge, 13,520; Abilene, 6,746; Ellsworth, 2,361; and Caldwell, 1,788. Ibid., pp. 25–26.

[7] Board of Agriculture, *Annual Report . . . 1875* (Topeka, 1875), *passim*. In March 1875 the city contained 2,482 residents. Kansas Manuscript Census, 1875, Sedgwick Co., City of Wichita.

"Wichita is one of the best cities in the state," conceded Ellsworth's envious editor in late 1872, adding: "Texas cattle built it."[8] This correlation of cattle and urban prosperity overlooked another important stimulus to Wichita's growth in the 1870's—its highly advantageous position for fully seven years as a railroad terminus from which freight moved overland to more southerly communities and to the posts and reservations of Indian Territory, and where many migrants into south-central Kansas disembarked. But this happy circumstance was largely a by-product of the community's intention to become a cattle shipping center, the determination of Wichitans to exploit the cattle trade having drawn the railroad down from Newton in the first place. Thereafter, Wichita's tenacious grip on the cattle trade—retaining it "beyond a time that seemed almost incredible," as Dodge City's Daniel M. Frost remarked—revealed the importance Wichitans attached to it.[9] Their liberal expenditures of both private and official energies and funds is sufficiently impressive testimony that the cattle trade benefited the communities it visited.

But specific economic arguments aside, argued William S. White (Wichita's anti-cattle trade farmer turned pro-cattle trade editor), if the Texas trade did nothing else for Wichita there still remained "those advantages . . . derived" from its effect in "directing public attention all over the land to this section of the Arkansas Valley."[1] The importance of this intangible contribution to urban growth was not lost on the cattle town people, although,

[8] Ellsworth *Reporter*, Nov. 21, 1872.
[9] Dodge City *Globe*, Nov. 26, 1878. Frost also insisted that it was the cattle trade that had made Wichita "the city she now is."
[1] Wichita *Beacon*, Feb. 9, 1876. A similar acknowledgment occurred at Dodge. "Dodge City is the best advertised town in Kansas," wrote Samuel S. Prouty, listing as the primary cause "her extensive cattle interests." Dodge City *Cowboy*, June 27, 1885.

as we have seen, the quality of the advertising stimulated by the cattle trade increasingly came under attack by social reformers concerned with a "proper" community image.²

[3]

IN 1910, when Senator O. H. Bentley, Wichita's first important historian, briefly characterized the rise of his community, he did so in terms of a cohesive vitality. "The city," he wrote,

. . . had no special advantages geographically over any other part of the state. It so happened, however, that an aggregation of men constituted its first inhabitants who were wide awake. . . . Around this nucleus of pioneer heroes came later on other and younger men of the same character, *who promptly joined hands with those who laid the foundation of the city, and together, and in harmonious accord*, pushed the city to the front and held it there. . . . Thus, *by reason of a remarkable unity of action and purpose on the part of all*, a city has been builded of which its architects are justly proud.³

Having examined the social process at early Wichita in some detail, we know this statement to be false: from the

² As Abilene's V. P. Wilson put it following his partially successful moral crusade: "Every newspaper man, whether editor or reporter, who has ever visited the town, and said anything about the 'dens' existing in this locality, has written of Abilene in a very unenviable light— often, it is true, exaggerating the facts. Hereafter, when others speak of us truthfully, they will represent Abilene in a better light—the light in which her people have determined she shall remain." (Abilene *Chronicle*, Sept. 14, 1871.) For the other view that almost *any* publicity (even that which was unfavorable) could be considered good, see Wichita *Eagle*, Dec. 12, 1872; Dodge City *Times*, July 26, 1879.

³ O. H. Bentley (ed.): *History of Wichita and Sedgwick County* (Chicago, 1910), I, 1–2 (italics added).

very first its leading businessmen fought one another with vigorous abandon. Senator Bentley had lived in Wichita long enough to know the facts. Why did he falsify? What significance is there in his idealized portrait of entrepreneurial solidarity?

The first explanation springing to mind is that local historians like Bentley simply respected the individual reputations of early citizens, many of whom—or whose immediate descendants—still lived in the city. But this explanation loses merit when we realize that the tendency of community historians to conceal divisiveness is at least as old as the Florentine historians about whom Machiavelli complained.[4] There is, it seems, something more important operating here. The central impulse would appear to be a public relations role of wider application.

In its American form this impulse can be traced back to a contemporary public relations program. In the Darwinian struggle for urban status and metropolitan dominance, the notion expressed by the rubric "unity above all" became a principle intimately associated with "progress." One sees underlying this principle a certain rationality: internal divisiveness represents an inefficient expenditure of community energies in light of the corporate job at hand, of which the most important feature is the attraction of population, capital investment, and industry. These urban prerequisites might, to some extent, be put off by displays of internal disunity. At the least, publicity about local violations of the unity principle normally cost a town prestige and dignity. Its rivals were

---

[4] "After having diligently read their writings in order to see what plan and method they had adopted, that our history might profit by their example to the benefit of the readers, I found that in the descriptions of the wars waged by the Florentines against foreign princes and peoples they had been most exact, but upon the subject of civil discord and internal strifes and their consequences they had been entirely silent, or had written far too briefly concerning them." Niccolo Machiavelli: *Florentine History*, trans. W. K. Marriott (London, 1909), p. 1.

apt to seize on such information with great delight. As a Kiowa, Kansas, editor remarked of Caldwell's internal conflict following the Frank Noyes lynching:

> The city of Caldwell has reached that condition which ends only in ruin. "A house divided against itself cannot stand," is a prediction old and true. . . . The proud Queen City of the border, who's glory was the theme of every tongue, is in the throe of deepest anguish; the sack-cloth of woe are her garments and the ashes of dispair are upon her head. In sorrow we mourn for the beautiful city, and we listen in dread for the tidings of her destruction.[5]

Caldwell had violated the unity principle; the consequence abroad was a mocking prediction of disaster for its metropolitan pretensions.

Publicity about local divisiveness, in short, was considered to be as bad as divisiveness itself. Stifling evidence of conflict was therefore one of a local newspaper editor's most important jobs, an integral part of booster journalism. But this task contradicted yet another, that of transforming conflict into consensus, which often meant admitting that conflict existed. And as we have seen, if strife assumed major proportions even the most sophisticated editor might be drawn into it. This proved especially true when more than one local newspaper was in business, tempting rival editors to assume rival positions on conflict issues. Then total concealment became impossible.

When local historians recorded the beginnings of their communities they tended to obey the old taboo on divisiveness. In retrospect, social conflict assumed an even more irrational and ridiculous appearance, totally out of keeping with a dignified presentation of the origins of local progress. And without immediate issues to resolve, historians could, more freely than their journalistic predecessors, indulge in manipulating evidence. To re-

[5] Quoted in the Caldwell *Journal*, Jan. 7, 1886.

turn to Senator Bentley's motives for encapsulating Wichita's early history as he did, the surprise is not that he emphasized entrepreneurial solidarity but that he was willing to include in his book Kos Harris's memoirs of the Main Street–Douglas Avenue contention. For this lively material Bentley's statement is an implicit disclaimer.[6]

[4]

THE LOCAL HISTORY TABOO on social conflict comes down to us from nineteenth-century amateur writing, but professional scholarship perpetuates it. Historians of American urbanism, for example, insofar as they have produced "city biographies," or case studies of successful urbanization, write in much the same vein. Like the local historian, the city biographer makes progress his controlling theme. He assumes that it occurred only within the context of community harmony. He views occasional conflicts as disturbing social aberrations to be overcome before further progress could take place. He feels called upon to apologize for them as embarrassing instances of urban immaturity.[7]

[6] The curious ability of local publicists to transform the record of conflict into one of cohesive progress was brought home to me by a personal experience. When my article on Ellsworth during the cattle trade era appeared in the *Kansas Historical Quarterly* in 1961, it was abstracted for local consumption in the town's two newspapers. Although I had made town-country conflict one of the central themes of the article, and both reporters acknowledged this, one of them concluded by translating what I had said into an account of purposeful development toward the town's current status, implying the existence of a strong, undifferentiated consensus. "And so the story continues," he wrote, "frontier lore of the richest sort, the story of struggle and hardship, failure and disaster, yet always with determination overriding to bring Ellsworth ahead as a substantial agricultural community." Ellsworth *Messenger*, May 10, 1961.

[7] For example, the first volume of Blake McKelvey's history of Rochester, New York, one of the most ambitious and distinguished of the city biographies produced by recent scholars, is shot through with periodic evidences of social conflict. Possibly only that concerning

The experience of the Kansas cattle towns strongly suggests the precise opposite: social conflict was normal, it was inevitable, and it was a format for community decision-making and thus for change—or "progress," if you will. At the cattle town conflict and cooperation were equally valid aspects of the same social process, to be treated by the historian with equal gravity. The cattle town people in most instances cooperated in winning railroads and cattle trails, adjusting to violence, and preserving the cattle trade. At the same time, their external conflict with farmers and their internal warfare—business factionalism and moral reform politics—demonstrated anything but a thoroughgoing solidarity.

If conflict and cooperation seem mutually exclusive and therefore incapable of existing simultaneously, we must remember that we are dealing with human behavior, which does not always bow to conventional logic. And yet there is nothing really strange here. The cattle town, despite its relatively small population, was hardly a simple social unit. Despite internal agreement on many important themes, each community was a truly pluralistic society with a fairly extensive range of attitudes. Whether townsmen cohered or clashed depended upon the degree of consensus surrounding particular goals. To repeat: not

religious schisms and antagonisms is satisfactorily placed within any sustained context. Business factionalism, in particular, is treated in a peculiarly oblique manner. The flavor of the author's approach can be conveyed through a few sample quotes: "Apparently the threat of strife was averted and harmony restored, for the progress of the settlement continued." "Rival factions with conflicting standards and divergent interests quickly gained a foothold, and the settlement was distracted for several years by bickering internal quarrels." "[Conflict ensued,] revealing that the village had yet to develop an urbane self-restraint." "Yet dissension failed to check the growing village." "Unfortunate events disclosed bitter factional jealousies, and only with great reluctance was the necessity for accommodating individual interests to the community's welfare recognized." McKelvey: *Rochester the Water-Power City, 1812–1854* (Cambridge, Mass., 1945), pp. 58, 71, 76, 85, 136.

even collective progress was something producing an automatic consensus.

The modern historian of the local community—"urban" or otherwise—would do well to acknowledge the functional relationship between community decision-making and community conflict. Until he does, the standard characterization of the early population center will continue to be that dear to the local history tradition: cohesive, sociologically simple communities swept forward by the dynamics of growth.

In actuality, was not many a frontier community—like the typical cattle town—a self-identified commercial metropolis in embryo, anxious to embrace local agriculture only when a more dynamic economic base failed to materialize? Were there not other times and other places in which townsmen and farmers differed strongly over natural resource utilization, the allocation of public funds, control of county government, the community image and crop disaster? Was not business factionalism endemic in many a flourishing settlement where the economic spoils seemed worth fighting over? Though the circumstances might be less dramatic than at Abilene or Dodge, were there not times in the life of every frontier town when the desire to impose moral uplift created social divisiveness? And was not a concern with community advertising and public relations everywhere a controversial factor in local efforts to attract those urban prerequisites an outside world yielded so reluctantly?

Decision-making, the behavioral side of the social process, the mechanism by which the cattle town people strove to influence collective directions and collective destinies, involved a complex interplay of divergent motives and perceptions. To acknowledge this is to abstract the experience of the cattle town people at the same time we clothe them in flesh, blood, and human nature. That so few of their individual life experiences have survived is the tragedy they share with all the common folk of history. But in their vivid corporate reality they still live, telling us much of themselves and of social change in their America and, in microcosm, of that mighty frontier adventure that shaped the American West.

APPENDICES

APPENDIX A

The Elkins–McKitrick Thesis

IN MORE THAN ONE RESPECT, I think, this book implicitly takes issue with what is probably the most influential theoretical writing in recent years about the frontier community: Stanley Elkins and Eric McKitrick: "A Meaning for Turner's Frontier," *Political Science Quarterly*, LXIX (1954), 321–53, 565–602. This important article has been partially reprinted in George Rogers Taylor (ed.): *The Turner Thesis* (rev. edn.; Boston, 1956), pp. 96–107, and Edward N. Saveth (ed.): *American History and the Social Sciences* (New York, 1964), pp. 379–99; it is fully reproduced as No. H-64 in the Bobbs-Merrill Reprint Series in History.

Since the Elkins-McKitrick thesis has not yet been criticized in any extended fashion, I should like to comment explicitly, if briefly, on it and how I conceive the cattle town experience to relate to it.

The authors sought to test Frederick Jackson Turner's hypothesis about the frontier origins of American democracy by examining the pioneer experience at the local level. They began by acknowledging an inspirational debt to a sociological study by Robert K. Merton, Patricia S. West, and Marie Jahoda, which they consulted in manuscript form at Columbia University. Merton and his associates had explored social behavior in two World War II housing developments. Unfortunately for present purposes, the Merton study to date is still unpublished, but it is conveniently summarized in the following words in

James S. Coleman: *Community Conflict* (Glencoe, Ill., 1957), p. 2:

> One town (called "Craftown" by the authors) was beset by early physical inconveniences: poor electrical equipment, no sidewalks, bad streets, and many other problems stemming primarily from contractors' malpractice. This community established a pattern of meeting problems collectively, through community organizations. Once the pattern was established, and the initial efforts met with some success, it was continued. Long after these community organizations had lost their original reason for existence, they were still strong, and played an important role in the management of community affairs. And when new problems arose, as they do in any community, these organizations provided an ever-ready means for handling them peacefully and democratically.
>
> In the other community ("Hilltown") such a pattern had never been established. There were fewer provocative incidents in the community's early days, and those that did occur were not met collectively. This, too, established a pattern—one of non-participation in community affairs. Management of the community was left to a few.

In sharp contrast to Hilltown, Craftown—a newly founded community faced by various problems needing prompt solution—seemed to Elkins and McKitrick closely analogous to the pioneer settlement of history. They therefore hypothesized that American democracy had emerged out of countless Craftown experiences on the frontier. They proceeded to identify democracy as

> a manipulative attitude toward government, . . . a wide participation in public affairs, a diffusion of leadership, a widespread sense of personal competence to make a difference . . . [that] evolves most quickly during the initial stages of setting up a new community; it is seen most dramatically while the process of organization and

the solving of basic problems are still crucial; it is observed to best advantage when this flow of basic problems is met by a homogeneous population.

To the authors "homogeneity," as witnessed at Craftown, meant "a similar level of social and economic status and aspirations among the people," and also the absence of "a traditional, ready-made structure of leadership in the community"—that is, political homogeneity as well.

Elkins and McKitrick then measured the Craftown archetype against the local experience on the frontiers of the Old Northwest, the South, and New England. They concluded from this test that democracy had evolved most fully where the early population was most homogeneous and the range of problems greatest: in the Old Northwest. It was mainly from the frontier of the Old Northwest, they noted, that Turner drew the inspiration for his famous hypothesis, and they offered their own findings as verification of it.

At least one historian has seen difficulties in making the Craftown model conform to frontier realities, especially respecting socioeconomic homogeneity (see Allan G. Bogue: "Social Theory and the Pioneer," *Agricultural History*, XXXIV [1960], 27–28). It would also seem true that political homogeneity as a precondition of democracy catches the thesis in a serious tautology—democracy requiring the existence of political homogeneity, but political homogeneity presupposing democracy. The use of Craftown as a model is also questionable. If it was merely a "bedroom community," as the evidence suggests, then it could hardly be called analogous to the typical pioneer town in the Old Northwest or anywhere else. Finally, the use of amateur writings and conventional local and regional histories for historical verification of the Craftown archetype could scarcely yield anything *but* proof of collective, peaceful, and democratic decision-making, since this is precisely the retrospective image early writers customarily sought to create.

These general criticisms aside, the experience of the cattle towns suggests the existence of four important conceptual or interpretive errors in the Elkins-McKitrick thesis. The cattle towns, of course, did not lie in the Old Northwest, and thus on technical grounds may be barred from commenting directly on the thesis. Yet, as shown in Table 2 of Chapter VIII, the single largest U.S.-born contingent in the cattle town voting population was made up of native midwesterners, or migrants from the area where presumably the Craftown mechanism had long been active. Would not these migrants have carried it as cultural baggage to the Kansas frontier? In any case, the following criticisms do not depend on the cattle town experience alone.

1. *The authors view the typical frontier town as self-contained to the point of being almost hermetically sealed.* Their conception of the irrelevancy of "cultural and religious" issues will be considered in a moment; let it only be noted here that they cannot conceive of an "external" issue like prohibition reform making any important local impact in the presence of entrepreneurial rationalism and solidarity. Nor do they acknowledge the major role played by public opinion from outside the community. Last, they fail to acknowledge that surrounding farm populations could impinge on community decision-making; they instead go so far as to remark on "the ease with which the basic agrarian experience flowed into that of commercial small-urban enterprise."

(For a supporting sociological discussion of the self-contained stereotype see Charles Tilly: *The Vendée* [Cambridge, 1964], pp. 58–59; for rural antipathy in historical perspective see Robert R. Dykstra: "Town-Country Conflict: A Hidden Dimension in American Social

History," *Agricultural History*, XXXVIII [1964], 195–96 and notes; for the continuing tendency of townsman-farmer conflict to be closely similar to conventional industrial strife see Coleman: *Community Conflict*, p. 6.)

2. *Elkins and McKitrick conceive of the pioneer settlement in terms of the "community organization" stereotype of an older generation of sociologists.* This view presents the community as a kind of formal organization striving to achieve well-defined goals in a rational manner. It recognizes neither the possibility of internal economic conflict nor that of any "nonpurposeful" (noneconomic) community behavior. Community decision-making therefore displays all the earmarks of decision-making within a business corporation. Local politics, unencumbered by cultural or social issues, becomes only a collective search for the best men to fill administrative jobs at hand.

(For the errors inherent in this conceptual approach see especially Edward C. Banfield: *Government Project* [Glencoe, Ill., 1951], pp. 234–38; for the universality of nonpurposeful local behavior see Coleman: *Community Conflict, passim.*)

3. *The Elkins-McKitrick thesis assumes that as at Craftown, community problems—given the existence of population homogeneity—routinely led to collective and peaceful decision-making.* It is, of course, a sociological commonplace that floods, aircraft bombing attacks, and other forms of "total disaster" give rise to cohesive local responses; but the invariably temporary nature of the social results is also well known. More important, I think, is the difficulty surrounding the authors' conception of a community "problem." Clearly community problems can be as socially divisive as they can be cohesive—in other words, often enough problems are really *issues*. Problems faced by the cattle town people included such matters as providing access to the cattle trail, enforcing the law, and promoting community reform, all of which were capable

of provoking individually differentiated responses. Even "routine" problems in the Craftown sense could be issues so long as there were different viewpoints respecting their solution. Wichita's Marshall M. Murdock put it this way (Wichita *Eagle*, Aug. 23, 1872):

> As babyhood is doomed to vexatious maladies before it can attain a perfect manhood or womanhood, so all new towns must have a run of a certain set of ills, inconveniences and experiences that time, courage and enterprise will alone overcome. . . . Wichita is having her first run of these distressing distempers. Persons and things are tending to their proper level; streets must be graded and regraded, guttered and reguttered; sidewalks laid and relaid; churches built, additions added, and then all replaced by more imposing edifices; frame business houses built one week and torn down the next week to give room for something more permanent, and so it goes until many get out of patience and feel inclined to kick up. "What's this subscription for?" "Why this expense?" "Why is this officer or person allowed to do this or that?" . . . Some of us want Main street better graded, and want it guttered and curbed; others want Douglas avenue served in the same fashion; this one thinks a "fire district" should have been erected long ago; that one thinks our city government too expensive, etc., etc.

4. *Elkins and McKitrick would also appear to err in insisting on democracy as a peaceful mode of community decision-making.* At the cattle towns, as I suggested in the conclusion to Chapter VI of this book, the most democratic format was typically conflict. Moreover, in his brief but incisive essay already cited several times, James Coleman's view of the proper extremes involved in decision-making is not that of democracy and nondemocracy, but rather that of the "ordinary democratic process," on the one hand, and community conflict on the other. The most clear-cut example of social conflict as a democratic

mechanism occurs when the overthrow of "unresponsive" administrations in power is at issue. In such cases conflict represents the mobilization of a hitherto passive segment of the local population—often the majority—that is usually acquiescent but not actively supporting the incumbent officers.

Though some of his conclusions seem tentative or even equivocal, Coleman presents cogent reasons for thinking that conflict may have been the *dominant* type of democracy in frontier settlements:

(*a*) It is in small rather than large communities where citizens are most "involved." Although "involvement" helps mitigate conflict, it also causes conflict to be most widely spread throughout a given community. (Coleman: *Community Conflict*, pp. 3, 21.)

(*b*) Towns with "self-contained economies"—that is, where men both live and work, including towns dependent on agriculture—are the types of communities most likely to breed economic conflicts. (Ibid., p. 6.)

(*c*) Large and rapid immigration into a community stimulates conflict, since the newcomers inevitably import divergent values and interests. (Ibid., p. 7.)

(*d*) New communities are not likely to have established procedures of public administration. When rapidly growing they are ripe for political conflict because there will be antagonistic viewpoints on how the town ought to be run. (Ibid., p. 17.)

(*e*) The smaller the community, the more likely its citizens are to be drawn into conflict irrationally—that is, by personal attachments and existing clique loyalties. (Ibid., p. 19.)

(*f*) High "organizational density" (a large proportion of residents active in voluntary associations), while serving to "regulate" and "contain" conflict, is also known to *stimulate* conflict in important ways. (Ibid., p. 21.)

Now do these several criticisms negate the Elkins-Mc-

Kitrick thesis? Not fully, perhaps. Surely the most important contribution of the thesis has been to identify pioneer town-building as productive of democratic mechanisms at the grass roots. But from what type of experience did these mechanisms most often develop? Which was the more typical decision-making apparatus on the frontier, the "ordinary democratic process" of Craftown or the community conflict of the cattle towns?

My own thought, informed by the cattle town experience, favors a conflict interpretation. But of course the question will only be resolved definitively—if it ever is— by many more good local studies than we have available at present.

APPENDIX B

A Note on Methodology

IN SUCH A HEAVILY DOCUMENTED BOOK as this a formal bibliography would probably serve no very important purpose. Judging from discussions with colleagues and students, a commentary on certain aspects of this book's methodology may be more useful, particularly so for those interested in local history techniques.

In speaking of local history I do not have in mind those forms of historical analysis that probe some specific question at the local level—Negro slavery, grass-roots economic democracy, ethnic voting patterns, land speculation, and so forth. These usually entail their own appropriate methodologies. Rather, let "local history" simply mean an exploration of the relative totality of "what happened" in a certain locality over a given period of time. This is the purpose that motivates the typical local historian, a purpose entirely legitimate.

The trouble is that the local historian characteristically lacks specific guidelines—something in mind that will circumscribe or regulate his open-ended purpose, allow him some initial assumptions, and lend him ideas for general thematic emphasis. My own extended encounter with the cattle towns has moved me to some considered observations on the problem.

Experience has cautioned me that what ails local history will not respond to simple solutions, given present knowledge. Take, for example, a recent formula for urban history in Eric F. Lampard's "American Historians and the Study of Urbanization," *American Historical Review*,

LXVII (1961), 49–61. At first glance it contains nothing apparently precluding its adaptation to localities of all kinds. The author champions an approach borrowed from the radical social ecologists by which, he insists, community studies could focus on "the changing structure and organization of communities in terms of four specific and quantifiable references": population, environment, technology, and social organization. But Lampard offers us no real solution. Other objections aside, analyzing even present-day communities under the terms of this ecological formula presents insurmountable difficulties in quantifying such things as, say, social organization. (See, for example, Peter H. Rossi's negative comments in the *American Journal of Sociology*, LXV [1959], especially p. 149.)

My own suggestion, noted in the introduction to this book, is that the local historian recognize the "social process"—defined as the interaction of impersonal factors and human factors—as a commanding theme. Treating impersonal factors largely boils down to accommodating economic, political, and social circumstances (prevailing national and regional ideologies, laws, policies, organizational forms, and the like), as well as specific "external" impingements on the local scene, such as national, regional, and state issues of various kinds. Local citizens could not hope to exert much influence over these impersonal factors, and could at best only try to modify them at the community level.

Treating the human factor is a more complex task. We simplify it usefully, I think, when we acknowledge that the most critical activity in the exertion of any important human influence over the local environment is decision-making. Important decisions are those that affect the community in the collective sense, but they can be made both by influential individuals (that is, leaders) and by groups. From this follows an emphasis on two related and interacting themes: leadership and politics. These terms as meant here include any and all individual or group attempts to direct the course of local affairs—something normally reaching beyond formal electioneering and voting.

In this context decision-making lies at the heart of all things that impel a community through time; from it stem all the conventional evidence of "progress" as defined from any possible angle—economic growth, population increase, improvement of social quality, and so forth. It is well to remember that even impersonal circumstances and external issues gain their importance on the local scene because of the individual and collective responses they evoke, and responses, broadly perceived, are also decisions of a kind. In short, no major community preoccupation could rightly be overlooked under the aegis of this emphasis on the human factor as decision-making, and decision-making as leadership and politics.

As for specific procedures, my own preparation included a familiarization with pertinent sociological literature, especially those classics of community sociology ranging from Robert S. Lynd and Helen Merrell Lynd: *Middletown* (New York, 1929) and *Middletown in Transition* (New York, 1937), through Arthur J. Vidich and Joseph Bensman: *Small Town in Mass Society* (Princeton, N.J., 1958). I also found Floyd Hunter's *Community Power Structure* (Chapel Hill, N.C., 1953) initially very stimulating, but soon learned that it should be assimilated with caution. Not only did the cattle town experience promptly contradict Hunter's notion of static "power structures," but the book has provoked a deluge of sociological criticism. Those interested can sample this literature in such empirical and theoretical discussions as Richard A. Schermerhorn: *Society and Power* (New York, 1961); Nelson W. Polsby: *Community Power and Political Theory* (New Haven, 1963); Robert Presthus:

Men at the Top (New York, 1964); and Edward C. Banfield: *Big City Politics* (New York, 1965), especially chap. i. Generally speaking, I found the literature on local conflict also very instructive. James S. Coleman's *Community Conflict* (Glencoe, Ill., 1957) provided the best assessment of this material.

In approaching the cattle towns themselves I proceeded into the primary sources with as detached an attitude as I could muster. Even so, after weeks of exposure to local newspapers I found myself having to suppress a mental picture of the cattle towns as pleasant utopias—which was just the image editors tried to sell nonresident readers. An even greater hazard proved to be the shameless circumspection of editors on social controversy. Let me cite an example. I began my research with Abilene, and only after studying Dodge City did I become aware of the powerful influence of prohibitionism at the cattle towns. On returning to the Abilene *Chronicle* for additional notes I discovered that editor Vear P. Wilson had effectively pulled the wool over my eyes. Strangely enough, in view of the shrieking publicity he gave certain aspects of local moral reform, Wilson had been unwilling except in the most oblique way to mention the existence of a powerful prohibition sentiment in his town. His studied evasion, combined with my failure at first reading to comprehend the significance of citizens banding together under the initials "I.O.G.T.", had caused me to overlook Abilene prohibitionism entirely. This error of omission can be observed in my early article on the movement to abolish Abilene's cattle trade: "The Last Days of 'Texan' Abilene: A Study in Community Conflict on the Farmer's Frontier," *Agricultural History*, XXXIV (1960), 107–19.

In order to penetrate the smoke screen shrouding many aspects of local decision-making—something requiring the patient tenacity of a trial lawyer interrogating a hostile witness—I was forced to take notes in a volume often far out of proportion to the information derived. Since nuances could be significant, this effort entailed typing out verbatim transcripts of any possibly important items. And since the complexities often did not make sense until all notes had been collected and sifted, the relevant material was not always immediately obvious. In the long run, probably the most consistently helpful newspaper items were of two types: (1) local voting statistics, and (2) lists of names—members of organizations, signers of petitions, attenders of meetings, and the like. From both I could frequently ferret out insights where editorial comment was not forthcoming.

Local historians, I found, were hardly more straightforward than editors with respect to things controversial. The very few truly uninhibited restrospective accounts that I discovered all took the form of personal reminiscences not consciously offered as local history. Such items as the Kos Harris memoirs of Wichita's business factionalism or T. C. Henry's lightly cynical appraisal of his own leadership role in Abilene proved to be rare sources. Those working in relatively recent periods, I suspect, could usefully seek out living informants for interpretive data not likely to appear in published form.

A final warning. If decision-making is to be emphasized, as it is in this book, then of course the need is to expose as fully as possible the individual or group motives behind decisions proposed and made. This requires a certain aptitude for reading between the lines, as well as a countervailing skill in withstanding neat but wholly imaginary interpretations. The sources themselves must always lead. If guiding assumptions and thematic emphases are legitimate—as I submit they are—the investigator must be willing to diverge from them wherever warranted. Only in this manner will local research, as with any historical endeavor, tell us something faithfully reflecting the way things were.

ACKNOWLEDGMENTS

MY GREATEST OBLIGATION is acknowledged in the dedication. Allan G. Bogue, now Professor of History at the University of Wisconsin, directed the seminars in which my research first took shape. His careful conviction that the cattle town experience might have something important to say about American social development was my chief inspiration; the interdisciplinary approach he champions was my general method. I hope this book fulfills whatever good expectations he may have had for it.

The book is a revision of my doctoral dissertation presented at the University of Iowa in 1964, which in turn grew out of a master's thesis. Joel H. Silbey worked through the dissertation draft with his customary vigor, offering numerous suggestions for both current and ultimate revision. In either its dissertation or thesis forms the material was similarly read by Lawrence E. Gelfand, Paul W. Glad, Samuel P. Hays, Jeffry Kaplow, Alan B. Spitzer, and J. Richard Wilmeth. I am deeply obliged to them all. George H. Daniels provided literally the last word in comprehensive criticism, suggesting several useful changes in the revised manuscript.

Of those who aided in the solution of various limited problems I should like to single out three for special thanks: Moses Rischin, who offered suggestions for relating this study to general urban history; Norman Sage, who helped interpret some of the economic details of the cattle town experience; and Robert P. Swierenga, who helped gather and interpret a portion of the quantitative data.

The staff of the Kansas State Historical Society, I discovered, not only operates one of the finest research facilities in the nation, but also goes out of its way to make it the most hospitable. Devoting themselves to my needs far above and beyond generous interpretations of duty were Nyle H. Miller, Robert W. Richmond, and—most especially—Joseph W. Snell.

The editors of *Agricultural History* and the *Kansas Historical Quarterly* graciously consented to further use of material from three preliminary articles I published during the course of the research. The Free Press, a division of the Macmillan Company, similarly granted me permission to quote a lengthy passage from James S. Coleman's *Community Conflict* (1957).

For financial assistance in support of this project I am indebted to the Social Science Research Council of New York, to Ralph H. Ojemann of the University of Iowa, and to the University of New Mexico Research Allocations Committee.

INDEX

Abilene (Kansas): founded, 11–15; beginnings as cattle town, 15–30, 36–7; business enterprise and the town economic base, 75–6, 79–81, 83, 86 *n.*, 87–92, 98–102, 104, 106–9; composition of work force (table), 108; property valuations by occupation group (table), 109; violence and law enforcement, 117, 123–6, 129, 144; cattle trade preservation effort, 153–4; factionalism, 209–10; social reform, 257–263; last years of Texas cattle trading, 294–307; in present day, 355; population growth, 358, 359 *n.;* concern with "image," 361 *n.;* and local history, 382–3
Adel (Iowa), 164
Alamo Saloon (Abilene), 102
Allison, Clay, 142
American Society for the Prevention of Cruelty to Animals, 174
Anderson, George L., 84 *n.*
Appelbaum, Barney W., 92–3
Arapaho Indians, 344–5, 353
Arkansas City (Kansas), 347, 349–52
Arthur, Chester A., 350

Atchison (Kansas), 270 *n.*
Atchison, Topeka and Santa Fe Railroad, 48–52, 55–7, 60–62, 68–72, 80–1, 157, 168, 171–3, 196, 201, 205, 221–222, 274, 326–9, 349, 359
Atherton, Lewis, 4, 111 *n.*
Atwood, George A., 163–6, 169, 177, 187, 207, 308–309, 311–15
Augustine, Jacob, 296

Bank of Dodge City, 85
banking, 78, 82–5, 185, 210–211, 213, 229–30, 232
barbed wire, 39, 297, 344
Barber County (Kansas), 180
Baxter Springs (Kansas), 19
Beard, Ed T., 106
Beatty, Peter L., 215, 219
Beatty and Kelley Restaurant (Dodge City), 215–16
Beebe, Jerome, 91 *n.*, 134, 138
Beede's Hotel (Ellsworth), 97
Beeson, Chalkley M., 339
Bell, James, 300, 303
Bentley, O. H., 361–2, 364
Berry, Samuel, 175, 246
Beverley, Henry M., 94–6, 155, 339
Bieber, Ralph P., 17 *n.*
Billington, Ray Allen, 111 *n.*
Blair, Enos, 288, 290, 292

Fraker, James C., 229, 256, 324, 327
"Front Street Replica" (Dodge City), 355
Fringer, Herman J., 332
Frost, Daniel M., 217–24, 265–6, 276, 332, 335–41, 360

Galland, Samuel, 267, 276–7, 280
gambling, 103, 106, 113, 121–122, 126–7, 128 n., 134–5, 139, 244–5, 254, 256–7, 260, 265–7, 269, 272, 273 n., 274, 281, 286, 292
Gamgee, John, 29
Garden City (Kansas), 279
George, Eli, 306 n.
George, Moses B., 98–9
German-Americans, 188, 218–223, 264–5, 267, 271–2, 276
German Immigration Society (Dodge City), 333
Gilbert, Charles F., 231 n.
Glick, George W., 174, 273, 335, 337
Goldsoll, Mayer, 91–6
Gore, James W., 98–9, 136–139, 141 n.
Gore, Mrs. James W., 98–9
Graham, S. L., 302
Grand Central Hotel (Ellsworth), 97 n., 99
Grangers: *see* Patrons of Husbandry
Grant, Ulysses S., 199 n.
Great Bend (Kansas), 60, 93–94, 140, 321, 327, 341
Great Western Store (Abilene), 89
Greenbackers, 188, 222–3, 225
Greiffenstein, William, 45–7, 229–33
Griffin, Albert, 279–80

Gross, Charles F., 17, 20 n., 28–9, 163
Gryden, Harry E., 222
Guide Map of the Great Texas Cattle Trail, 170

Hardin, John Wesley, 142
Harris, George E., 256
Harris, Kos, 233 n., 364, 383
Harris, William H., 271–2, 279
Harvey, James M., 36, 54
Harvey County (Kansas), 53 n., 329
Haynes, John James, 100–1
Hays City (Kansas), 58, 165, 215, 268
Hazlett, Henry H., 24–5, 91 n.
Henry, Stuart, 307 n.
Henry, Theodore C., 27, 117, 294–7, 299–300, 303–4, 306–7 n., 383
herd law, 40, 53–4, 62, 172, 181, 297–8, 305, 308–9, 311–16, 318, 325–6, 329–330 n., 336 n., 342; *see also* night herd law
Hersey, Timothy F., 12, 26, 209–10
Hickok, James B., 124, 143, 147, 261, 262 n.
Hindes, George F., 75
Hitt, Samuel N., 163
Hodgden, Perry, 226
Holliday, Cyrus K., 50–1
Holliday, Doc, 142
homicide, 112–14, 128–9, 132, 139, 141–8, 254 n., 278, 285–6, 289–90
Hood, John H., 154
hoof-and-mouth disease, 331
Hoover, George M., 102–3, 113, 217, 219, 221, 223 n., 277–9, 331
Hope, James G., 255, 324
Hot Springs (Arkansas), 90

hotels, 96–101, 154, 161–2, 185, 212, 231–2
Howard, Jacob C., 311–12
Hubbell, W. N., 91 n., 155
Humboldt (Kansas), 45
Hunnewell (Kansas), 107, 157, 173, 347–9
Hunter, Floyd, 381
Hutchinson (Kansas), 56
Hutchison, William B., 54, 346

Independence (Kansas), 346
Independent Order of Good Templars, 258, 262, 270–1, 382
Indian Territory, 10, 21, 28, 36, 42–3, 45, 63, 181 n., 196, 338–40, 342–54; see also Cherokee Strip; Neutral Strip; Oklahoma
Indianapolis (Indiana), 147 n.
Ingersoll, J. W., 310
Inman, Henry, 312, 315–17
Isaacson, S. E., 93–4

Jay Cooke and Company (New York), 77
Jewett, William T., 325, 327
Johnson, Andrew, 43
journalism, 6 n., 36, 41, 69, 145, 149–50, 152–3, 163–166, 169, 174–6, 182–3, 189, 193–5, 197, 200–4, 224, 244, 250–1, 258, 262, 265–6, 274–6, 288, 296–301, 315, 332, 336, 340–2, 346, 352–3, 361 n., 363, 364 n., 382
Junction City (Kansas), 12, 21, 26–7, 30–1

Kansas Central Relief Committee, 191
Kansas City (Kansas), 270 n.
Kansas City (Missouri), 78, 81, 83, 134, 152, 159, 335

Kansas City, Burlington and Southwestern Railway, 69–70
Kansas City, Lawrence and Southern Railroad, 70–1, 157
Kansas Pacific Railway, 30, 35–8, 51–2, 55, 62, 80–1, 153–6, 160–1, 164, 167, 170–1, 295, 297 n., 321–2, 329; see also Union Pacific Railway, Eastern Division
Kansas State Temperance Union, 279–80
Karatofsky, Jacob, 89–90, 93
Kelley, James H., 215–16, 219–20, 264–8, 271, 277, 279
King, W. M., 308, 314
Klaine, Nicholas B., 201, 203–205, 216–17, 240, 245, 270, 274–8, 282, 331 n., 332–3, 338, 340
Knox, Leonard, 312, 314
Kohn, Sol H., 83

Ladies' Aid Society (Wichita), 193, 196–8
Lamb, William H., 15, 23–6
Lampard, Eric E., 379–80
Lane, Charles H., 94, 96
Larkin, Arthur, 227–8
Larned (Kansas), 201
Las Vegas (New Mexico), 242
law enforcement, 116–48, 240–241, 245, 254 n., 257, 260–262, 265, 269–70, 272–3, 279–85, 287–92; see also homicide
Law and Order League (Caldwell), 251, 291–2
Lawrence, W. W. H., 45 n.
Leadville (Colorado), 242
Leahy, David D., 290 n.
Leavenworth (Kansas), 56, 270 n.

LIBRARY MEDIA CENTER
ALBUQUERQUE ACADEMY